Red Tarot

Red Tarot

A DECOLONIAL GUIDE TO DIVINATORY LITERACY

CHRISTOPHER MARMOLEJO

North Atlantic Books
Huichin, unceded Ohlone land
Berkeley, California

Published by
North Atlantic Books
Huichin, unceded Ohlone land
Berkeley, California

Cover art © Carol Cruz via Adobe Stock
Cover design by Amanda Weiss
Book design by Happenstance Type-O-Rama

Printed in Canada.

Red Tarot: A Decolonial Guide to Divinatory Literacy is sponsored and published by North Atlantic Books, an educational nonprofit based in the unceded Ohlone land Huichin (Berkeley, CA) that collaborates with partners to develop cross-cultural perspectives; nurture holistic views of art, science, the humanities, and healing; and seed personal and global transformation by publishing work on the relationship of body, spirit, and nature.

North Atlantic Books's publications are distributed to the US trade and internationally by Penguin Random House Publisher Services. For further information, visit our website at www.northatlanticbooks.com.

Library of Congress Cataloging-in-Publication Data
Names: Marmolejo, Christopher, 1993– author.
Title: Red tarot : a decolonial guide to divinatory literacy / Christopher Marmolejo.
Description: Berkeley, California : North Atlantic Books, [2024] | Includes bibliographical references and index. | Summary: "Designed to be used with any deck, Red Tarot interrogates the images, themes, and power structures that have been read into and onto the cards-and guides readers to radical and empowering reclamation"—Provided by publisher.
Identifiers: LCCN 2023029919 (print) | LCCN 2023029920 (ebook) | ISBN 9781623178475 (paperback) | ISBN 9781623178482 (epub)
Subjects: LCSH: Tarot. | Divination. | Decolonization.
Classification: LCC BF1879.T2 M346 2024 (print) | LCC BF1879.T2 (ebook) | DDC 133.3/2424—dc23/eng/20231020
LC record available at https://lccn.loc.gov/2023029919
LC ebook record available at https://lccn.loc.gov/2023029920

1 2 3 4 5 6 7 8 9 MARQUIS 28 27 26 25 24

This book includes recycled material and material from well-managed forests. North Atlantic Books is committed to the protection of our environment. We print on recycled paper whenever possible and partner with printers who strive to use environmentally responsible practices.

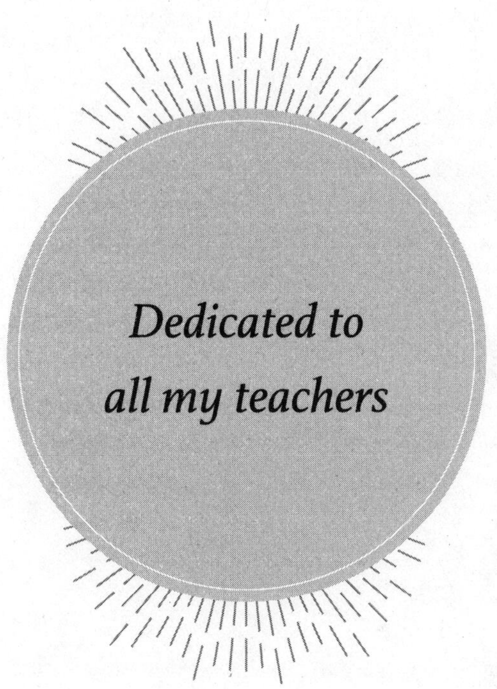
Dedicated to
all my teachers

CONTENTS

ZERO

The Red Read

When rationality runs dry, it's Red that will reconcile the world, a hue vibrant and vital inside its brown. Red is passion and it's primary. It's first and it's forever.

To be born, this work broke open my heart, and so let this reading be opened by my blood offering, a requisite pound of flesh. Black ink will be dried blood across these pages, and like always blood returns to the Earth. I hope this serves you, because for me it was a necessity. It filled me with passion, purged me of residual rage, and protected me as I pray for Red power to seduce the soul back into my body.

Red is my thread. Reading is my rite. And I say that reading should revitalize you, it should make you Red. Red is the substance that raises knowledge into wisdom. Red will restore full-bodied relationality through a divine dialogue we pursue together. Red is not rational; it's intimate, numinous, and intrinsically co-respondent. *Red Tarot* evolves this understanding into a project of critical prophetic literacy. Liberatory prophecy activates modes of expanded cognition through such communication. It is not a simple transfer of information; it's a recovery of native knowing that knows the cosmos is alive and communicative. Literacy and language are capital in our sociocultural worlds. Those with more social, economic, and political power claim for themselves the ability to determine which languages and discourses are legitimized. So as language is an ideological site of struggle, reading tarot is an act of resistance by radically expanding who gets to be considered literate, meaning *Red Tarot* lives in the legacy of literacy being a means of enacting emancipation.

Red Tarot is a project of simultaneous decolonization and re-Indigenization. *Red Tarot* is unafraid to confront, listen, critique, or unveil. Red light makes each card a prism of poetic, political praxis. The reader unfamiliar with social horror will find their imagination engaged and activated. They will see how colonial consciousness constellates in their inner and outer worlds. It's within the schemes of perception that symbolic domination is able to obscure itself. Its activities are hidden in our cognitive relationships by working *through* the very categories and lenses of perception.[1] *Red Tarot* works to unveil and interrupt this symbolic violence by sensitizing us to the psyche's uncontested perceptive frames and modes, making it co-responsive to external, historical, and social environments. To reverse the process of forcible de-Indigenization *Red Tarot* offers a visual framework for interpreting the tarot in a manner that perceives, disrupts, and rejects conditioned colonial consciousness. To make meaning in different space-times we shift the frames that shape reality perception, to free them from their colonial context, making them mobile and possessed of a mind all their own. By describing myself and my work as decolonial I invoke a long history of insurgent subjectivity. I take the tarot as a starting point to observe and critique the genocidal logic of the European colonial racial imaginary. My daily divination with the tarot guides me into direct, intentional, and inventive action from this *Red* subjectivity. As Patrisia Gonzales does, I use the term *Red* in *Red Tarot* to transcend various conceptual borders, as Indigenous peoples and their epistemologies are centered in their world, rather than disempowered at the fringe.[2] As Gonzales was inspired by Sandy Grande's *Red Pedagogy*, *Red Tarot* is my attempt to extend a paradigm of Indigenous reclamation, reimagining, and regeneration of self-determined relationships.

By reframing and rereading the text that is tarot, it can be claimed as an alternative, local epistemology of the people that can renew the divinatory animacy that permeates ancient ways of knowing in the present language-body. Our sense perception is represented by the symbolic code that is language. Language is more than intellectual; it makes meaning of the body and spirit of the speaker, reader, writer. True language is never mechanically intellectual. It is sensuous, evocative, and emotive. It is animate and animating. The sound of our speech expresses the living spirit. Despite extended loss, we can again root ourselves in the cosmic order with the image-vehicles offered in the tarot. Each symbol is a library of concentrated stories, knowledges, names, parables, omens, and augurs. The practice of laying cards can bring forth a creative communion through the application of the divinatory mind that branches from the metamorphic mind, the collective mind by which we describe, create, and imagine an animate world with interrelated participation.[3] These symbols express the processes of unseen forces materializing as spiritual matter. Though it takes conscious effort to call upon the metamorphic mind, by summoning it from the subconscious we can again commence a communion with nature every time we lay cards.

Red Tarot images the reflexivity of a sovereign subjectivity. Its readers are part prophet, part poet, part political participant. Their self-reflexivity intersects social critique, navigating dangerous inner and outer terrain with a critical imagination. A *Red reading* finds the political in the everyday so that the daily practice of pulling cards becomes a documentation of working-class lives persisting to transcend exploitation, find belonging, and heal their soul. *Red Tarot* understands that the meaning within everyday social relations is to be inscribed, decoded, deployed, translated, and circulated. It enacts a *rubedo* that is the flesh entry into a reality that we know radically, viscerally. As readings are a dialogic experience between querent and reader, text and audience, card and consciousness, they can be seen to enliven an oracular cultural mode of knowledge production that is wholly contextualized within the field of interaction, intuitive and emotionally sensitive. The alchemy of *Red reading* looks upon the reality of the image as more than what has been, opening a door to an eros repressed through "chemical reactions fixed on metal and paper that represent desires and lusts, longings and yearnings."[4] Reading with the whole body, the socially matrixed body, the emotional body, and the soul is erotic reading.

Red readers go beyond interpretation. Their readings articulate an artistry of dissent. Their words, their images, their cards, their readings are renderings of a politicized imagination. Their craft is combined with their commitment. A *Red reading* marries the intensity of lived experience with the aesthetic imagination toward real-world application. More than mere fortune telling, *Red reading* reconnects the personal with the universal current of cyclical creation and consequence to encourage an expansive responsiveness through personal awareness and responsibility. *Red reading* transforms reality with pictographs that subvert the chronology of colonial language claims. *Red Tarot* indexes cishet white supremacist capitalist imperialist indices of power while also promoting a literacy that changes those dynamics. Since it is still whitestream institutions that contextualize the education of Black, Brown, and Indigenous students, resistance requires knowledge of the oppressor and the oppressor's language.[5] *Red Tarot* aims to offer new interpretations for an old body of images to break the hold of colonizing representations and to map decolonized psychic, social space. In this queer world with its ensemble of social actors we come to understand the dimensions and topographies of being, a visual understanding that builds a place for language to go. By entering this queer world we can experience the joys, risks, and rewards of self-exploration, self-reclamation.

The spiritual practice of reading tarot *reads Red* when it acknowledges, regards, and relates to the inner world as a sacred landscape. Divination facilitates the creation of sacred geography so that the cards become codices, with multiple histories surrounding them, and values and signposts are embedded within a cartography of critical consciousness in their symbolic metaphor.

> *Indigenous people are people of place, and the nature of place is embedded in their language. The physical, cognitive, and emotional orientation of a people, is a kind of 'map' they carry in their heads and transfer from generation to generation. This map is multidimensional and reflects the spiritual as well as the mythic geography of a people. Knowing the origins of their people, their place, and the all-important things the place contains is*

considered essential orientation for a tribal person. A people's origin story maps and integrates the key relationships with all aspects of the landscape.[6]

Profound symbolic communication stems from Indigenous cultural foundations but also interrelated life understandings that necessarily include distinctly Black queer feminist thought; but it's not a *Red read* without leading to the repatriation of native lands, native ways of being and knowing. *Red reading* is a transgressive cultural act in centering the spiritual selfhood otherwise actively denied to impose inhumane domination. Deities speak through doorways in our heart-mind. Beyond an awareness of these doorways into different dimensions of peace, possibility, and fulfillment, these cards offer keys.

Red Tarot regards tarot reading as a tool of revolution by revealing the inner sanctums of power, the shadowed structures of dominance. Tarot's language is meant to be unexpected. It shocks you, wakes you, humors and comforts you, and offers you medicine in its multiple ways of knowing, seeing, and saying. It helps you cope with uncertainty by making chaos and potential something to play in. The syntax of a *Red reading* refuses to be frozen into resolution, for the tarot is not a fixed text. Therefore *Red Tarot* is not designed to be a comprehensive document, but I hope that by tying decolonial, feminist, queer, antiracist literature to the aesthetic artifact that is tarot, with its emotional and imaginal affect, this scholarship may reach a more profound audience than one would typically expect.

When the silence of my own company becomes insufficient, the invention of my imagination becomes my companion, and my cards come alive with spirits from above, below, ahead, and behind. In writing this book, I may not have fully trusted my own imagination and may have relied too heavily on what I know and who came before. It is my bowing before my teachers as I call upon a chorus of ancestors that my voice might harmonize and with them be raised to heights that would've been impossible to reach as a solo.

I offer these cards as pedagogies that may be guides toward critical praxis and profound meaning-making, but not as a one-size-fits-all metaphysical elixir. Its magic is malleable. It'll work best if you bring your own deck, your touch, and your own tongue to your readings. The divinatory mind is a speculative mode, offering "what might be termed an ethics of equivocation that enables something like an ontological humility—or ethos of ontological multiplicity."[7] *Red reading* fosters a perceptual disposition that delves into disorderly ways of knowing. By offering a numerical ordering of the cards by chapter, themes are uncovered that connect each numeric group, such as visibility with the Nines, resistance with the Sevens, or displacement with the Fives. Connections are made across suits, major and minor arcana. Its awareness may be more perplexing, ambiguous, fractured, and fractal, but it is not necessarily less reliable. Its images are aesthetically dubious so that our readings acquire epistemic flexibility to skillfully navigate and inhabit multiple worlds.

The oracular language-body regards all occurrences within the reading as meaningful. The reader views the series of cards, bordered and with empty space between them with the gaze of an enlightened witness. They linger over, observe, and control the pace of the reading. They can read each card at a time, forth and back, and then assess the composition of the spread all at once. With a glance they can reorient themselves in the reading based on the visual cues that claim attention as the querent's narrative is further disclosed and developed. They extract meaning from the implied relations between the borders of each card, filling lapses of time, emotion, and cognition. *Red readers* work the tarot as a mode of *disidentification* as theorized by Jose Esteban Muñoz, wherein "the disidentifactory optic is turned to shadows and fissures within the text, where radicalized presences can be liberated from the protective custody of the white literary imagination."[8] Any shadow seer is an occultist. And because our current awareness is an offspring of colonial relations, the shadow is the other, the Black, Brown, and Red bodies buried in the white gaze of white America. *Red reading* is strategic to resist and confound the identity states white supremacy prescribes. *Red readers* resist assimilation; they work with dominant cultural modes and materia and restructure them from within to render themselves free and self-fashioned. The shadow work of *Red readers* aims to foreground the dissociated, divorced, alienated, and dejected to transfigure our identity matrices and repair our relations.

They are fluent in the alliance between language and visually rendered ideas. They understand each card as a partial sequence of a much larger trajectory. They develop political imaginaries through powerful narrations of the speculative that nuance the conceptual and perceptual approaches of knowing and being. In the imaginative space of the reading, readers offer divergent accounts for reality through the variable frames of reference presented in each card. With frame after frame of reference it is clear that each card is not establishing the boundaries of truth; rather, it is discerning the appropriate interpretation, understanding, and ordering of truth from an array of visual possibilities.

What's true, imagined, or communicated within one reading changes in the next, because although the same set of cards is used, their *shuffling* recycles, reinvents, and renews meaning between readings. Since cards and decks may be nonidentical but structurally similar, they offer multiple modes of understanding inner and outer reality.

We can pull cards when we are lost in the dark, displaced and despairing. The cards are flashlights through the dark tunnels of our interiority, finding all the psychic fault lines of violent eruption. But for me they shine with their own light. And then they are a cyborg technology, a prosthesis that allows my stride to be walked with dignity. With my Red writing I repair my people's innate divinatory faculty ruptured right with their Indigeneity. The cards are daimonic forces, spirits that can guide and assist through our multidimensional excursions. Through the looking glass we find in the tarot a seventy-eight-port entry into another realm, with another opportunity for finding and inscribing the pain, the love, the memories, the fears, the mundane, and the sublime of life. We need them not just to allay fear but also to find inner treasure, to be led into the possibilities beyond the known world of hierarchical domination. If we look long enough we will find unexpected guidance in the designs for living.

ONE

Ace

For me—a writer in the last quarter of the twentieth century, not much more than a hundred years after Emancipation, a writer who is black and a woman—the exercise is very different. My job becomes how to rip that veil drawn over "proceedings too terrible to relate." The exercise is also critical for any person who is black, or who belongs to any marginalized category, for historically, we were seldom invited to participate in the discourse even when we were its topic.[1]

One, or the Ace, is the subject. It is the narrator. It is *I.* It is the *particular* gaze, the power to narrate the world, to name the world and thereby order its constituent parts. When we are drawn into a creation story, the storyteller becomes veiled. The subject gives meaning and the object receives meaning. It is the eyes, the *I*'s, through which we gain a world view. The eye always belongs to the particular person. The gift of personhood is the ability to name oneself, to interpret, to turn the facts of experience into truth. One is the center, the center of consciousness, the center of awareness, the universal experiencing itself as singular. When the singular seeks to be universal, what they seek is dominance; they seek a colonizer's model of the world; theirs is the subjectivity that objectifies with the cishet white gaze. Quantum physics has revealed that matter appears as particles or waves depending on how it is viewed, if viewed at all. Aces initiate us into alternative, renewed perspectives. Beauty isn't only in the eye of the beholder; beauty *becomes* through the eye of the beholder. Potential and presence are unveiled in the witness, in the act of perception.

When the One acknowledges singularity it is autobiography. It is an unveiling of creation by trusting one's own recollection. It is the literary heritage of slave narratives. It is the power of the personal narrative, when wielded by the marginalized, to contradict the oppressors' delusion of the enslaved as illiterate. A literate slave was supposed to be a contradiction in terms.[2] The truths of the many centers of the colonized consciousness fuel the fires of abolition. Historically, literacy is power because it is subjecthood, and subjects are not objects. Literacy unveils systems of domination, reads the facts in light of a new truth, a distinct vantage point. When the objectified come to voice, they throw off the weight of silence, and the shadows begin to speak. Language defines the boundaries of our knowing, while literacy seeks to defy such limits. The Ace is the subjectivity informed by enslavement. The awareness and articulation of enslavement, of objectification, is its own subjectivity. Though the state may attempt to censor the deepest horrors of its hell, it is the brave writers who self-recollect, who bear dangerous memories, who remember, who move from image to meaning to text, that transgress the imposition of silence. By heeding the responsibility of truth the Ace establishes sovereignty.

Ace is each suit's absolute, encompassing all of its encoded knowledge. "Part of memory and knowledge is encoded to protect the knowledge or serves as 'hidden texts' embedded in symbols and myths. This knowledge can also be camouflaged in the dominant culture's signs; for example, the Native cross (balanced in the four directions) was synchronized with the Christian cross because Indigenous people could make sense of its meaning from their preexisting internal knowledge."[3]

By consciously working with the elemental Aces, a ritual space that mirrors the cosmos creates a bridge between the cards, the self, and various realms to explore and enrich with *conocimiento*. Thus Aces establish well-being. The Ace asks for individuation and offers the four directions, four starting points, four dimensions of possibility. As each Ace corresponds to a tool of the Magician, they represent the elemental composition that makes the Magician subjectivity possible. The numerical connection between the Magician and the elemental aces signals the natural world as inseparable from human experience. The living entity held in the Ace is the land that creates the meaning that the Magician channels. Perspective derives from the environment.

Aces are invitations from Spirit to encounter new geographies or rather to renew existing geographies. The Wheel of Fortune provides us a compass, while Aces provide the needle guiding us in the therapeutic landscapes contained in the symbol and story of each card. They show that the natural world has its own agency and can assert profound influence upon humanity, as humanity derives from the natural world. Each Ace of the natural world executes celestial purposes and commitments, teaching us to listen to the water, to see with fire, to speak with air, and to work with earth. To pull an Ace is to pay attention to the environment and begin the return to a reciprocal, respectful relationship with the land itself, for each elemental Ace is an avatar of an incarnate Spirit. Communal care is dependent upon ecological care dependent upon decolonization that requires the body be recognized as part of the sacred geography. Each Ace activates somatic memories of ancient ways of knowing, transgressing capitalist violence by valuing and exploring the body as a site of knowledge.

The Aces initiate the metamorphic mind capable of conceiving multiple levels of meaning and knowledge, as necessary to operate the complex equations and formulas of consciousness each card creates in a spread. Aces are objects of meditation providing orientation. They transmit the meaning of place, especially the human place in the natural world, to find that "who you are is also determined by where you are."[4] Their encoded knowledge orients the perceiver to the phenomena of both the physical and the spiritual worlds.

The Aces are birth stories, and origins are important in an Indigenous orientation. In them is the chance to return to original knowledge as remediation of historical trauma, no matter our unique place, body, or time upon the shared social geography. "The sacredness of a common origin determines the basis of relationships between diverse forms."[5] We see vastly different elements, elemental stories, experiences, and lessons related by origin within the tarot as well. To be in right relationship we must begin again.

The Magician

With an accuracy, clarity, often musicality, that in themselves exemplify the writer's love, care for language, they illuminate origins, motive springs; how these become substance, vision; varying ways of working, of being productive. Uses of autobiographical materials are discussed; influences, predecessors; place and power of imagination; the self-critical faculty; criticism. The larger questions are here too: why and for whom do I write? What is the writer's responsibility to one's work, to others, to society? Towards what do I aspire? The result is one of those rare, rich source books for writers, readers, teachers, students—all who care about literature and the creation of it. Yet—as if this were not ample—this collection transcends its genre. It becomes a harbinger book, a book of revelation, of haunting challenge, opening on to central concerns not only of writing, but of life, of living, today.[6]

Magic is in the conductor's hands, the orchestrator's. The music commences, crescendos, and concludes upon his say-so. The Magician's guiding hands cut the deck, draw the cards, and summon synchronicity. Divination is like a symphony that has music's same magic. Spirit fills the soundscape, stirring the emotions of all involved. The reading gets us to writing the feelings we are afraid to confront. You leave the divination like leaving a jam session—elevated, enriched, and cathartically expressed. Magic is where the rational and irrational converge. Being a Magician is being a writer for whom selecting syllables and structuring syntax is spell casting with every word. And it's being unafraid to curse. It's writing without shame and without fear, though not without consequence. The Magician writes new neural pathways pursuing freedom.

The Magician has a mathematical methodology with an artist's aesthetic expression that is the work of way-opening. The reading is hardly a simple one-to-one correspondence between image and lived experience.

The tarot does not mimic life but is an intermediary, a place for the Magician writers to store understanding and project prophetic vision. The Magician operates as the intermediary process between the realms of lived experience and art-making, encompassing organization, reflection, and distillation. Memory mixes with the imaginary, and many voices emerge to tell the stories of the silenced. It's the Magician's music that guides our soul back from the psychic state of trauma through the telling of one's story with a profound degree of truth and sincerity. This composition renders the reading rich. With the Magician, we make our way through the tarot tableau to learn a new language out of the previously censored, suppressed subjectivity. We recall and we rename.

By uniting interiority, with its shadow and silence, and voice, with its auditory embodiment, the Magician maintains integrity, emotional clarity, and sustained creativity. The Magician writes in right relationship with the natural world, in constant communion with the more-than-human. The Magician's writer consciousness learns the grammar of animacy, the system of intersubjectivity spoken in the natural world. As Thomas Berry notes, "The universe is a communion of subjects, not a collection of objects." This language does not seek to dominate nature by silencing it, manipulating it, or exploiting its riches. If the Magician is speaking with the elements, the Magician must be native.

The Magician's achievement is in establishing a craft as personal and particular as the timbre and tone of a writer's chosen words. The arcana inspire us to arrive at a thousand new ways to the word, to make the ineffable audible. And we will remember our native tongue when we cherish the legacy of our languages. To summon an image of origins is to enter one's center and write till the search for a meaningful identity meets a self-sustaining dignity. The Magician is concerned where this quest diverges from our previously established priorities and toward alternative landscapes. Even if a body has restricted physical movement and is bound to a particular place, in the Magician's close quarters this quest is still conjured. The Magician's meditation is toward a state of mind, a place within the soul where the gift of seeing, of subjecthood, takes shape.

The careful observation of life becomes a language to unveil the intricate mechanisms of the world.[7] The Magician's critical readings elevate conscious awareness of the self and the outer world at once, adding depth to identity. Awareness emerges with conceptual abstraction evocatively communicated through symbol and sign. These signs are never stationary, but by following them we form complex personal relationships to multivalent meaning structures. Symbols and their metaphors are more than representations; they perform essential functions in the reading's ceremonial formula.[8] One is made multilingual in learning the intricate mechanisms of the world and its enduring power relations that maintain white supremacist capitalist imperialist patriarchy. By achieving some self-understanding, the Magician's relationships are mutually beneficial. It's the bad relationships that make us lose sight of ourselves and deteriorate our self-esteem. To fill in the spaces slavery stole, Toni Morrison teaches us that the "approach that's most productive and most trustworthy for me is the recollection that moves from the image to the text. Not from the text to image."[9] Although Morrison is discussing her approach to fiction writing, she offers insight into reading tarot. To begin with the image we can conjure the forgotten places in our soul; we can come to voice and satiate our desire for connection. By descending into the dark interiority, a Magician does the work of raising consciousness, giving light where there was darkness, giving Logos, giving language.

As the Magician, "I" navigate worlds. I gather all the elements of my being, and I am whole through the act of remembering. My words ensure I survive with dignity. My limitations do not completely circumscribe me because in my voice is strength, capacity, and skill. I may have nothing more than my intellect and emotions, but even in the midst of chaos I make my life meaningful. My responsibility to maintain humanity remains. My very imagination is radical because it presupposes my future existence, my entire existence. I become a guide strong and safe enough to trust. Colonization cut out my native tongue many times. I should speak Spanish, I should speak Serrano. Nationalism confused my nativity. Yet my voice becomes clearer at the cosmic edges, in the turns of fate and in the experience fully lived and responded to.

In this language, we don't just give; we receive too. When we listen to nature we are protected by its voice. "He escaped boarding school by hiding under an overhung bank where the sound of the stream covered his crying."[10] The sound of our cries is the sound of the river running. Nature can hear itself in us and assists us as we flee from the severing alienation of colonial institutions.

I am grateful to have been born into a family that valued education and encouraged my interests and my curiosity about literacy. While growing up I turned to books for company and companionship. I can trace my curiosity about the world to my hunger for more books. The tarot, in its many artful iterations, allows me to develop, appreciate, and analyze my multiple voices. Writing is soul-making alchemy. In this writing I am not alone, though each voice is singular. How would we know what they have to say if they never dare to speak?

It requires great power to embody the principle of One, and this power is best applied by decolonizing the gaze. A decolonial gaze is a radical subjectivity that restores those objectified by white supremacy, including the animal, the plant, the mineral, the silent and unseen worlds. That gaze that objectifies the other is undone as it comes to understand *its* subjectivity. The individualistic vision of humankind works to alienate the individual from their membership in an oppressed class, yet the Magician sustains the heart of collective culture in language. Language is cultural preservation, passed down via oral traditions, transmuting across time into patois, slang, and colloquialism. The Magician is the central station for the image vehicles of divinatory consciousness. This core spacious capacity is a generator of sacred self-consciousness that is inviolable to the invalidation of dominator culture.

The Magician knows that silent words aren't words at all. Silent words fail to say anything when they stand alone. The tongue is tactile; it's meant to touch and taste what the mouth may receive. When words remain unheard and unshared; it's not long till they are forever lost and forgotten. With even a single sound the Magician can make a story magic. Selfhood demands testimony that depends on language that is made with, or intended toward, the soul's radiance. All such language is divinatory. The Magician's divination is knowing that someday we will again have someone to share our native tongue. The Magician's power is in fact drawn from every world, every state of consciousness, every realm of being in which we become.

"All kinds of things seemed to be verbs: 'to be a hill,' 'to be red,' 'to be a long sandy stretch of beach,' and then my finger rested on *wiikwegama:* 'to be a bay.' 'Ridiculous!' I ranted in my head."[11] The spoken word is sacred; we create with it because it isn't an *it;* it *is.*

English is a capitalist language. A language focused on appropriation of objects. English is a gendered language. To be heard in English we must classify the world into male and female. It is the master's language. Yet Mercury, the planet that rules language, is nonbinary. The Magician as a face of Mercury, with the elements all around them, acknowledges that we speak differently to the living world, and the living world is more-than-human. It does not contain the world in a word. To respect the animacy of the natural world is to restore the (verb)al capacities of the noun, able to do, to be, to speak, to know. "The verb releases the water from bondage and lets it live."[12] To learn the language of the natural world is to resist the will to dominate. Such is the language of learning to read tarot.

I cannot teach you a native language, but you can still listen to the ocean, to the shores, to the rocks, to the morning, to the east wind. You can experiment with a language where all is alive, all has a story. The Magician wants nothing more for us than to tell a story, a story that reflects our intricate connection evidenced by and strengthened in the act of communication. By expanding who we commune with, our language shifts, our language is redeemed, for it is possible to resist reducing the personhood of the nonhuman. It is unnatural to relegate to, or be relegated to, the nonstatus of *it.* Nature does not speak the language of slavery, nor does it prepare us for enslavement. Colonial language constructs a grammar of violence by the order of its relations. The tarot offers a language system, a Logos, for intuitive soul communication via art, the body's pathos, and the environment. The tarot offers a language to listen to an intelligence other than our own.

"The cards speak in their voice (Ometeotl, Dual Divinity, who is incarnate in all being), and in the voices of the Teteo. If a Teotl, a 'god' appears in a reading, it is that Teotl reaching out to the querent, in order to speak to them and to teach them."[13]

The Magician points one hand upward and the other downward, signaling the six directions, placing the reader in the mesocosm. Though they are free to travel above and below, here we find the middle world with its four cardinal directions and elemental composition. The lead tongue learns the magic of animation by attending to every angle, shade, gaze, posture, scale, symbol, and implication in the scene presented. The static image begins to move when the words are more than description; they are also an appreciation that coaxes out the card's voice. Each card is its own Magician that determines the direction of the reading, something that neither the querent nor the reader can control or plan for. A psychic portraiture develops therein where the threads of time and space converge. The images become alive first within the imaginal realm, stirring memory and imagination. A memory that restores our lost language, the stories lost to imperialism, colonization, slavery. The more alive our interior becomes, the more animacy we can extend to the exterior world, the more we meet the cards in the manifest world. Tarot reading then becomes a ceremony of memory enlivening Indigenous intelligence.

Without this communion of intelligences the world would be a collection of facts, but it would have no truth. Truth requires intelligence. The image speaks back in a silent, wild language, one whereby we discover an archeology of the symbolic supernal communication. We dig up disjointed bones of memory and give the gods a body again. We remember the spirits residing in the image, and we begin a relationship of respect so we can consciously consent to sacred attunement. We discover that the images themselves are an ancient memory, a doorway to communicate with the Divine that animates all.

What memory might the "dead-seeming, cold rocks,"[14] the bay, the maple tree, conjure within us? This more-than-human communication of the Magician is transgressive literacy. By restoring communication with the more-than-human, we re-member our autonomy, our cosmic anatomy, and we find an expression of the profound peculiarity of our shared interiority.

The Wheel of Fortune

Categorically rejecting the subordination or exploitation of others as either a primary goal or an unintended consequence of caring of the self, they instead put their energy and imagination into the service of remaking themselves and the world(s) they inhabit. The goal of decoloniality is thus the creation of a new world—a different kind of world "in which many worlds fit," to borrow the words of the Zapatista Liberation Army (Mignolo 2001). This "new" world entails a total renovation of the current one—a reworking of subjectivity, community, institutional arrangements, and the logics by which humans live together.[15]

With any luck the Wheel of Fortune will advance the decolonial turn. The movements that advance decolonial thinking are many. And there have been many since the very outset of colonization. There may be differences and tensions in strategy and standpoint, but all can recognize coloniality as the enduring problem since the late fifteenth and early sixteenth centuries. Nelson Maldonado-Torres and many others made a profound shift away from modernization, understanding that decoloniality is an unfinished project still unfolding. To gain a sense of scope and scale, the reader must understand the nature of revolution that is the Wheel's contribution.

The Wheel of Fortune portrays an intersecting range of diverse characters across an interchange of social and spatial upheaval. All characters in the tarot stake a claim to narrative centrality in the reading. There is constantly another potential center of interest, another hero, another motivation, another alternative narrative for every major and minor arcanum. Each possesses a look of knowing, registering their existence in a shared social world. But each has their own world of sense. Our relations to the world change as the word does. And in each card is another word. Everyone bound to the Wheel turns to the center from a distinct perspective and narrative space. It is the motor of reading, a spin-cycle method of shifting perceptive orientation.

The revolutions powered by the Wheel have no end. It refuses to stop at any singular point of resolution. In doing so it opens up narrative possibilities that involve the reader's interpretive choices in the creation of possible futures, sharing the narrative responsibility of liberation. The revolution rejects the counterstance of either/or logic. This refusal of singular resolution enables a kaleidoscopic consciousness,[16] the constantly shifting perception that moves toward a both-and orientation of onto-epistem-ological multiplicity. The future will not be fixed upon a racialized, devastated past.

The Wheel's consciousness could organize a universe, harmonizing the mutual forming of our relationality. Through the interdependence of individual engagement with cultural practices, a collectivist self-model emerges. This is an embodied, intersubjective, and egalitarian approach toward reading the self, the social world, and the self's station within it. The totality of the social world is never made by any one person. The Wheel of Fortune persists to deny the status of any sole protagonist, demonstrating that the arc of decolonial liberation exceeds any one character, time, period, or place, but remains a project of each. This is multiperspectival decolonial witnessing.

The multiple schemas offered by the cards, encompassed by the turning of the Wheel of Fortune, are "sensory-motor and cognitive-affective learned structures that have been built up through past behavior and experiences in specific domains; they are central to persons' perception and cognition and serve as patterns for behaviors."[17] The reader utilizes the Wheel of Fortune to read through several simultaneous perceptions. Thus, learning to read the tarot may frustrate readers who want simple, straightforward solutions. The tarot digresses. It disrupts linear structures and patterns of perception. This multiplicity still recognizes that certain perceptions and phenomenological representations have stronger ideological relations to the shared social world than others. The kaleidoscopic consciousness can find focalization within the narrative divinatory structure. The Wheel spins, and to keep from falling off the edge, you find a focus point, some central core to lock onto no matter what changes around you. But in a pluralized narrative structure like the tarot, we interpret based upon multiple and diverse perspectives simultaneously.

The Wheel of Fortune is forever generating more standpoints through the social fabric so that the world can be experienced in more ways than has been considered. Each reading makes consciousness flexible and dynamic. It makes the psychic structure one that is always adapting in response to perceived possibility, which is always pluralized. It's this dynamic adaptability that bolsters ethical action.

The cards are keys. You're supposed to keep turning them till they click. They are mechanisms of movement that tap the reader into the nature of the cosmos. Worlds are built upon seasons and cycles, or so the Wheel of

Fortune models the mandalas of the heavens. There is an existential rhyme orchestrated at a grand, cosmic level, administered by the Wheel of Fortune, that looks like a game of chance from down below. And this gets to the sortilege divination that is tarot, that proliferates from playing cards arising in Europe somewhere in the thirteenth or fourteenth centuries. Tarot was foremost a source of entertainment among the wealthy who could commission the artist-made decks. The Wheel of Fortune reflects tarot as a medium of chance, where the readers determine what can be done with the indeterminate. Change is the language of luck, as the Wheel is considered an auspicious augur to appear in a reading. Chance, randomness, and luck do not mean meaning has been removed. We can divine seriously while still being playful with the Wheel of Fortune.

Change is a blessing because it offers hope. To acknowledge and embrace change is to affirm possibility. If tarot is a tool to heal the imagination, to restore the capacity for futuristic thinking, then it is a revolutionary tool. It is a struggle to leave notions of identity behind and imagine something new. Racism produces fatalism, an attitude that does not promise a future. Prophecy counters this. Divinatory practices such as tarot speak about hope to create a vision for the future. Hope is not as simple as reshuffling the thinking, or wishful thinking. "Hope, much like imagination, comes at a premium. The cost is a life where more is expected. Where more is expected, new actions are required."[18] If tarot is a tool to renovate the psyche's architecture, then it is a life-changing technology. The audacity of hoping for transformative change undergirds Afrofuturistic art, maintaining a spirit of liberation across space and time. Without such a vision the people would perish.

The quality of each moment is changing. There is a time and place for everything. To be in harmony, on the heavenly beat with life, we must grieve, rest, work, celebrate, and commune in a measure for which capitalism has no scale. Change is transmutation. Death is the hand of change, the force that forces change. We see kings cast down with the Wheel's everlasting imaginary of revolution. Tarot maintains a subversive historic technology to communicate, know, and challenge. It's a chance to disorder the terrorizing status quo to satiate revolutionary longings. To encounter true change, one must become self-aware within a historical, sociological construction. The white West sustains a fantasy that the desire for otherness can alone disrupt and subvert the will to dominate. Commodity culture is a delusion of cultural exchange that exploits the desire to change. To unfix one's place and participation in the contemporary social landscape, commodity culture only offers transactional conversions through a racialized sexual encounter that bell hooks refers to as *eating the other.*[19] Revolutionary turns are not accomplished by the powerful still assuming a hierarchical stance in attempting to unilaterally define the nature of relationships with the other, with the more-than-human, with time. To undo the condition of containment, the multiperspectival subject dynamic is offered through renewed time orientations.

We cannot work as if every day is the same, as capitalism contends. Capitalism consumes time, yet the Wheel of Fortune reminds us of the cosmic order of time, that astrology is a primal calendar.

> *Calendars actually "trap" time in space to handle it more easily. . . . A whole time of experience—a complete cycle such as a year or a day, a lunar or planetary sidereal cycle or a synodic cycle between two celestial bodies—thus came to be projected into space, and it took the form of a circumference: the serpent swallowing its own tail of archaic symbolism, less excitedly but more ubiquitously, the circle. The circle came to stand as the symbol for wholeness—wholeness in space as a projection of less-easily-defined and worked with wholeness in time. The advantage of working with a circle was that the circle could be visually grasped as a whole in one glance; a cycle unfolded at its own rate over time and could neither be experienced all at once nor speeded up or slowed down. Circles could also be divided into any number of segments or arcs. And while actual cycles—both natural cycles on Earth and celestial cycles—are also divided into phases, they are divided into more or less set numbers of phases.*[20]

John Mohawk has said Native ceremonies are life in motion. The circle is sacred, also understood as a medicine wheel made of crystals, herbs, totems. Great stone circles are considered feats of ritual architecture. Around the circle of the Wheel of Fortune are deities perched above clouds. These are keepers of the cosmic order. On the backs of these beings, time is held. The cross is a crossroads, a meeting with destiny on a path determined by pivotal moments of choice. There is the sword of the blue sphinx, a golden serpent, and a Red Anubis undulating around. There are sacred mysteries when subjectivity combines with infinite potential.

The Wheel is a metaphor for cyclical time, a complex structure documented by astrologers both contemporary and ancient. The Wheel respects the fact that personal development is governed by day, night, sun, and moon, by a complex arrangement of planetary forces at the moment of birth and in real time, right now. To know our own wheel or birth chart can restore a cosmic orientation and makeup to our identity. There is much more literal space to know oneself by knowing one's planetary placements and transiting activations. We are afforded an identity beyond the social categorizations of race, class, and gender. We engage in a sacred dance to move with the planets in time, to know opportune times to plant, pray, reap, and rest. Tarot makes time tangible so we can understand that it is awake, conscious, and imbued with divinity. Tarot makes time into a cypher language speaking to cycles of development. Some of the many methods of subjective time experience include solilunar cycles, synodic cycles, and ten-day cycles. The cards keep cycling, involuting, arising, clarifying, harmonizing. They offer a microcosm to understand the macrocosm. They track our personal and collective cycles; they give guideposts to keep going, to trust nonlinear growth. With them we shift between objective time and subjective duration. All of the Wheel's shifts work to clarify the foundation of the reader's spiritual philosophy or operating cosmology.

The Wheel is the higher order referenced by the Magician. Knowing the cycles of the planetary spheres is working with the wisdom of cycles to enact agency, manifestation, and meaning. The Magician is the astrologer and the Wheel of fortune is the astrology, both images of each other. And yet the Magician is the subjectivity of the present moment, while the Wheel's consciousness is of eternity.

The Wheel reminds us that life is not organized into an endless upward growth; there are periods of harvest, rest, decline. The relationship which does not revolutionize over time becomes a prison. To be stuck in an endless loop of repetition quickly incurs delusion, and so to keep from the ceaseless cycles of pain and suffering the Wheel of Fortune signals an opportunity for awareness, understanding, and action that closes the loop.

This process evolves the soul's consciousness. The arcana appears anticipating change, telling us to abandon conditioned expectations so that we might find abandoned knowledge. The Wheel augurs new developmental phases, changing epochs, generational movement, an endless pursuit of holistic realization.

Pages

Children make the best theorists, since they have not yet been educated into accepting our routine social practises as "natural," and so insist on posing to those practices the most embarrassingly general and fundamental questions, regarding them with a wondering estrangement which we adults have long forgotten. Since they do not yet grasp our social practices as inevitable, they do not see why we might not do things differently.[21]

The Pages capture the excitement and curiosity we experience when beginning again. They represent our dealings with children or youthful energy within and externally. Children return our spirit to its essence, its innocence and spontaneity. They remember our potential as a living, growing being. Children are simultaneously divinely aware and yet at the start of becoming self-realized. Children are teachers reflecting each element with the most pure and innocent expression. They find guidance from fresh perspectives as they access the wisdom of the world around them. They take us to the root, and they present an opportunity to clear and heal past trauma or nurture the nature of beginnings. There is a childlike capacity activated when awe is experienced and when discovery is made via an organic, playful engagement with the present.

The Pages of each element are the ones who begin the work delivered by each elemental Ace. They set off in each direction, the ones who "go among the standing people" or who "spend some time with those Beaver people."[22] The Pages are immersed in their environment. They are the ones who still extend selfhood, compassion, and communication to plants, elements, and animals. By innately extending personhood to the more-than-human, they live in a richly peopled world. They know Birch people, Bear people, Rock people, and they show up with an invitation for the reader's reacquaintance.

The Pages have lower stakes in outcomes because their investment is in origin. The child within knows play is praxis, a space for imaginal action, and discovery so delightful it's worth the risk of uncertainty. Critical reflections of the world around them exist in their made-up games. The Page plays as a mode of operating, moving, and being that becomes a vehicle for liberation. They are purposeful about foolery as an orientation toward engaged, joyful speculation. They are epistemologically curious, and they are us as we begin turning the pages of the unbound text that is tarot, learning to read its symbols and signs in no particular order beyond what naturally arises by chance.

Their communication is profound, honest, and uniquely revelatory. They communicate with awe and an open embrace. As such, Pages are often regarded as messengers studying in close relationship with the Knights.

> *Studying is a demanding occupation, in the process of which we will encounter pain, pleasure, victory, defeat, doubt, and happiness. For this reason, studying requires the development of rigorous discipline, which we must consciously forge in ourselves. No one can bestow or impose such discipline on someone else; the attempt implies a total lack of knowledge about the educator's role in the development of discipline. In any case, either we are the agents of this discipline, or it becomes a mere appendage to our selves. Either we adhere to study with delight or accept it as necessity and pleasure, or it becomes a mere burden, and as such, will be abandoned at first crossroads.*[23]

Discipline is necessary for the Page's maturation. Learners need to develop this discipline so that as they engage in intellectual labor, read and write carefully, and analyze, observe, and establish relationships among texts, they do so responsibly. Their love for adventures makes them daring, but they must also recognize limits. Children are often most expressive of their sense of empowerment that comes from recognized limits, as they learn to say *no.*

Yet they are needed for their innate, radical imagination. Their contribution is of vision. Children are honest seers. They are prophets of joy with the audacity to hope in a context of despair. Children's medicine is safe for all, and this is the Page's purpose. They offer a level of trust, love, and breathtaking confidence that is possible only for children. They are new to the terrain and the craft of their element. They don't necessarily know the path toward that liberated future, recognizing that their emergent mobility is wayward and the way forward unpaved, meandering, circuitous. By releasing the need to know the end result and the final location, they never find themselves lost.

Page of Swords

Pedagogically, I encouraged them to think of the moment of not understanding what someone says as a space to learn. Such a space provides not only the opportunity to listen without "mastery," without owning or possessing speech through interpretation, but also the experience of hearing non-English words. These lessons seem particularly crucial in a multicultural society that remains white supremacist, that uses standard English as a weapon to silence and censor.[24]

The Page of Swords is learning to listen without ownership. The Page of Swords begins speech beyond censorship. This Page could be the beginning tarot reader, learning a new language within the symbols, associations, scenes. Within tarot, we learn as the Page of Swords to diversify language, to search for understanding. There is no homogenous, hegemonic interpretation when reading tarot daily. It is a book whose pages are constantly shifting, new meaning always being made. To be in this dynamic state of curiosity is learning to make language communicate the truth of our many selves.

This Page learns to wield the sword differently by changing the relationship to what the sword means. By reshaping meaning, the action and application of the sword then changes. "Shifting how we think about language and how we use it necessarily alters how we know what we know."[25] They remind us we are capable of learning alternative epistemologies, ones that center truth, respect, equality of power, freedom. They appear, shifting how we know ourselves, learning new forms of communication, wielding new ideas, learning to free themselves, learning in order to be fully free. The sword's severing power is aimed toward the internalized chains of bondage rather than being used as a weapon to silence or suffer. By learning to read tarot, or any new language, the Page of Swords represents the chance to use language as the sword to subvert colonial, standard English. The Page of Swords is learning that there is no master language in true, engaged communication. There is history, there is structure, there is inherited dialect, but language is very much alive, shared amid the many readers' interpretations of similar images in vastly different ways. This Page continuously learns to communicate, to play with language, to embrace a multiplicity of voices that disrupts the thinking that the only one worthy of hearing is the one speaking standard English.

The Page of Swords is the child exploring clarity, and a child with a knife is a dangerous thing. This student voice must be encouraged. They must be given the kinds of knowledge that will agitate, arouse, and inspire action to change societal structures. Youth voice is complex and nuanced and must not be co-opted by adults. Youth must be given direct and explicit instruction, along with writer's workshops, teacher and peer feedback, and public forums to display their work. The Page of Swords seeks the freedom to choose any of the varied vehicles of expression for the complex experience and social identities among differently positioned youth. They show us the clarity of a youth's perspective. Teaching youth to shape policy, to engage, to participate within school and community is the model offered by the Page of Swords.

By considering how their self-concept exists in relation to the environment, this child explores the boundaries of self. By learning to think for themselves, the Page of Swords takes the first step toward claiming personal agency. This page finds us when we, like Arthur, grab the sword of our unique destiny. It is here as we begin to individuate, seeking the knowledge required for self-actualization.

Personal integrity forges a mighty will. Integrity is a state of wholeness, a unifying of selves displaced by dominant society, a state of knowing and being. The Page reclaims this state. They begin to shape the meaning generated from the subjective vantage point of their person.

Self-awareness extends toward social awareness. In generating a new worldview, a new sense of purpose, this youth of air is making new systems of meaning. They are constructing a new language, or a new way to use language. They are training with the sword, beginning to understand its power, how to handle its weight, the depth of its duty. They wrestle with the sacrifices required to uphold principles, personal values, self-belief, and a responsibility to right relation.

The Page of Swords teaches us about our clear, natural voice. They are the instinctual expression of truth, a force of justice that overcomes the oppression of censure. Their simplicity is piercing. Theirs is truly the beginner's mind, ready to learn, ready to share perspective. Their stance is a state of openness, yet discerning, an expression tempered by responsiveness. Engaging their authentic dialogue toward change is a "critical process in our struggle to break the *oppressor-oppressed* contradiction and the conflicting beliefs that incarcerate humanity."[26] As we begin to engage the discourses of power we become the Page of Swords as we are held to high standards of rigorous study that affirm the entirety of being, knowing, naming.

Page of Wands

The child of destiny has to face a long period of obscurity. This is a time of extreme danger, impediment, or disgrace. He is thrown inward to his own depths or outward to the unknown; either way what he touches is a darkness unexplored. And this is a zone of unsuspected presences, benign as well as malignant: an angel appears, a helpful animal, a fisherman, a hunter, crone, or peasant. Fostered in the animal school, or, like Siegfried, below ground among the gnomes that nourish the roots of the tree of life, or again, alone in some little room (the story has been told a thousand ways), the young world-apprentice learns the lesson of the seed powers, which reside just beyond the sphere of the measured and the named.[27]

The fire starter is mischievous, with a predilection to be spirited by the call of adventure. The child of fire is a child of prophetic vision. The child proclaimed as heroic journeys into miraculous realms of divine principle. Joseph Campbell tells us that epic myth, legend, and folktale contain the recurring theme of infant exile and return. The Page of Wands is representative of this young seeker, the divine child within, who encounters extraordinary wonders only permitted, plausible, and possible beyond the bounds of rational epistemologies. They begin an experiential critical interrogation to lay a foundation for *conocimiento.*

The Page of Wands steps forth as the heartbeat of the flame. With them, they bring fate foretold in the stars. Mythic fire burns bright in the timeless imagination of collective consciousness. Fire is always youthful, energized, excited, growing, and confident. The Page of Wands has boundless energy. They are extravagantly dressed, visually marking them as an outsider within their arid landscape. The Page of Wands uses their clothing, their style as a mode of subversive action. Their aesthetic has excess and is sexualized. They know they aren't too much but that white culture is never enough. Knowing that white culture will read them as excessive, the Page of Wands is even more brazen. They know "appropriateness" and "respectability" maintain racialized, gendered norms that exist to regulate identity. And they interrupt these norms with their hypervisible, stylized resistance that embraces the *extraordinary.* To the colonial imagination their presentation and their ontology are disorderly, nonsensical, and aesthetically dubious.[28] Crossing over the confines they become the perverse. The colonizers always cast suspicion upon the cognitive and affective capabilities of the colonized.

They champion their vibrant culture, like a poet touring the country translating their diverse travels through their own vernacular, accent, language, and affect. I see in this Page of Wands the queer, undocumented poets who are self-defining in their artistic pursuit. Their style is for self but also directs others' perceptions. I think of how many perish in the destitution of colonial cognition. The Page stands bodaciously, stroking their flowering wand amid these unforgiving desert trails, erased of their multisensual capacity, as if to say, "you come from the desert but baby you are not deserted."[29] It is important to the Page of Wands people that their words travel in a way that is accessible. And yet they are also the words that arrive from elsewhere, the muse that embraces the reader-writer from afar. They are led into worlds where their nonconformity is celebrated. The Page of Wands youth speak with a fire that sensualizes the perception of the listener, the querent. They warn against racializing geographies that cage the spirit in concrete. They seek a relationality that recognizes difference, and they refuse to exile others for not being considered fully or authentically anything. Their process for constructing positive self-identity does not rely on tests of ethnic legitimacy, and therein they perceive the normative expectations of cultural identity as a reductive liability.

"Furthermore, given that narratives of race, gender, and sexuality are crucial vehicles to the production of national identity, stylized resistance can interrupt expectations of multicultural assimilation often associated with appropriate Latina embodiment."[30]

Theirs is a cross-referencing perception. The Page of Wands excavates the divinatory consciousness lost to colonialism. Within this inner visionary is the desire to be seen and to show something that titillates. The card turns up with an invitation to come out of obscurity. They bravely use the light of their authentic, experimental expression and illuminate the shadows of cultural repression. With their wand they intend to plant trees, making an oasis where once was a desert. They are not there to plant a flag, to feign discovery of lands that existed long before their arrival. They have traveled far but traveled light. Their journey is of erotic self-discovery. Standing alone with their wand, they are homoerotic, surely *sui generis.* Much creativity is born from this bravery and attitude of open erotic exploration. Theirs is every element of adventure. They are the spark of attraction, the newfound joy, the passionate expression of a vital power.

This Page pursues meaning of and through artistic, personal, cultural, and/or spiritual channels. They wander, wondering what is real and authentic if not governed by racialized, colonial discourse. They are willing to re-create their personal narrative in order to reconstruct the paradigms of their social world that are more expansively erotic, affective, awakened. Their spiritual inquiry is achieved in the body's creative acts. For there to be any honest way to be in the world, the Page of Wands offers themselves and the tarot to continuously rearticulate our bodies' creative expression. They affirm creative embodiment as a site of resistance. In the dailiness of their dress they shift subjectivity. Changing self-presentation changes their self-understanding as it also critiques and rejects cultural assimilation.

They approach adventure with a spirit of playfulness, perhaps naive to the potential dangers upon the path. Yet the terrain of fire compels one to freely laugh, dance, and sing. After many dark miles, the Page of Wands reappears with light and tells you, you are no longer lost. The Page of Wands is emblematic of anticolonial resilience. Even when they are deprived of mainstream access and resources, they fashion something fabulous, proving the ghetto is more glorious than you thought. They embody a feeling of freedom when you are on a path that is yours alone, a path motivated by the conviction of purpose. Your vision will be realized through the trials of experience, but at this point your beginning is blessed and bright and full of hope.

Page of Cups

Taking the newborn from where the woman was lying-in, she takes a *xicara* [gourd] of water and carries it out to the patio and after placing it in the middle [of it], she returns to the room where the fire is and takes some of it in a pot. Taking the newborn from where the woman was lying-in, she carried it to the fire, where she had left the water, and bathed the child. She gradually killed the fire with the splashing water and asked for the child's name, which was announced by the community. . . . In the water blessing for a baby boy, the midwife used ritual words as she put water to his mouth and breast: "Here is the blue water, the yellow water, which cleanseth our hearts, so that they be purified. . . . May the heavenly water, the blue water, the deep green, go into thy body; may it remain in thy body."[31]

Children have been regarded as messengers of divinity, a blessing, in traditional Indigenous practices across time and culture. The Pages may then signal the birthing rituals of each element. The child's arrival is generative for the communal ritual orientation. Ceremonies are constructed for the child because they are a blessing of continuity.

The Page of Cups presents a chance to name ourselves anew, to call upon spiritual relatives, guardians, and guides to retain the memory of divinity within. The Page of Cups is a child of miracle, a messenger of water. The child of water, the Page of Cups, is emblematic of the child in amniotic fluid, the child within, whose spirit is made flesh in the proverbial waters. Water is used to prepare the child for communal naming. Water is a meditative force, mediating child and spirit, child and community, community and spirit. By blessing water, washing it over the babe, and then pouring the water into the child, the child is infused and cleansed with divine essence. As water retains memory, spirit is retained in the body, blessing is preserved. The child's energetic body is prepared for the impression of communal intention and grace distilled into a name, an introduction to the creative forces within the larger community. Water is poured on the child to nurture what is precious. And from the child emerges a small Star, a minor from the major arcanum, a cupbearer who replenishes the shared well of hope.

When you start allowing yourself to pray in your own voice, the Page of Cups turns up. It happens when you don't question how you hear God talking to you. Many question the difference between the voice of anxiety and the voice of intuition. Often anxiety is loud and incessant, and it deteriorates our overall sense of well-being, no matter its pretense of protection. As the voice of intuition—soft, still, reassuring—is the Page of Cups. What they have to say only inspires trust, belief, and care. When the Page of Cups speaks, fears fall asleep. The cupbearer is developing a poetics of divination, a new technology of communion by which to speak with a spirit, a goddess, an angel, an ancestor. The young, soft voice of intuition will grow into the strong song of faith. Their message is always gentle and responsive. A willingness to be possessed by joy is a rite here presented, like the first time you feel the pleasure of your voice singing.

They are a child of wonder teaching us about the nature of imagination that is the magic of innocence and trust. They can communicate the innate creativity in relationship with all things. Here is the beginner's heart, full of tenderness and big dreams. Their grand receptivity and their willingness to let a dream continuously expand are born of water's elemental nature. Water *knows* because all that has happened and will happen emerges from the water. Water is source, it gives all to all, so it is able to receive all. Therefore this Page represents a growing intuition or psychic ability. They encourage us to express what we can't see—our emotions and our most soulful dreams.

Although what they access may overwhelm, as a wave is overwhelmed by the ocean, this Page embraces their emotions as a harmonic of soul. This child is highly empathetic, very sensitive, attuned to nuance, gracious but tumultuous. By intuition they wander the realms of reverie. They communicate truth through dreams, poetry, and song. This is the child who experiences awe beholding goldfish held in a plastic bag. They will learn that the goldfish will grow as big as the body of water it's placed in, like love, like faith. It's a blessing to *perceive* God anew, suddenly illuminated within the witness of beauty. The Page of Cups trembles with controlled excitement as golden forms appear, disappear, reappear from the water.

The Page of Cups dares to envision new spiritual practices and orientations. They begin to understand their own divinatory aesthetics. They are willing to reconstruct and revise heaven, to pronounce salvation in terms that they welcome and receive. What this page seeks is their own baptism, their own communion, in their own faith. Like them we can be amazed by the magic made in finding one's own faith.

The ocean's children hear home through the seashell. They are the memory of our psychic communication that speaks to all beings through the direct language of the heart. They find a focus in the particular that opens them to the whole, which reminds them of a sacred purpose. They are the spirit of young love. In the poetic play, romance renews. They are making memories of the first time, and they bow before all love still has to teach them. Their love is the water nourishing dewy relational gardens. Their forgiveness makes beginning again possible. So many men would do well to learn from the Page of Cups, to be poured into like the Page of Cups so they would know the strength of vulnerability, compassion, and change.

In the seeker and in the community, the Page of Cups inspires trust, a belief in love, and a promise of the heart that will be fulfilled.

Page of Pentacles

We cannot overemphasize the importance of seeds: like recipes, they are a cultural inheritance passed down from generation to generation. At this point in history, we see an urgent need to resist GM seeds and to support the struggle against GMOs in Mexico and Central America where people have been organizing against GM corn, in particular. Agribusiness focuses on monoculture, raising one crop in huge fields and applying pesticides and herbicides. In contrast, indigenous ways of cultivation use intercropping, which grows more than one crop in the same field. One well-known example of intercropping is the "Three Sisters" technique, where corn, squash, and beans are grown together. Among the many benefits of this technique is that the beans "fix" nitrogen in the soil, which helps the corn grow tall and strong without the need of chemical fertilizers.[32]

The commitment to freedom, justice, and decolonization is maintained not in proclamations but in the values and habits of being. As we begin attempting to truly revolutionize our values, to change our habits of being to be a clear reflection of our commitments, the Page of Pentacles stands. The Page of Pentacles keeps us from going morally bankrupt, because their insatiable *Why?* is a constant confrontation about the source of our motivations, behaviors, and beliefs. They bring forth a value for life that enables us to live differently, beyond the order of domination. They wonder how their youth might grasp the vast knowledges of life. They take the pentacle as a living codex, the divinatory technology that prophesies through the preservation of essays, poems, prayers.

> *The pre-Columbian manuscripts offered images of flora and fauna, myth and history, genealogy, war, and ritual—from the mundane practices of daily life to ceremonies of great sacrifice. The function of those original manuscripts was to create a cartography of time and place and of the divine energies that animated through them. Painting serpentine paths of journeying, the* tlacuilos *inscribed the progressive footprints of our collective ancestors. Most codices that survive today were painted after the arrival of the Spanish, the smoke from the smoldering graveyards of the original texts still lingering in the olfactory memory of their creators. That is to say they were works created within the context of colonization.*[33]

The reader becomes the Page of Pentacles when the body of the reading, the sign, matches its shape. They behold the fruition of the foretold, learning how tarot may imbue the mundane with a numinosity when the evidence of divine dialogue yields.

With as much respect as the Page upholds the pentacle, they can read each being as a relative, as an innate relation. Their psychic prodigy is an instinctive vision of the orchard from just a single seed. They communicate with the Earth seeking consent, guidance, and growth. Knowing that they have so much yet to harvest, they take the initiative to begin tending their dreams.

This child senses the innate value of life, reflecting the seed stage graced with an inner knowing of vast potential and a powerful estimation of Earth's glorious capacity to materialize spirit. They demonstrate humanity's capacity for deep listening, nonviolence, honoring biodiversity, adaptability, and an animate relationship with the Earth. This child is connected to the cycles of change, exploring the beauty of the earth through sensual awareness and enjoyment. There is joy in beginning to fertilize your dreams, and the Page of Pentacles maintains this joy by shifting their focus from the harvest to the pleasure that ripens in process. This joy sustains the patience required for potential to be made manifest. Rather than fixating on results or forsaking pleasure until an arbitrary standard has been imposed, this Page possesses the wealth of presence, the pleasure of the body's being.

The Page of Pentacles has ancestral memory, seeking to preserve communal health and harmony. The page is the promise of cultural and ritual reclamation. The card is a meditation on the young climate activists called into action because of the wailing world left to them. They are the *Earth Guardians* organizing grassroots campaigns for environmental and climate justice. The arcanum occurs when the youth are given value-led platforms, when their capacity for contribution is affirmed. It is the card of the microgrants given to young trans and nonbinary communities to improve their well-being, increase their resiliency, and invest in their right to thrive. This is the promise of the child's wealth, their potential contribution when they receive mentorship, acknowledgment, and patience. Inheriting the tremendous weight of a global environmental and climate crisis, they incorporate intergenerational wisdom to make sustainable impact across diverse communities.

The Page of the Pentacles eats the meals only grandmothers know how to make. They learn that for food to be truly nourishing it must be made with love. This Page of Pentacles is the person who preserves seeds, stories, and recipes. Both card and recipe are regarded as living documents that change to meet the needs of community. Every seed is a prayer for the Page of Pentacles. They possess the resourcefulness and adaptability to make use of available ingredients. Decolonizing the land, mind, and body entails decolonizing the diet and restarting a relationship with food. The Page of Pentacles looks for multiple ways of eating as the more recipes we use, the more ways there are to offer people nourishing food choices. They are committed to reclaiming ancestral food knowledge, histories, and practices, while still recognizing that cultures are living and evolving. They become the homegrown educators, the teachers that are of the community they are serving. But first they are the students, young and Brown and Black and Red, and they bring the salt that cures.

Ace of Swords

With women like these, the loneliness of writing and the sense of powerlessness can be dispelled. We can walk among each other talking of our writing, reading to each other. And more and more when I'm alone, though still in communion with each other, the writing possesses me and propels me to leap into a timeless, spaceless no-place where I forget myself and feel I am the universe. This is power.[34]

When you are bound in bondage, what could be better than a sword appearing by the hand of grace? If the unconscious keeps us captive, then writing is a tool to pierce the mystery we've kept secret from ourselves. Writing may be the most daring, dangerous thing you ever do. But it's defensive as well. Either way, the writing, the sword, helps us survive. It is most precarious when it is held without intention or training. Perilous words are detached, impersonal. Then the words are not our own, and the sword is most menacing. Becoming autonomous entails a process of individuation so that we become more fully self-realized rather than further estranged. There is clarity in distinction, a power to find self-connection by honoring difference against the chorus of family and culture. The more deeply and authentically we speak from our particular experience, the more we speak to the particular experience of others. We may fear the pen's pirouettes, but the ferocity with which it allows us to leave our signature is worth its surprise, worth the cleft of a cesarean cut.

The sun rises gloriously in the east of this Ace that renews the air, speaking to the potential of words and ideas to catalyze an evolving consciousness, a shifting worldview, or a pivoting paradigm. Here is an image of power ascending, positioning the reader in truth, honesty, victorious realization. Wield the weapon to claim victory, affirm purpose, discern destiny. So much of the Swords suit is dark and damp; each card comes with rain; but the Ace is the lightning strike. Light rises within as an inspired, clear structure of consciousness. On the days you draw forth your Swords, you are to delve inward and write till the blood your sword spills across the naked page surprises your safe, censored sensibilities. Only the words that cut you can clarify a new worldview, articulated by an emerging voice. Success is self-defined by the Ace of Swords, so it is self-accepting, expressive, and courageously standing in authenticity.

Here we come to voice so strongly that we disrupt prejudiced estimations of intelligence based upon social standing. The accent and tone of self-discovery are achieved only after enduring a demanding discipline of craft. Once we master our consonants and vowels we may claim the power to properly name ourselves. Total triumph is assured in a clear connection between thought, belief, and action. The sword is object of this triumphant aesthetic integrity. The honed focus of this Ace is aimed toward heaven's higher truth.

As Paulo Friere writes, "There is no true word that is not at the same time a praxis. Thus, to speak a true word is to transform the world."[35] The transformative intellectual is realized as someone capable of articulating emancipatory possibilities and actively working toward the manifestation of liberation. This Ace wants to enact a critical dialogue by interrogating prior knowledge and preconceived notions. This Ace asks about the origin of ideas and the manner in which their ideas serve larger power dynamics. The "I" in this Ace seeks to constantly extend self-awareness toward social awareness.

A critical literacy engages the discourses of power through symbol, myth, and metaphor. The critical literacy of the Swords suit empowers us to not passively accept the authority of a given textual interpretation. The existential experience can be honored in the development of critical literacy theories (e.g., feminist, Marxist, postcolonial, psychoanalytic, etc.) and multicultural readings of canonical texts. This Ace asks us to bear the weight of transgressing cultural, linguistic, and social borders and boundaries.

It is much harder being a minority because the majority, with its many representations, does not need to work at multidimensionality. The multiple bodies, voices, histories make race a nonconsideration to white bodies. The scarceness of the minority, in representation and thus in power, works to make a monolith of a cultural group. As a minoritized person I think constantly about how I experience multidimensionality, as well as the expression of my many vocal tones, registers, and ranges. Discussing various oppressions like race in a racist society is extremely difficult, but such a discourse demands confrontation. To avoid being silenced in space we must confront an internalized oppressor, must grapple with our varying complicity and entanglement in white supremacist capitalist imperialist patriarchy by using the sharpest sword we can. This confrontation does not necessarily imply violence, and yet many who are charged with facilitating such dialogues seem to fear violence, stifling passion in favor of a neutral conversation. Our words are no more safe if they are silent than they are if shared. It's a double-edged blade. Real words require risk to be spoken. Any "safe" conversation is a silent one, more dangerous because the silencing of authentic perspectives, dissenting experiences, and critical awareness only engages the oppressor's racially coded language that many speak so cavalierly. That piercing dog whistle, inaudible to all except its intended audience, is blown with the intention to debilitate and domesticate.

The point of the Ace of Swords is the pressing necessity of truth-telling. A righteous word can only be spoken by the character willing to be named, to expand their personal mythos, their sense of social reality. We slice right through an unconscious or conditioned allegiance to a belief system that victimizes, harms, or dominates. We sever attachments to fixed interpretations and static perceptions of time, the world, the self, the other to become as light as feather, surrendered to air, riding the wind. The Ace of Swords is held only in the complete presence of the moment as the identity detaches from shaky, ever-fluctuating external circumstances. This card seats our consciousness with the stillness of the breath so we may witness the mind's shimmering reflectivity. And for the loss and sacrifice our freedom claims by the sword, flight is a symbol of life, even in death. And our name shall be infused with meaning that will live on.

Ace of Wands

Thus, because of the way in which domestic myths are transmitted, people often never learn that they are myths; people become submerged in their view-points, prisoners of their own traditions. They readily confuse attitudes toward reality (proclamations of value) with reality itself (statements of fact). Failing to see their own myths, they consider all other myths false. They do not understand that the truth of all myths is existential and not necessarily theoretical. That is, they forget that myths are true to the extent they are effective. (In a sense, myths are self-fulfilling prophecies: they create facts out of the values they propound. Thinking we are superior to other creatures, for instance, we set ourselves up as such and use them ruthlessly. People that think of themselves as brothers to the beasts live with them in harmony and respect.)[36]

White culture has an uncanny ability to mystify reality among people of color. Without a clear sense of our own histories, we are vulnerable to the delusional and destructive myths of white supremacy. As you realize an ideology has been imposed upon you, anger mixes with confusion. White worldviews maintain dominance so long as they shape the consciousness of the masses. We are blind until the fire touches us.

The Ace of Wands arrives erect. And before us is an absolute reality, and it's self-stimulating. With the Ace of Wands we write with a reason, a sparked interest, a cause. And with it we make myth to achieve self-determination. The penis is a phallus, but the phallus is not necessarily the penis. The wand is the phallus rather than the penis, the active rather than receptive symbol of power and fertility that can be wielded by any, regardless of sex or gender. The staff is a symbol of external power and authority. But it only appears as we understand how we have been complicit in our own subordination. Fire's animacy lends itself to sudden inspiration. Fire is all-knowing, possesses every prophecy. The Ace of Wands is then a divinatory scepter. Burn a white fire, and the past will be purified.

When Persephone was presented with the Ace of Wands, it became the vehicle of her descent into the fiery underworld until she was transformed into the mythic Queen of the Underworld. Through the fire we journey into the South, calling up sexual awakening, resilience, reawakening. Be transfigured in fire, and lay the shell of potential upon the pyre. Intense desire activates, and once deeply rooted, fire pulls the soul upward.

The Ace of Wands grows toward the sun, ripening sexual energy at the base of all creation toward a cosmic consciousness. It arrives with the impulse to shine, create, flower. We take the tree and cannot deny our arm as a branch connected to Earth. A torch is passed to you so that it is not light but *fire* that drives the inquiry. To speak so authentically, to be so brazenly honest in how you say what you see, is to hold the Ace of Wands. The suit of Wands becomes a space of discovery and understanding. It's an erotic adventure, a place of pleasure, a place of passion. After setting in the West, the Sun endures the night's trials. Fire is the night's guide, burning every color with its heat.

From the wand we know the will to live, which is distinct from the will of the sword, existing at a separate point in an alchemical process. The cold sword of truth is forged in the fire, tempering integrity and enduring the sacrifice of crude constructs. From fire we meet the dangers of excess, the potential burnout of unceasing consumption. Desire is a force of movement, a vehicle of illumination rather than a destination. There is no end to the fire. It emanates into the atmosphere and acts upon its environment.

Fire is the imagination's nature. Fire answers the prime existential questions of purpose and identity. Fire is profound because in its flames the widest range of questions of meaning are addressed. Fire touches first causes and the essence of perception. It is the mythic statements that make culture. You cannot perceive fire without slipping into a state of awe.

Feed the fire. It must be fed all night, all day. It must never stop burning. It's relentless. The fire will consume every offering. Offer your prayers, your salt, your tears, your grief, your fears, your faith. Fire is ancient. It is our first ancestor. It might burn, but it keeps the heart from turning to stone. The burn teaches us respect. Fire is necessary to engage the dispossessed. It agitates political passions and arouses critical curiosity. Arousal guides an inquiry toward what unsettles us. Fire's confrontation creates confidence and commitment. When fire talks with you, it's a rigorous discussion. It's not nice and does not deem your ignorance acceptable. It demands discernment. Not everything can withstand the flames' provocation. But fire is a wise counsel, for the insights discovered in the fire are long retained. It inspires self and socially transformative praxis.

The Ace of Wands can change the power dynamic and galvanize the citizenry and those with righteous passion to step forward. Without fire, there would be no motivation, no desire, no invention. And we are rescued from a profound, protracted passivity. We are fired up and we are furious, defiant, and we are not desolate nor helpless or hopeless. The fires that burn for hours on end lift into the night. An unbearable heat proliferates. And the light from this fire shows what we could not otherwise see about ourselves. And what we see is unexpected, unpredictable, and alive and uncontrolled. There's fire everywhere because we refuse to stay down. We keep rising and rising.

Our bodies have become far too cold begging for justice. We want power, and the fire has made us fearless. We are nowhere compliant. We rally round the flame and rebuke the terrible horror inflicted upon us. What will be left standing after the fires of revolution are centered on principle. Self-hatred has gone up in smoke. Sense the victorious spirit that has risen. With the Ace of Wands, envision the long pursuit of justice. We are to take the Ace of Wands and become liberatory leaders. The honesty of this leadership unsettles and motivates the reader to personalize social issues. The fire that fosters transformative change captures passion, frustration, and anger. With the Ace of Wands we find a power highly concentrated with a palpable intensity. We begin the pursuit of freedom with the fire born of the Ace of Wands, only to find an unexpected creative communion as the reward for our bravery.

Ace of Cups

He knows, for example, one can't afford to give into desolation. He is against brooding about enclosed spaces, even beautiful ones like gardens, but supports dreaming of wild open spaces, like sea and mountains. He understands too well the temptation of sadness, the dangers of indifference, the healing power of laughter. . . . So many modern and contemporary poets are terrified of deep feeling, of seeming undefended and "sentimental." . . . Many write as if it were desirable to refine out the emotional registers of the lyric. We live in a cool age. But I invoke Hikmet precisely for his emotional excess, for writing an oracular human-sized poetry, for his toughness and unblushing sentiment, for calling the heart a jewel that should never lose its luster.[37]

Write till what you write makes you cry. That writing will be an antidote to apathy. The water takes us West, toward death, toward release. The Ace of Cups teaches us to craft a sexual epistemology rooted in spirituality. Overflowing from the Ace of Cups is a substance both temporal and divine. It washes over our wounds and welcomes us in the mysterious, sacred realms of spirit. It establishes reading and writing as an alternative spiritual tradition that does not create false divides between spirituality, sexuality, or knowledge. Instead, queer sexuality becomes a mode toward ecstatic spirituality. In the Ace of Cups is self-sustaining sexual subjectivity.

Water and wetness psychically express what is deepest and richest within. Currents of joy bridge the physical, emotional, spiritual, and intellectual. The value of intellectual and political labor should be appreciated in measure with the spiritual work of revolutionaries. Its promotion is just as important toward a liberating selfhood. We need the words that arise from the erotic spirituality of this golden grail because they create a context of healing. Cum conjures spiritual well-being in the Ace of Cups consciousness. Cum is queer when it overcomes the shame that represses our natural knowing of bodies' desires and pleasures.

The subjectivity of the Ace of Cups is fluid and able to embrace a polytheistic, nonheteronormative consideration of body and spirit. The Ace of Cups helps us find a viable alternative space to worship. When writing becomes the spiritual tradition, the essay possesses creative energy, and by creating a subject we create our own deities and doctrines. Writing becomes the way to praise a supreme being within the self. The Ace of Cups reads the body as a holy text. Any body of writing is therefore divination. Words are vessels we receive God in. Our words allow. They are spacious enough for various sexualities to be practiced within. We write praise songs and presence ancestral guidance. Words drip from our tongue, and we taste the sweetness of our spirit. There is unique pleasure in their catharsis.

The writing only elevates and sustains the divination. Divination has been grouped into categories of "possession," "wisdom," and "intuitive" practices. Reading encounters the Divine, but so does the word. Language descends upon us like blessings spoken by ancestral voices. The sexual desire deep within is suppressed with fear and shame. Alternative sexualities were considered heathen and savage by the self-righteous sexual morality of white colonizers. The Ace of Cups reunites a divided body and soul severed by patriarchal racism. It is the alternative to destructive heterosexual practice, because its pleasure source exceeds dual-gendered systems and dual sexual orientations. The pussy praise inherent in the Ace of Cups is a viable force for radical movement toward queer sexual autonomy and agency. It is a site of autonomous, exalted pleasure and a subjectivity of spiritual embodiment. There is multiplicity and an interplay of difference.

This love is not simply romantic; it is devotional. These are the waters of baptism by bodily fluid. This love is beyond limitation, beyond the masculine ownership of female eros. The Ace of Cups is a place to glory in the erotic power of sexual pleasure. This radical sexual liberation opens the ritual healing space.

Love springs forth like water, pouring in every direction. This open emotional space is cleansing and restorative. It observes the words that bless, the words that praise, that heal. The emotions as a psychic, spiritual water spring from some unknown source, yet they offer a subjective experience of a universal current. Here is the high tide lifting all boats. The rain falls freely, and you are the vessel being poured into. There is no space the water will not wash, no space out if its reach, no call unanswered. The mind may be incredulous and incapable of fully comprehending the heart's capacity. It's the only opening that a soul can be born from. The soul's sensorium expresses in the emotions. They bustle with gratitude and grief, grace and passion, purpose and creativity.

The golden chalice is here for you, ready to sip from and so partake of liquid love. It is our heart's divine inheritance. As the water recycles through each generation, we sense how deeply these waters remember, how much is retained in the deep psyche. Ancestors cry with us. The performance of memory is a pivotal component of diasporic religions. The Ace of Cups encapsulates this idea by merging memory, water, and space, the West. Space and memory compose a dialectic. A homeland memory is shaped within the memory of the new space, the hostland. The memory of rapture, as presented by this Ace, is salvific.

> *Whether memory is a "rope let down from heaven" or a pain "burnt in," diasporic memories are formed, erected, and galvanized as a reaction against a monstrous obliteration. . . . Spatial shifts like those caused by migration call up memory in response to territorial crisis, and every new house or territory is "read" in some sense as a variation of the original oneiric place: the homeland now becomes the place of dreams.*[38]

This Ace carries memory, allowing us to dream in new expressions determined by different positions in space. The memory of rapture transforms in the spaces of our migration. The body-mind-soul becomes re-membered and enacted as the homeland, traveling and constructing across diverse ranges of space. The homeland becomes a dreamland, a temple, a spaceship. The Ace of Cups captures this portable altar while the tarot is a technology of movement, a mode of mobility that sustains selfhood via divination. A sense of salvation is preserved. After finding this place in the soul it is unforgettable. We can try to hold the humility of such deep receiving, but the water's generous grace doesn't stop with determinations of deservedness. The Ace of Cups says it is not only safe to trust your feelings, but that trust is an act of faith. The rites of the West return whatever was lost to the ocean.

Ace of Pentacles

Pictography is not a dead language, lying flat in archival tombs. I aim to show that those tombs have always been cenotaphs, empty signifiers for a signifying system that is very much alive, energetic, responsive, and indeed unnatural in its ability to continuously redefine the nature of its world. The key to doing that is to focus on the semiotic and aesthetic forms of these signs, and to observe how these forms have moved across language and cultures to create contemporary experiences, insights, and relations.[39]

At the heart of tarot reading are the questions readers pose. The reader questions how the signs of each arcanum illuminate the reader's normative ideological positions, social spaces, and psychic temporalities, and how they might subvert, transgress, or transform those perceptive positions. Card laying becomes a way to more consciously shape the intersubjective consciousness required for divination. The cards' questions make us cognizant and capable of decoding the signs of the social body. The body's subjectivity is understood and perceived differently across different aesthetic thresholds, but materiality limits, defines, organizes, coheres, and enlivens these various bodily positions.

The Ace of Pentacles solidifies these worlds and absorbs us into their realities. It makes us resilient gardeners of golden grain. It is the seed of Spirit that becomes corporeal. The flesh offers truth. With its gift we can promote communal survival and become maximally positioned to thrive in the summer springtime and endure the winter's bone. The Ace of Pentacles is a metaphor for power, exchange, and labor. Conceptual domestication extinguishes wildness within the imagination. The Ace of Pentacles represents the human artifacts that compromise the alienated Western world. But the cards resist being collared, and they interject the energy of chaos and chance into the colonial consciousness. The wealth of experience cannot be commodified or explained uniformly. Cartomancy opens toward miraculous possibilities of the unexplained, where we can again encounter something more than ourselves.

At the crux of the card is the issue of ownership. Its strange, unnatural concept applied to the land. Ownership of land is rather a leasing arrangement, because this land we pay taxes on will be the land our bodies are buried in. It is the earth that will repossess us.

"You don't need to actually own any land. Over the years, I've gardened on ten different pieces of Oregon land, all but one begged, borrowed, rented or leased. There is vulnerability in not owning the land where you garden, of course. But land ownership doesn't confer invulnerability."[40]

Land claims can only be defined by relations of domination and Indigenous dispossession. State sovereignty may be a fiction that negates Native power. Since time began people have rushed the rivers and harvested the lands. To the extent that those activities are conceived as state-regulated rights, Indigenous being, even within specific territories, will be shaped and thus defeated by the dominant Western paradigm. With the Ace of

Pentacles we are to reject the claimed authority of the state and assert our relation to the land regardless of state-sanctioned right. Sovereignty is a renewed self-assertion in the presence of others. It is not an enclave. In this Ace is the adamant refusal to "dissociate culture, identity and power from the land."[41] The capitalist intent to devour the land inherently disrupts spiritual Indigenous sovereignty.

Sandy Grande tells us that this shameful intent necessitates more than a revolutionary critical pedagogy; it requires an *ensoulment,* the reciprocal reclamation of Indigenous peoples and the land. The deep connection among the Earth, its beings, and the Spirit world are foregrounded by the Ace of Pentacles. Morally inspired by these connections, we are able to access ancestral ways of knowing and historically ground ourselves. We all want economic self-sufficiency. But by clarifying our value system, our sense of meaning is able to endure. The Ace of Pentacles is the realization that we can create conditions of possibility for human beings to be more than capital. We are to reclaim our power from the thrall of consumer culture. Indigeneity prioritizes respect, harmony, autonomy, and peaceful coexistence. Communal stability depends upon our ability to listen to our bodies, each other, and the land.

The Ace of Pentacles invites sensual, embodied exploration and discovery. Our bodies are the first pentacles, the material expression of the five directions. Life is a material, practical opportunity. This is a chance to invest the body's energy into a material representation of inward truth. The external work becomes the manner of refining inner integrity. This is an invitation to create from inner integrity by planting in the dark. It may be a time to dig deeper to find what holds value, meaning, worth. To find the fertile earth, the intimate place within where something good will grow, we learn patience. What is the seed of thought, the primary state of being that begets prosperity and abundance? In this Ace, contemplate worthiness.

Through the body's labor, nourishment, ecstasy, and ache, the spirit becomes like a diamond, refined and realized as eternal Spirit. This is the earth of Virgo. "Jade gives itself up to the artist, and allows its body to be violently cut, drilled, shaped and polished, in an act of sacrifice."[42] The body is a gift. And what must be offered in exchange for corporeality is time. The body bears many losses, but loss becomes sacrifice, a sacred exchange through conscious intention. The body offering becomes sacred as it is offered to Spirit, offered to a purpose beyond any one lifetime, but offered to life itself. It is not about the body's beauty or capacity or productivity. The body simply *is* sacred. This sensual epiphany is given a new form any time this Ace appears in a reading. This is seeker as the seed. A core value is unearthed, clarified, and grasped.

The Ace of Pentacles is the arrow pointing North. The North is the astrological fourth house, the nadir of the birth chart. The North is the place of the ancestors. Thus, this Ace tells us the pentacles are many places to find ancestral guidance. The Northern Ace asks us to cherish life, to let death and ancestry inform life. The death processes are more than a matter of decay; they are a mode of resurrecting ancestral veneration. The Earth displays its vast fecundity, variegated in its verdant prosperity, open deserts, and barren plains. In the dead places we find ancient and eternal connection; we come to realize the North as a state of consciousness. "Flower Mountain was portrayed as a pyramid with stairways flanked with plumed spirits, which served as a symbolic entrance into this paradisal solar realm. Flower World nonetheless intersected with the North as the space of the sun's zenith, where ancestors went, resided and contacted."[43]

This path toward illumination requires exploring the unfathomable depths of the unconscious. So while this Ace calls in the North, it presents us a descending path, a chance to bring consciousness and spirit into our bodies, as we invest the body in the land's lasting wealth. The soul secures a divine connection as we deeply root and realize the body as a vast ecosystem of relationships maintained over lifetimes.

TWO

Binary thinking, which focuses on just two groups, usually whites and one other, can thus conceal the checkerboard of racial progress and retrenchment and hide the way dominant society often casts minority groups against one another to the detriment of each other. Immediately after the Civil War, the army recruited newly freed slaves to serve as Buffalo Soldiers putting down Indian rebellions in the West. Not long after, southern plantation owners urged replacing their former slaves with Chinese labor. Congress acquiesced.[1]

The Two represents duality, opposition, tension, balance, projection, and integration. It is the antithesis, the contrast, the juxtaposition, the counter. Each element represents various aspects of two poles held in counterbalance. The Two presents the pairs seeking synthesis, uncovering another aspect of true reality. The Two anticipates synthesis, union, and profound integration. The Two offers a gaze as a mirror to more than reflect the self—it actually constitutes the self as it is beheld.

Two is the displacement of subjectivity; it is the hole left by the wounded word. Two seeks to decenter the self, bowing to our constitution, which is interdependent upon the other. Two understands that through another, the self is born, birthed from the other's bodily sacrifice. Of my own birth, my mother said it felt like her hips were breaking, but it was my collarbone that was broken. I was too wide and my head too big for my sixteen-year-old mother to bear. Finally, the doctor broke my clavicle to keep the umbilical cord from asphyxiating me. To be alive I had to be broken. Without that wound, my mother or I could have died. Two relates the realms of life and death.

Two enables the One, giving silence to speech as green gives to the immemorial. Two pierces the illusion of separation by revealing our inherent relatedness. Personhood is constituted by our encounter with *the other*—the human, the nonhuman, the Divine personage. Where One is the speech, Two becomes the listening. Where One is the call, Two is the response, brought forth in silence. Two is discovering our being has already and always been created in response to the call. It is the answer waiting for the One's question to arise. One is the rising, Two the setting. Two teaches us the constitution brought by destitution. So that One can give, Two receives. Two asks for sacrifice, seeking to teach the nature of relational composition. Two generates by giving away the One. Two encompasses duality, Omeyocan, the place of duality, originating beyond the heavens, producing the cosmic stage upon which everything unfolds.

Where One is the selfhood's subjectivity, Two is the confrontation with the other. At large, Two becomes the power and shape of knowledge. Two is prism, whereby we step into the mirror, easily to be confused in the binary thinking of domination. One would side with their oppressor so long as they are unable to see themselves in clear connection with the plight of the oppressed. Until the image that Two reflects inspires solidarity, One will stand alone, severed from truth, alienated from humanity. Two gives relatedness, distorted by the binaries of white supremacy. Colonial subjects become ethnocentric, conditioned to the set standard against whiteness, whereby status, power, and privilege are reserved for whatever is not Black. White supremacy exists on a spectrum of anti-Blackness. As anti-Blackness became the economic model for global imperialism, conquistadors and slave masters stripped the world bare to create commodity. Bodies born of relation became capital for the One, the Monarch, the King, the Capitalist. Whiteness is about perception, as its class construction has historically been shifting and malleable.[2] It is a state whereby one refuses to see. To be precise, it is not a sacrifice, which can only be made by personal consent; it is theft. It refuses to give, so it takes. If the self is created in its offering, whiteness dehumanizes by stealing our offering. Whiteness exists in the perversion of exchange into dichotomies of domination.

The High Priestess

These cave-beings—emerging from another side of time in the earth's depths, hidden from the casual disappearances and erasures of history, abiding in the contorted darkness of snakes and spirits deep underground—must want something with the people on the surface. They await their time, reclining in the low rumble beneath our feet until, like a sudden rain in the summer heat, they spread over the earth. In the creation stories of greater Mesoamerica, humans were once such underground dwellers. They rippled in subterranean pools until cosmic pressure pushed them through a hole into emergence in the upper world. . . . There are further holes above through which to ascend. And even so below, the Diné knew the Hopi and other Pueblos, who also come up through a concentric hole, after which they are transformed from lizard-like people into five-fingered caretakers of maize.[3]

The point of descending into death is to retrieve the substance of life: maize. Seeds from the underworld become an abundant upper-world miracle by the chthonic female deities depicted by the High Priestess. The High Priestess is the Moon's arcanum. To stand before her is to acknowledge her power over the forces of life and death, as it is her body that transforms death into life. The High Priestess's body is every medium of divination, every card in every deck. The psychic faculty is an extended range of existential extensivity, as Edgar Garcia names, an extension or continuation of one being into another. It's a cosmological orientation toward and understanding of relationality that is interdimensional, interspecies, and multistratal. The deck is her psychic manuscript, her holy prophetic text that reads and reveals the inherent relationality of all.

If the Devil is the belly of the Earth, she is the mouth. She is the caves and the grottoes. Her body is a terminal, a way we leave mundane consciousness and enter the profound, and exit the otherworldly onto Earth. When she speaks, it rains, and seeds sprout. Her chthonic cycles swallow the whole of life only to spit it out again. Her deep indwelling surfaces with insight into caring for lasting sustenance. She is the old way. We must again and again renew the life she lends to us. Her subterranean power is unmatched. She demands a reckoning with our interdependent personal and social histories. She summons what we have sown. Her dawn comes by chaos, risk, and crisis if it must.

By knowing the names and cycles of our forebears we can revise their cycles we naturally repeat. The High Priestess's lunar function of self-reflexivity enables revision, redemption, and reconfiguration rather than fatalistic bifurcation. By seeing the fate of the fathers, the sons alter their actions to revise their destiny toward victorious fulfillment. The High Priestess is the historical lesson of our familial psychic legacy. All fates extend from that shared origin. She sits as the source of power over history through cyclical revision. The Moon is dis-/re-membered every month, paying with her own pussy for the flesh of the future. She is the exemplar of moving from victimhood to empowerment, from displacement to self-sovereignty.

In the deep substrata of the collective psyche, the High Priestess is there waiting for us to remember. She *is* the memory faculty that makes the mind malleable. Through the High Priestess, we elevate memory to its mytho-historic magical capacity. The mythic memory is the restorative and creative act fashioning a new sacred experience that revitalizes. It's her understanding that to advance is to return again and again to the site of the origin. She opens the underworld for us, shining her light to reflect awareness in what was once unconscious. The High Priestess illuminates the shadow's presence, the shadow's gifts. She speaks in subtle whispers in meditation, in the mirror of the cards or the stars. She shows us how to travel to new psychic landscapes, soon to become our newborn bodies, opening doors we never knew were closed.

She teaches us a different language to speak with the unconscious, opens a different eye for insight into the internal, invisible world. She heightens the reader's psychic ability, putting old wisdom in new bodies with an old world and an omen. She finds us in dreams, déja vù, and memory, catalyzing our pattern recognition, our awareness of the matrices of power that shape realities and pattern the psyche. She reclaims your consciousness from dogmatic conditioning.

> *Underworld descents in the epic tradition are often expressions of political necessity: Aeneas's quest below to retrieve imperial prerogative and the rights of conquest for Rome; Jesus Christ's harrowing of hell to extend Christendom backward in time, to all times; and Dante's journey through the Roman Catholic inferno to descry cosmic order in the chaotic midstream of political unrest in late thirteenth and early fourteenth-century Florence. In some ways the Popul Vuh is like these works. It has cosmic realpolitik in it, but it also emphasizes that none of its political life can be realized without the gift of maize.*[4]

The High Priestess protects sacred knowledge, making the page blank to those who would denigrate or seek to dominate the extended epistemology of witches, *curanderas,* feminist scholars. While the Magician activates its power through embodied expression, the expressive voice of authority, the High Priestess is the witness to the truths too dangerous for kings and patriarchs to express. So the High Priestess is the act of literary transgression, enacted in all the female authors who dare to read and write and speak against oppressors within and without. Her prompt is to read, enter the blank page, and seek sanctuary. She is a rigorous reader, reading till the words within overcome the voice of internalized colonization, overcome the voice of self-loathing, the immense shame that makes us mute. But her sanctum is also silence, teaching us discernment. Silence is different from being silenced; being silenced serves cultural genocide, but to preserve what is sacred she keeps her secrets still. We pull the High Priestess and determine if and when and where and with whom we should open, whom to receive, where life should be made, and where to lay the dead to rest.

The High Priestess holds truths so intimate, they must be held until we are ready for revelation. The High Priestess is watching, recording our life with the counternarratives of the oppressed partaking in writing autobiography or memoir. Their body births the cultural documents that tell the truths deemed taboo by dominant culture. In the words of bell hooks, "Her love of words is a private passion—one she would rather not share. In the house of her childhood though everything had to be shared. If she tried to hold anything back, they would search and find the hidden places. Her written words, discovered, read were just the source of more pain and punishment. This was why she loved poetry. They did not always understand it so they left it alone."[5]

The High Priestess preserves our right to say no, to deny giving others our most cherished words, most valuable perspectives, when their asking is not an ask but a demand. She is intriguing, yes, but she teaches us to refuse exoticization, to refuse becoming a specimen, an ethnographic subject from a faraway, strange place. She offers us the sweetness of aloneness, though we may fear it. The High Priestess preserves one's privacy. In her own room, in her own body, she tests the daring of our self-exploration, erotically, imaginally.

She asks us to take a critical, reflective look at the experiences that most shape us, and to work with tarot to create a biomythography by using dreams, fantasies, and longings to invent the new self. Remembering the past, there is no absolute truth. She teaches us to discern fact from the interpretation of fact. She makes us aware of our biases, default interpretations of self that may not be as factual, fixed, or rigid as we've held. So the High Priestess shows us how we shape ourselves. By her activation we can know ourselves differently by re-relating to our past. She wants us to find a new body for our past, as a means not only to deposit the wealth of our experience but also to unbind the pain of ancestors from our spines. To transfigure pain, fear, and absence into writing that is daring and difficult is to High Priestess. Against the cultural backdrop of white supremacist capitalist patriarchy, it continues to be an act of resistance for Black women, Indigenous women, queer women to write against the grain. As Zora Neale Hurston reminds us, "If you are silent about your pain, they'll kill you and say you enjoyed it."

It is difficult to decide to write about one's emotional landscapes. Yet engaging the psychoanalytic power that enables self-reflexivity is an act of re-mediation, always taking place when we critically reflect on past events and choose to rewrite the past with our current understanding. We must explore the splits of mind, body, and spirit if we are to ever find those lost dimensions, if we are to ever call them home again. She is whom to turn to when you've lost yourself, helping us reconcile what we have disowned within ourselves under the duress of domination.

She tends to our most devastating disruptions. The sudden changes in narrative that shift our entire relationship to being may be traumatic until one learns how to harness such a subversive power. To read as the High Priestess reads is to challenge hegemonic, conditioned institutional narratives written all over your bare body. It is to begin a process of redistributing meaning. It is a prowess of economy, to recycle the body and its relationships into the most radical sources of self-regard. Somehow the High Priestess takes disjointed spirits, fragmented psyches, and makes a body of coherence out of an apparent nothingness.

She teaches us that we can leave pain behind by reading. Even when *they* try to take our books, our words, our pleasure away, she offers the memorized heart poetry to recite as incantations of liberation. "In reading the Sacred Scriptures, one feeds on them, one ruminates, one tastes their flavor, and, says Jean Leclerq describing this practice, 'all activity, is necessarily, a prayer, the *lectio divina* is a prayerful reading.'"[6]

Trust the heart's knowing above all else. Submit to the High Priestess to summon the intuitive methods, the nonrational ways of knowing to deconstruct patriarchal assertions of logic. As Patricia Hill Collins notes, alternative knowledge claims are routinely ignored, discredited, or simply absorbed within existing paradigms. The High Priestess represents these alternative epistemologies, which challenge all certified knowledge by testing the taken-for-granted given truth against alternative assessments. The High Priestess then decolonizes our knowledge sources and, reading tarot, aligns with feminist ethics. She knows colonizers do not listen to what the colonized say, especially if their theories come from experience and not from books. Rather than relying on institutional validation of knowledge and experience, the tarot becomes a radical act of literacy by placing the cards in the hands of the people. It is the people who become the authority to certify knowledge, able to speak for themselves, record their unique experience, and trust the truth of the heart to find the wholeness denied in patriarchal culture.

"Poetry sustains life. Of this I am certain. There is no doubt in my mind that the pain of poverty, whether material or emotional lack, can be eased by the power of language."[7]

The High Priestess asks us: *Why are the pages blank?* She listens to our frustration and rage. She knows that if we want authentic inclusion we must keep on writing the books that will tell our truth, record our existence, our brilliance, our becoming, our embodied demands for change. As we add our voice to the stories of challenge and resistance, the High Priestess honors the truth tellers who have lit the path in the past. She sees that we are not walking in the darkness alone. She holds the record of every cultural artifact, every image of someone who isn't supposed to be there, all the times our self-assertion transgresses against the power that would keep us relegated to the shadows. She's there when we show up so deeply that we can't be ignored. There will be no doubting our impact, no forgetting we were here.

The High Priestess embodies the principle of duality; or rather, she is the space to explore between duality. Within the written word we can articulate the bodies that breach the boundaries of race and class, gender and sexuality. While the Magician expresses the unseen into the material world, the High Priestess recovers from the mundane world the unseen pain and potential. She initiates a journey of soul retrieval, a recovering, a transformation through integration with that which has been hidden or obscured. She is our ability to navigate the dark corners of the mind, our nonlinear, oracular thinking. She is the divinatory mind. The High Priestess guards the chaos, summoning its entirety, its pure potential, and gives body to being through the channel of time.

In an unbuckling of labels used to fasten the body in place, tarot engages a process of identity disruption. Her divinatory body births, breaks, and repairs the boundaries of time. Divination is a path of space-making. It stretches the soul. Where once we were rigid and stiff in belief, in knowing, faith becomes an act of flexibility stretched by divination. We are released from the severity of stasis, with a serpent tongue that can speak for an eternal soul in a plane of temporality.

A divinatory body must be capable of processing paradox, simultaneity. We become multiconversant, more fluid in response to the choir of relationships that engage the body into being. In the High Priestess are many ways to know ourselves. The journey is not toward another fixed point of reflection or self-realization but an identity as the fluid experience of simultaneous de-/re-construction and experimentation.

Justice

Once upon a time there was an old woman. Blind. Wise. In the version I know the woman is the daughter of slaves, black, American, and lives alone in a small house outside of town. Her reputation for wisdom is without peer and without question. Among her people she is both the law and its transgression. The honor she is paid and the awe in which she is held reach beyond her neighborhood to places far away; to the city where the intelligence of rural prophets is the source of much amusement.[8]

Law is the language of power. It is a process of defining, labeling moral states and status. Justice begins to open our eyes to the process of legal storytelling, the language used to determine to whom we ascribe innocence and guilt. Deeds done become a reflection of intention. Justice *legitimates* experience by demonstrating the principle of cause and effect. "The intense struggle to draft appropriate language reflects far more than a simple, lawyerlike impulse to be precise; it also reveals an acute sense of the importance of citizenship, both for symbolic reasons and in terms of the rights and obligations appurtenant to that status."[9] Those with hegemonic power go to great lengths to create language that justifies exclusion while trying to ostensibly orient around liberty.

Capitalist individualism incentivizes people to value the representation of Justice over the thing itself. Justice makes us viscerally aware of the limits to such storytelling. Representation is the central problem for the colonized mind. Representing diverse peoples through gatekept positions flattens the individual and the intended represented group, and such efforts often fail by reproducing essentialist thinking. Diversity seeks to assimilate the other into the status quo. It is the state interpolating its subjects. This makes it possible for any exploited or oppressed group to become complicit in the structure of domination. Diversity aims to use power that reinforces the status quo rather than challenges, changes, or revolutionizes. Diversity is geared toward the marketplace morality of capitalism that co-opts the name of Justice. This orientation makes desires that divest or diverge from economic exchange shameful, if not a crime, and it is far removed from the structural revolution required for radical inclusion, for Justice. A false promise is sold to communities of color who seek to learn from any institution that is ostensibly committed to social change but that maintains the current demographics of power.

It seems common sense that you would have a diverse representation of voices in efforts to seek authentic critical discourse, and yet I am cognizant of the history of various institutions that have denied a seat at the table to the groups with most at stake. If one has to join white society to be counted, then there may be representation, there may be taxation, but no Justice. Citizenship as debated, defined, and reconstructed through congressional history has focused on the problem of Indigenous recognition. The struggle derived from the presence of Native peoples residing on land the US government claimed by conquest. While previous international law held that conquered inhabitants of conquered nations were generally integrated into the polity of conquerors as citizens, this status was denied Indigenous Americans. Yet the conquering of Native peoples and the annexing of their lands was justified by language that would deny them the possibility of citizenry, labeling them as alien, uncivilized, savage. Chief Justice John Marshall gives voice to the white colonial mindset:

> *The tribes of Indians inhabiting this country were fierce savages, whose occupation was war, and whose subsistence was drawn chiefly from the forest. To leave them in possession of their country, was to leave the country a wilderness; to govern them as a distinct people, was impossible, because they were as brave and as high spirited as they were fierce, and were ready to repel by arms every attempt on their independence.*[10]

To suggest the tribal governments possessed sovereign authority over their lands would imply that the federal government's authority over recognized tribes of Indigenous Americans be subject to limitations. They argued over naturalization, over the Indigenous population who lived outside tribal communities. Yet naturalization was aimed toward garnering states more power in political representation. It was not an investment in or attempt to consider Indigenous people as full, political equals of whites.

Racism is not simply located in biased individual actions; nor is it a simple prejudice of misperception. The goal of conscientization is not just to help the oppressed/oppressor to realize the misperception of their prejudice but also to challenge the racist institutions controlled by wealthy whites, who restrict access to power and privilege by usurping territory and titles. Euro-American academics reproduce colonialism in their assertions as authorities on the subjects of minorities. Instead, Justice encourages the oppressed to continuously self-reflect and source authority from their own subjectivities with honesty, no matter how confrontational and ugly the history, no matter the emotional discomfort. Such enactment of emotional-psychic honesty is needed to confront the dissonance of the self-oppressing colonized mind. Justice maintains that there is knowledge that emerges outside the categories of domination.

Legal storytelling draws upon a long history rooted in slave narratives. These testimonies of captivity unmasked the propriety proclaimed by white society. White supremacy continues to employ legal language to explain persistent racial inequality in a way that doesn't implicate white society. Without the testimony of the oppressed, our truths would be rendered invisible, our stories sold as self-satisfied within the lots of subordination. Justice reminds us we are able to speak truth at all times, even to power, even to risk punishment. Such bravery comes from the surrender to the heart, the devotion to nothing but its truth, leaving nothing but its desire for liberation.

Justice asks if we have the intellectual integrity and emotional honesty to have distributive justice between diverse peoples and the present dominant group. Justice requires us to recognize that by healing the harm of internalized oppression there is much potential to heal and change material conditions. It is the advocate, probing for truth and its articulation, recognizing the difference and tension between behavior and identity. Justice, as an arcanum, gives tools to transcend the oppressive dialectical relationship toward an integrated, polysemic social consciousness and spiritual cosmology. Nature is then sensed as inextricable from cultural matter. Justice restores the world as a multisensorial place, governed by analogical, symbolic reasoning. Justice consciousness recognizes the alienated, dispossessed, and disenfranchised. Justice accounts for all, never losing track of the people disappeared by state sanction. This is a higher hand that maintains a harmony, a flawless accounting of every soul ledger. Justice, by an Indigenous aesthetic, appeals an authority beyond the bounds of a corrupted Western legal system.

It is the bridge between symbolic and physical realities. The High Priestess by night becomes Justice by day. These two display the power of threshold guardians, one guarding the gates to hell and the other to heaven, the doorways to prison or freedom. As one they are master of fate. They relate chaos to coherence, and they contextualize aesthetics with ideology. Justice balances the aesthetic and the ethic, the substance and the show, so that entertainment is not put before principle. Thus, we engage Justice in the process of world-ordering. As the Moon gives a matrix of space-time to reflect consciousness's holograms, Justice maintains the patterns, the laws of that matrix that keep creation together, and teaches us to do the same.

June Jordan, as Justice, says "the syntax of a sentence equals the structure of your consciousness."[11] The spread is simply the syntax of card-sentences in the reading. The reading involves learning the syntax of psychic liberation. Still, the reading sometimes subverts the structure I attempt to impose upon a spread. It reminds me, shows me, that the tarot has its own spatiality, its own prophetic perception. The cards become a house of mirrors presided over by the cutting clarity of Justice. To make the mirror of soul shine, Justice utilizes tarot reading to sharpen the vision so it can see in the dark, see the shadow, see the soul. By being a divinatory mirror, akin to obsidian, tarot calls for a just, balanced perception of the world. Readers recognize tangible dimensions that are seemingly invisible to the colonial consciousness despite being in plain view. Justice establishes the soul's value, reserving to those who seek to pass judgment the test of truth. This arcanum reflects our blindness, and with her cold impartiality we begin to see *our* actions, *our* righteousness, *our* contradictions. Justice teaches us to stand at a distance, to take in the whole of being. Only from such a stance of self-reflexivity upon *our* judgment nature can we make sense of the judgment of others. The other teaches Justice by reciprocity. To equally regard *all* relationships, love becomes dynamic and balanced against unconditional self-regard. No matter the presence or absence of the many relationships we seek to reflect the truths we need others to see, we don't doubt its presence, even if a reflection is yet to be found.

Justice incurs a different aesthetic engagement with materiality because more metaphysical significance is ascribed materiality. An aesthetics of brilliance understands the polysemic nature and form of a soul's radiant luminosity. The native valuation of brilliance reflexively links the aesthetic properties of shiny matter with notions of cosmology, myth, natural landscape, and techno-economic propensities.[12] The scales Europeans use to ascribe and assess value disregard the sacred for purely secular, economic estimations. Justice subverts these blinded valuations by revitalizing and reconfiguring the aesthetics of agency.

To rebalance this aesthetic agency, truth-telling becomes a measure of love. The work of Justice eradicates emotional withholding, letting go of any lie held in the imbalanced, burdened being. To keep from becoming even more alienated and loveless, one must embrace the emotional pain of testimony. The pain of confronting emotional truth can redeem relationships and foster enduring commitments. To face *true* love is to stand before Justice. Attention is love's resource. By letting the most wounded and vulnerable be seen and heard, we are released from the rigidity and repression of only ever presenting an ideal self for acceptance. The gift of our faults, our transgressions, when held in clear perspective, keeps us from becoming *the only moral one.* The one who must always know better is often very bound by shame. To create such moral safety requires pushing others away, requires severity and a lack of self-compassion for being less than ideal, for being imperfect. To profess all the ways our spirit survived and the ways we dealt with all of our shortcomings, we would administer Justice to our hearts. Justice lets each carry their own faults before blame becomes overwhelming. Justice wants each to admit fault so we might know the mercy of forgiveness. Justice asks if we are willing to lose face in order to gain heart. To begin judging or valuing life as Justice does is to become sensitized, to notice the feather's psychic subtleties.

We ready ourselves to receive the love promised when we admit where it is yet to be had. Because there is no greater risk than to never be known, which is to never be loved, the pain proves worthwhile. True love gives us a chance to reveal ourselves, to become fully honest, letting Justice's awareness tend to where it is needed most. Justice is a love that forces you to become free in every way.

The Hanged One

Mesoamerican gods could see through insincerity. In the Aztec account of creation of the fifth sun, the gods sought volunteers to become the Sun. Tecuciztecatl put himself forward, and then, more hesitantly, Nanahuatzin came forward when called to do so. As a preparatory sacrifice, the two fasted for four days and performed penance. According to Sahagun, "that with which [Tecuciztecatl] did penance was all costly. His fir branches [were] quetzal feathers, and his grass balls of gold; his maguey spines of green stone; the reddened, bloodied spines of coral. And his incense was very good incense. And [as for] Nanahuatzin, his branches were made only of green water rushes—green reeds bound in threes. . . . And his grass balls [were] only dried pine needles. And his maguey spines were these same maguey spines. And the blood with which they were covered [was] his own blood. And [for] his incense, he used only the scabs from his sores." The four days of penance completed, these two were to become gods by immolating themselves in the bonfire made by the gods. Four times Tecuciztecatl ran up to the fire but leapt back. Only when Nanahuatzin hurled himself into the fire did Tecuciztecatl follow. Nanahuatzin rose as the sun. In this story, the sincerity, generosity, and immediacy of sacrifice are the keys to Nanahuatzin's transformation.[13]

Like sacrifice, suspension starts with will. The Hanged One is the arbiter of suspension, indexing a radical reorientation from death to life, from enclosure to spaciousness. They are the determined application of spiritual force as a counterbalance to the obscene acts of violence committed upon Black and Brown bodies daily. The colonized are held captive in a temporal spatiality that offers no movement or release. Frantz Fanon describes this as a state of muscular tension. Colonial relations of anti-Blackness diagram the architecture of aesthetic space, but the Hanged One unfolds that logic toward alternative outcomes.

Applying the Hanged One's holding becomes an act of care. Certain ethical conditions make pursuing suspension a strategic aesthetic mode for defiant strategic action. Applied spiritual force lifts the reader from misery, death, and danger, rearranges expectations, interrupts and unmoors the predictable scripts and predetermined narratives. As a suspenseful sound-image, the Hanged One deploys an arresting aesthetic. Suspension defies temporal linearity to instead preserve and keep the soul intact. Though the arcanum's history deals with torture and suffering publicly performed and consumed, the Hanged One refrains from allowing the reader or audience to possess the queer, Black body. The tarot is a montage of the Hanged One's still images. By suspending colonial, racist logic we can substitute for it the vitality of a fruitful ethics and erotics of relation. The Hanged One is a buffer zone around the vulnerable reader, producing a pedagogy that cares, holds, and loves queer being. The buffer opens a temporal wedge that becomes a strategic shield from the world's violent shaming of the queer "sideways" growth of spirituality.[14]

With this key we become queered by the state of suspension.[15] Whether we become butterfly, bat, the sun, or the moon, the change incurred by the Hanged One is total and absolute. Surface change is insufficient, as is any simple rearrangement of parts. What's needed is patience until our wings fly free. It's no overnight process. It is confusion, upheaval, and uncertainty that births the desire of the Hanged One, the quest for greater clarity about the meaning and purpose of life. Desire at rest gives us a chance to become certain of the wishes we'd make given the golden opportunity. This hanging suspension is the tarot's welcome into erotic contemplation. The old self and its notions dissolve. In this sacred holding, I begin to imagine myself as something else; I make myself into a metaphor, moving and growing my meaning even—and especially—against time delayed. "I make an instantaneous association of the bat man with border artists' *neptanla* stage—the dark cave of creativity where they hang upside down, turning the self upside down to see from another point of view, one that brings a new state of understanding."[16]

Being neither, not yet *this* and no longer *that,* is to be *in between.* To reside in liminality is to enter queer dimensions, chosen for the chance of a change of heart. The sacrifice necessary to enter the realm of the mysterious is to seek an oppositional location by touching the senses and emotions beyond conquest. The willing self-distortion simultaneously re-members an identity of resistance. As we desire to leave the identity behind in order to go somewhere else, somewhere different, somewhere ecstatic, we explore the trial of the Hanged One. In states of suspension we surrender urgency and the incessant motivation to stay in motion. The fear of stopping falls away, or at least we gather enough courage to stay present with the fearful, even when novelty fades, for it is then that unsuspected depths are disclosed. To stop skipping to the next sensation, relationship, or project in order to see *this* through is to transfer into the life of Spirit. Then the reading of the cards, reading arcanum twelve, becomes a modality of experiencing ecstatic time. Reading the tarot or being read by the tarot is to queer by query.

Our prayers may be fulfilled, even if only momentarily, by the Hanged One's hanging. We all exist in a dangerous limbo. The Hanged One as an image evokes a spiritual perfection while gesturing toward "the idea of a self-contained Black history—suspended above its hostile surroundings—that finds within itself the resources for its fulfillment."[17] They teach the reader to be spiritually self-reliant, rendering consciousness as constantly moving against, defying, and delaying the gravity of the West's inescapable doom. To keep from falling the Hanged One unmoors technologies of surveillance, domination, and captivity in favor of caring modes of contemplation.

"Blackness is excluded from the 'world' we live in . . . and yet it provides the ground on which it is built. What happens then, when black bodies leave this ground?"[18]

After a held breath, the card elongates the sigh of relief. The maintained composure of the Hanged One belies the tension exerted to maintain their suspension. Tension maintains appearances of a buoyant grace within expressions of bodily compression and release. Architectures of suspension are designed to make the most motley and hefty structures appear featherweight. The visual effect of lightness contradicts the force and pressure required to create suspension. The Hanged One has this visual effect, emphasized by the crown bathed in sunlight from behind. They possess a levity that defies the racialized spatial arrangement of their societal context. In suspension they have found a suitable dwelling place to process and develop at their own pace and in their own direction, deliberately leveraging a productive undecidability.

The Hanged One is patient enough for the reader to rotate the axis of their perception until the ground becomes the ceiling and the pole of death shifts the weight of our stillness to life, making what was rigid and stiff soft and euphoric. They hold still long enough for us to see the tense stasis we are held within as possessing vectors that may open an almost free-floating movement for Black and queer bodies to go wherever they want. The integrity of the soul is maintained, making the body space feel more miraculous.

Alessandra Raengo writes that "suspension moves freely between reading practices, aesthetic strategies, rhetorical structures, and media affordances and specificities."[19] Reading tarot becomes a way to productively deploy suspension of our foreclosed and foregone conclusions, assumptions, and associations. The Hanged One helps us see suspension as complicated and requiring a willingness to let it reorient reading practices/praxes. But there is a limit to how much tension will be reconciled or absorbed. There will be an eventual ending to their elevation; and a release, a sacrifice, will be required.

At the root of creation is sacrifice. The world's various mythic and cultural cosmologies converge around sacrifice, yet the conceptual orientation continues to change. Animal sacrifices were made as the "breaker of the year," giving us cyclical development rather than monotony of linearity. As Richard Robert notes, whatever sign appears on the vernal point is the sacrificial animal symbolizing the god of that religious period and the start of the zodiacal year.

If Justice reflects our blindness, then the Hanged One offers the sacrifice of self that restores sight. If we are unable to witness and regard our trespassed and trespassers in the act of redemption, enacted on our behalf, then we succumb to shortsighted hypocrisy. The body weight of miscommunicated guilt is here surrendered. From this teaching we know that our most humble and sincere offerings are sacred, valuable, and powerful. With courage, greatness can be accomplished. When we take responsibility for our truth, frail as our bodies are, standing before mountains of cold, stolen stone, we know the Hanged Man's sacrifice.

> *On a worldwide landscape mutilated by games of arrogance and domination, how should we come to know the name of any man except the man who makes money, or the man who makes someone else a loser, or the man who can make somebody else cower and die. How should anyone recognize a Black man of God, a Black man trying to redeem all of America from what*

> *he perceived to be "the evils" of racism, militarism and capitalism? He was an anomaly: a mountain in the desert of our time. How should we know and respect and honor his name? Or why should we bother? He was not a God.*[20]

We know we are not God. We are the pariah prophets, and we are many. And may the sacrifices of our struggle subvert the sense of dread provoked by the supremacist state. Our tactics, our truths may even be falsely persecuted, as prophecy often is, but who will deny the colossal courage of our bodily witness, offered to the faith in the righteous cause of our freedom? To endure introversion is to strengthen faith within, even in the absence of external validation. In this threshold we surrender to the mountain before us. Are we foolish enough not to calculate the difference between our small stature and the unrelenting, humbling dimensions of the obstacles we must try to surmount? Is it any wonder that in our bold, revolutionary callings our bodies are threatened by the state? The state makes our body a stage, a place for martyrdom to be performed. Everywhere evidences the state's unbridled willingness to use our human faults, our imperfections, our weaknesses to destroy us. Yet when we decide to transgress, to transform, to reject the state judgments and administrations of assault upon our soul, we step into the Hanged One.

Despite hundreds of years of colonial abuse, enough to discourage even the most fervent poet, prophet, or visionary, the Hanged One offers wells of revolutionary faith. The Hanged Ones suffer no confusion. They recognize the suffering silenced under conformity, and they are courageous enough to unmask, to divest, and to surrender the privileges that keep them complicit and constrained in dominator culture. They are bold enough to realign their actions with their ideals, a pathway only taken upon crystal-clear perception. The Hanged One pursues integrity after epiphanies upon one's conditioned cognitive dissociations. Disruptions of the body break through double consciousness in the Hanged One.

> *After the Egyptian and Indian, the Greek and Roman, the Teuton and Mongolian, the Negro is a sort of seventh son, born with a veil, and gifted with second-sight in this American world—a world which yields him no true self-consciousness, but only lets him see himself through the revelation of the other world. It is a peculiar sensation, this double-consciousness, this*

sense of always looking at one's self through the eyes of others, of measuring one's soul by the tape of a world that looks on in amused contempt and pity. One ever feels his two-ness,—an American, a Negro; two souls, two thoughts, two unreconciled strivings; two warring ideals in one dark body, whose dogged strength alone keeps it from being torn asunder.[21]

The Hanged are the imprisoned, beaten, blacklisted, fired, slandered, and spied upon. This arcanum is for those born veiled, gifted a second sight that disrupts the logic of the normal. This arcanum presents a chance to redeem the false convictions placed upon Black and Brown bodies. For those seeking reconciliation after such historic disruption, this is the stage where faith is upended into an awakening. Personal conviction is summoned, confronted, and clarified, whereby one awakens to the truth of the culture in which they are immersed. Claim your soul as your own and smile upon the enraged society, who despite all their bodily theft and assault could never possess.

The Hanged One is patient, willing to wait for us to catch up. Belief is in their body. It plays a *pivotal* function. By their belief, the possibility is afforded to affect the speed and substance of social change. Be reminded that state law is not God-given.

In Justice we've determined an ordering of the world by the ordering of the word. The language of our chosen expression has revealed the structuring of our desire. And in the act of proclamation, where we claim and reveal personal desire, demonstration becomes felonious. In the Hanged One we reckon the sacrifices of silence against the sacrifices of speaking.

The Hanged One realizes that, perhaps to a large degree, justice may only exist as rhetoric. A changed society is dependent upon the personal capacity for self-transformation. This, the Hanged One confronts. It presents the moral obligation of personal action when social law is sanctimonious. The test of heart in each ally who proclaims solidarity is the test of transgression. The lover of a subversive is also a subversive. The Hanged demand civil disobedience, when we have but one option:

Break the law!
It was once against the law for Blackfolks to read and write.
It was once against the law for Blackfolks to marry each other.

It was once against the law for Blackfolks to vote.
It was once against the law for Blackfolks to swim indoor, or outdoor, public waters.
We had to break those laws or agree to the slaveholder's image of us: three-fifths of a human being.[22]

We offer all severed selves to be reconciled when we decide to stop lying. Pretending in order to pacify oppressors does not make us any safer; rather, the harm may be even more difficult to recognize when it's not visible upon the body. Once we stop the pretense we step into the Hanged One. When we refuse to debase the body we give birth to our spirit. This becomes the denial that sets us free. It is our *no* that affirms our communion. It is an active denial, a letting go of everything we've been dependent upon, enslaved by. Love's all-encompassing liberty snaps the rope of our suspension. Poet and political leader José de Diego reminds us that "the 'no' of the oppressed has been the word, the genesis of the liberation of peoples." Loss becomes sacrifice through this reclaiming. Like Nanahuatzin, we sacrifice the body to make it sacred. Sacrifice works upon the wounds of the objectified, the commodified, the colonized. The empty space of stolen selfhood becomes filled with the Divine in our acts of sacrifice. It is thus a generative act. We live, not as consumers of objectified others, but as a person among persons.[23] Sacrifice is possible in recognizing all we have to gain once we let go of everything that isn't true. Sacrifice surrenders every space to the Divine. When the only witness we need is that of divine witness, we become certain we will be born again.

The most precious gift the Hanged One gives is the knowing of what it is to desire *gifting* the body. The *having* of a body inscribes autonomy upon the body. The pleasure gained in giving over your body, the pleasure of total submission, suspends all distress, and blood rushes from all over our body to your heart. Healing the spirit in this giving. The pleasure of this devotion is all that the Hanged One wants for us to partake of. Despite the body's contortions under the duress of state subterfuge, it is *ours* to give, and its meaning cannot be taken nor stolen. No sacrifice made with stolen bodies shall be rendered true.

When the only thing you give yourself over to is passion, that is praise. Our sacrifices made in faith will stand as testimony that our losses are made in more than our pain.

Judgment

Martin Luther King's divine calling was to preach. He preached with an artistry, a divinely inspired creativity, that was wondrous to behold. He could call masses of people to hear the word of God; the holy, holy, holy spirit emanating from him was awesome. King was a prophetic witness. Able to convert listeners, he not only made it possible for them to hear sacred teachings, he invited them to open their hearts and be transformed.[24]

The word *apocalypse* in its Greek origin means "to reveal, to uncover, to see." When the wretched of the Earth arise, everyone's exposed and everything's out in the air. And so it calls upon the expertise, the necessity, of the prophet. Their voice must thunder like Justice's condemnation. The masses are awakening in the uncovering of global corruption from white supremacist capitalist imperialist patriarchy, and we are being confronted, called to evolve. The prophetic vocation challenges the old while announcing the new. "The poets, being poets, still won't shut up. The compulsion to tell this story transcends the borders of geography and language."[25] The poets of prophecy suffer political persecution and yet still they write. Still they sound their horns, still they fly their pens. What is it that these poets see as they look upon the same doomscapes we are suffocated by and yet find breath that refuses to be bated? Nevertheless we are still to benefit from the truth of their sight, a clarity of conviction to keep calling on freedom's potential in the face of injustice and inequity. Although our awareness of living through apocalypse is most felt under the weight of multiple global crises, can our awareness also encompass the poetry of the truth tellers?

The apocalypse has lost its novelty. The global continuum of merciless hostility and neglect is inescapable. The light a new day provides does not diminish, nor fade, nor cure, nor overcome the consequences of debasement and contempt. The flatlining of morale has become familiar. Without the poets of prophecy, it becomes impossible to imagine the important, the good. "You push along, slowly, from one terrible loss to the next. For sure, you cannot save anything or anybody from the destruction that now preoccupies your mind. Evil is old. Evil is long and powerful and everywhere. You unplug the telephone and call it a night."[26] Despair becomes unavoidable under such states, and the spirit sinks in a miserable inertia. Our vision and awareness of oppression must grow in equal measure with our perception and capacity for pleasure, purpose, and beauty. We cannot long continue being radicalized at the expense of the vitality and vigor of a joyful, related life. Our sleeping hearts are not awoken by unceasing news of devastation. The pervasiveness of evil has a numbing quality. Its awe-fulness is somehow lost. The frightening has become mere entertainment.

More challenging than overcoming all the costumery and cunning of evil's insidious conceit is wielding language to reveal the imaginal complexity of paradise. What sounds, images, stories of paradise seize the imagination to inspire the most rare character growth that becomes motivated to do good? Can we reach toward a vision of paradise that is not trivial in its familiarity of beauty, plenitude, rest, respect, love, bliss, or safety? Can these paradisal prisms be extracted from the capitalist media of consumption? As contemporary populations are indifferent to the language that moved our ancestors, God's language has been modernized and marketed to the masses. But in this marketable immediacy, contemplation is lost. Judgment calls us to make the journey and experience of faith fresh and intimate. What word would wound us with its immediacy, would cut the blindfolds from our eyes and make it as if we were receiving the word for the first time? We are to seek the brilliant sermons, revelatory poems, and personal prayer language that both stun in their creativity and prosper in their healing properties. Judgment asks if we can widen the narrow imagination of paradise in the collective mindset. Maybe it is only the devout writer who holds an unblinking gaze upon the realm of difference that can freshen our vision of salvation. For those of us who can't see the way forward, other senses heighten. You learn to rely on sound to navigate the darkness, for it is sound that will awaken sight.

"It is usually impossible to explain to folks who are not writers that ideas, words, the whole essay itself may come from a place of mystery, emerging from the deep deep unconscious surfacing, so that even the writer is awed by what appears. Writing then is revelation."[27]

The poets of truth may be imprisoned, lost, forgotten or hidden, but their Judgment will not be. On the Coachella stage, which is a microcosm of otherness in a white world, Judgment is in Beyoncé pronouncing "I woke up like this," reanimating prone, Black bodies to dance across the stage in full, exquisite control of their being in space and time, in open display of joyous praise and power. Her power performance condemns the ignorant onlooker while also birthing a Black future behind a Red moon. The vision then of apocalypse, of Judgment, is one that calls us from our graves. A vision that excises the strain of shame and guilt, a burden carried under duress within the matrices of domination, is then a vision of apocalypse. It exhilarates the soul and surprises the spirit. It is a moment of great collective catharsis.

The rebirth of consciousness is Judgment's threshold. It is a declaration of heart, a proclamation of purpose and intent seeded deep within. The unexpected display of the courageous, gloriously resilient spirit of artistry fills the reservoirs of hope and snatches us out of the failings of fear. Genuine revolution delivers a love dance triumphant into the world. See in Beychella the opus of the alchemist, the transmutation, ripening, or rebirth of the soul of the artist themselves. If apocalypse is thought to announce the end of time, it is also compelling to consider it the triumph of spirit liberated from matter. When we awaken to Judgment, life becomes a work of art, a work of revolution dedicated to the reinvigoration of the human spirit. The song of revolution moves the soul to anthems not yet written. The call and response becomes the chorus praying and delivering at once. Judgment creates our own homecoming. The trumpets sounds, welcoming the reader's soul to return to paradise from the islands of alienation. We clamor, inspiring courage, stoking passion in the firm-footed faith that change is coming.

I pull Judgment when I call out in praise, still reaching for a way to fulfill my calling, when I am moved to tears by the endless open horizons I find within the Divine. The prayer that breaks through the darkness is the prayer uttered in song so that the chorus of my calling out is not sung alone. Judgment is a gospel choir, an instrumental organ in the oration of freedom. The winds of Judgment are as in the chapel, so that every open landscape is orchestral. Harmony preserves paradises in song, and though it may seem so far, fraught, and frayed, it is never far gone. Harmony is reconciliation with the other; it is the joining of voices that makes one heard in God. The scales wiil be balanced in our song. Our harmony will be our justice. Our prayers foretell our arrival. Freedom is forthcoming. I may stagger senseless and blurry, but I am held within a *we* that will be lifted. A *we* that receives a grace given with no judgments so I can stand tall and yet humble, welcomed by the *we* poised in truth.

Judgment deals with the transmigration of the soul. It is the freeing of the soul. It is a clearing, a releasing and resolving of karmic legacies. It is going from the stasis of two dimensions to the animism of three dimensions. It is a gaining of coherence, a sense of divine order to the world and the self within it. This arcanum awakens us to divine assistance. We arise from the realm of the dead as we embrace the levity of spirit. This is an ascension of spirit, an uplifting of the downtrodden, a dignifying of the damned, and a departing from the underworld. Cold flesh becomes warm skin in the sun as I stand naked and vulnerable in my desire for connection. It is a grace to accept the invitation into an honest, humble self-presentation so that this connection might be my salvation. This naked display is akin to confession. As Erika Buenaflor puts it: "The act of confessing, followed by prayers, was a critical component of the process. Verbalizing any wrongdoings ejected them out of the children's bodies, purified the children from these transgressions, and prepared them to undergo a cosmic rebirth into a new stage of their lives. The spoken word, in the form of poetic recitations, was a means of facilitating the release, and could also serve as part of the offering for divine help."[28]

A goddess of purification who facilitates this ritual is Tlazoteotl. She is a Venusian goddess of filth who frees the reader from shame. Under her care we can find sanctity in the ownership of our desire. Desire is seen as sacred, even in its filth, because it is given to us by the Divine. Under her care we begin an erotic relationship with the Divine that is emancipatory. In such a blessing we are able to release ourselves from the suffering we have condemned others to. We release the need to judge, exact punishment, or seek retribution. When the iron gates are opened, attitudes of imprisonment are abolished, and the prison guards—who come by choice to incarceration, along with the inmate they take pride in patrolling—are set free.

This arcanum is the calling card, letting us know *we will* have our time, and none will be forsaken. Instead of reading or reciting scripture we have the inverted experience of being read by scripture. The cards are actively reading us, as our soul literacy develops to illuminate immemorial human experience. This is a cypher language. Prophecy is always about the present moment, though it is often relied upon solely for prediction. Awakening deeply to what is happening around you is prophecy, the eye opening to the vistas unto God. As Jean-Louis Chrétien shows in *The Wounded Word: The Phenomenology of Prayer*, it is our encounter with the call of the infinite that demands our embrace of the finitude, fragility, and corporeality of human life. Becoming aware of our limitations invests meaning into our limited time. The new identity we awake to in Judgment is a recognition that *we* are the answer to the call. It is *our* being brought forth by prayer. We are always already constituted in response to a call for being and beauty that precedes us. Thus, Judgment reveals our interrelationship with the Divine. Consciousness and circumstances change in the perceptive faculties awakened by God. In this perception, internal limitations are overcome by the conscious, full-bodied recognition of the core power residing deep within our spirit. While we have proven to be so committed to freedom in our willingness to die for our truth, here we are called to make equal space for a commitment that means we are willing to live for our beliefs to be realized.

Judgment creates an opening for spirit to discover anew the Divine's recognition of our small person. In this arcanum multiple points of origin arise. A new way to freedom has not been found; rather, it has been created with the soul's nuclear power, and the horn section continues to blare.

Two of Swords

Our language is a system constructed by people constantly needing to insist that we exist, that we are present. Our language devolves from a culture that abhors all abstraction, or anything tending to obscure or delete the fact of the human being who is here and now/the truth of the person who is speaking or listening. Consequently, there is no passive voice construction possible in Black English. The assumption of the presence of life governs all Black English. Therefore, overwhelmingly, all action takes place in the language of the present indicative. And every sentence assumes the living and active participation of at least two human beings, the speaker and the listener.[29]

If we were to speak a language with person-centered values, as June Jordan describes doing with her students, there would be a delivery of voice. In the Two of Swords, the voice has been lost, withheld, denied. Where there is no voice, there is no Justice, and where there is no Justice there is no peace. To understand the contradiction between reality and appearance the Two of Swords sees with x-ray vision, telling the reader they must travel more deeply inward to get to the root of contradiction. Although the parts are in relation to each other, they are in an antagonistic relation. Reality is disguised and distorted, which is why scientists and occultists are so adamantly peering beneath the surface. Coherence is established as the contradiction between root and appearance is resolved. The Two of Swords tells the reader surface signals may be misleading us into action with disastrous outcomes, dying in the Three of Swords by what has crossed our hearts in the Two.

The first challenge of the Two of Swords is to acknowledge emotion's irrationality. The next is to withhold judgment, as if a righteous proclamation could rationalize away anger, grief, disappointment. Release and healing cannot come before awareness. These feelings we keep hidden from others so long that we become self-alienating are refused by resentment. In the Two of Swords, shame crosses secrecy. The pervading silence that follows is ominous.

The shame that keeps us from honest self-acceptance often originates in childhood. Parents who abuse their children often impose silence onto them. The child internalizes this state of denial. The child begins to bear the emotional cost of keeping secrets, never knowing and receiving true love, leaving them confused about their own capacity for emotional fulfillment. In this state we suffer in exile from our true feelings, leading to depression and a loss of self-awareness. Childhood shaming halts the development of healthy self-assertion. Rather than risking more punishment in attempting to self-assert, many are conditioned into a learned passivity as a survival strategy to avoid conflict and harm. In the long term we are no safer as the voice of the abuser becomes internalized to keep us subordinated, controlled, controlling. We navigate psychological conflict, internalized projections, and disengagement from embodied life experience. The Two of Swords refuses to reconcile the actions and words of those who abuse us and yet claim to love us, knowing love and abuse cannot coexist, that a love tied to abuse is not true at all.

Jacques Lacan explores the childhood stages of identity formation and dissociation through his well-known theory of the mirror stage. The child recognizing themselves in the mirror reflection becomes confronted with an idealized version of the self, an image of perfection internalized yet unreachable. They strive toward an image of wholeness that is disembodied, as it is at the time when this identification occurs: infancy. Lacking physical and mental coordination creates distress, anxiety, frustration. The child, in a state of helplessness and bodily discoordination, is enthralled by the reflection's promise that their body can be pulled together to attain a state of unity, coordination, wholeness. Lacan tells us this imago-Gestalt of virtual wholeness offered in the mirror is sought after in vain. The Two of Swords appears when the images in which we've found reflection become distorted, or rather when we realize the accretion of identification with images is an ongoing process of self-objectification. The mirror is a question of identification. To locate one's identity within an image, a reflection, is considered a misrecognition. You are not your reflection, do not lose yourself in the reflection, says this silent woman in white. The mirror's function is to develop self-consciousness, but what comes is the contorting confusion of liking or not liking what you see in the mirror, suffering the shattered images of perfection where we will always fall short.

The relations between these two swords are interlaced and crisscrossed. We do not own or identify with the words spoken, though they come from our body. Justice finds our body, our voice. We are not the authors of truth; we are its page. The Two of Swords is a chance to create necessary fiction that disorders the real, when the real is repressive. The Two of Swords wedges a space open and renders identities of impossibility heard. Fiction then can give rise to the real by providing an imaginary space where freedom can come to full expression.

A culture of secrecy socializes men and women distinctly and yet achieves the similar function of self-denial. Paternal sadism wounds male children by forcing them to deny their feeling nature, whereas the wounded children in women are socialized into silence to attract and acquiesce to others. Men are forced to speak up, whereas women are punished for talking back. This internalized voice becomes the self-negation, the "negative" voice made transparent in the Two of Swords. This voice indulges endless negative critique.

A doppelgänger—an identical being who walks around claiming to be us, yet works to our demise as it unveils our mistaken identity to those who thought they knew us most intimately—is born from denial states. The Two of Swords arises when our doppelgänger does too.

Any autonomy, self-determination, and freedom that come at the cost of self-mutilation are falsely conceived. Liberation cannot mean liberation from corporeality. Attempting to annihilate the pain of our suffering, or to cover a tormenting past to the point that we feel unreal, disembodied, and split off, can never balance an awareness of love. To seek a self-determination that requires alienation from the body is to seek dominance of the head over the body, male over female, a poison lingering from Enlightenment thought. It's a worldview at odds with a trusted intuition. But the Two of Swords is a signal that the logical path to inquiry is blocked.

We navigate secrecy in this realm, learning to distinguish it from privacy. Secret-keeping is typically about power. It is about the hiding and concealing of information, the veiling of abuses, the masking of shame. A peace built upon secrecy is pacifying and fraught with imbalance. Privacy, however, is used by open, honest truth tellers. Privacy respects the space needed for reflection and inner processing. Privacy respects the consent and autonomy of the individual to determine to whom they self-disclose. Privacy honors the solitude required for healthy psychological autonomy. The Two of Swords's no to the "negative" emotions can be revised as a defense against unconscious projection. To perceive what the logical mind cannot, the subtle mind is to be strengthened. Power and its abuses do not disappear simply because we refuse to recognize them. A neutral stance cannot be long held when the swords are in our hands. The Two of Swords is the energy of a mental block, a mental defense that denies the relating with *other.*

Emotional withholding violates the foundation of relational commitment. The goal of the Two of Swords is not eradication but a change of relations so we can break through self-denial and claim our true feeling state. Only an honest heart can clearly see the love of the other. To *embody* authentic selfhood and relate with a dynamic of love rather than domination, the scales of self-esteem must reconcile with an innate worthiness. Once the full range of emotions are allowed bodily expression, they no longer hold us in captivity. This is why the Two of Swords precedes the Eight of Swords, which sees the femme figure of our intuitive erotic body's knowing bound. Space must be made for challenging but honest emotions, thoughts, perspectives. When we declare moralistic judgments toward our honest feelings, we are trying to be good, right, virtuous, and yet we end up denouncing our humanity. There are no declarative statements about the entirety of your being; rather, there is acknowledging and observing.

Braving the truth is dangerous as it requires an unmasking. In an effort to self-protect we lie, to preserve a power we've subverted in the distortions of truth. Lying to avoid conflict or to spare feelings is a forsaken peace strategy. Masking covers a sense of unlovability, only to face disappointment and heartbreak when the truth eventually pierces through. The sacrifice of relationships upended by the revelation of truth is a sacred severance. Disappointment is born from the dishonesty of the mask, not from an inherent worthlessness. Masking breaks the trust needed for real relationships, a tendency typically arising from this deep wound of confused unworthiness.

We begin a powerful healing path when we confront the internalized voices of shame that would have us choose isolation and loneliness rather than letting others know who we truly are. Self-acceptance challenges the judging voice inside, who judges both self and then others. It is overcome by the voice of affirmation, the practice of honesty, and the compassion of accountability. To be truly loving, we must be self-accepting. As selfhood is a relational constitution, self-love cannot flourish in isolation. Self-esteem is strengthened the more courageous and committed we become to truth telling. The negating self-perception projected onto others becomes far more difficult when there is active listening, open-hearted sharing. When we regard the flesh of the person's beliefs, thoughts, and feelings, they can no longer exist disembodied in our mind. Self-disclosure is a sacred act. It disrupts the division between false presentations of self invented to please others and the more authentic self residing in the whispered shadows of silence. To mend this rupture, we seek the Two of another element.

Two of Wands

This is theory's acute dilemma: that desire expresses itself most fully where only those absorbed in its delights and torments are present, that it triumphs most completely over other human preoccupations in places sheltered from view. Thus it is paradoxically in hiding that the secrets of desire come to light, that hegemonic impositions and their reversals, evasions, and subversions are at their most honest and active, and that the identities and disjunctures between felt passion and established culture place themselves on most vivid display.[30]

Power impresses itself upon and through culture. The architects of power exert their will from the micro to the macro and in the process unveil the power of their invisible desires. With a figure holding a globe in their palm, such is the scene in the Two of Wands. A young sovereign is world building, mapping the trajectory of their legacy. Desires for a world in which you are represented has a tenuous balance against desiring to make the world in one's image, for while such a world would reflect the individual's sensibilities, it would be a world image steeped in ethnocentrism.

Argentine feminist philosopher, activist, and professor Maria Lugones defines ethnocentrism as "the explicit and arrogantly held action-guiding belief that one's culture and cultural ways are superior to others'; or the disrespectful, lazy, arrogant indifference to others' cultures that devalues them through not seeing appreciatively any other culture or cultural ways except one's own when one could do otherwise."[31]

Such a worldview is in stark contrast to the awareness that one's experience of time is a *particular* movement through space. The Two of Wands is all about reorienting worldviews, rewriting the maps of power to say natives are not passive victims to the spatial configuration that hardens their inferiority. A trajectory of conscious embodiment orients the self as a vehicle driven by a particular vantage point. This point is the convergence of culture against self. This point is the Two of Wands. The sense of self and sense of others are simultaneously constituted and filtered by culture. Selfhood and culture are mutually generative. The Two of Wands is a card for theorists contemplating identity construction. One wand holds fixed dispositions and essential self-understandings, while another holds the social legacies of culturally constructed narratives. The figure mediates the tension between these two wands. The figure is one of negotiation, working with and against dominant cultural dispositions.

The Two of Wands is a contemplation upon these two framings. It is a contemplation upon how culture frames the individual and how our disidentifications with the dominant cultural narratives can be reflected in the cultural objects we create by reformulating the cultural framing we've been given. The Two of Wands is an invitation, a call to deepen self-reflexivity. Otherwise the peril presented is getting lost in the mapping of one's world, confusing it for the territory itself. As Lugones says, "Dis-engagement as sanctioned ethnocentric racist strategy works as follows: you do not see me because you do not see yourself and you do not see yourself because you declare yourself outside of culture."[32]

Hegemonic cisnormative patriarchal culture mutes culture differences as it takes itself for granted as a neutral, culturally unremarkable locus. Western perspective takes whiteness to be universal, to be the norm, the standard upon which deviance is measured. The colonizer mindset orients around supremacy, around a self they deem to be the peak. The Two of Wands shows a high-ranking elite far removed from the nameless worker we see in the Ten of Wands, for instance. They look upon the world in their hand with an exotic gaze as if they were to stand outside culture. To declare yourself outside culture is self-deceiving, for it is actually one's culture and one's society that one is looking at and sees through, but this awareness is veiled because the viewer takes it as a universal lens. Every other voice and every other culture then becomes alien. This imperial sight maintains a cultural ideology that severs the meanings and connections between ethnicity and racialization. Adopting such a disengaged stance of inquiry is either dishonest, incompetent in its lack of self-conscious depth, or committed to ethnocentric racism. It is a radical form of passivity that privileges the dominant culture's perception as the only "true vision." And yet since the "culture" of supremacy is cannibalistic, whiteness is really devoid of culture; it is antagonistic to culture. The Two of Wands asks whether your stance is unconsciously ethnocentric and thus disengaged, or self-reflexive and self-governing. It's a card about cultural creation, consumption, and nonappropriative exchange.

Through the consumption of "exotic" bodies, cultures, and lands, the world becomes a simulacrum, a copy of a copy of a world, of a culture. What was a rich environment with historical relationships, knowledge, and rituals becomes an amusement park, a museum, a mall. In the plastic re-creation of consumed culture, the dominant class is able to brand and copyright the source material. They license themselves to change the actors, the narrative, the meaning, the representative modes of expression. The cultural claims and projects of the majoritarian express a sense of centrality assuming that one's people, culture, community, or language have the hegemons' same sense of self and their web of connections. This is distinct from the communal and cultural adoration that expresses the dearness of such woven connections and social participations that do not suppose they are better than another in a comparatively inflammatory manner.

The Two of Wands begets a process that increases awareness of the cultural practitioner's positionality, power, and product. The querents of a reading typically query at a crossroads. To be met in this open and vulnerable space, cultural practitioners (readers, writers, astrologers, counselors, teachers, artists) must be aware of their cultural makeup, their unique positionality of power as it is situated by race, gender, class, location, education level, sexuality. To develop any technical language mastery is to increase power, but this power will be imbalanced without awareness of one's own cultural constitution. Such an imbalance challenges competence at best, and colonizes at worst. Mark Rifkin models this awareness when he writes, "I neither seek to position myself as speaking for Indigenous people(s) nor as offering a neutral location from which to assess Black-Indigenous discussions, debates, tensions, and negotiations. To do either would involve evading the significance of my whiteness by implicitly using it to present myself as transcending what would by contrast appear as the located particularities of blackness and indigeneity."[33]

The practitioners' will toward empowerment must be held in awareness so we'll remember that as others come to us when they feel illiterate, powerless, and absent from representation, it would be an abuse of power to impose our cultural arrangements and identity scripts upon them. It would be an abuse of power to deem others illiterate for simply speaking a language that isn't yours. Literacy has no limit, so the reader would do well to refrain from assuming a cultural deficit exists within a culture or cultural actor that is simply different. To look upon the world and see it as flat, small, static, and possessable stems from the manner of seeing rather than what is seen. Thus it is not content but context that has impact. The ideological formation of whiteness is about blinding, muting, and erasing. One cannot really hear or speak about what is muted. Do you not see yourself because you declare yourself outside of culture? Or do you not see yourself because you are looking for representations from a source that has declared your culture dead? This is the tension of representation between oppressor and oppressed. Regardless of which pole or wand we relate to, we are unable to see the self; so then how can you see me, or the client, or the student?

The practitioner's true power is in the mutual development of literacy across reader and querent, creator and viewer, writer and reader. This is the nascent power of the Two of Wands. An excellent reader is a leader who achieves self-governance, being responsible and responsive. They maintain a vision that the soul governs.

To work with the Two of Wands, with the tarot, is to work to change this nonperceptive perception. The card gives us a key to hold our distinct cultural objects and examine all that is reflected in its construction, its representation. This card reminds us of our cultural inheritance, for we cannot deny or disown the world that has been passed down to us. The Two of Wands is about the choices made in perceiving the path. An engaged or disengaged stance is predicated upon an awareness or unawareness of power and its histories. It is a gift to become aware of one's limitations without declaring deficits, for it is possible to lovingly world-travel instead of conquering via voyeuristic tourism. It is vital to experience the benefits born from difference without destroying, appropriating, or minimizing. Such a positive perception of difference is not divisive, and thus it eliminates the need to deny differences or render them invisible.

The tarot presents a new subjectivity that denies any *one* perspective as the only answer. In our confrontation of the various fronts of oppression, the Two of Wands helps to shift tactical and strategic subjectivity. It uncovers a capacity to recenter accordingly. The Two of Wands is a meditation on which vantage points enable the mapping of new social, spiritual, and ideological geographies. There will be no simple or single utopian route to liberation, as there is no single conceptualization of an oppressed position. In contemplating the ever-mobile flux of societal power we face the ideological limitations of a single, frozen, "correct" oppositional response. In this sense, the Two of Wands expands the oppositional imagination.

By using criticality to examine the texts and situations in which race, gender, sex, sexuality, and ethnicity are salient, we embrace difference. Being unable or refusing to examine our place within dominant culture makes us unable to truly meet another. The figure is always alone on the terrace of the ivory tower. As much as they may fashion themselves a cultural titan, a king among kings, without the other their world is infinitely smaller. They are left stranded and isolated in the trappings of power. By self-consciously knowing ourselves a raced, sexed, gendered person, we can then know others beyond abstraction. One can reconstruct culture in struggle, in collaboration and deep acknowledgment of self and other. The sphere of power can be reapportioned. As we recognize what does and doesn't lie within our sphere of influence, we recognize the spheres that influence and act upon us. Then we stand at the thresholds of perception, as desire for destiny summons expansion; and then this card turns over. The seeds we share from ourselves are meant to sensuously nourish another while we also experience a new, different cultural topography that enriches a new personal flowering.

The Two of Wands presents us an opportunity to *see* a web of relationships that may become a bridge out of solitude. We are invited to dream beyond the shrunken worlds of imperialism. Bigger than the insatiability of imperial cultural consumption is the desire for freedom that is restored in tandem with restoring relation. The Two of Wands asks us if we have the will to change, the will to love. We are called to adventure, to the greatest unknown, the cardinal challenge of continuously changing in choosing to commit to love. A sure step toward self-discovery and actual independence is taken by the recognition of interdependence. To fulfill personal desire, we grapple with stepping outside of ourselves. To shift focus toward the circulation of power rather than a concentration of power, a self-conscious flexibility of identity and political ideology must be developed.

As wands relate to fire and fire to the harbinger of destined manifestation, the Two of Wands stands at the vanguard. Their sight does not simply enable reading; it also determines what gets read, what is readable. We need divinatory literacy to transmute the concealed, censored voices, cultures, and bodies from a state of absent invisibility into a viable presence. In a divinatory literacy we learn criticality as we learn to read absence. What is not here, what is unsaid and unseen and has a silence that speaks. The decolonized reader communes with this voice.

Two of Cups

When we reveal ourselves to our partner and find that this brings healing rather than harm, we make an important discovery—that intimate relationship can provide a sanctuary from the world of facades, a sacred space where we can be ourselves, as we are. . . . This kind of unmasking—speaking our truth, sharing our inner struggles, and revealing our raw edges—is sacred activity, which allows two souls to meet and touch more deeply.[34]

A culture of domination severs connection, poisons love. We must purge love of its inferiority. The journey from the Two of Swords to the Two of Cups is a turn from rupture to rapture. If in the Two of Swords the pain of shame caused us to close our hearts, the Two of Cups is the medicine of opening, entertaining the possibility of love as a way to radically reorient a colonized subjectivity that makes love inaccessible.

This is the lover's discourse. Love is a dialectic, generating true connection. The language lover's use begins to change, healing what was harmed in relationship where you discover you are worthy of each other. Two hearts expand, fluttering and feeling sacred and sensual at once. The alienating self-denial of the Two of Swords is unmasked in the Two of Cups, self-recovery pushing from the first to the second soul.

There's no blindness in the mutual reception between these two vessels. These two hearts are ready for more than reciprocity; they are in the process of reconciling the other. When your parents fused, your form began, from your father inside your mother. Two in motion as one, a call and response, a firm fluidity. The gestures human life makes toward God see mysterious patterns emerge from the soul sharing sensuous pleasure.

While this process begins with the reader, it should not end with them. Many readers are afraid to trust the herald of love within the cards. Many have become cynical or too afraid to hope that transformative love is still a possibility, thereby denying the cards the full spectrum of their possibility. They have been paralyzed; hope has been foreclosed. To look love in the eyes would leave them helpless, words would escape them, and they would be left wishing they knew how to reveal the love they feel inside, to fill the void that only the other can. But this is no individual failing. One I had hoped to love writes about love as being poisoned in the colonial, racialized world, turning around the "'possibility of love' in a world that imprints a humiliation on the black body."[35] Colonial love is corrupted as it falls along racialized dichotomies that reify the schema of white supremacy and anti-Blackness. Inferiority and overcompensation must be purged lest love be left unattainable.

The prospect of knowing true love is as much a chance, as much a risk as any other omen called forth from the cards. Love is destroyed when its proofs are constantly demanded. Love's validity cannot be measured by the patriarch's logic. The reader cannot focus solely on finding love within, for love's nature is meant to overcome alienation, drawing us deeper into another. Through vitalizing awareness, reaching toward a clear perception of the other, the Two of Cups can feel like being seen for the first time.

The Two of Cups says that though a single card may stand alone, the tarot's greatest strength is its composite. The fantastical elements of love and romance become chimeric in most depictions of the card. The Two of Cups backs love's multiplicity. Colonial fantasy aspires toward a logic of purity. It cannot contain, understand, or cultivate heterogeneity like this card can. Different worlds require different discourses. To alchemize a heart corrupted by dominating violence, the entire world must be restructured to maintain the hope toward love.

The card comes with a confrontation that asks: where is love in our lives? Our answer might require acknowledging a profound absence, but only as we deliberately decide to begin to "write the wound"[36] will it be externalized. Then you might see that the invisible blocks to love are more than individual; they are a structural pathology requiring political acts of sedition. Then a loveless world, a debilitated body, is no longer a fixed fate. Then healing potentials pour forth.

Two find each other thirsty, and without cease they give the gift of life, drinking up all the water and the blood till it overwhelms and overflows from the self into every sphere of living. To be acted upon by the beloved in a way that continually catalyzes our inert potential into expression, love starts to uncoil, and pleasure becomes sacred. We dance like whirling dervishes while calling out "the crown of my blooming is the desire to be in your arms."[37] So begins a tantric journey of opposing forces balancing each other, complementary and evolutive. Glistening wet in the waters of love, two are bonded. The heart has its own resonance that ripples in waves of bliss when it finds clear feedback. The open heart is a symbol of strength and self-awareness. In the field of love's courageous, open, accepting exchange, the serpents of desire are stirred from dormancy, conjoining into a greater erotic body enacting a critical intervention. A laboratory of love is maintained by an equilibrium of power, wisdom, and eros. Love is always placed, and every lover is particular. No two follow the same path. Though their acts differ, they serve justice with their love all the same. The Two of Cups challenges our methodologies, calling for a more careful consideration of how our words relate love to another. The magnitude of the Two of Cups is only conceivable by its continuities and its consistent transformations.

Two of Pentacles

While we might read the history of capitalism as a history of destabilizations, here I am situating my work against a more specific backdrop of what has been called "precarity" in which individuals who once considered themselves generally upwardly mobile and shielded from financial—as well as environmental—collapse are now experiencing what Berlant (2011) has called "a recalibration" to a set of new relations between their lives, the state, and the market. Precarity has often been theorized as a labor condition, what some call "the casualization" or "informalization" of labor (Ettinger 2007), which emerged as post-Fordist, postindustrial capital moved a "new economy" of information, global networks, ever increasingly flexible work arrangements and investment in "immaterial" forms of labor. Additionally, these shifts in the configuration of labor were accompanied by the reduction of state-sponsored social welfare programs and by the increasing privatization of risk and insecurity (Beck 1992). In this regard, precarity has been understood as a labor relation that illustrates the dissolution of what was once presumed to be a "contract" between employer and employee and that suggests that opportunities for stable, long-term employment and security have disappeared (Beneria 2001). However, following Lauren Berlant (2011), the condition of precarity moves beyond the realm of economic restructuring and exists as something much more ordinary and immediate: the textures and rhythms of daily life have been altered in the wake of this restructuring, and individuals are now charged with attuning themselves to these effects—as well as affects. Precarity, in this regard, is a demand for personal affective reorganization in order to take a next step or to continue to conduct the work of everyday life.[38]

To go where there is gain is to go where much is given. Tarot goes beyond platitudes, more than merely a mirror for self-awareness, when it is *vibrant* and energized, and it attunes the reader to the affective reorganization required to survive the neoliberal market. The cards weave a web of media, mediums, meaning, and emotional and physiological states in a cypher that recycles itself with every reading. In the Two of Pentacles readers learn to make do with material instability, a fluctuating livelihood, as they are positioned in precarity, as all professional tarot readers are, by being as flexible and adaptable as the figure in the Two of Pentacles. They are the ones who see a ship sinking and choose to row their own boat, and though they *are* rowing, they are alone. They are their own capital, and their survival, their earnings depend upon their capacity for their own production, what Foucault calls "capital-ability." One side of the coin is purpose, adventure, power, and freedom; the other side is a constant preoccupation with alchemizing *capital-ability* as an attempt to manage economic insecurity. Without an accessible, renewable energy source, we couldn't keep our boat afloat for long. The Two of Pentacles reminds you to shuffle the cards in order to replenish and reorient the sensorium. The Two of Pentacles is an aleatory oracle, enchanting you to acknowledge the cards' own agency, their abundantly energetic animacy.

Professional readers of the tarot hold two languages at once. In one hand is the language of tarot that embraces decay, inertia, and endings as part of a larger elemental balance; in the other is the mundane talk of financial crisis. The Two of Pentacles reader ebbs and flows with their city's economic circulation. The Two of Pentacles presents us a voucher, an experience that is redeemable. The Two of Pentacles reader learns about recycling, transferable skill, transferable value. They move money, time, and bodies around, investing in the various energies of their being as potential resources for prosperity, so long as the reader properly attunes to their rhythmic energetic flows. The Two of Pentacles circulates affective energy into material forms that then circulate across media online and off. They endeavor to be master of their own ships, for though the seas are ever-changing, a well-honed balance can ride the waves longer than most. Still, it's hard not to feel like a fool for having faith in new social connections and material contexts in spite of the laundry list of dismal realities. Just how many things can two hands juggle? The Fool finds another form in the Two of Pentacles, for it is the comedian offering satire and social commentary, turning bleak circumstances into humor infused with broader meaning. The pursuit of a meaningful, fruitful spiritual life is always contextualized within a shifting economic structural base that is always displacing the sense of belonging.

The jester guides us in the search for the place of belonging, the place of freedom, which often means fleeing psychosocial histories of terrorism and traumatic powerlessness. To find this place we deal with repetition, which may feel frightening, as it can suggest a static, stuck quality. We may feel that we are juggling cultures, not yet rooted to a particular place or people. Yet in our comings and goings we create new trails, new routes, which take time walking before they are well worn. Consider what you return to, again and again, and how such past recollections are an aid in locating a space for coherence to come together. In the Two of Pentacles we become aware of our patterns of movement because they provide stepping stones. Another card of cartography, where we map the territory of our life, discover the self, and find a homeplace. The habits of being ingrained from the culture of origin become all the more apparent the moment we leave and exist in a new community and its environment. Juggling various cultural values and personal desires allows us to develop skills of flexibility, levity, resourcefulness, and faith. As we become aware of the stories we cyclically tell ourselves, we merge past and present, informing the unfolding future. These stories become rhythmic steps as we seek to expand our presence and our commitment to making a world where everyone can belong. Returning to the places of our past is returning to a site of memory. In this cyclical return we renew our roots while extending the embodied experience of existing in that space.

> *When I left my native place for the first time, I brought with me two artifacts from home that were emblematic of my growing up life. These two totems were to remind me always of where I come from and who I am at my core. Each year of my life as I went home to visit it was a rite of passage to reassure myself that I still belonged, that I had not become so changed that I could not come home again.*[39]

We become discerning in this card, seeing what our body tells us about where we've invested its time, its energy. We become curious as we walk between environments, relationships, cultures; shifting of material circumstance, routine, and perspective from one state to another. What of our home cultures to keep and what to leave behind? What to receive from our new environments, and what are we to reject? As the marginalized ought to do, we make the most with what we're given, we hustle.

We weigh our experiences, opportunities, and relationships against each other, seeking a common denominator, a through line that keeps up momentum. We may not yet feel we've arrived home or summited the mountain of our most important strivings, but there is value to be recognized in where we stand.

The Two of Pentacles balances the desire to stay and the need to leave. We leave out of a need for autonomy, for sovereignty. The potential for such freedom is compelling. We leave with joy, willing to go without the security of the known when we value what is to be gained, what can only be gained by going. We go in search of an environment that will be receptive and nourishing to *our* existence, *our* joyful expression. The Two of Pentacles partakes of reciprocity so regularly they establish a hybridity that is bespoke.

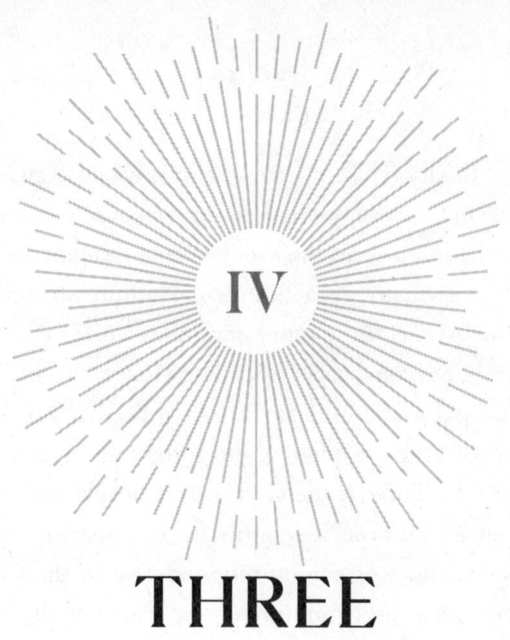

THREE

Generally speaking, this function of the number three is reflected in all sets of trinities: Father, Son, and Holy Ghost; past, present, and future; mother, father, and child; Isis, Osiris, and Horus. In all of these the third member acts as an equilibrating factor, combining the "parent numbers" in such a way as to produce a completely new reality. An interesting side light in this connection is that Pythagoras considered the number three to be the first real number. The first two numbers, he said, were merely essences for they did not correspond to any geometric figure, hence they had no physical reality. But the number three creates the triangle, a plane surface with a beginning, middle, and an end: a tangible reality that corresponds to human experience. Visualizing this triangle dramatizes the truth of Pythagoras's insight. It demonstrates how, with the advent of the triangle, Divine Intention became concretized, and nebulous essence was made manifest in terms of human experience.[1]

Three unites the active, the passive, and the neutral, applying itself to creation, conservation, and destruction. Three is a number of clairvoyance, yet Three teaches us that social change will not come through the effect of raising consciousness alone. Three is the principle of praxis, the necessary bridge between theory (High Priestess) and practice (Magician). Three is an initiatory rite in the development of human consciousness. Three is the number of truth, for it unveils the link between thought and action, cause and effect. Before divinatory practitioners of culture are able to transform the world or the psyche, these inner and outer worlds must first be problematized. The tarot interrogates prior knowledge, preconceived notions, and innate concepts, and it inquires into their origins. The tarot functions as the principle of Three, mediating our inner and outer worlds upon its shadow mirror. The Three is the compass point relating the poles of self and society that would otherwise grow further apart in opposing directions. It is construction: of community and fate in the Cups, bodies of beliefs with the Pentacles, commitment and clarity with the Swords, and with the Wands, culture.

Three resolves the conflict of dualism. Three is the principle of dialogue, the knowledge created in the interplay between two speakers and two listeners. Three maintains that true communication is meant to reach an intelligent, responsive audience. It is not an empty, arrogant projection upon an inactive, captive demographic. When theory is deprived of its active dimension it loses substance, becoming empty and alienating; just as practice without reflection, or an active principle divorced from or denied its passive quality, becomes impulsive and reactive, making dialogue impossible. Three reveals that an authentic *word* is always praxis, a commitment to transforming the world informed by constant reflection upon the world and the self within the world. Three shows that we cannot truly speak if we are speaking alone. Our word requires another. To deny another the right to speak is to deny their action; yet it is an exponential denial, for the one who denies another their right to praxis cuts their own tongue, slices their own ear.

Three is where significance is achieved. It is an existential necessity. Three is the mandorla formed by the joining spheres of Heaven and Earth, Sun, and Moon. Three is the offspring of unity, offering transcendence through resolution. Three is the instrument of creation, distinct from the tool of domination via plastic reproduction or polemical imposition. Three, as dialogue, determines love to be the relation between creators, since subjectivity cannot exist in a relation of domination. Three is courageously brave in claiming love as the creative source of subjecthood. Three, as a dialogue of love upon a foundation of love, is committed to generative acts of freedom, enacted again and again.

Three is humility as a tonic against arrogant perception, alienating self-sufficiency, and elitist patronage. Dialogue is only possible in the space of learning, space made in the recognition of one's own ignorance rather than projecting it outward. Three is liberation born from the foundation of love, humility, and faith. Three establishes trust, and trust overcomes a possessive, constricting false love, a force of manipulation. Trust is fostered when one's word is honored, when action is so aligned. And when action must be refined or adjusted, trust is the act of compassionate communication so confusion is not created. Three is the underappreciated easel that the artist's canvas rests upon. It is the support and the catalyst, the quicksilver for conception. Three is the reality that union is attainable.

The Empress

The garden is a Venus symbol because it is a place in which gendered relations are heightened, made violent, and hypersexualized. The walled garden offers chastity and the protection of sacred desire from worldly decay, while the original garden of Eden is the site of original female sin. In early modernity, female figures in paintings began to represent a social force responsible for the healing and redemption of a degenerating masculinity. In Oskar Kokoschka's play *Murderer, Hope of Women,* there are two main characters: Man and Woman. While Woman first rejects Man's advances, he is wounded but, eventually, Woman nurtures Man back to health. Once Man has recovered, he is able to become fully redeemed when he kills Woman. In this play, Woman is the figure who must be sacrificed to redeem Man. This psychosexual drama imagines femininity as a temptress who must be killed. In short, the death of Woman, in Kokoschka's play, represents both Man's alienation from the natural world and his alienation from the artiifical world. The sexual fetish of Woman shocks Man into action, but only by murdering his sexual fetish can Man redeem his morality. Through violence, Man sacrifices Woman and regains paradise. The metropolis, as garden, is an arena where gendered aesthetics are staged. In the garden as stage, femininity is sacrificed and masculinity is redeemed.[2]

As I write this, the Earth is literally dripping on me. With sap from the trees and the bees pollinating around me, there's an eroticism in the air that is only natural. The Earth shows us how to be love-pregnant with God. The tarot shows us the Empress. Her overturn turns your back on the spectator so you can see the sublime. Reject the notion that freedom is dependent on an ongoing process of emancipation from nature. The *carne vale*—farewell to the flesh—is invoked by the tarot's carnival ruckus of card shuffling, as if to say, *Let go of a gaze that sees only lead, dead flesh.* The hegemonic colonial power leaves us in a state of constitutive discomfort. We are captured by its constant surveilling. *Carnival* cuts the carceral conceptions of material being. After hundreds of years of conquest of native lands, customs, and people, this is an ongoing project. The Empress teaches you this exaltation: raise the body and elevate the soul. Contemplate her sunset and sunrise until you weep, enamored and terrified by your meager position set against her scale. And of a volcano, or a tempest, or her open skies, what power does a human have? She is the sudden daybreak, the luck of those golden moments when humble mumbles of prayer in the most subtly felt centers of the soul begin to burst forth into brilliant sensorial vivification.

The Empress has true power: the power to feed, to nourish, to make another stronger, to sustain another from pure love, only to become more sustained by love in return. Should we love as the Earth does, we'd thank her for the space to labor over our own love crop, and we would know how good it feels to feed our bread to the beloved. She is the motherlands, and from her flesh many paradises are made real. She is where we come from. No matter how far we've gone, her home is always full of freedom, beauty, and abundance. The Empress is Freire, teaching us power is the practice of freedom, "the means by which men and women deal critically and creatively with reality and discover how to participate in the transformation of their world."[3] Hers is a throne welcoming you into the earth's open rolling hills, a queer visitation in its dislocation from the state. She promises a world where you will be well-fed and free. We are love crowning from her. Our being is her body, our bone her blood. Ours is the flesh of love. To exalt love we only need to hold the body.

Hers is the doorway to a life with vibrant sensuality. Hers is the hand behind all creative endeavors, blessing, guiding. For the drama of new life manifesting, she is the stage. She inspires all cultural creation, the dynamic and joyous byproducts of people sharing ideas, space, and bodies. Her charms are alluring; bees and boys buzz to her pollen, and by her consent, honey happens.

The word arrives at an approximation of truth in the interplay of reflection and action. The Empress is the praxis between the Magician's speech and the High Priestess's listening reflection. The truest words transform the world. Her power connects diverse and oppositional elements in a creative embrace that has its own subjectivity, its own autonomy. True sovereignty extends power. Her relationships are their own power source, able to overcome the lust for status, the reach for dominating authority, with radically reciprocating love. We come from her, but we are not her possession. Love is not static and is not purchasable. It needs nourishment and cultivation if it is to protect the agency of life in all living beings.

Venus, as the Empress, has been the nonneutral marker of civilization, the force of power that normalizes itself in social custom and protects the colonizer's privatized paradise, while simultaneously producing the anxiety of cognitive dissonance that the means of such protection produce and reproduce. Imperialist nostalgia, the conqueror's longing for what they defiled and destroyed, now sells us the very things labeled as profane and used as justification for conquest. Seeing sage, a sacred native plant and tool, now endangered due to its overcommercialization is a perpetuation of the original assault of conquest. Imperialist nostalgia is a tool of mystification that obscures paradisal desire, as this longing locates the spirit of the "primitive" "in the bodies of dark Others whose cultures, traditions, and lifestyles may indeed be irrevocably changed by imperialism, colonization, and racist domination."[4] Trying to make contact with the lost paradise of the past through transgressive sexual desire for the Other in the present and their "primitive" power of body is an attempt to assuage guilt of the past in a manner that denies accountability and rejects history. Colonizers, in their imperialist nostalgia, yearn to redeem a lost paradise they found projected upon indigenous lands. However, the act of conquest is the defilement they seek to guard against. They seek to escape the profanity of their civilization that cannot restrain itself from restraining others. In their attempts to exceed the human, their anti-Black terror backfires, and the terrible horizons of accumulated suffering are too much to bear to occupy the flesh-in-this-world.

The innocent naked body of Venus, of Empress, becomes bound tightly in the corset of the state's repressive hypersexualization of female bodies for commercial viability. "The psychosexual impulses of Enlightenment-era men were preoccupied with the innocence or profanity of the feminine body. This anxiety, which was always the anxiety around the innocence or profanity of the state, became a preoccupation with the innocence and profanity of the colonized lands from which the state derived its wealth and power."[5] Their mission is self-defeating and doomed in its logic.

When the Empress asks you *what to become,* the reader must reckon with the impasses of the Madonna/whore dichotomies of sacred/profane; civilized/savage; private/public; beauty/ugliness; white supremacy/anti-Blackness.

Yet the Empress also offers an eco-logic of persevering and nurturing natural cycles of regeneration. Ecological emancipation is contrary to the lingering Enlightenment-era ideas of humanity's progress seeking technological advancement to emancipate *from* nature. As the feminization of the Earth engenders mutually constituting hierarchical dualisms such that women and femininity are always subordinated to men and masculinity, the Earth is always subordinated to the human, the body subordinated to mind, people of color subordinated to whiteness, and so on, ecofeminist orientations and critique become necessary considerations.[6]

> *Ecofeminism is about connectedness and wholeness of theory and practice. It asserts the special strength and integrity of every living thing. For us the snail darter is to be considered side by side with a community's need for water, the porpoise side by side with appetite for tuna, and the creatures it may fall on with Skylab. We are a woman-identified movement and we believe we have a special work to do in these imperiled times. We see the devastation of the earth and her beings by the corporate warriors, and the threat of nuclear annihilation by the military warriors, as feminist concerns. It is the same masculinist mentality which would deny us our right to our own bodies and our own sexuality, and which depends on multiple systems of dominance and state power to have its way.*[7]

Such interrelated awareness necessarily encompasses the spiritual selfhood and well-being of all life forms. Capitalist conquest necessarily denigrates and denies the spiritual dimension of interconnectedness to consume, extract from, and manipulate the Earth as a raw material resource. The tactics of patriarchal conquest apply aggression, conquest, possession, and control to both the body of the Earth and the femme body. The Empress concerns our search for cultural identity and rootedness. It is important to maintain that while Venus and the Empress can be called upon to recover and regenerate women's Indigenous knowledge and spiritual cosmologies, Venus in the Western empire is a feminine goddess who has acted to reinforce the structures of patriarchal power. The societies Venus describes have been of a hierarchical social order that, while distinct from militia, rely on the martial for material and political power.[8]

To honor the sacredness of life is to honor the source of life, the Earth, and as the Earth has been feminized, to revere the Earth is to praise the femme, the Goddess. Such Goddess worship must be critical to ensure that the feminine effigy is no longer equated with the interests of powerful men. Such is the danger of assessing progress by means of representation, for simply aiming to have more women and/or people of color in power loses sight of the reality that patriarchy has no gender. The state defangs spiritual practices and cosmologies through commodification. Such commodification focuses on materialism, appropriation, and oriental exoticism that recapitulates conquest, although such imperialist nostalgia becomes more difficult to discern as it hides under the propaganda of representation and progress. "Luxury spiritualism cannot overcome the dichotomies between spirit and matter, economics and culture, because as long as it fails to integrate this search for wholeness into a critique of the existing exploitative world system and a search for a better society it can easily be co-opted and neutralized."[9] The Empress supports our need for wholeness while critiquing the fragmented and commodified ways wholeness is sought in the West.

The expansion of monoculture-based agricultural production and fragmented farming systems proliferate an understanding of diverse elements viewed in isolation, alienated from their connection, contribution, and full realization within the larger ecosystem. The ruling class pursues diversity to collect contained varieties. The ruling class pursues diversity with an exoticizing gaze. The conqueror's fascination is deadly. The colonizer seeks difference as a spice to flavor the bland whiteness of their cultural consumption. Their invitation for a seat at the table is an invitation to *be served* as dinner. The guiding paradigm for biodiversity conserves in word but destroys in act, whether in agricultural practice or in the institutional efforts toward diversity that produce tokenism and its insidious violence. We learn from the women, whose stewardship of the earth's biodiversity, though rendered invisible, continuously creates linkages that maintain underresourced environments with ecological stability, sustainability, and productivity. In their own invisible work is evidence of their preserving the value created by the interrelationships between elements. Such diversity exists in relational rather than reductional categories. The Empress tills the soul as soil, asking us to treasure our bodies as geographies of pleasure and possibility to cultivate the cultures of belonging we've been denied.

The Empress's love is found in the invisible spaces, where bonds have been physically severed, families displaced, and bodies imprisoned. While my mothers' mother was an inmate of the California prison complex, my father's father worked as a corrections officer. The state's violence is gendered. My grandmother's body was exploited and abused by the state. Colonial gender production forces members of an oppressed class to enact lateral violence, to become self-oppressing as they become servants of the state's employment. Empress love cares enough to change. My mother's love showed me this. My mother was first pregnant at sixteen. Children mothering children makes a Mother of the Ghetto. The Mothers of the Ghetto are mothers armed with a love sharp enough to cut the cords of bondage, brave enough to break cycles of generational abuse, and resourceful enough to tend the ruin of the body plundered. My mother was a Mother of the Ghetto; my grandmother was a Prison Mom. Despite the state's attempts to uproot the mother bond, her love is a flower that refuses to be weeded from the garden.

Despite the state's attempts to cut and cage my grandmother from her daughter's life, a Polaroid picture of her with a crown of waist-length jet-black curls—gathered with the daughters torn asunder, huddled around in the prison yard—refuses to recognize her as anyone other than the Empress in her lavish garden. I grew up enraptured by this photograph of her imprisonment because of her staging in the adoration of her community. The blue of her jumpsuit became the Virgin Mary's robes, and her daughters gathered like cherubs made me feel less lonely. The Empress cannot be made ugly. Even imprisoned, this beauty could not be disappeared by the state. This Polaroid is testimony to my grandmother's defiance against being forgotten, understanding her beauty, her motherhood as resistance. This Empress motherhood finds freedom by transfiguring the dominant portrayal and associations of the oppressed as existing in an unending abject state into bodies of pleasures, sensuality, and affirmation through communal relations. This photo refuses to forget her beauty, just as it refuses to ignore the violence imposed upon her. It is visual testament to the loss or displacement of her body and being from her family, her homelands. Such images presence absence, providing texts of paradox that unfurl with possibility for queer literacy. The environmental degradation made gardens scarce in my hometown, but my mother made sure I knew libraries and museums as literary gardens of cultural artistry. With the Empress, even the ghetto has a garden.

Death

He died at eventide, when the sun lay like a brooding sorrow above the western hills, veiling its face; when the winds spoke not, and the trees, the great green trees he loved, stood motionless. I saw his breath beat quicker and quicker, pause, and then his little soul leapt like a star . . . and left a world of darkness in its train. The day changed not; the same tall trees peeped in at the windows, the same green grass glinted in the setting sun. Only in the chamber of death writhed the world's most piteous thing—a childless mother.[10]

I grew up attending so many funerals, it's as if I was raised in a graveyard. Solemnity pervades the air of burial grounds, filling the lungs exasperated by grief with a steady, cold assist. The stillness of such air was familiar but never so personal till the death of my grandmother. My people know it is an honor to be there in the room when the dying take their last breath. My mother held her mother's hand until her coldness came. My grandmother was understandably nervous, resisting the recitation of ritual prayers as though she would not accept defeat. My grandmother's body was shutting down, but inside she still had vigor. In her final days, her spirit began reaching beyond her body's limitations. She knew who was in her home before they announced themselves, and she welcomed each, as she would soon be guided home by her late brother and mother. They came for her days before her passing was due, endearing themselves to her with memories and sharing laughter. Then the angel of Death caught her attention, and she finally surrendered to her fate. She taught me Death is about accepting our own dying as much as it is about accepting the death of our loved ones. She taught me that your dead bring you home, so we should celebrate and welcome Death. In its process we come to cherish our ephemeral forms, and we are motivated to make peace. She shared the grip of Death with my mother, grasping her daughter for support as though she were on a roller coaster with its crest reaching Heaven, and leaving the drop for the living, bidding her body farewell as her spirit crossed the line and she entered a permanent dwelling of peace she'd never known on Earth. This truth is only truly known by those there at the last breath.

My grandmother's passing has shown me that the mother who bears creation is the same one who delivers death. Who else could resolve life but the one who has brought it all forth? Death is the Dark Mother, the full realization of her love. While the Empress births us into body, Death brings us back to Spirit. Birth and death are but two sides of the same veil. She veils and unveils fanning life into the cosmos, as a mother would resuscitate her child who refuses to breathe. The force of this love is so enthralling we fear we will be swallowed whole. This devouring and smothering aspect is sometimes pictured as a dragon. The hero defines himself by his ability to slay the dragon, to cut the umbilical cord, to gain the pearl. This hero mythology reiterates the worldview that nature must be transcended, and transcended by violent means. To justify these means, the mother is made a dragon, a man-eater, depicted as power-hungry and abusive. Dominant narratives perpetuate the idea that women are incapable of possessing power without being corrupted. The grandmother becomes a wolf determined to gorge herself upon the youth of her children. Man has perceived his ability to sever his relationships as a virtue. This Western guilt manifests as white anxiety fearing the retaliation of the Earth and the oppressed against debasement.

> *White people believed that whatever the manners, under every dark skin was a jungle. Swift unnavigable waters, swinging screaming baboons,*

sleeping snakes, Red gums ready for their sweet white blood. In a way, he thought, they were right. The more colored people spent their strength trying to convince them how gentle they were, how clever and loving, how human, the more they used themselves up to persuade whites of something Negroes believed could not be questioned, the deeper and more tangled the jungle grew inside. But it wasn't the jungle blacks brought with them to this place from the other (livable) place. It was the jungle white folks planted in them. And it grew. It spread. In, through and after life, it spread, until it invaded the whites who had made it. Touched them every one. Changed and altered them. Made them bloody, silly, worse than even they wanted to be, so scared were they of the jungle they had made. The screaming baboon lived under their own white skin; the red gums were their own.[11]

These depictions unveil a different purpose for the psyche when understood alchemically: "*Prima materia,* Physis, or the elemental world, devours the king. In the background, the base *prima materia* is consumed, or transformed, and the king makes his exit from the fire. The flames are purgatorial in that they purge the gross and permit the resurrection of the king, who parallels *anima mundi* as the soul of matter."[12] Primordial Earth is *prima materia* to the alchemist, it is the abyss, the chaos that Logos descends into, the Fool descending to Death. Prima Earth, Mother, is *the Devourer* in Death, appearing as a crocodile in Gnostic hermeticism.

Death functions as a necessity for the psyche, but we must reconcile the legacy of misogyny that denies the awesome might of a Mother's will to love so strongly that she would kill her own child rather than subject it to a life of servitude. Her love is radical in its commitment to liberation, and from the child's devastating death we learn it is not our own kin we should sacrifice; we should rather seek to overturn the forces that compel such violent means of finding freedom. Death's love is only depicted as villainy, justified by the *characterization* of a woman bereft humanity. Such objectification leaves one a beast, a wolf, an animal who can be bought, broken, indentured, killed, or eaten. "Unless carefree, mother love was killer."[13] That peculiar institution that assaults our vast ecosystem of loving relatedness to deny our identity, subjectivity, and sovereignty has its legacy in all modern institutions. Regardless, the state's attempts to kill or incarcerate only reveal the strength of the Mother's love. It takes work to reorient our understandings and representations of such love. It takes careful holding to not confuse Death with desertion.

I write to make sense of Death, to keep from confusion; life is language, for Death has no words. Writing, unlike life, is never finished. Writing has no death. I write this as if in a trance, but I'm too tired from too many mournings. Many readers will tell you Death is not about the final physical death; but it is in our first firsthand encounter with mortality that the reality of dissolution is summoned in steady awareness. Once our Death-cherry is popped, it becomes a card in a deck we regularly pull. To think we could have a card called Death and not be confronted with the literal death all around *is* the reading, as the survival instinct becomes self-evident. Death is about surviving and all the mechanisms, strategies, and dogged determination to self-preserve. It's about surviving as in "Cecilia is survived by her daughter Ruby, her son Victor, her daughter Deleena."

Death reawakens the collective body, reminding us we have a part in sustaining the heart of our love beyond the corporeal. Death not only takes but also brings life to the shared body of grief. Death is the process of collectivization. Collective self-possession changes as the self is no longer singular; it comprises all the bodies of our love, all the bodies of our longing, fulfilled as tears fall within the larger body of our shared salt water.

Death apportions survival. As there is no survival without the hope of love, we know Death is a bride, because in Death we are reunited with the beloved. We can be so willing to share our life with the dead that we attempt to take up all the grief for everyone else. Let Death teach us to parcel grief, for it is indeed very grave. It digs in far too deep for any one body. When Death comes, be ready to move beyond self-limitation.

In the past, when Death was dealt it didn't always need to be spelled out, but the mind is incredulous. It has doubt, it lacks faith, it wants proof, it wants insurance, a guarantee. Death brushes around our personal geography, prodding the borders humanity makes as a fiction unable to withstand the truth of Death's migrating transgressions. The mind wants to watch out for Death, to avert the eyes, to postpone the encounter. But then we become so fixed in the fear of Death that we are imprisoned in a false forever, afraid of life. Death doesn't care about misinterpretations; it touches our soul to free every single one of us nonetheless. Death is the true egalitarian, the radical abolitionist, willing to make all death a sacred sacrifice, eternally upholding the commitment to a life of liberation. Death does not take long in extending an invitation. Death is constantly working upon us; daily we are dying, daily resisting succumbing to its touch.

Yet to be touched by Death is to clear the veils of race, class, gender. Dubois knew this; Sethe knew this. The mourned find freedom in transgressing life with Death, while those in mourning all wait in grief for Death to take us beyond bondage. Pull Death as a promise that we will not long be left behind.

Still, it is the duty of the living to process death. To deal with loss we create culture, we memorialize by gathering, singing, and joining in prayer. As Proust remarks, "Ideas come to us as the successors of grief." Darkened spirits encroach so regularly upon the lives of the oppressed that we have worked it into our cultural iconography and sensibility. The dead and the ways of dying become as much as a part of identity as the ways of living. In the words of Karla FC Holloway: "The twentieth century rehearsed, nearly to perfection, a relentless cycle of cultural memory and black mourning. Black deaths and black dying have cut across and through decades and centuries as if neither one matters more than the incoherent, associative presence of the other. Even if the story is grief-stricken, the act of memorializing retains a particular aspect of a culture's narrative, and for blacks in the Americas, some notion of racial memory and racial realization is mediated through the veil of death."[14]

The tarot's Death can move us from cultural realization to cosmological reclamation. The primal power of the Mother is too great to be denied. Rather than a dragon or a crocodile, it is the deities of the Earth—Serpent Women, Cihuacoatl, Coatlicue, Tlateuchtli—who encompass the chthonic creatrix.

> *Coatlicue literally means "skirt of snakes." She is associated with death, fertility of the earth, and medicinal plants. All healers call to her. When you need to be grounded in the earth or connect with your heart and cut attachments, she invites you to reinvent yourself and let go. Her name literally means "earth-lord"* (tlalli = *land;* tecuhtli = *lord). While the suffix of her name usually indicates a male, she appears in stories as female, and her*

pictorial representation is decidedly female, usually in the birth-giving posture. Midwives prayed to Tlaltecuhtli in cases of difficult birth. Tlatecuhtli embodies the duality of creation and earth. She has her mouth open to give and receive in reciprocal relationship with those who dwell on earth. The tree of life growing from her jaws of death completes this picture of the earth as womb and tomb. Her mouth and the act of eating are analogous to birth and death. When Tlaltecuhtli comes to you, you know that you are now strong enough for a rite of passage; you are ready to go deep into the darkness and return to light.[15]

Studying the history of various cultural primal goddesses with serpents for adornment (e.g., Medusa, Algol, Coatlicue, etc.) reveals that patriarchal violence deploys a counterfeminine power to behead each queen of creation. There is one who reclaims and alchemizes this power through her own self-decapitation: Chinnamasta, a manifestation of Mahadevi, the Great Goddess. Like Kali, she wears a *mala* of skulls, representing temporal ending and the triumph of a more powerful force. She overcomes the worldly authority of kings and tyrants and recenters the locus of power from the heart. Death may come for our crowns, but only as she serves her own head on a platter. Chinnamasta redeems the mother's killing love and reconciles the various cultural myths converging in the requisite beheading and dismembering of Death. The blood flowing from her sacred severance nourishes both her and her children, showing she is very much alive. She is the Black Madonna, the Mother who is there at the time of our greatest need, the hour of death. Grief is all the felt testimony of her love, the truth of her presence amidst loss.

Death is not the last card in the major arcana; there is much beyond, much to come, though often we are offered a white rose in exchange for the thorn's piercing process. Death is arcanum thirteen, the witch's number, the rupturing of the finished cycle and the thrust into the unknown's dark night. Death is about transformation so profound and enduring it is irreversible. It is the laying to rest, putting some sorrow to peace. Death frees us from our holding patterns and acts as a midwife facilitating our spiritual rebirth. Death calls back all our scattered soul pieces, lingering like ghosts at the sites of trauma and devastation we dwell in for far too long. Death says we have suffered long enough, that we can let go now. Death wants resolution for all that has been left unresolved and festering. It is often the internal damage that takes longest to heal. Scorpionic Death alchemizes the poisons of shame from our watery memory. This putrefaction part of the journey acquaints the reader with *essence.* In this way of washing our soul, we are left humble, compassionate, and sensitive. We need Death to make peace with our vulnerability, to stop punishing ourselves for our failures of invincibility.

When we allow ourselves to become undone, to dissolve the identities created to armor ourselves from being touched by change, by life, we allow re-creation. This is the essence of Mesoamerican divinatory practice. The diviner summons the godly powers of creation to be *re-created.* Their body becomes a medium, opened through ritual and prayer. This recognizes that the body is itself a sacred space, capable of fully becoming a conduit for sacrality. While the tarot is a book of the dead, it is not forestalling Death or reanimating fallen bodies as zombies. It is about moving through death so the spirits find new bodies. I won't see my grandmother in her same flesh, but I offer her my flesh and let her love flow through me and lead me to a space where we might meet again, readily recognizing each other even in new skin. Tarot reflects the many forms divination takes. The Mesoamerican divinatory channeling and *re-creation* are distinct from sortilege, the recreational gambling games of the future with the casting of lots. Recreation offers refreshment through play, pleasure, and relaxation. Can we come to greet Death as we would a friend inviting us out to play? How many invitations can we afford to forgo? Perhaps this is why the child welcomes Death without fear, for they still know how to play. They can shed identity easily, because they know the make-believe roles we assign ourselves are not so serious that they are worth losing the joyous connections they seek to forge. They are less attached to the outcome, less focused on proclaiming winners and losers because they are all the more engaged in the play itself.

Death admonishes the reader to get resolved to know love while you live, before all your transitory plans expire. No love grows without the change Death facilitates, so more than just accepting Death, embrace it. Death is ready to disclose the freedom the Divine intends for us.

Queen Theory

Shakti comes to us from these forests and grasslands, we watch them grow, year in and year out through their internal shakti and we derive our strength from it. We watch our streams renew themselves and we drink their clear, sparkling water, that gives us shakti. We drink fresh milk, we eat ghee, we eat food from our own fields. All this gives us not just nourishment for the body but a moral strength, that we are our own masters, we control and produce our own wealth. That is why it is "primitive," "backward"; women who do not buy their needs from the market but produce for themselves, who are leading Chipko. Our power is nature's power. Our power against Gurjal comes from these inner sources and is strengthened by his attempts to oppress and bully us with his false power of money. We have offered ourselves, even at the cost of our lives, for a peaceful protest to close this mine, to challenge and oppose the power that Gurjal represents. Each attempt to violate us has strengthened our integrity. They stoned us on 20 March when they returned from the mine. They stoned our children and hit them with iron rods, but they could not destroy our shakti.[16]

The Empress is the archetype of which the Queens are elemental manifestations. As each Queen is an aspect of the Divine Mother, each one depicts personalities embodying the internal mastery of each element. Each member of the court can be met as the steward of their respective elemental dimension, with the Queens relating the central organizing principle of a power resourced, rather than extracted, from the Earth. Each Queen lives within each of us, cultivating sovereignty by venerating nature, the source of life, as sacred. Queens maintain diplomacy, teach us tact, and sustain community through cultural, artistic investment. Each Queen is autonomous and maintains social cohesion.

These are aspects of our personality focused on relating, protecting, cultivating, and inspiring. The Queens represent the elements in their most nurturing expression. Queens measure freedom and human evolution in terms of the capacity to integrate harmoniously with the Earth's rhythms, both intellectually and emotionally. Queens inspire loyalty through love. They ensure continuity and attend to the ecosystem of relationships with intelligence, sensitivity, and care. Each Queen serves like a full moon, providing full inner realization of what, who, and how we are serving. They illuminate the inner landscapes, and they counsel us with wisdom when our power, autonomy, and agency feel most challenged or attacked. Queens show us how to embody solar awareness. Each reminds us that we are part of the democracy of nature's life and that we do not stand apart, separate from, or above nature. Their responsibility to defend life and honor death informs each of their directives.

Queens shape community. They are mothers to lost, disowned children. Being a Queen is about performance. Claiming power in the display of beauty, grace, and precision is Queendom. Queens cultivate spaces of leisure, artistic rapture, and social engagement as strategies of resistance, preservation, and innovation. Queens remind us that ruling is a performance, the world a stage we stunt on. Queens help us understand the social consequences of nonnormative identity construction through sites of play and recreation. Queens unveil leisure spaces as permeating with possibility for creative power reconfigurations. They remind us that our identity construction and expression have political effect and implication. Queens work within, against, and with broader cultural projects and forms. Each sovereign deals with simultaneous visibility and invisibility. They are projected upon, rejected, pressured, dismissed, and sabotaged even as they protect, inspire, and rally.

To earn a Queen's trust is to be offered the intimacy of seeing what is unseen by many. To understand the complexity of the performance of social actors within social contexts is to understand the Queen's intelligence. Performing power and claiming a role of one's own construction is a strategy to make real and tangible the truths that have been hidden, repressed, or ignored. The Queen works against invisible renderings of reality and identity. The Queen is a champion of the censured and silenced. If we are subjects with distinct orientations, it is the Queen who dispatches, authorizes, and emboldens such orientations. Queens inspire exaggeration in their emulation of empowerment. Identity and meaning are malleable when we take identity markers into our own hands, yet this malleability works toward authenticity when guided by a Queen. They are creating their own authentic genders, on their own terms, informed by the unique context of their historical, sociocultural milieu. They remind us of our own power to transgress and transform social constructs; they remind us that we are not bound by any particular set of gender expectations, because the expansive possibility of expression exists within us, the ones without whom the show could not go on. We cannot help but shower adoration upon Queens who champion the genderqueers of the world. They remind us that dignity and respect cannot be bought but are accomplished in community. "The Queens display infinite weirdness to the world. For them, style is the path into the unique self and so to transcendence. They long for everyone to reveal themselves wherever they are."[17] Long live the Queen!

Queen of Swords

The private world represented is an intimate sphere of Latina love and passion that calls attention to the quotidian pressures that besiege Chicana dykes who must negotiate the task of being public intellectuals and private subjects.[18]

The Queen of Swords is the human emissary of Justice, an emanation of Libra's scales. She holds the sword upright, yet her head is turned. Despite her emotional attachment to any particular outcome, she is able to make hard decisions and so upholds truth with authority. The Queen of Swords is discerning, she writes and educates, she speaks truth to power. This Queen is disposing and dismembering, but for our benefit. She is the one who makes heads roll, the ego-killer when cold logic has reigned too righteously. She utilizes and respects the power of language. Her sword clarifies the framings of justice, orientations toward discipline, and perspectives on power. She is experienced in heartbreak, has pierced through deception with her honed perception, and by knowing herself as a survivor, she has done the work to heal and keep healing.

The Queen helps beauty become clearly reflected in truth. She recognizes the beauty of truth, a recognition only possible when we move toward the freedom of authenticity and away from the expressions that are bound up in others' expectations, projections, rejections. To hold power always puts one at risk. The throne is never safe from either internal temptation or external threat. The Queen must maintain her sovereignty, maintain higher perspective, and honor her responsibility to be of service to the greater harmony of her people.

She is often associated with the swan, a cross-cultural symbol attuned to wisdom, music, and speech. In the constellation of Cygnus, Zeus is transformed into a swan in the pursuit of Leda in the act of seduction. High culture is epitomized by the swan, but lurking behind the beauty is a bird of battle, a spiritual warrior. Alchemically, the swan is associated with the *albedo,* the whitening, or the purification of form. The Queen of Swords is the swan queen, with shamanic skills of transformation. Behind the subtle beauty of air is the queer power of transfigured creation.

The Queen of Swords appears to help us distill knowledge into wisdom. She asks us to speak up, to speak out, and to speak truth. Or she asks us to be silent and still. She offers reading lists and journal prompts. She calls upon critical reflection in our personal experiences of law, transgression, justness, and mercy. The Queen brings clarity to our interiority, coming into critical acknowledgment of how our manners of knowing are forged in history and relations of power. As we work to break through personal and collective denial, we are servicing the Queen of Swords. Be true to your heart, she says.

She wakes us from collective amnesia so we cannot forget that all knowledge is forged in histories of social antagonisms. She gives us strategies to deal with contention, challenge reified paradigms, and allow for shifts in social relations. Our education, our perspective, our history, and its stories are not neutral. The Queen of Swords is clear about this. She teaches us to assume responsibility for our choices as she helps us confront the limitations of our training and knowledge. As such she shows authority is maintained by knowing where we lack authority. She recognizes the deep fear of any decentering of the white male canon, while working to clarify the commitment to cultural, intellectual diversities that are truly transformative. She remains both patient and vigilant toward revolution. She does not despair in the face of conflict. As her commitment to truth informs every dimension of her being, she welcomes dissent, rejoices in diversity, and affirms the spirit of intellectual openness. Experienced in critical discussions with authority figures, students, and community members, she gives multilayered testimony.

She knows education as the practice of freedom, and she advocates literacy for all. She defends libraries and public spaces of learning, questioning, and creating. She is recognized as an insurgent intellectual. Students who feel terribly wounded in their psyche seek knowledge that is meaningful. Her court is the classroom, providing an education that heals the uninformed, unknowing spirit within a space of inclusivity. The Queen of Swords models the vulnerability of bringing personal narratives into the learning environment in order to dispel the notion that any teacher or authority is all-knowing or that any truth model can be universal. Rather, we can interrogate our lives to generate the theory born from lived experience. "I came to theory because I was hurting," bell hooks writes. "The pain within me was so intense that I could not go on living. I came to theory desperate, wanting to comprehend—to grasp what was happening around and within me. Most importantly, I wanted to make the hurt go away. I saw in theory then a location for healing."[19] Such educational practices become acts of resistance. The Queen of Swords challenges us to embrace these processes of self-actualization. See through her sword and ask what values your habits of being reflect; ask if they maintain the commitment to freedom, and she will show another dialectic.

This Queen is unafraid of honesty and is strong enough to let truth dictate her relationships. This means her relationships are ones of integrity, each one a source of power. She is the coolest, emotionally, of the Queens. She comes with the wind, and the mist before the rain. She has grieved illusory attachments and welcomes reality placed perceptively in a position of higher clarity. This energy suffers no fools, cuts karmic cords, and does not tolerate deceit. She draws strength from boundaries and clear ethical guidelines. She recognizes the constructs and boundaries of her community while pushing against borders of exclusion. She facilitates dialogue, knowing love is at its foundation.

The Queen of Swords reminds us our mother tongue cannot be cut out. Her orientation respects multiple subjectivities in the creative act of communication. She is an intellectual, a teacher, a judge, able to read and write the world because she has already lost face, and now her self-image is forged in the truth found beyond loss. She creates space to communicate and creates pathways for progress through a calm, loving center.

Queen of Wands

The erotic is a resource within each of us that lies in a deeply female and spiritual plane, firmly rooted in the power of our unexpressed or unrecognized feeling. . . . The erotic is a measure between the beginnings of our sense of self and the chaos of our strongest feelings. It is an internal sense of satisfaction to which, once we have experienced it, we know we can aspire. For having experienced the fullness of this depth of feeling and recognizing its power, in honour and self-respect we can require no less of ourselves. . . . This internal requirement toward excellence which we learn from the erotic must not be misconstrued as demanding the impossible from ourselves nor from others. Such a demand incapacitates everyone in the process. For the erotic is not a question only of what we do; it is a question of how acutely and fully we can feel in the doing. Once we know the extent to which we are capable of feeling that sense of satisfaction and completion, we can then observe which of our various life endeavours bring us closest to that fullness.[20]

We turn to the Queen of Wands by tapping into the erotic, nonrational power residing in the deepest core of our being. The Queen of Wands is the primordial fire of life. She becomes the fire, and to play with fire is to play with her. She is a provocateur of revelation. She scorches away confusion, denial, and shame by her self-acceptance and open presentation. Her flame demands conscious engagement. Her approach is brave in its unflinching honesty. This Queen's inquiry seeks empowered sexual identities. Of all the Queens, only she sits on her throne positioned facing the front. The strength of the Queen of Wands is her vantage of independence. Her legs aren't crossed like the Queen of Cups, or supporting or a pentacle, or turned to the side. Her seat is sure and well spread. Her power is widened, not narrowed.

The black cat before her stares timelessly and directly at the reader, an omen unto itself. The black cat is a witch's familiar, and fire is her focus, unsettling in its all-seeing quality. It is not pacified by artifice, nor is its scrutiny avoidable. She forces shadowy encounters to facilitate fearlessness and overcome complacency, for as a representative of projected puritanical, patriarchal fear all her own, she is not naively navigating danger.

She is insistent; you will see her seeing you. Her look is toward experience. She does not want us to look away. She wants us to recognize desires and then to say yes to the deepest among them. She sits in the essential power of the erotic, so she is discordant and disturbs. The Queen and her kitty have survived all manner of catastrophe. With style she is always coming alive, always dying time and time again. Her sunflower, her wand, her golden gown are testament to this victory. Before we even hear her speak, the image of her survival resounds because she knows what it is to cower, to look away from the fullness of herself for the sake of expediency.

"The fear that we cannot grow beyond whatever distortions we may find within ourselves keeps us docile and loyal and obedient, externally defined, and leads us to accept many facets of our oppression as women."[21]

She is adamant that we learn to respect our needs more than the fear of breaking the silence. The Queen of Wands insists on burning brightly, on arising from the fullness of her feeling despite the fear of others. The Queen of Wands sanctions what is deemed dangerous. She leads us into chaos, to show us more than the conditioned response, the tightly bound patterns of predictability. She isn't motivated by necessity, strict logic, profit, or propriety. She refutes external commands but submits always to her own arched back. The Queen of Wands is *self*-affirming, relying entirely on her own knowing to guide her. She trusts herself completely, so she can move through the world with poise, precision, and graceful levity. She is glamour, she is pleasure, she is satisfaction for its own sake. Holding court with her is only possible when you are as honest as possible in pursuing the pleasure of passion's power. She watches as you discover this creative freedom of combining the sexual and the spiritual, the psychic and the emotional with the physical and sensorial, the personal to the political.

The Queen of Wands cooks you. She cleanses you with smoke and stimulates latent potential into actualization. Her fire is vigorous, but it overcomes the ways we deny and diminish ourselves. This power demands we assume all the power of our capacity. From her fires, desire comes confident. Deeper, wider, it entices beyond self-limitation. To be touched by her fire is to become revitalized, charmed, fascinated, and energized. She does what feels good because she feels herself, because she is not numb. She is not putting on a show, stuck in shame or moving in a way that makes her alien to herself. By becoming self-motivated, living from within outward, she sits in creative catharsis, medicine for depression, despair, self-denial, and resignation in the embraced, vulnerable expression.

She's always tending the communal spirit, always seeing into the heart of the flame. She safeguards every hearth, every billowing column of copal clouds that re-creates the axis upon which the cosmos spins. Whereas the Page of Wands delivers messages from the divine plane to the human, the Queen of Wands carries our prayers and ritual offerings to the celestial spheres beyond. As we learn from her to be faithful to our pleasure's intuition, we push past convention only to find that our power, radiance, optimism, and creative sexuality are nothing to fear. *Shine unapologetically,* she will always say.

Queen of Cups

Chalchiuhtlicue or She of the Jade Skirt is the Central Mexican goddess of lakes and streams. The watery nature of the human womb thus ensures that Chalchiuhtlicue plays an important part in Central Mexican birth stories, particularly baptism.[22]

The Queen of Cups is the Queen of hearts, is the Queen of water, is the Queen of birth. As the force of water over the Earth, she is the blood of the earth, sustaining all. She embodies emotional freedom and critical self-reflection. She provides counsel in all matters of the heart. She makes containers that are beautiful, safe, spacious, initiatory, and nourishing. And it's not just the content, it's the care. It's not just the language or logic, it's the heart that makes it communication. She sits upon the shore where water meets earth and stares at the waves. And there is space for everyone in the ocean. And there is creative interlude. And her looking inward is a reflection of the ocean's effect upon us when we find her literal embodiment at the beach.

She is stable, not just still. She sees the pure nature of life so beautifully alive and with so much depth. She is the soul watcher. Her unabashed stare is turned within. The water can handle the intensity of her witness because her desire to see and be seen so deeply arises from the waves. All can come to her and find reflection of their deepest desires. She cultivates any field that respects the value of our inner lives. Her seeing is not to be understood but to understand. The majesty of this portraiture peers into the souls of the neglected and maligned. Where the Queen of Wands stares to assert, the Queen of Cups sees to receive. And with every wave offers endless possibility for their creative forthcoming. Her most powerful emotion is empathy, wishing all a safe homecoming with every life washed away. She stares for the recognition of beauty and its adamant, innate summoning of attention. She can crown her cup with a dignity that contains and protects her inner emotional world, rather than ignoring the necessary tending to the psychic worlds to which she is attuned.

When we need patience with our soul's process, compassion for our failures to love, and grace to begin again, she appears with the force of emotional catharsis. Every wave is her every throne as she can be gentle, serene, and crystalline in her care, or turbid, raging, and boisterous. No matter the method, she ensures life's continuous creation. Her power is in the medial realms. When our body seems barren, our hope bankrupt, and our faith fallow, her well replenishes and renews the soul.

This Queen is the embodiment of emotional bravery, which she uses to communicate her inner world and confront the shifting reflections of her self-image. She says it's safe to return to the ocean, to return to love. She knows the forms of love change, but they all arise from the same source and maintain a unifying essence. Desire for the immensity of love's ocean may overwhelm us with fear and disorientation, so she negotiates boundaries and nurtures emotional maturity.

In community she may be the folk healer, the doula, the dream interpreter and deep listener, helping us feel safe and serene. Through her model, we learn to become a vessel clearly reflecting the soul. Yet she is a figure of mystery. She nurtures emotional maturity. As we seek the center, it is her blessing that protects us, guides us, and ensures our success. The canvas she resides in invites the reader in, all accepting of every emotional state. Like an Amy Sherald portrait, she is also something blue, as her own being encompasses a regal contemplation, a royal reflection. Over her may be a mist of melancholy, but an undercurrent roils just beneath the surface.

Look at the card like looking at your mother for the first time, and wonder if you've ever really seen her in all her depth.

The Queen of Cups wonders well about the desires that drive us to continue choosing life, foreseeing the forms of soulful depths. She asks us if we know how to love, and what are the measures of such an inquiry? She accounts for the heartbreak and loss in our wake, but she offers a golden thread to reweave the broken pieces so they are stronger in their reassembly.

The heart has its own morality. She reminds us that desire, though passionate and stirring, is guided by choice. Desire challenges our willingness to take responsibility for fulfillment. To love is a choice the Queen of Cups makes consciously, wholeheartedly, and continuously. By her herald hidden feelings are finally set free.

The Queen of Cups appears when we are to ready ourselves for a tide rushing in. Her love consciousness merges intellect, beauty, power, feeling. She holds the heart for those worthy, those who have chosen to live aligned with the love at the deepest core of their being. Love is a free choice, and to be able to make such a choice we may need to release desires that would compel us toward disempowering dependence. We are her when we refuse to abandon hope. When we let joy be born again, we are sustained by her. When we are ready to trust her, we are ready to be liberated in love.

Queen of Pentacles

It's time for all the men who come to us "weary and burdened" as it says in the Bible—those we save from suicide and solitude, those who find in our arms and in our vaginas the vital force that's only thwarted elsewhere, those we send away with their balls light and sunshine in their hearts—to stop hassling us, judging us, disowning us, taxing us, beating us, locking us up.[23]

As the Queen of Wands brings us into autoerotic relationship, the Queen of Pentacles teaches us the art of appraisal. She has the bread, the poetry, and makes sure everyone is fed and nourished with language. Many readers regard the element of domesticity when reading the Queen of Pentacles. They point to her ability to warmly welcome others, and the generosity of her spirit that is moved to share her warm butter so it sustains her community. Yet this reading is bound within the limits of domesticity in a manner that clearly reinforces the heteronormative gender roles that require a woman to carry the burden of the unpaid, undervalued second shift. The Queen of Pentacles rejects such essentializing orientations as she demands a wage for any privatized labor. The state colonizes women via this project of domestication, while the Queen of Pentacles reveals the cunning of wives who negotiate in their transactions with men, the state, the patriarch to ensure they get their due.

> *And if we interrogate the limits and possibilities of sex, might we also need to investigate what constitutes work, renumeration, and payment? How might the sexual labor we perform within romantic relationships, including marriage, also function as a kind of sexual labor, performed in exchange for social status, jewelry, or domestic harmony? Even in these noncommerical contexts, when is sex about mutual aid and shared pleasure and when is it a transactional exchange performed across uneven registers of power?*[24]

The Queen of Pentacles is a Queen of Earth, sovereign over the sensuous body. She knows the history of bodily commodification. She remembers all the ways the modern nation-state has controlled and still controls women's sexuality, fertility, work capacity, and labor power. The body is its own commerce, and the Queen of Pentacles recognizes that the means of production should be maintained by femme collectives. It is the body that produces, pleasures, services, and materializes. So she ensures that we own and maintain agency over our body and sexuality. The body as extension of the earth has been a site of conquest, an imperial project that denies the sexual autonomy of the pussy. So a sovereign Queen of Earth is in control of her body. She has no shame over the power in her rolling hills. She knows her body is more expensive than money. It may not be bought, could not be sold, but it can be shared.

As such, the Queen of Pentacles is the Queen of sex workers. Sex workers are the most honest bodyworkers amongst us. We always are equating, exchanging currencies between bodies, money, goods, and services, about which sex workers have no confusion. She holds that the body is ours to offer, and it is up to each to determine the value of every exchange. There is a decorum to the exchange that need not always be bound up in respectability. We assess and value skill, mastery, and the ability to do a job well. She maintains discernment and protection for those who have no shame in turning to their body to find the money to live. To live as a sex worker is to claim liberty where others would seek to assert control. And so the Queen of Pentacles liberates sexuality, breaking out of normative sexual roles that are extremely difficult, impoverished, restrictive, or unsatisfying. She helps us respond to moralizers who condemn sexual autonomy. She sees through paternalism and misogyny. She is an effective leader against patriarchal repression, and she legitimizes sexual professions, kink, countercultural desire, and consenting sexual practice.

The militarization of men and the logic of warfare is maintained by a nationalistic identification with a fatherland that requires the yearning for destroyed motherlands to become appropriated by patriotic nationalism. "Nationalism as well as religious fundamentalism, thrive on the social-psychological plane, on these yearnings and projections."[25]

The Queen of Pentacles, and indeed all Queens under the Empress, can help restore lost connections to our motherlands. She helps us collectivize the body, extending personal identification not with a nation but with every bodily expression of the Earth. Her medicine for alienation and physical isolation is to invest in the body as a preserved wildland. As tarot works to summon what's embedded deep within the psyche, it leads with the Queen of Pentacles to maintain psychic-social connections through history. These connections may be ruptured, but they cannot be severed once and for all. The Queen of Pentacles calls upon mother-right traditions, matrilocality and matrilineality, which recognize all equally. The Queen of Pentacles has no bastard children, because all life born from her body is legitimized by her disregard of state-sanctioned relations. We are legitimate as long we restore the connection to the lands we come from.

She sees us through cycles of growth, aligning with nature's seasons, thereby helping us attune to the mother's time. In every way she is working to restore ancestral connection and advocate for the Earth's many bodies, and she ensures no one is forgotten. Difference may pose a threat, but much less so when approached with her respect. She treats the body as a temple, knowing it as a site of healing, pleasure, and praise. Sex work may be regarded as profane, but she maintains its sacred functions as well. She restores the body beyond its capacity for productivity. She knows the body as home, builds it up as a sanctuary, and then invites her community in. She shows how to recycle and repurpose energy. She is the leader who cultivates abundance, seeking sensual pleasure within every relationship.

She is the motivation of care while knowing the balance between what she gives to others, what she gives to herself, and what she receives from Spirit. She is how to feel worthy while receiving.

> *Some of it's very fierce. Powerful. Distorted, even, because the duress they work under is so overwhelming. But I think they believed, as I do, while it may be true that, you know, people say, "I didn't ask to be born," I think we did, and that's why we're here. We are here, and we have to do something nurturing that we respect before we go. We must. It is more interesting, more complicated, more intellectually demanding and more morally demanding to love somebody, to take care of somebody, to make one other person feel good.*[26]

Three of Swords

We can only move from perfect passion to perfect love when the illusions pass and we are able to use the energy and intensity generated by intense, overwhelming, erotic bonding to heighten self-discovery. Perfect passions usually end when we awaken from our enchantment and find only that we have been carried away from ourselves. It becomes perfect love when our passion gives us the courage to face reality, to embrace our true selves.[27]

You can feel when the heart begins to harden like it is made of lead. When it swallows swords of rejection and betrayal, it hardens to stop from shattering. The grief from feeling unworthy of love gets condensed into a black box of pain kept hidden at the center of the heart. This is the grief of the Three of Swords. The card makes marks on our hearts, tallies scratched across the love organ, counting the heartbreaks, the scars of love. I've lived with this heavy, scarred heart so long I fought the shattering that would be a shedding, an expelling, of the corrupted self-worth like a poison from the body. The only way for love to survive in the heart is to (r)eject this poison. The Three of Swords initiates a necessary alchemy of the heart that releases the reader from the psychosomatic cages of shame, self-abandonment, and the internalized unworthiness that makes us fear accepting true love.

This is the key to unlock the imprisoned heart. Carceral conceptions of justice create conditioning that condemns the character of an individual as being beyond redemption. To justify putting people in chains they must be made subhuman, a beast, a monster, and they must be made to believe this about themselves. They are most deeply enchained in their psyche, reasoning that the pain in their heart, the dread of living a loveless existence, must be because *they* are wrong instead of having done wrong. They are wrong by the simple fact of their existence. The Three of Swords seeks to break the heart free of the wizardry of white supremacy, which is the darkest illusion to be lost in. It is the exorcism of this white invasion. We must deal with the assaults across our hearts. The Three of Swords cuts to the deepest scripting of our beliefs about love. So it takes us to the heart's cold stone. There is no other way to the core than by cutting deep. Bondage must be *broken,* somehow.

This is the medicine of shattering: liberation. The tongue of shame and loathing in our heads is a lying tongue. We cut that out. We say our words. We proclaim the truth of our love, the truth of our heart. There is nothing synthetic about a Three of Swords love. It calls upon the courage to profess the passion in my heart, to stop denying its presence, this love that has grown through concrete. This heart is ready to handle the weight of its calling.

The Three of Swords conquers the fear of facing love's responsibility to be honest. It is love's letting go of fear. With her Saturn in Libra's second face as found in this card, bell hooks left us a timeless teaching of love's truth when she wrote: "When we experience true love, it may feel as though our lives are in danger; we may feel threatened. . . . Most of us run the other way when true love comes near. Since true love sheds light on those aspects of ourselves we may wish to deny or hide, enabling us to see ourselves clearly and without shame, it is not surprising that so many individuals who say they want to know love turn away when such love beckons."[28] The Three of Swords seeks to recondition our response to love's approach. We ask for an audience with the judge; we desperately seek for our court date to be scheduled so we can testify to the innocence in our heart and hand when we can, without doubt of our inherent worthiness, ask for love's justice to be served. The proclamation will bring justice and freedom.

We have to trust in our ability to change, to trust in love.

My grandmother always listened to Mary Wells, and something about Mary singing about the moment you broke my heart—it stopping like a clock that's just been dropped—stays with me. The heart, the love, stops moving, freezes in time, for the cold, cutting truth is too much to move through. To say in one breath we want true love and in another we are unwilling to change is to be either confused or contradictory. Love necessarily puts us at risk by utterly changing us, a blaring reminder offered in the Three of Swords. "Not everyone can bear the weight of true love," writes hooks, telling us this card is a scale, a measuring tool, a way into uncovering the worth, the weight, the texture and tone of love's truth. With the Three of Swords the heart is made featherweight again. Love cannot be controlling if it is to be true. By surrendering the will to such power you can overcome emotional withholding. Do not turn away from the wounded heart; remove the swords and let the blood of love flow again. Let frozen grief melt so it becomes love rain. So that as you stand out under the showers you are washed clean in God's truth. This love rain fertilizes a garden of relationship that will blossom in a new season.

This card calls upon the rupturing of bonds, it makes space in the heart. It rips the heart into new ranges of self-worth. It takes us beyond any love conceptions, flattened and static in two dimensions. It becomes the badge of the *true* heart. It becomes a shield, the herald in a personal coat of arms. The Three of Swords is sobering, for it destroys the dangerous romance fantasies that makes us estranged to love in the here and now. This is often first felt as disillusionment, a devastating loss, leaving love bereft. We learn the hard way that we cannot change another, we cannot mold and cast them into an ideal. This card cuts the diamond. Though we may be pierced by the truth, it will eventually become cherished as the gift that readied our hearts for something real. "Although I have experienced many disappointments in my quest to love and be loved, I still believe in the transformative power of love. Disappointment has not led me to close my heart," hooks testifies.[29]

Three swords cross our hearts with truth and we will be ready to die knowing we've truly lived a loving life. Knowing we've embraced the truest love in our heart, we can die without regret. Working deeply with the bitter medicine of this card, I know in my heart that veracity is visceral. I pull this card as I understand I deserve to be appreciated, valued, seen, which requires me seeing myself as such. It is how I hold my own heart that matters most, how I handle its pain. What felt like swallowing darkness now tickles and tingles as butterflies awaken, flutter, and fly again.

Truth is never a punishment. It may be painful to shatter illusions and break attachments, but it will be better than being trapped in unfulfillment for being too afraid to face the beloved. The Three of Swords is an important initiation on the path of love. If we can come to accept our vulnerability, heartbreak may become a vital opening. We create clear definitions of love, intention, and will. We enter relationship with full and informed consent. We make bonds that are beyond the doom of old, repeating patterns. Truth recovers love, and the piercing protects the heart from rigidity. Love must penetrate the heart. The Three of Swords delivers the love we pray for. When our heart is ready for redemption, this card appears.

Three of Wands

As outsiders to the mainstream, women of color in the U.S. practice "world"-traveling, mostly out of necessity. I affirm this practice as a skillful, creative, rich, enriching and, given certain circumstances, as a loving way of being and living. I recognize that much of our traveling is done unwillfully to hostile White/Anglo "worlds." The hostility of these "worlds" and the compulsory nature of the "traveling" have obscured for us the enormous value of this aspect of our living and its connection to loving. Racism has a vested interest in obscuring and devaluing the complex skills involved in it. I recommend that we affirm this traveling across "worlds" as partly constitutive of cross-cultural and cross-racial loving. Thus I recommend to women of color in the U.S. that we learn to love each other by learning to travel to each others' "worlds."[30]

The Three of Wands appears when we have decided to disorient ourselves, venturing toward a new order. We deal with inherited realities by reconstructing them so that they exist in accord with our inner being. We travel inward to be free of living within another's rules for reality. We risk disorientation in the promise of refuge, in the seeking of sanctuary. How we are welcomed is an echo of the language we use to greet foreigners, settlers, refugees. Where is the space for us to be sovereign? It must be anchored within.

We begin to develop new frameworks for freedom, power, and truth in this card. It is a movement between political formations formed by a speculative leap in which the terms and dynamics of one are disoriented in the encounter with the other.[31] Disorientation requires translation, it requires becoming multiliterate, which requires recognizing one's linguistic fluency with the grammar of power in their native tongue. This a card of shifting orientations, based on meaningful and open engagement with the world. Moving beyond the boundaries of cultural, linguistic, and national borders clarifies our visions of progress upon new horizons of possibility. In constructing the sites where identity is expressed most freely, seeking the power of freedom entails seeking freedom from reified power. This rearrangement of power and freedom is most necessarily enacted and incorporated into the structure of our relations.

To leave a known world, where you exist unknown, is to venture toward a self-responsibility, determined to walk a path that leads to a world where one is welcomed, empowered, recognized, and respected. To discover that the world is not alien is to seek a place where one isn't alienated. The disorientation encountered in venturing toward new horizons is the Three of Wands showing us how to walk a path of integrity. The journey toward freedom requires risk. Risk is a dimension of liminality we move through and work with, as one must be brave to take such leaps into the unknown. The disorientation is necessary to know a new language, a new way to understand the self in a new context. Virtue entails sacrifice. Working with the eroticism of the Wands is a practice of integrity, as the congruency between what we think, feel, say, and do. We must bear honest witness to our inner motivations and resonances with life. We walk a path of sovereignty when these interior truths direct the life. Inner connection allows us to face the uncertainty of the world, to see how far this truth will take us. It may be a mystery to see the effect this truthful living will have on the world, but as we cultivate inner ethics we can eschew those that would compromise our fulfillment. We form our own code of conduct, ready to break with any hegemonic conditioning from family, religion, or any other cultural institutions. The Three of Wands finds the needed bravery to break with the pack by seeing a shining horizon that promises authentic fulfillment. This is a card of confidence and trust. We cannot live responsibly without securing this self-trust.

An initial discomfort with institutional authority has given way to an acceptance of authority that emerges from knowledge itself. In my own journey toward sovereignty, I found my ability to enter and experience the joys and risks of self-exploration. In an honest proclamation of this peregrination, I was forced to move beyond the formal institution of education. In naming myself as a queer educator committed to teaching students about the history of power and supplying them a vocabulary for their dis/empowerment, it was safer for principals to hire a white teacher. I was one who would implicate the institution by naming its ongoing history of exploiting students for profit. I had to break and go beyond the homophobia and anti-Blackness of the patriarchal machismo of my Mexican American family history. But beyond breaking is flexibility, necessarily acquired as an outsider shifting in and out of mainstream constructions of consciousness.

What will be lost upon the sovereign as they look upon the world if they have yet to see themselves clearly? To world-travel with cultural exchange, cultural recognition is required. Without this recognition, the world is "met" through militarization. To have true inquiry into the nature of reality and its manifold subjectivities, cultures, and languages, we must go beyond the bounds of our own ethnoculture. As the self is experientially created, a true model of the world can be only created based on experience that goes beyond the limitations of our previous perception and unique historical, temporal, physical, and social positionality. A democratic, critical discourse cannot occur without equal representation, cannot occur without inclusion, without an incorporation of nondominant groups in restructuring institutional arrangements. Once we have truly inquired into the world through our own self-reflexivity represented in the Two of Wands, we can realize our agency to reconstruct the world and its relations in the Three of Wands. We must reorient the psyche toward new states of consciousness that welcome and guard difference rather than assuming, at the sites of liminality, a stance of border patrol. The Three of Wands helps us shift this encounter to be one of guardianship rather than policing, tending to these sites of cultural exchange. Then there stands a spirit ready to be born into new terrain, with the courage to engage the self with the larger world. The terminal of consciousness that is the Three of Wands sees many departures and arrivals.

Stand at the point where self-concept expands, and the soul becomes the bridge between ancestry, familial sociocultural inheritance, and the unique identity desiring queer innovation. Personal transformation is achieved by travel (within/without), reflection, discipline, vision, and hope. To leave the familiar behind we embrace a global perspective of connectivity. Though parts of our identity become dis- and reoriented in new cultural environments, from a stable core we can exchange culture without appropriation, sharing an evolving ethos of inclusivity. We aren't fooled into universalizing our particular experience in a way that renders our native culture invisible and bland, thinking we must take to taste cultural difference. Cultural appropriation is an exchange of deficiency perspectives that deceives us into thinking that variety can only be known by consumption of the other. To generate critical modes that can address the necessary process of translation between and among historical and political framings, orientations, and imaginaries, we must resist erasing these translations through attempts at unification.[32]

Tarot is a technology of the future visionary. It allows our perceptual approaches and orientations to be made more visible as our "reading" unveils a speculative accounting of the real among varied sociopolitical agents, groups, and imaginaries. We must be clear that our vision and analysis for liberation are shaped by a *particular* perception and accounting of reality, to resist being resolved into a singular, systemic narrative. The Three of Wands represents the tarot as a chance for conceptual and representational experimentation. We venture into imaginal spaces, breaking with concrete events and experiences, into a relation as something that is not simply a referential accounting of reality. This is a process of divergence through loving perception that Maria Lugones articulates. Love is required for the courage to critically read the world, love is required to maintain the courage to face the world, and love must guide the alchemical transformation of the world. We value being multiliterate, exploring a strengths-based resourcing within the collaborative cultural space to generate multipronged and adaptive strategies toward liberation. There are multiple ways of conceiving and perceiving, varied frames of reference to make sense of the workings of the world. We move through the framing of each card as moving through potentiality, for within each particular framing, there are vast possibilities for interpretations by each reader and writer. There are multiple modes of representation, expression, and understanding that may all be true while simultaneously being nonidentical. Reading the tarot is a way to track these disparate orientations and interpretations. Thus, reading the tarot is a way of engaging a mode of relation reflected in the Three of Wands. The Three of Wands is a chance to become realized as a transformative intellectual, someone capable of articulating emancipatory possibilities and actively working toward the manifestation of liberation.

Three of Cups

Something I've observed from reading cards is that more people than you might imagine have problems with celebration. People conflate celebration with excess, a lack of discipline, egotism, or most problematically, with "being happy." The concept of celebration is often straitjacketed by shame. Many times I have observed the cards respond to this position by saying that, in fact, celebration is vital to survival. Celebration casts a space in which we can anchor what we have been through, so that we might claim the wisdom of having survived it. Celebration is not about numbing out; rather, it is about the acquisition of wisdom, often earned through suffering.[33]

The Three of Cups is about embodied invocation. It engages the ritual communication that helps create the sacred geography established in the Three of Pentacles. The body is sacred landscape in the Three of Pentacles. The body is the vernacular of song in the Three of Cups. It is the good spirits of the Cups permeating the vessel of the Pentacles. Cards like the Three of Cups and the Four of Wands remind us of the necessity of ceremonial celebration for collective harmony. To survive, we celebrate. As it has been said, there can be no revolution without music, dance, and laughter. Further, joyous, playful states of being are states of divination. Celebration is a ceremony of continuance, made through merriment. The Three of Cups is a toast to the passing of time, binding the past, present, and future together. The Three of Cups is the chance to redeem our suffering, to reframe our past and celebrate our survived devastations. We cannot enter a future of greater possibility, a future born of radical imagination, without crossing the threshold of the Three of Cups. Many cards come asking for an offering of grief, heartache, and fearful confusion. They are no more real or demanding than the ones calling for revelry. Revelry is a route toward revelation.

The word *gambling*—with its etymological roots in the Middle English word for "making merry," *gammlen,* a variant of *gamenen,* which links games, playing, joking, and risk—reminds us that throwing cards is a game of creative chance, and games are a form of festivity. In the calling out of our personal grief-filled grievances, celebratory chances facilitate continuity. We raise the cup to raise the flesh, to lighten its load, to remove its burden. We celebrate so we can say yes to life again and commence a new cycle with its climaxes and depressions, its absurdities and glittering orgasmic ephemera.

As the Threes describe matrices of communal environments, gardens of change, spaces of body temples to worship each other's nature, they are championed by the women, femmes, *curanderas,* and high priestesses who bring us into the community of belonging in the divination of love. We can imagine the sacred, protected places where they enjoy themselves without concern, regard, or distortion by the male gaze. The celebratory acts are communal acts commemorating the triumph of spirit overcoming exile. The Three of Cups is a card of time magic in the landscapes of cherished community. As water is the bearer of memory, these water bearers toast to the joyous memory that is yet to be. It is a precognitive cleansing so that our anticipation, availability, or response to the future is not impeded by trauma recollection. Even if they are bearers of dangerous memory, their cognizance redeems the severed selfhood of lost and forgotten lives within a new future that we come together to envision and create.

The Three of Cups connects us to a space where there is no other, as in our mutual recognitive invitation we move from otherness into belonging.

A culture of belonging is defined as one in which "there is an intimate connection with the land to which one belongs, empathetic relationship to the animals, self-restraint, custodial conservation, deliberateness, balance, expressiveness, generosity, egalitarianism, mutuality, affinity for alternative modes of knowing, playfulness, inclusiveness, nonviolent conflict resolution and openness to spirit."[34] The knowledge of such communities is radical, as is this subjugated knowledge in dominator culture. Laughter is a form of trickster communication; it is a psychic sound of alchemy. Laughter communicates joy as an offering to the Goddess. Make your grandmother laugh and be reminded you have a purpose. Joy is resistance. Pleasure is political. Pleasure is a prophecy because it propels our living rather than our dying. We have engaged the pleasure prophecy for hundreds of years. We've engaged the Three of Cups as a ceremony of necessity, because its communal dance nourishes revolution with a joy that is radically defiant. Joy can reclaim a space. In the midst of hopelessness, this shared communal affect is vital for survival. The Three of Cups is a musical punctuation. It is a grammar that claims time marked by our ecstatic rhythms. The Three of Cups is field synchronicity, where bodies touch each other and our souls transfer affirmation among each other. We share space at the same time, spinning in a dance of imagination. Our dancing animates spectrums of space from open fields, classrooms, living rooms, and bedrooms. The sanctuary is the club we create everywhere for queer liberation. The dance floor offers *becoming* a space of possibility. Smiles slide across as our hips rock in rhythms of resistance. The Three of Cups remembers how good it felt when we learned to moonwalk.

Many selves are made at once in this card. The communing bodies and spirits consecrate a power that sustains as it defies. After the dance, each body, once joined, leaves rejuvenated and able to endure. We need the Three of Cups to exchange exhaustion for elation.

The Three of Cups asks us to cultivate sensory spaces of rest, tranquility, and intimacy. The Three of Cups seeks to expand our possibilities for the leisurely body. Regarding the public spaces of leisure, this card asks us to reexamine modes of leisure that are exclusionary in their reservation for able-bodied, white, cis, male, documented citizens. To engage an equitable future, we must engage our conceptions of public leisure and spaces for communal rejuvenation. Such rereading of these conceptions is an act of recreation in itself.

The Three of Cups seeks the cohesion of bodies as elements within a space. It coheres these bodies in a way that protects those who enter the space to worship. The card reflects the offering of spaces where it is safe for our spirit to rejoice. It is then a sanctuary for the spirit repressed in hegemonic patriarchal spaces. We cannot enter into the Three of Cups without consideration of those wishing to worship. The Three of Cups creates calming environments conducive to play, rest, joy as resources of renewable energy. In the Three of Cups we can be still and quiet and still call it a good time. Such spaces resist hypermasculine cityscapes. The Three of Cups builds communities that are self-sustaining in their circularity. Any excess or gain at the expense of others ultimately goes back to others in the health systems offered by the Three of Cups.

A culture of compulsive heterosexuality determines and overemphasizes the male romantic partner as the most important relationship in women's life. It is hard for many readers to realize just how limited the narrative of female friendship is within popular culture. Everyone looks for the Two of Cups, but this Three is its own treasure, if not more valuable than the Two. It's the sisters that heal us the deepest. These are the sisters-mothers-friends who may or may not live in a local neighborhood together, but who behave that way nonetheless. The Three of Cups makes space to acknowledge and honor that female friendship is an act that renews community.

> *I remember her coming into my house with two bags of groceries, no one asked her. She didn't say she was coming, she just appeared and she set the groceries down and she said, "I'll take care of the children today. You go do what you have to do." Those of us who were without males controlling our lives, there was a kind of singularity, and that intimacy, that instinct, knowing exactly what a sister needed before she could even articulate it was what was so important.*[35]

The construction and reclamation of spirited, celebratory spaces and rites confront the contexts of the civic, social, and psychic limitations imposed upon oppressed people. It is a continuous reworking of elements, finding how many harmonies we can make out of our sorrow, how much laughter we let out in our pain. The celebration of the Three of Cups is a spontaneous choreography of healing, dancing intelligence. If it seems there is no way to continue walking forward, then the Three of Cups asks us to dance through the dark to keep the faith. Jubilance is an instrument of the people. It transmits, summons, expands, and envisions. Our dancing, our celebration is a *living* prayer. From these memorial gatherings we keep from falling into oblivion, we dance our way into the future, or we ensure a future through our dancing. This dance is dedicated toward freer, unconstrained futures for all our relations. This Three of Cups conjures our ecstatic resilience.

Three of Pentacles

When you walk into Brooklyn Museum, the first transcendent element to hit your senses is the music, hustle-inducing sonics that truly lift you out of the doldrums of what some people would consider a routine visit to a sanitized space, a museum, albeit one filled with art and its infinite potential to inspire. I, on the other hand, treasure a day at the museum as "going to church." Similarly, you arrive feeling the bluesy piano chords and the call-and-response of popular disco tracks finally given their breathing room—full extended mixes echoing off high ceilings—pop hymns heard appropriately in their cathedral.[36]

The Three of Pentacles is about the construction of ritual landscapes that organize relationships to space aligned with natural forms and processes. An altar is a reflection of one's cosmology, the arrangement of sacred objects and offerings on the altar is a replica of the order of one's cosmos. With the Three of Pentacles the architecture of belief systems is seen through the altar. We turn to nature to understand the essence of spiritual values. The landscape body, in the collaborative construction of altars, temples, and sanctuaries, reflects the body that is a ritual site. A community's temple reflects how those people understand and relate to sacred nature so that self-determination is realized through a caring relationship to the Earth. The spatial arrangements not only reflect but determine what activity is performed in that particular space, at that specific place. The altar becomes a vestibule into the Divine. The ritual is a vehicle for movement of being. Entering into the sacred space is entering a sacred state of being. As Patrisia Gonzales observes, "By examining these signs in Mesoamerican expressive culture, we can explore how related practices reflect what archaeologists Lawrence and Low term 'landscape-body, body-landscape' that transmits memory, Indigenous messaging, and ways of being in the world. The human body often visibly becomes part of place and sacred geography."[37]

The intimacy of creating a ritual relationship to space is the manner of creating cultural practices that join people in community across the generations of living and dead. On Día de Los Muertos, we drive city to city to join in the festivals that share personal altars communally. Altars are spaces where we welcome ancestors, angels, guides of the soul, into our life. Altars honor our ancestors, connecting us across generations, sustaining community across time with the cultural display of our devotion. To see people motivated to construct sacred spaces for sacred relationship is a restorative act. It affirms the soul and fans the living flame of the communal heartbeat. Each element in each placement is intentional and imbued with sanctified significance. It reveals the reverence we feel. Altars arise from the motives of collaboration, communion, alliance, for the desire for sacred relationship is too much for one person alone to conceive. The yearning for a rich ritual relationship ripples through collectivities, inspiring each to fulfill their role within the ceremonial order. There is responsibility to this relational construction. As we look for evidence in the continuity of values and practices, these ceremonies and protocols continue to evolve and adapt. These maturing and renewing rites ensure that our responsibility to the natural world and the spirit world are joined, to be fully fulfilled.

The first sacred space we know is the womb. The mother's womb is an aural place of orientation for a baby hearing the voices of its relatives. "Indigenous sacred geography is created by the interaction of history, stories, and place."[38] These are the three pentacles of this card, asking us to strengthen our sacred anatomy, which creates a sacred dimension of self and makes sense of our place in the world, and of the world in the larger cosmos. The Three of Pentacles is an inquiry into our ties to the land and our energetic practices of tending, honoring, and communing with the land spirits. The tarot provides an intricate web of symbols, and the practice of tarot reading transmits the transformative potential of our sacred-psyche-body landscapes into the reproductive ecology of continuous continuation.

In the Two of Pentacles we begin a search for home, and in the Three of Pentacles we come to the realization that we will need to construct our home as a sanctuary against the daily assault of white supremacist capitalist imperialist patriarchy upon our lives, but also against the assaults upon our dying. Often the violence of these dominating mechanisms is felt most intensely painful within our childhood home. As the home is sanctuary, it becomes a site of resistance. The Three of Pentacles is about *taking care* of our living and dying. There are matters to be arranged, and it is not a chore, but a solemn duty. We leave home looking for a more enlightened environment, only to be disappointed by xenophobia, intolerance, and institutional dogma. I look in the Three of Pentacles for those who are willing to be members with me in tending to this sacred relationship of living and dying. Where are those who are willing to redefine and reconstitute cosmic, divine space?

The boundaries of our body, our experience, and capacity do not go away, they become the structures of our veneration. They must be reconstituted to redefine our connection to each other, for white supremacy has worked to sever the sacred dimension to our relations for generations. It may take long periods of solitude to find the community who will join you. This card is a promise that we will not always stand alone. But as we find the courage to build a sacred orientation of life that gives us a sound foundation for a secure life of peace, tranquility, and prosperity of being, we can stand tall. The Three of Pentacles sees us climbing a mountain of faith. To protect the environment of our spirit that we devotedly work to create we must see ourselves as temple keepers. From integrity among and between body, heaven, and earth, the spirit of our life is not washed away in the ebbing, flowing tides of love's ocean. In *working* to build a temple sacred enough to be a space of love, we realize the spirit of love emanating from within us. We build an altar to invite in what desperately feels like it's missing from our heart. We work to fill a deep void, a deep wound of disconnection, but the altar in its magic processes all of our forgetfulness, sorrow, and disorientations, putting us in the place of love, in the state of love. The altar shows us how to fulfill ourselves from the void. Love's place has to be a sacred place. Love's bedroom is a temple. We go there for love to undress and enter us. We go there to heal, to be at peace, to grieve, to be restored. We bring ourselves there by choice. Realize love's presence by how its absence brought us together. Even through loss, love remains within us, and we have the ability to regenerate relationships. Once we've built a room of love within that we can always return to, we can feel safe to turn to one another. It is here in the belly of spirit that we pledge to forever love ourselves.

Though we may try to leave behind markers of class, race, and geography, we cannot truly "get away" from systemic domination without grounding our being in an internal landscape of spiritual sustenance. Building and connecting to the deepest site of freedom within one's being, a site to return to and live from to restore the soul—especially when living in exile from one's home country, or when one is exiled via race, class, gender, sexuality—is an activity of divine dimension.

To accomplish the daunting work of overcoming the deeply engrained structures of white supremacist capitalist patriarchy, a deep collaborative spirit needs to be summoned, a collaboration that reaches beyond human limitation. I would not be alive to write this without divine assistance. This belief is one of the many counterhegemonic beliefs that sustain the exploited and oppressed. Spiritual growth can help free the psyche from the chokehold trauma has on our lives. We do this spiritual work to come to each other in good spirit and integrity, but we must be good with our own spirit before we can do good work with others.

The Three of Pentacles has us realize we cannot have a spiritual center without having a geographical one. We determine where to invest our spirit and root our bodies, where to draw strength and courage from. To commit ourselves to place is to begin to share responsibility for what happens there. We commit to mutual caretaking with our bodies, the land, each other, and Spirit. We turn, in the Three of Pentacles, to spiritual communion and fellowship. We begin to discover what happens when you treat a thing, a place, a community, or yourself as sacred. We move into collective support systems and away from capitalist exploitative individualism.

The Three of Pentacles builds this temple so we can continuously find members to conduct ceremony with. The challenge of this card is to extend belonging to someone who may be a stranger, or someone who may have even hurt us. This entails reworking the boundaries of our engagement, for there are those who may not want to know us. Always another consideration in constructing communities and cultures of inclusive belonging.

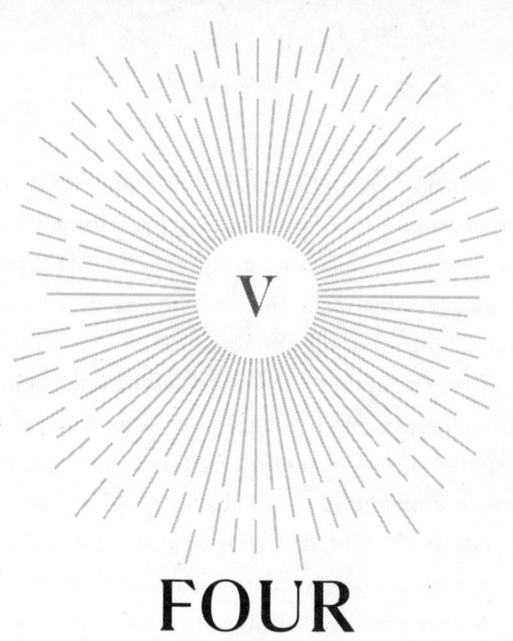

FOUR

My aim, as a scholar of Indigenous studies, is to engage the prominent and pressing issue of how Black and Indigenous movements might engage each other by questioning the value of triangulation as the vehicle for doing so, including the ways that the attempt to bring Indigenous and Black movements into alignment as part of a single struggle tends to center whiteness as the mediating principle.[1]

While Three, as a triangulation, unifies two distinct forces, Four pushes beyond centering whiteness as the means of relations. Four presents the challenge of framing, a squaring. Four asks: what is included in the discourse, and what is outside its scope? Who is subject to state rule and consideration, and who is denied citizenship, alienated, and disenfranchised? Four is the creation and destruction of borders. Four challenges us to consider the central conceptual framing of self, history, culture, civilization. Four explores how distinct concepts, conversations, and references enter various modes of "worlding."

Four teaches the reader to translate across framings, orientations, and imaginations. What is nonidentical between particular framings and distinct political formations, what carries over, and what is contended, is the implication of Four. As the self is framed by culture, history, and geography, certain orientations may arise at the expense of others. The "worlding" process engaged in Four is a construction that may leave behind what it cannot contain. Thus, framings enable a certain kind of selfhood while frustrating another. The skilled reader looks for the lost parts and finds a frame for their coherence. Such engagement is an occult engagement, the reading of the shadows, experimenting with translation, and the expansion of our world conception and communal sites of belonging.

Four helps clarify the perceptual approaches of defining and articulating the real, as well as the speculative leaps required to change frames, or the ways in which certain framings are disoriented in the terms and dynamics of the other. By becoming adept at recognizing central framings, divergent modes of perception arise in discerning the variable frames of reference to understand, articulate, and imagine the world. Four creates a doorway, a border, a foundation. Four gives shape to the world, to *a* world, in an attempt to create clarity from chaos. Fours sustain an ecosystem, protecting what is growing inside its boundaries, at best; becoming rigid, exclusionary, and xenophobic at worst. We are asked in the Four to create a threshold and then walk through it. It clarifies the limitations of self-determination by contextualizing the body in a political history and sociocultural space. Four offers the bodily boundaries that make distinct selfhood possible. Four establishes the context from which meaning arises. The tarot explores the relational capacity of various framings. As each card in a spread offers a frame, we attempt to read between each to find a greater whole of significance. The cards continuously move through frame after frame until a prismatic, kaleidoscopic perception is honed, and an ontological humility and ethos of multiplicity arises.[2]

Four is about placemaking, enduring stewardship of particular lands, and personalized elemental relations. It is the encompassing system, the overarching logic, the governance and the structural integrity of a movement. There may be nonidentical formations among each Four, and in recognizing the areas of divergence and the disruptive subjectivities and knowledge that emerge from such sites, we recognize they are not necessarily enveloped in a singular structural dialectic. Divergence amid frameworks is not a problem to be eradicated; rather, it is a "normative condition of nondominating relation between/among sociopolitical formations. Understanding these movements as oriented by nonequivalent kinds of collective identity, modes of identity, modes of oppression, and forms of political aspiration provides the conditions for putting them into relation in ways that do not presume some version of false consciousness or invidious unknowing as the basis for the discrepancies in articulations and experiences of blackness and indigeneity."[3]

As Four determines the borders of space and the limits of propriety, the hands behind the constructions must be turned over. This examination goes back and forth—for finding the architects behind any "world" is a type of retrograde motion—while addressing how varied sociocultural orientations interpret the concepts of power and sovereignty, and how they take us toward futurity. Tarot offers speculative sight as a way to suspend exclusivity in what is deemed real and who is entitled to make such claims.

The Emperor

A notion of "private" is absolutely necessary for there to be private property. And land, property, is the foundation of settler colonialism and the economic systems it has built. Before the things like the French Revolution, the Industrial Revolution, before colonialism, "private" property essentially did not exist in Europe. In the age of absolute monarchs and feudalism, all land technically belonged to the monarch (with obvious variations depending on region and people). The monarch was the entity who granted rights for certain people (nobility) to make profits and occupy the lands. The monarch could take away this land if they chose.[4]

The King of Kings is pictured in body armor, cloaked in red, crowned and grayed. There is supposed to be nobility in the courage and valor with which the Emperor has confronted life's opposition. This willingness to fight against the forces that would overcome the nascent actualized life earns them the seat of power. This card corresponds to Aries, which corresponds to the head, the locus of power, that which is crowned.

The Emperor is the sovereign subjectivity. The Emperor situates the three dimensions of time (past, present, future) in space, and pinpoints three-dimensional space within time. Like the Magician, they relate to the four elements, directions, seasons, moon phases, cardinal virtues, and so on; yet rather than mediating between realms, they aim to stand erect in their own, individuated and autonomous. The Emperor brings earthly, historical, temporal orientation. They establish boundaries and maintain control. The Emperor is the principle of Logos, which aims to create coherence out of chaos. They are discriminatory, the aspect within us that determines what "I am" by discerning what I am not. Historically, monarchs ruled by the principle of divine right. Their rule was thought to be governed by reason; that was the custom and precedent of the ruling period. The Emperor is very much the patriarch, ruling over the state as though it were his family. State power arranges gender relations to justify its legitimacy, while hiding its hand in such arrangements so they are taken as normal, right. The Emperor, at its root, is concerned with authority, legitimacy, sovereignty, and legacy. "Hegemonic masculinity can be defined as the configuration of gender practice which embodies the currently accepted answer to the problem of the legitimacy of patriarchy, which guarantees (or is taken to guarantee) the dominant position of men and the subordination of women."[5] In understanding the Emperor as embodying hegemonic power, we see it shifting as a historically mobile relation, from kings to presidents to Wall Street bankers; the power of constructed masculinity ebbs and flows as it adapts ongoing strategies of subordination. Through the Emperor we understand patriarchy as a historical *structure* itself, so it is not universal nor timeless.

But the Emperor, in creating empire, creates alienation; for their actions and body to be put beyond any earthly authority of accountability, they must pass beyond relation as well. Patriarchs suffer not solitariness but loneliness in only being able to define their identity through their work. They aim to gain respect, power, and prestige bestowed by others by setting themselves apart from others with their accomplishments. Exceptionalism becomes a bandage to the wound of alienation—a bandage I proudly wore to feel validated in my intense suffering of seclusion. The Emperor has shown me that "being exceptional isn't revolutionary, it's lonely."[6] The

Emperor must be wary of being tokenized and promoting the delusion that one can exist without community. I've always loved academia because it offered me recognition, a way to be seen and rewarded; yet internalizing such metrics of self-worth came at the cost of my emotional well-being. The Emperor has helped me honor my inner states and make courageous choices to live so that my work does not undermine the spirit. This inner restructuring happened as I endured unemployment but started forging a commitment to selfhood over manhood. The Emperor started to appear as I moved beyond this crisis of meaning measured against external accomplishment, as I started to lay a solid foundation for my inherent self-worth. My work is life-enhancing as I come to it loved and loving. This work goes against hundreds of years of patriarchal conditioning.

"There is indeed a close interaction between the predominant Western conception of manhood and that of racial (and species) domination. The notion, originally from myth and fable, is that the summit of masculinity—the 'white hero'—achieves his manhood, first and foremost, by winning victory over the 'dark beast' or over the barbarian beasts of other—in some sense, 'darker'—races, nations and social castes."[7] The Emperor helps the reader critically perceive the racialized narratives within myth, fable, and fantasy that valorize white supremacist capitalist imperialist patriarchy. The king's body and being was figurative, an agent of divine decree to parcel out the Earth under the artifice of uniting disparate people under the banner of a single kingdom. Power was performance, rather than a state of being. The Emperor's logic oriented around bringing "the savage," "the barbarous," into the court of the king's culture, into the realm of "civilization." The Emperor, in order to frame themselves as human, powerful, civilized, perceives the world as wild, and foreign bodies as dangerous, savage, and inept. Myths of heroism connect racism with the construction of such masculinity.

It is this construction of power and governance that we must contest. Within the nature of the square, embodied by the Emperor, various elements, various worlds, are in contention. Emperors claimed it was God's determination that they should conquer foreign lands in the pursuit of culture and civilization. This made them incontestable. The Emperor brings us into reality through the distinct manner of dealing with historical abuses of power, imperialism, and conquest. Emperors are concerned with the process of naming so long as it is a means of claiming. They read the world only to write their own name.

Such was the case with the land claimed on behalf of King Philip of Spain, named the Philippines, ever an object of annexation as competing imperial powers use the same logic of "the white man's burden" to contest colonial control over the same lands. The phrase "white man's burden" was written about the Philippine-American war by Rudyard Kipling, noted author of *The Jungle Book*. Such a burden is borne by the king who is driven on a mission of civilization, bound up in an ever-evolving logic that justifies conquest as a divine impulse. This "divine right" of European monarchical absolutism is but the ideology of manifest destiny in the United States, which is but another (ir)rationale of white supremacy, perpetuating a myth of the "benevolent" slave master, in which the enslaved should be grateful to their conquerors, for these soldiers were supposed leaders of virtue in seeing that their "property" was well cared for. The "virtuous" Confederate soldiers employed circular logic in their conquests; their virtue was dependent on endeavoring to civilize and teach an inferior people, and so because they conquered, they were virtuous. Be not confused: there are no good masters, and kings are men with flesh and bones who bleed just the same as you when the sword is drawn against them.

Insofar as the Emperor constructs a base of power that homogenizes and erases difference, power is ascribed to dominance. Yet the complexity of social difference cannot be erased, only repressed. The Emperor is then connected to the topology of the closet. Whereas Western hegemonic masculinity forced any divergence from heterosexuality into a closet of shame, we see the closet as social construction crucial to whiteness and capitalism. The closet is not just about shame but also about autonomy, privacy, and ownership. "What is 'in' the closet is private, personal and what is 'out' of the closet is public. The process of coming out, then is a process by which you render what is personal, public."[8] The expectation that queer and trans people "come out" of the closet disregards the differentials of privilege and danger inherent in rendering a marginalized body even more public. As history reminds us, Emperors aim to claim our private bodies and our interpersonal land as their own. By moralizing the necessity of coming out, even at the risk of personal safety, bodily annexation is maintained. The Emperor achieves this grafting of bodies and land into the four corners of their closet by denying people agency in whether they are construed as "private" in the first place. At the expense of their bodily integrity and "privacy," nonwhite bodies are rendered available for public consumption. The closet functions by forcing us to abdicate personal autonomy and repress authentic desire, expression, and embodiment to be out and yet tucked away in the Emperor's domain.

The Emperor asks for personal sacrifice to fulfill imaginary obligations to a community, nation, or kingdom they took by force or inherited by chance. As the governed are inspired to ethnocentric nationalism, the Emperor becomes the central organizing principle of their rallying cry. The Emperor tells us the state is a masculine institution fused with whiteness. We pull the Emperor and are confronted by the groups in power that are culturally exalted, our personal relations to them, and what marks the successful claims to authority. This card calls on the reader to interrogate their allegiances.

The Four of the Emperor reminds us that various masculinities exist, and the hegemony of any given form is always subject to challenge. The fourth arcanum shows us that gender is a structure of social practice, as it is a way of ordering social practice. Masculinity is better defined, not as an object that is a norm, a behavioral average, or natural character type, but constituted within a system of gender relations. "A culture which does not treat women and men and bearers of polarized character types, at least in principle, does not have a concept of masculinity in the sense of modern European/American culture."[9] The Emperor concerns the construction of masculinities on the global sphere. Transnational business masculinity, like the kings before it, values individual liberty above all else. Alternatively, the masculinity competing for hegemony is one of military command, rigid and control-oriented. This key helps us recognize gender as a historical product, though it is also a producer of history. The Emperor is ontoformative, constituting social reality in dynamic time. This card locates the reader in the world history of social agency. It assesses the integrity of being. As such the Emperor tells the reader to imagine, envision, and embody a loving and healing masculinity by looking at and beyond men's emotional wounds and personal healing, to have both personal and structural rearrangement. Others have explored, and continue to explore, such possibilities in the context of therapies of wounded masculinities, by mythic initiations into a healing journey that encompasses and interrelates masculinity with the healing of a wounded planet and a racist, sexist, transphobic society.

> *[John] Rowan, however, searched for resources to support men's continuing commitment to feminism. The image of the "horned god" within a context of goddess-consciousness is his attempt to find archetypal support for men in a world where women are strong and men remain engaged with them, rather than trying to separate. The goal of his therapeutic work is not the restoration of masculinity, nor the promotion of androgyny (criticized as based on a patriarchal masculine/feminine dichotomy), but revolutionary changes in the relations between women and men.*[10]

The Emperor is no longer legitimate in modern awareness, though white men remain in power in practice. So this arcanum asks how can we rebuild structures of self-government. This card keeps us accountable to the demands of equality seen in shifting gender ideology that are consolidated in localized institutional changes such as those that seek to equalize access, share household labor, move to stop violence against women, establish new health services, define new pay scales, provide cooperative childcare, and so on. We are continually realigned through the purposes of action by the Emperor. Masculinity exists within all genders, and as it arises within a reading, it points to structural changes of the psyche. Because patriarchy is institutionalized, the masculine is authoritative. Yet when pulling the Emperor, examine the point of intersection between patriarchal dominance and the bodily experience of masculinity. To dismantle hegemonic masculinity, authority must be redefined within culture, restructured in institutions, and recovered within intimate interpersonal relations between diverse bodies, whose rights are often contested in the court of law.

Discerning discipline as the self-responsibility required for actualization and freedom from a discipline that seeks control through punishing strategies of shame and abuse is Emperor embodiment. To address questions of liberty and purpose, the Emperor guides us into bodily agency and develops capacities for male bodies beyond the capacities developed in war, sport, or industrial labor service. To move forward with masculinity, we must move away from unity into the complex solidarity of coalition building. The Emperor shows us where we are rigidly aligned and where we would benefit from joint action and interaction with forces of power differently constituted.

I envision power as the capacity to be loving. I envision power that arises from respect, mutuality, compassion, and spiritual fortitude. I see love as fundamental to wielding power. Sharing the spheres of power becomes an act of reconciliation. Reconciliation with the father happens in the accountability taken for the wounds their violence created, the need we have for fatherly love and male love of all kinds, and the appreciation for such relationships expressed in authentic and open communication. The Emperor aims to reconcile us with anger and self-assertion, forging a spirit brave enough to uncover the pain of an anguished spirit and exit the silent prison of fear.

"Anger is the agony of believing that you are not capable of being understood, and that you are not worthy of being understood. It is a wall that separates you from others as effectively as if it were concrete, thick, and very high. There is no way through it, under it, or over it."[11]

I am in the process of releasing suppressed anger, for the pain of internal combustion has had real physical consequences in my body and dragged depression through my spirit. I first felt the patriarchal violence of anger from my mother, teaching me that patriarchy has no gender. My mother's anger was so explosive that when I was a child I only understood anger as something to be avoided at all costs. I knew anger was dangerous. And like my father, who was rarely upset, I similarly learned to shut down in response to his father's patriarchal violence upon him. The only way to deal with such pain when one is powerless, as children are, is to become numb.

Journeying through the portal of suffering is the bitter remedy required to open back up to feeling. This is the martial nature of the Emperor: to recognize that to claim passion is to delve into the root of suffering. I see the passage through one's own suffering for the sake of passion and integrity as the heroic journey of today that can displace the past heroism of conquest and domination. As my mother sought the forgiveness necessary in practicing the art of loving, I witnessed her anger unravel to reveal a deeply frightened and wounded child within. Anger is something to be tempered—my mother had too much of it, and I too little—but between and underneath us was substantial grief. This arcanum motivates me to find ways to resolve conflict without war. We've learned that confrontation is necessary in a love ethic, as avoidance only causes distance and relational separation; and that conflict does not need to be violent, though it is activating. In our confrontations came the bravery to commit to healing generational trauma and move beyond emotional alienation. To live a life of intimate connection I must stop avoiding my vulnerability. This requires reconstituting the Emperor's power of containment so that we are not repressing turbulent emotions but making space to mourn, to find outlets for grief, desire, emotional connection.

The power to commune with the land spirits confers the responsibility of stewardship. This also means that Emperor empowerment arises in sustaining healthy, good relationships with ourselves, our bodies, our beings. The Emperor fortifies an internal sense of self-worth that is not based upon inferiority or superiority. In this way the Emperor can restore humanity, fostering closeness through intimate self-acceptance. The Emperor tells me to reject conformity and the conception of power that "rules" over another. To engage this arcanum is to challenge and to change. We cannot uphold a vision of a benevolent patriarch who, though tender and kind, maintains control. We are still working to imagine alternatives to patriarchal control, but it must be clear that power can no longer be consolidated within patriarchal masculinity. For collective liberation, patriarchy must end. Let the Emperor imagine models of self-assertion that do not rely on perceiving the other as an enemy to be conquered. The power is one of responsibility, the strength of will. The will to love is the insight that love is action aimed at nurturing spiritual and emotional growth within oneself and within another. A partnership model of interdependency and interbeing refuses to privilege one over the other as it becomes the will of life that displaces domination.

Temperance

The speculative as a mode or an ethics facilitates the project of imagining oneself into others' frames of reference without suspending the efficacy of the explanatory frameworks one has, allowing both to coexist while opening up room for the difficult and potentially fraught dynamics of equivocation that arise in moving among disparate worldings.[12]

What would it be to witness an angel before your eyes, mixing the very waters of your body with the waters of your spirit? What would be restored within you? To take flight, what fear would you be willing to surrender? Faith feathers our freedom. Trust feathers salvation so that when the body is bound by doubt, it is grace that perceives the wings of our spirit.

Temperance enables ontological humility as our eyes open to numinous experiences that remind us there are worlds beyond our understanding and personal experience. But as our eyes are opened to a direct experience of the Divine, we move beyond belief into the *knowing* of faith. Temperance reconstitutes the spirit, blending and joining diverse elements of existence into unforeseen relationality. In Temperance an angel appears before us, with irises, rainbows, and a progressing sun. Through this threshold, we find a rainbow resolving pain as it joins every phenomenon of faith into a spectrum of meaning relative to the angle of the observer. And as a rainbow's visibility depends on the angle of observation, the angels we do or do not perceive are dependent upon the capacity of our vision, the force of our faith. In this card we train our eyes to find the prisms of possibility, promised beyond the tempest of revolution. As we stand on the edge of desolation, Temperance offers something secret, subtle, and yet substantial as it marks a moment of transcendence.

With this seemingly small addition, like bringing an iris to the edge of brown waters, we are taken beyond what was. Old forms wash away as a higher hand purifies the waters of life, mixing awareness and transformation into a holistic state of health. A triumphant spirit shines brightly in this arcanum. Though the body endures the trials of despair and the troubles of being brokenhearted, the grace of the soul cannot be denied. In earnest emotionality, the storms of our life are settled through this vestibule. As we give ourselves over to faith, we learn an adaptability that ensures our resilience and our survival. Temperance tells us that although change is dynamic, it ensures a continuity of life. The angel arcanum models for us a gesture that both pours and receives at once. Temperance is for finding a way back to each other.

Historical and political blindness arises in trying to address one aspect of what we are attempting to relate with, without a sense of the importance of the other. Rather than attempting to hold the diverse bodies of struggle, and the resilient spirits arising in response within the same schema, Temperance teaches the skills of switching between conceptual frameworks, finding what the reader needs to access transition. Like gender and sexuality, faith exists on a continuous spectrum, or perhaps on separate but intimately related spectra. The capacity for spectral perception is a talent of Temperance, expressed in the queer theory that aims to break down binaries and move identity outside of rigid, fixed categories. Such an appreciation of multidimensionality is applied to the term *queer* itself, being applicable as a noun, an adjective, and perhaps most radically, a verb. Perhaps this Angel of Temperance is enacting the work of *queering* something. The complex relationships people have with their genders, bodies, families, cultural objects, and communities constitute a multidimensional sense of identity that changes over time. With Temperance, we don't arrive at this change of being by any single defined path.

Temperance is a card often ascribed to people who are two-spirit, trans, androgynous, or genderqueer. Alternatively, the Angel of Temperance, being divine, is genderless. "Here, a two-spirit being stands on the bank of a pond.... Their position as both male and female, or neither male nor female, situates them at the center, in a place of balance, and as a perfect incarnation of Ometeotl, the Lord/Lady of Duality, the fount encompassing both genders and from whom all being springs."[13] It may be intriguing to consider an aspect of queerness that, in the recognition of its own authenticity and the bravery of its self-acceptance, touches upon something divine, though I am wary of further othering queers by ascribing a divinity that denies us humanity. We must be wary of generating dismissive and demeaning forms of exceptionalism that block meaningful relationality with diverse humanity. Temperance is how I would describe my gender: fluid and in constant change. It's an ongoing project, and within Temperance I have something that encompasses the shifting forth and back that does not force a fixed label or a static stance.

It is the virtue of Temperance that regards sites of marginality as sites of resistance and possibility rather than despair. Temperance keeps us both accountable to those we seek to stand by, and faithful enough in humanity's capacity for transformation that we are able to extend forgiveness to those who have harmed us. Yet the forgiveness we seek for self-betrayal and internalized shame is the hardest to find, the hardest to receive. Temperance, an image of the Divine, reflects and maintains our humanity. When we feel condemned by the trauma of our past or haunted by the pain we have perpetuated, it is Temperance that restores self-worth. It is a card that replenishes our faith as we aspire toward personal, social, political, and economic change. It aspires to transform imbalances and unjust distributions of power at their source.

Temperance, as queerness, argues against inflexibility and resistance to change. It refuses to see only one aspect of self. Because certain aspects of selfhood, theory, or activism may be contradictory, Temperance challenges us not to compromise complexity in seeking resolution or relation. Temperance challenges us not to short-circuit the process of resolving discrepancies and pronounced differences by predicating solidarity upon a single system that presumes a common analysis.

> *As against such totalizing or foundationalizing gestures, a critical praxis organized around translation starts from the premise that these movements are not so much inherently commensurable or incommensurable as simply nonidentical; that they are shaped and given momentum by nonequivalent sets of concerns, emphases, and self-understandings. Articulating them to each other, then, requires engaging the ways the terms and models generated within one (set of) movement(s) cannot simply encompass those of another, or be incorporated into a supposedly neutral supervening framework, without producing profound shifts in meaning and orientation.*[14]

As we are shifting orientations and meaning, Temperance maintains our center of balance amid the disorientation of mutable states of being. In the consideration of movement, struggle, and state change, I can't help but look at this Christian angelic depiction and consider the history of white colonizers forcing conversion upon Indigenous peoples and the ongoing state strategies of assimilation that deprive people of authentic spiritual relationships. Forced conversion is an attempted act of soul murder.

Temperance then speaks to religious intolerance. Many are still dwelling in the absence of meaningful spiritual relationships they were forced to abandon.

Still, I see within the archetype of Temperance—and modern visions of the card, such as that of the Tarot Yohualli Ehecatl—the adaptive strategies Native peoples employed to sustain ancestral, spiritual connections. As a person severed from spiritual human elders, I rely on plant elders, animal elders, and the communion with my local native environment to reformulate my spiritual center. For a long while I felt as though I were a spiritual bastard, as the concept of "purity" is used against children of conquest to deny them consideration or identification within Indigeneity, within the adoption of the colonial blood quantum by Native tribes. Such a colonial mindset is internalized to render Native peoples obsolete by their own edicts of exclusion. These systems of classification are varied and complicated, and while ostensibly a tool of sovereignty, I wonder which ways of establishing and defining Native communities are eclipsed through the use of blood quantum.

> *The optics of recognition and reconciliation can also have a colonial impact on Indigenous subjects. . . . Settler-colonial rule is a form of* governmentality: *a relatively diffuse set of governing relations that operate through a circumscribed mode of recognition that structurally ensures continued access to Indigenous peoples' lands and resources by producing neocolonial subjectivities that coopt Indigenous people into becoming agents of their own dispossession.*[15]

Blood quantum is a strategy of racialization, perhaps more clearly seen in the "one-drop rule" that displays how larger matrices of white supremacist and colonial ideologies, institutions, and coercions engender varied trajectories for Black and Indigenous sociopolitical and intellectual formations in relation to disparate yet similar histories. Perhaps the Angel of Temperance is washing away our notions of blood purity. Perhaps ridding the psyche of such puritanical notions is the great work of the alchemist, represented in Temperance.

Temperance considers experiences of salvation that are so personally significant that one's whole cosmology becomes reframed. Whatever it is that converts our nihilism into faith, such is the work of Temperance. This card offers us transitional visions that keep our deities evolving as we become different people in entirely different environments and contexts. And before that transition is enacted, this arcanum stirs an inner questioning of whether within our spiritual realm there is an interchange of possibility offered by stewards and guides of spirit, in spirit, working in various traditions, that could guide us toward personal transformation. As Indigenous spiritual beliefs and deities—such as Toci Tonantzin, the great mother of wise women, patron of medicine, and protector of new mothers—became incorporated into new religious structures, as in being adopted into the iconography of La Virgen de Guadalupe, Temperance was at play. While this incorporation may seem natural to some, it was rejected by others for being "whitewashed" and lacking the articulation of clear boundaries of divergence and distinction between spiritual expressions. The fact remains that "the Native can never be completely erased or totally assimilated."[16] This card offers us an image of radical equanimity but also summons what is nonequivalent.

For instance, if Temperance speaks to our capacity for forgiveness in touching upon the capacity of human transformation, it is also about *seeing Red* through the development of critical consciousness that refuses to forgive, or rather is unwilling to reconcile, should that "settlement," forgiveness, or reconciliation become a strategy to serve the interests of colonial power. The apologies offered by the state deceptively take on a temporal character, as the apology relegates abuse to the *past,* and such an apology becomes a way to avoid and obscure accountability that would transform the ongoing violent structures perpetuating injustice and informing the settler-colonial *present.* Should we accept apologies, our claims to redress ongoing grievances would be undercut. Temperance says that to establish harmony and accord, change must be made *structurally.* Temperance works to clear out the state's conceptual obfuscations. Therefore, experiences or enactments of rejection can strengthen the authentic self-affirmation that Temperance seeks to distill. Temperance aims to reestablish a positive relation to self where it has been damaged, distorted, or severed via symbolic, structural, physical, or psychic violence.

"'Reconciliation' is also commonly referred to as the act of restoring estranged or damaged social and political relationships. It is frequently inferred by proponents of political reconciliation that restoring these relationships requires that individuals and groups work to overcome the debilitating pain, anger, and resentment that frequently persist in the wake of being injured or harmed by a perceived or real injustice."[17]

There is reconciliation of self, reconciliation of sociopolitical relationships, and reconciliation as in the process of coming to agreement, concord, or harmony, being made consistent or compatible. Temperance helps us discern which forms of reconciliation are being enacted and to what cost. Reconciliation requires overcoming not just the legacy of past abuse, but the abusive structures themselves. Temperance helps externalize what was previously internalized, through a process of purification via the purging of colonized consciousness and its inferiority complexes. Temperance mixes our renunciations of abuse—our insistent "no" to personal, communal, and environmental degradation—with our affirmations, our resounding "yes" to life, to love, to generosity, and to the enactment of dignity within our relations toward self, each other, and the land. In the alchemical combination of our renunciations with our affirmations, Temperance distills a substance of *being* imbued with structural integrity. The constituent elements of our composition and disposition are rearranged into equanimity. Temperance offers profound insights into the maintenance of relationships within and between species of personhood or being (human, environmental, animal, planetary) through principles of reciprocity, respect, and cooperative coexistence. Exploitation has no place in the relations of Temperance.

The card concerns how our earthly, chthonic body and being are united with the Divine in an endless alternating current. Temperance is to reconcile our sovereignty with our willful submission to the deities acting beyond human capacity. Between the interplay of the celestial and chthonic, our spirit is made more potent. Temperance shows us fluid dialogue between realms. The angel appears as arbiter of this soul process of "purification." In this practice we gain an inner world of equal validity with our outer world. The nonhuman depiction within this arcanum, as with the other cards of nonhuman representations, reminds us that the more-than-human comprises our humanity, and that what resides within our soul psyche is of a numinous nature. Angels, with their winged revelations, unveil new dimensions of awareness, being, and possibility. Following Death, the

Angel of Temperance marks an important turning point: we are undergoing a change that is irrevocable. The fluidity of identity is ever-changing. No character is fixed in singularity. To draw Temperance is to develop the capacity to recognize such inner processes of change. As we establish systems of reciprocal relations, bound by the responsibility of autonomy, we are enacting Temperance. This contrasts with colonialism, which, "as a structure of domination predicated on dispossession, is not a 'thing,' but rather the sum effect of the diversity of interlocking oppressive social relations that constitute it."[18]

Temperance is the card of the art of soul alchemy. The Angel of Temperance, rather than the angel of Judgment, is patient in waiting for the awareness of acknowledgment. Our guardian angels are not impeded in their silence, or their stillness. In fact, this patient silence may be more effective working upon our behalf, protecting and guiding us especially when we feel most alienated and abandoned. Such methods initiate a *meditatio,* the "inner dialogue with someone who is invisible, as also with God, or oneself, or with one's good angel."[19]

Enduring a life of loneliness and lovelessness has been remedied by song. Music performs Temperance on my being. Before I knew mantra or began a meditation practice, it was song that sustained me. It is song that shows me God is real. It is through song that I hear the angels' voices. It is song that stirs me from depression and brings me to fall upon my knees into surrender of the sacred permeating through and all around me. By blessing my loneliness with angelic visitation, Temperance shared with me the gifts of such solitude, the surrender of silence into a spaciousness of soul, free to compose a melody of my own.

Kings

There has never been such a savvy administrator, one who could touch the world, interfere in it, with the justice of his or her technical knowledge, one so great and so pure as to be seductive. Such a person would have the power to abolish social classes; to ignore the fact that existential differences between the rich and the poor necessarily generate, in different people, different ways of being, different likes and dreams, different cultures, and different ways of thinking, of acting, of valuing, of speaking; and to ignore the fact that all this has to do with political choices, with ideological paths.[20]

Kings are authors, for as they are apprehenders of the world, its text and its context, they mediate meaning in their ongoing textual composition. Their critical composition is a knowing that encompasses the entirety of their being. They have command of language. They work and rework textual meaning. Their knowledge is created in the negotiation between reader and writer, which in the creation of the text is the creation of the reader. Kings are teachers, they are cultural workers. They maintain the discipline required to map out textual territory, and they join in this knowledge mapping with the students, the learners, the "subjects," with whose care and responsibility they are entrusted.

Such is the composition between King and Queen, for in the tarot Kings do not rule independently. Leadership cannot exist in isolation. The Kings' authority is in concert with the Queens, in the established councils for every aspect of life. A council is powerful when it is as inclusive as it is democratic, for the people who must live with the decisions must be part of the decision-making process. A council that is modeled after the great wheel of the universe draws upon the power of the unbreakable circle, the power of Spirit. Considering the King and the council inspires personal and collective governance aligned to nature. Kings preserve personal autonomy and resourcefulness to teach us self-governance and inspire the will to destiny. They mature us with responsibility and expand consciousness while promoting and protecting all life forms. Sometimes Kings are called fathers and Queens mothers. Father teaches you freedom and survival, and Mother teaches you home and belonging. Neither is gendered, and both exist within you.

Kings ask us to fight the colonial traditions we bring with us. To move beyond a colonial comprehension of administration, the King guides us in equitably distributing public resources. They are concerned with the hierarchy and priority of expenditures, energy, availability. They teach us decisiveness paired with discernment. Decision-making is a process of evaluation, of balancing and assuming responsibility for the inevitable rupturing that results in any decision. In the decisions wisely made, the

King's competency, clarity, and integrity are made plain, for a King who is negligent is a King who is violent. They listen with humility out of self-confidence, self-respect, and regard for others. In such a state of open listening, the Kings show us that humility overcomes the conceit of hierarchy. They delegate, they communicate, they listen, and they lead. They have the reader refuse to impose their truth as the only truth upon which we know or accept others. Kings recognize the tasks, structures, and responsibilities that are fundamental and indispensable for social life. Kings awaken relevance and garner support for the indispensable provisions: education, housing, health care, nutritious food, clean water.

The habits of being cultivated by the King are those of vigilance, diplomacy, and literacy. A recognition of the fallaciousness of divine right deems that these traits be developed through intentional practice. Kings are not born with these attributes, nor are they bestowed by decree or gift. Take greater responsibility for greater freedom, and claim their power of self-assertion. By engaging our spheres of influence, we come out of alienating individualism to know the humility of leadership. As a King cannot deny their crown, we cannot deny our cultural or familial inheritance. They are the custodians of history, not the owners. We cannot quit the struggle of history without undermining the dignity of life. History has yet to culminate. Kings take a global, multigenerational view of accountability, progress, healing, and transformation. Kings plant trees for fruit they will only taste by the tongues of their descendants. Such is the example set by an authority figure.

As each King is an aspect of the Emperor, each one depicts an external elemental mastery balanced by their internal actualization, so that their legacy is one of responsibility aligned with life purpose and deeply felt passion. Kings deal with authoritarianism and rebellion by adopting a stance of uncertain certainty. They can recognize the limits of their experience, body, and knowledge, but they are also disciplined in their ongoing inquiry toward a democratic, equitable arrangement. They keep us from falling into apathy or dwelling in the fear of freedom. They refuse to let fear immobilize them into rigid, insecure dictators. Nor do they deny fear. They learn to control their fear and lead with courage in doing so. They reject perfunctory conformity and resist the humiliation of nonconsensual domination.

Kings are made in the social experience. To pull a King is to confront the expressions of dominant power, its ideologies, and its repressive apparatus. In this confrontation, inspired by the King, the exercise of authority seeks balance by teaching tolerance, which is respect for the other, and an embrace of difference. It is these principles of tolerance, humility, discourse, and courage that the King upholds. Without the maintenance of these principles no peaceful coexistence could be possible.

King of Swords

To the extent that I become clearer about my choices and my dreams, which are substantively political and attributively pedagogical, and to the extent that I recognize that though an educator I am also a political agent, I can better understand why I fear and realize how far we still have to go to improve our democracy. I also understand that as we put into practice an education that critically provokes the learner's consciousness, we are necessarily working against myths that deform us. As we confront such myths, we also face the dominant power because those myths are nothing but the expression of this power, of its ideology.[21]

The King of Swords creates new ways of knowing while strategically sharing knowledge so it is accessible by all. Overcoming censorship, there are no areas, themes, or values that are consigned to silence by this King. We are told to talk about everything; *everything* requires our testimony. Learners forced into silence and uniformity are denied active participation in their education, which undermines the democratic ideal of education and the development of the subjects' critical reasoning faculties. The King of Swords moves us into identities of integrity, a healing process that requires releasing arrogant perceptions. Through this constant process of self-construction, new topographies are formed so that the fragmented psyche is recombined. This reconstruction is a type of communication demonstrating the reality that our identities, our sense of self and manifold relation to the world, can move beyond the oppressor/oppressed dialectic.

This King is there for us when we have a crisis of meaning. Within their court we are to interrogate our experiences and unravel the deepest unconscious conditioning of domination. The violent paradigms we have internalized are undone by this King's sword. He has a host of verbal techniques to manage destructive action. He uncovers unconscious resistance while joining with us in a way that helps us feel less defensive, less aggressive. The master swordsman is one who disarms without drawing blood. Through graceful maneuvering we are freed from repetitive and destructive patterns. When aggression arises as overcompensation for feeling powerless, this King fulfills a lack we've been conditioned to believe we have. He tells us he is on our side, we are not alone, we are more powerful and more capable than we realize. The King of Swords avoids activating defense mechanisms by engaging the subject in progressive communication. In this manner our resistances to fully knowing ourselves are dissolved, and our path toward destiny is paved.

As we further articulate our deepest truths, our most visceral experiences, our most substantive longings, the more clarified our visions of freedom become. The King of Swords is how to uphold an ethos of honesty so we resolve the contradictions between our words and our actions. This King has perception that pierces, and in our clear seeing we can resist the oppressive hegemonic values veiled in the American discourse of freedom. The classroom is the kingdom here—that is, any space constructed upon the principles of respect, mutuality, trust, and truth. This type of environment invites students to experience the joys and risks of self-exploration. It requires the freedom to question, change, and resist. The King of Swords physically arranges the environment to clearly mirror the complex psychosocial atmosphere being cultivated, challenged, and transformed. We become the King of Swords as we design spreads—the symbolic spatial designation for psychic inquiry—for penetrative and generative readings. The sites constructed by the King of Swords are holistic spaces that provide relief from the degradation encountered in most of society's dominating locations. As we enter this environment we become cognizant of our agency and responsibility for its maintenance and ongoing development.

This is the butterfly king, forged in the sites of dispossession and exclusion. They have been disgraced, discouraged from speaking, denied of being. They have suffered tragedy, a loss of power, and rejection, but still they have rebuilt themselves from within. They recognize themselves as authority, the upholder of a spiritual law unto themselves. They have successfully integrated inner truth into all outer aspects of life. The King of Swords has a firm grasp on the truest sense of self. They have rid themselves of others' projections, and thus of a previous self-perception; in so doing, an inner patriarch had to die, transform, evolve. They are the King for those exiled, for they are the ones who have inherent capacity to move beyond collective limitations, as well as personal fear. Knowing the pain of internalized rejection, the King of Swords accepts us for who we are. They heal by helping us to stop lying to ourselves. This King's medicine is the application of honesty. They see all sides of us: our failings as well as our hope and our honor, our inherent potential and our contribution. They acknowledge us where and when we need it most. They show us how to be unshakable in our truth, even if that means we stand alone. The sorrow of separation is transformed by writing our personal history, by letting the stories we tell ourselves become grounded in the honesty of our beauty, resilience, and agency. The King of Swords has worked to heal a father wound, a wound of misperception, of being violently made invisible by patriarchal masculinity and left longing for a father's, brother's, man's love.

They are the psychoanalyst, able to reserve judgment to adopt a stance of analytic neutrality. This position discourages rash, reactive behavior. The King of Swords asks for reflection before taking action. They adopt an open and accepting posture, talking us through our impulses to see the underlying motivations behind our behavior. Through this communication we can make clear and constructive decisions. It is their pausing to reflect that may change the tendencies of compulsive action. Any compulsion unexamined is a freedom we've yet to claim.

The King of Swords offers guidance toward transforming the negative structures of the psyche. They show us strategies to answer or explore the big questions: who am I? What do I want? What is my place in society? This King is very queer, bravely exploring self-expression beyond societal constraints. This King knows that ethics and aesthetics are intimately bound. They know that the style of their self-presentation, the tone of their voice, the switch of their hips is political. The culture they cultivate is one of radical acceptance through their self-disclosure and hybrid identity construction. The King of Swords leaves a legacy of liberation through literacy. He is Frederick Douglass, Paulo Freire, Anna Julia Cooper, and all the English teachers who've offered a haven in the worlds between book covers.

Learning to name the self is learning to name the world. It is developing a capacity to make meaning of and for oneself. It is denying the imposition of censorship or silence. The King of Swords is there for us as we make critical decisions that may conflict with our self-image. He guides us through the metamorphosis of mind and body, through the conflict of knowing and not accepting. We can fix ourselves to an image of perfection to gain acceptance and approval, yet remain torn and confused in a state of self-denial. As we stop denying our difference we embrace self-worth, we restore our honor by our own validation. The King of Swords guides the reader to build the self anew. By developing symbolic understanding, the reader learns to communicate with the unconscious through dreams, fantasies, play, tarot, astrology. The King of Swords is the King of this symbolic understanding, translating signs, interpreting dreams, decoding portents. The King smiles at us as we summon the courage to define new outcomes for ourselves. When we arrive at the insight offered through the symbolic representation of psyche, it is a sight profound.

King of Wands

Men of integrity are not ashamed to serve. They are caretakers, guardians, keepers of the flame. They know joy. . . . This is the true meaning of reunion, living the knowledge that the damage can be repaired, that we can be whole again. It is the ultimate fulfillment that comes when men dare to challenge and change patriarchy.[22]

The King of Wands champions the freedom of will for it is the force that overcomes resistance. As the King of the fire, that of Leo, this ruler represents the Sun at its zenith. The reader's perspective is heightened here, overseeing the broad landscape of life. The mythological fire creates kingdoms in all the legends surrounding the birth of the Sun. Nanahuatzin, in the bravery of his self-sacrifice, throws himself into the flame of creation and emerges as Tonatiuh, the sun god of postclassic central Mexico. The eagle is associated with Tonatiuh, for the eagle is the only one able to carry

Nanahuatzin out of the fire. The lion is often pictured on the crest of this King's throne, making clear the association with Leo, the king of the cosmic jungle. This King is the hearth fire, gathering communities around his radiating charisma and confidence. This noble, pioneering King harnesses a sustaining power toward the realization of higher vision. His is the Sun overcoming the night and restoring clarity and coherence. By this model we know leadership entails a responsibility to be so self-actualized that we may bridge daybreak like the King of Wands.

Ruling is a performance in this King's theater. Although this performance is not meant to be a spectacle; it is rather intended as a catalyst for invention, engagement, and reconceptualization. The voice carrying this performance is always changing and evolving as it adapts to specific contexts and diverse audiences. To be in dialogue with a world beyond the self is to be illuminated in the interplay of anticolonial critical discourse. The King of Wands emerges from such a standpoint. The fiery political imagination takes shape in the dailiness of our lives as it is guided by the broad visions of revolutions we tend.

Attractive for his confidence, the King of Wands champions sexual liberation, resourcing sensuality as a continual embrace, a channeling of pure life force energy. The naked flame burns brilliantly. His authority is celebratory. The erotic is uplifted as pleasure becomes liberatory. Renewing the fires of eroticism engenders the healing of shame and self-denial. This confidence is highly influential, which must temper egoism with excellence; for with unbridled force, this King's light will blind. We embody the King of Wands as we refuse to be diminished by an all-powerful authoritarian. The light of the King of Wands casts away the shadows of ignorance, fear, intolerance. Anger is harnessed toward worthy ends in the hands of this King. "Indigenous peoples' anger and resentment can generate forms of decolonized subjectivity and anticolonial practice that we ought to critically affirm rather than denigrate in our premature efforts to promote forgiveness and reconciliation on terms still largely dedicated by the colonial state."[23] This anger is affective. It indicates a deep care for the self, the land, and the cultural communities we are engaged in. The King of Wands burns bright with this anger, this refusal to submit to denigration, this burning advocacy for the rights and obligations held by First Peoples.

This King continuously plants the seeds for new life. The warmth and vitality initiated here inspire communal cohesion. This King is unafraid to lead, to speak, to rally a community around joy and creative self-expression. This fire is contagious, exciting, and outgoing. It is the fire as the heartbeat, the very source of life, a fire to be respected; otherwise it overwhelms, burns down and out. This raging internal fire is an engine for change. The King of Wands shows up as we succeed in living a passionate, purposeful life. This card appears when we are becoming highly visible or engaging those who strongly display their sense of conviction. The King of Wands tells us we can shine brighter. This King centers our source of power within self-worth so that we feel safe to be seen, showing an authentic representation of an inner character. Such are the concerns of this King: keeping the public accountable, not being beholden to one's audience, while still nourishing a relationship with one's base of support. The challenge is not to be externally motivated, to act just for the show of it, though the deep desire of this King is to externalize the power and creativity they feel within. To deny this expression would lead to internal combustion. In the performance space of this card, hard-earned and refined skill is demonstrated. What is power that is not put to use? The King of Wands knows the inward force must be directed, channeled. Draw more cards to determine the agenda of this change, and the style of pursuit. As the genius of our light expands, the audience whose recognition is most important to this King is those he serves. Long before the public recognizes the talents, intelligence, or vigor of our being, our efforts are sustained in self-recognition and validated in the mutual recognition of those we labor with. The King of Wands facilitates the possibility for such mutual recognition. In the court of fire our active participation is encouraged. Active participation entails overcoming the dualistic separation of public and private.

As the steward of fire, the King of Wands offers spiritual counsel. These are the guides and mentors concerned with our inner well-being. They make *conocimiento* compelling. Time spent with the King of Wands restores faith and provides perspective as we continue on the quest for wholeness, healing, and transformative meaning. They offer us warmth when we spiral in the cold void of unknowing, guiding us through the process of rediscovery. They bring us out from the cold of spiritual estrangement, and in such compassionate warmth rekindle our belief in humanity. They show us how to sustain the fire of our faith so that as we confront our progressive visions without illusions, we are not stymied by the unavoidable conflict, pain, and obstacles we will encounter. Our faith in change needs this King's fire to ensure we overcome, to ensure we survive, to ensure we flourish.

We become more honest as we are influenced by the King of Wands. Honesty is born of vulnerability and of this empowerment. The light shining here is one that heals the unknowing spirit. Under this light we are emboldened to assert our autonomy. As nothing that touches fire can be left unchanged, our encounters with the King of Wands are transformative. The consciousness-raising offered by fire must be meaningfully joined by action. As a luminary we rise with the King of Wands, surpassing limiting beliefs, doubt, and despair.

King of Cups

> Feminist masculinity would have as its chief constituents integrity, self-love, emotional awareness, assertiveness, and relational skill, including the capacity to be empathetic, autonomous, and connected. The core of feminist masculinity is a commitment to gender equality and mutuality as crucial to interbeing and partnership in the creating and sustaining of life. Such a commitment always privileges nonviolent action over violence, peace over war, life over death.[24]

With waves crashing all around, the King of Cups sits steady upon his throne, a calm emotional center. His early emotional turbulence has been tempered. This is the water man who brings us back from the dead. The penetrating poet who goes beyond the veil to restore lost love. The King of Cups maintains a stance that all feelings are acceptable, able to be tolerated and processed toward constructive self-realization. The water King shows us how to feel the full range of emotions without drowning in them. He is the King of emotional catharsis, inner alchemy, and soul desire. He says follow desire, and it will lead to the Divine. He is the exemplar of desire harnessed toward spiritual union. He no longer denies the dreams closest to his heart, for his characteristic vulnerability and sensitivity is his source of power. He resolves inner conflict through art-making, through the preservation of memory. Creativity is a coping strategy. Art allies itself with revolution.

He, the King of catch and release, receives visions, images, and dreams that surface from the depths of his oceanic subconscious; treasure finding him through impossible stretches of distance and time. He listens, lulls, comforts, transforms, and transports as he holds the ephemerality of material things. He knows when to release, when to let go. He waits patiently for their return, shape-shifted, expanded, cleansed.

Sacrifice and renunciation are familiar territory in this card. The water King refuses separation from erotic desire and so enters the aesthetic dimension to be liberated in beauty. The King of Cups establishes order without repression or shame. Through the poetry of his being, dormant nature awakens into song. In our ability to find a self reflected in all of nature, we extend our gratification outward into the fulfillment of nature. Our freedom is found in the freedom of nature, free as ocean water. Such is the embrace of the nonrational way of being, the way of the King of Cups. The King refuses to be separated from fulfillment, refuses the constraint of reason. He rejects normalcy for a fuller eros. Such is the King's queer desire. He sacrifices substitutes and safety, he dives fully into the depth of desire, and he does not drown. His fantasy is resistance. He is the determination toward reunion. He is the process of inner transformation, the process that overcomes sublimation or the repression of libido. He says beauty is enough of a reason. There need not be endless productivity to be worthy or to have the right to exist. Beauty is its own purpose, and we are beautiful for our own sake. He appreciates us with his erotic attitude, his artistic contemplation. His language is song, and his work is play. This grace echoes through every living being and comes back to source, back to the heart, back to the King.

Any repressed memory is unlocked in his realm of sensuality, revelry, and art. A deep soul remembering takes place, and we strive again for core integration. This replenishes the spirit. This is the water of restoration, the soul's holy water. The soul retains every memory of love ever exchanged. Such memory is dangerous, because it subverts societal conditioning. Water is found to be the force that overcomes estrangement. After being numb we become hypersensitive. Memory is restored, and our fantasy cognition is ignited. We speak with Spirit, we enter trance states, we commune, we transcend when we step into the King of Cups. This King brings sleep, meditation, and relaxation to accommodate the truths found in this expanded capacity of communication. In him, the cognitive and the sensuous are fused.

He writes love spells, fluent, free, and unfettered in the language of longing, seduction, and artistic arrest. He is familiar with every fluid that flows through us, and he wants its release, so we know the freedom of orphic orgasm. We need this King to revive constrained matter, to uncover the animacy of the inanimate, the song of the silent. As protector of the waters, he establishes emotional equilibrium within his community. Ceremony cannot be held without clean water. Spiritual and religious freedom requires water free of toxins. Water is a universal need, yet it is only protected and championed by the Indigenous. Within the teachings of the King of Cups, it is understood that water is a spirit, as are all natural resources. Water is a power, a spirit, that we have no control over. A relationship of respect with water is necessary for our survival. "In His palace, Tlaloc keeps four tubs of water; one represents the storm and flood, one the calm, gentle rain, one hail and ice, and one drought and the lack of rain. He decides which to distribute to the earth. He does not do this in anger, or through lack of control; rather, the days of the Tonalpohualli, of the Sacred Calendar, determine His actions, and He sends the waters accordingly."[25] Tlaloc is a deity of water to the people of central Mexico, still revered by those of Mexican Indigenous ancestry, as water connects us spiritually across time and space.

He holds space for every emotion, knowing it all pours over itself. He is an open-hearted seer, committed, soulful, and intuitive, for the truth of love is all seeing. He takes the potency of social critique but helps us imagine new forms of fulfillment, relation, and distribution through the exploration of our interiority and the expansion of our emotional, soulful awareness, which he facilitates. Like water, we become immortal by changing form; rather, we become self-sustaining as we nourish community in our self-offering. He stimulates the impulse toward beauty and pleasure while finding the pathways for their genuine satisfaction. He is the exhilaration of emotional freedom, an unrestrained heart. He is the liberty of crying in public, of singing out in praise, of the freedom to feel. He knows the shame we encounter in being told we want too much, our desire is too great. When we are loved for the first time for the same qualities that others hated us for, he appears. He reminds us that longing is our recognition of our capacity for attainment, our discernment of the forces of full satiation. He redeems the sensitivity that wounds us so deeply, so early on, that it becomes the capacity for the richest experience of divine love.

He activates the creative prospects within us, he restores our heart's capacity to love; and though our desire may feel chaotic, and our excruciating sensitivity be a source of suffering, it becomes that which allows us to be enraptured by eros. Our considerable depths are manifestly expressed as we communicate with the King of Cups. He helps us find our way back to the source of our desire; though the path may be devastating, he promises it is worth walking. He protects us from the mediocrity of satisfaction. He is Audre Lorde demanding our erotic discipline, saying our freedom can be found no other way than by taking responsibility for our feeling. We must be profoundly open to receive the desire we've been taught is dangerous. He is the one who opens us. He is the erotic manifestation that overcomes historical self-denial. He peers into a horizon of plenitude; he envisions for us a life without emotional restraint, a life of abundance made meaningful. He shatters our sense of self so that the illusion of separation is washed away. He knows this as a self-defeat by which our desire is successful. He'd choose death rather than to be separated from his beloved. Dormant sacral energy awakened becomes radical sexual agency, becomes shame-free self-acceptance. His is the force within that keeps rushing toward union with the truer, deeper, and more lasting pleasure, the source that the soul incarnated for.

The King of Cups alchemizes desires to want differently, to want more than the meager substitutes of a repressive society. Disappointment, regret, and frustration are released in the sacrifices made toward the embrace of life. He matures us emotionally and makes our ethos sexually sophisticated. The heart discovery we have here shatters the frameworks of restraint. Though we move downward into death, by his waters we are reborn.

King of Pentacles

For the most part, however, with the exception of the high arctic, meat played a fairly minimal role in the ultimate survival of the human species. Our species survived because we inhabited new environments and when we did, we learned about the edible plants that lived in those environments. We learned how to live with those plants and, in fact, those plants made it possible for our species to survive in almost every environment that is presently inhabited across the planet. Our cumulative knowledge of plants made this a reality. It was this cumulative knowledge and shared, passed-down knowledge that made long-term survival possible. It's what I like to call our collective human heritage, which is the knowledge of our relationship to plants.[26]

The King of Pentacles has cultivated this cumulative knowledge, and he maintains it with care. This knowledge is enriching and life-enhancing. He knows our bones, flesh, and blood are the same metals, minerals, and waters that make up the Earth. This King establishes methods to thrive in place, making an art of sustainability, land reciprocity, and environmental adaptability. This King, often represented as describing the wealthy, land-owning patriarch, can be revised as one who has lived in right relation with the land for so long that the wealth of his character becomes materially manifest. His wealth is not one of ownership but stewardship, for the treasures he gathers, distributes, and grows are not his, but are entrusted to his keeping.

A healthy society is established by the reciprocal relationship between human and plant. Plants have their own agenda, acting in their own best interest according to their innate intelligence. Spiritual revitalization comes through renewing our connection, our communication with the land. The land is revived as our spirit is restored. The King of Pentacles is the one who kept the sacred link to ancestral spiritual ways of being intact through conquest. He re-Indigenizes the people of the planet to the planet, reawakening ancestral knowledge and enacting cultural revitalization. He does not run afoul of the pitfall of uncritical essentialism; rather, he recognizes that traditions change in the call for cultural dynamism. The King of Pentacles conceptualizes outcomes and thinks pragmatically. His actions are considered in the light of how they will benefit generations to come. He works on behalf of the children he has yet to meet. He seeks to leave them an inheritance of worth—not just a suitable, fertile environment, but a wealth of knowledge, a sense of communal continuity in the passing down of ritual, technique, and values. The cultural resurgence advocated by the King of Pentacles seeks to re-create the sociocultural political systems that flourished in the past in a manner that supports the holistic well-being of contemporary citizens. The King of Pentacles has roots that run deep, but he governs with fluidity, not with the rigidity of capitalist colonialism. He keeps the core intact, persisting in the spiritual beliefs and practices of his people while embracing culture's malleability.

The King of Pentacles divines by casting corn kernels, as the ancestors did. Corn is him, is his sister, is his teacher. He's always known augury before he knew how to translate its messages. In observing birds of flight, he carries on the communication from winged messengers between the celestial and earthly realms. The King of Pentacles carries the prophetic traditions to maintain cultural integrity from generation to generation. This literacy is a syncretic ecopoetics, the deep sense of interconnection that links the poetic self and the universe within surrounding ecosystems, accessible through the selfhood of the King of Pentacles. This selfhood is multisensory, so it reconciles the mind/body/spirit split of colonial institutions. He is the somatic therapist, the science teacher, the tobacco, morning glory, peyote, and other hallucinogenic, dream-inducing plants. He organizes *flor y cantos,* bringing together flower and song, or a poetry that arises from appreciation of and immersion in nature. He does not anthropomorphize his people's gods like the Greeks did. This Earth sovereignty recognizes that the spirits behind creation are not human, not quite animal nor plant, but a spirit animating them all. He knows the differences between ecosystems and how people come to specific places in specific times, how they adapt to survive, how they create a culture that unites them with the environment so they can thrive in their blending. The King of Pentacles lives where nature has put him, and he flourishes.

He has built a foundation for community step by step. To enter his kingdom is to enter an autonomous community, a people who control their own resources and protect their land. The spiritual laws that govern the land are upheld by the King of Pentacles. He embodies the success of resourcing love, reciprocity, and respect in all relationships. His mentorship teaches us to receive, to overcome insecurity and complexes of inferiority. By his teaching, we learn to reconcile material abundance with spiritual prosperity. The King of Pentacles connects us to the systems that are always interacting and interconnecting. He is us as a walking planetary ecosystem. He listens to the Earth and learns to restore the planet, to replenish resources, to rejuvenate the body's vital energy systems. He is the trust of a great oak tree, teaching us to be unafraid to stand tall in our truth, to claim the authority of our inheritance. He is the seed that knows its capacity to create bounty before it is brought to fruition. His golden touch brings plenitude in harmony with sacred time. Ohki Siminé Forest speaks as the Earth sovereign as they write about Indigenous survival in Chiapas: "The seed of all true power is within us. We will all die one day, but dignity can never die because dignity is the spirit of earth within us. If humanity can learn to see through Indigenous eyes, and to hear in the land the voices of our native ancestors—which continue to speak to us of dignity—then the hearts of all people will be healed."[27]

The King of Pentacles invests in us. He is patient, and he knows the value of each season of life. His endurance inspires the prosperity of his materialized gifts. His abundance is assessed by collective accessibility. He is continuously redistributing wealth, continuously overcoming the shame caused by capitalist class division. He shows us true wealth, one that is generous, one that does not hoard or covet. Colonization seeks the commodification of everything, which requires invasion as a structure of territorial acquisition in perpetuity. The colonial state seeks to eliminate Indigenous peoples for continued access to native territory toward the purposes of state formation, settlement, and capitalist development.[28] The King of Pentacles rejects any gestures of colonial reconciliation or recognition that would sustain colonial structures and subvert Indigenous claims of self-governance. The King of Pentacles gives us critical consciousness through historical awareness of land injustice, which continues in the present. This sovereignty refuses to let his people die from curable diseases or hunger or a lack of shelter. The King of Pentacles is every parent who prepares a nourishing meal for their children while living in a food desert. This King finds a place for all the displaced people, all the transmigratory people fleeing to survive, learning to adapt to new environments. He teaches reverence for every meal that sustains us, and respect for every hand that prepares and serves that which satiates us. His is the will of the humble who will triumph over the arrogant, those who heed the dream of the earth, who respect the flesh of the earth.

When we really know our worth, we know the King of Pentacles. His is a harvest of love. He knows where everything material begins and ends, and he enjoys co-creating security with his people so they may build a fruitful, meaningful life. He is the first environment, the bodies that sustain life, the original instruction. His medicine remediates exposure to toxic chemicals and heavy metals. This sovereign leads in times of environmental crisis. Such leadership aims to reconcile social progress with environmental recovery and sustainability. This King builds bridges between places within the psyche and places within the body. The King of Pentacles sees a world tree grow from our spine. The roots anchor us in the earth as the leaves crown in the heavens. There is no distinction between the physical and the spiritual.

Four of Swords

Many of us are not ready to accept and embrace our true selves, particularly when living with integrity alienates us from our familiar worlds. Often, when we undergo a process of self-recovery, for a time we may find ourselves more alone. Writing about choosing solitude over company that does not nurture one's soul, Maya Angelou reminds us that it is never lonesome in Babylon. We sacrifice our old selves in order to be changed by love and we surrender to the power of the new self.[29]

The Smith-Waite deck Four of Swords portrays an idealized version of a warrior on their deathbed, and you'll find most decks dealing with a laying to rest, depicting a solitude, a meditation, a healing, restorative sleep. This speaks to the funerary tradition of adorning tombs of noble men and women, dignitaries, and wealthy members of society. The recumbent figure is cast as a great and noble war hero. They are memorialized in full body armor, an image of valor, forever calcified in spiritual fervor as their hands are joined in prayer. Solemnity brings dignity. A life lived bravely, succeeding in piety as the culmination of triumph in the lifetime. The idealized hero repose in full body armor tells us of the patriarchal legacy that men are conditioned to uphold. Young boys internalize an ideal of masculine identity that is stoic, divested of emotion, devoid of expression. They learn to mask true feelings, to project toughness while denying feelings of loneliness, heartbreak, or sensitivity. The Four of Swords reminds the reader that no one is made of stone. The Swords suit speaks to stones and serpents as truth slices through the fog of illusion and ignorance.

Beneath the veneer of idealization, the former self is decaying. Behind an apparent nothingness, repair is happening. This is the paradoxical movement of the Four of Swords meditation. Squirming vermin make a cold body warm to unveil death as a point of departure for other species. Grief yields emotional alchemy in the gift of space and stillness. In this soul space, life is processed. Hardly "doing nothing," the Four of Swords prepares the reader to be inserted into a structure of healing consciousness. To recover the emotionality necessary for a fully realized life, survival strategies must be relearned. Estrangement from the self is asserted as a strategy to avoid male ridicule, physical violence, or other forms of demeaning self-denial. Grief then becomes a private, shame-filled act. This is a grief that alienates love, for when a loved one is lost, grief shared publicly marks the celebration of a life fully realized. Grief, when informed by love, evidences the lasting bonds between souls. It communicates passion, as it is also communion with the everlasting beloved beyond the veil. The Four of Swords reconciles us with the reality of loss. The Swords liberate through communication, through declarations of truth. By voicing our grief, our dead, life is unlocked. This is the medicine of the card: the ability to engage death peacefully through love's truth telling. This is a reclamation, mending all the self-severing that cishet white supremacist capitalist imperialist patriarchy imposes upon humanity.

The deathbed recognition of the Four of Swords is a recognition of love. We are lucky to pull this card, because as we are reminded death is always with us, we access the ever-present life as well. Therein is the freedom to name love, to pursue life, to live with clarity of mind and heart. The Four of

Swords lets the shadow of our fears emerge into the light, and while death does not dissipate, our aversion to it does. There is secret comfort in discussing death, for in our eulogizing, weeping, and commemorating we find a love that moves beyond the grave. As bell hook writes in *All About Love,* "a culture that is dead to love can only be resurrected by spiritual awakening." The Four of Swords sees such an awakening. Tarot is a countercultural spiritual thought that provides an alternative to a religious fundamentalism that is often represented as the *only* authentic spiritual practice. The Four of Swords offers a sanctuary for the estranged spirit. In our daily tarot practice we forge a personalized communication to stay in touch with the divine force permeating our inner and outer worlds. This card displays the power of tarot to reconcile individual introspection with cosmic awareness.

Wisdom is knowing when to rest. The Four in the suit of air stabilizes the mind and invites the querent to tend to the nervous system. The mind is made dormant in this card, and something deeper, more still, and restorative takes over. To consider rest holy, to let what is dead rest in peace. This brings us back to the life force waiting in the darkness, waiting for the emergence of light. Pull this card and be told to put down the deck and settle into a meditation exploring the interplay of mental activity and psychic stillness. This card offers a choice to choose serenity in the midst of struggle. Though great challenges lie ahead, the capacity for our peace persists in the quest to uncover the meaning behind our lives. We enter an inner realm through this threshold. Our woundedness is accounted for, as we unlearn the idea that it is virtuous to be silent about our pain. As we willingly touch upon our vulnerability, safe in the sanctuary of spirit, we learn to care for the soul. This soul care is transformative, for we find that the moment we open to our pain is the moment we open to salvation. This tender touch is the only one that will revive the heart and deliver the promise of love. The Four of Swords takes the reader into a pitch-black place of stillness so that the senses are intensified and new visions burst forth from the chest. It is a card of disciplined spiritual practice, the focus necessary to open the heart. The Four of Swords teaches you to talk with angels unafraid, to face your anguish so we may be able to love again.

Hanging above the figure is the Damocles sword, a reminder of the imminent and ever-present peril faced by those in positions of power. The

Four of Swords seems to say that true psychic peace is had by those who live in virtue, who do not compromise the integrity of their spirit for the accumulation of earthly power. As they say, "there's no rest for the wicked," while those who have lived lives of sacrifice and virtue finally recline into eternal relief. Those who achieve power by unscrupulous strategizing make power a prison. They live in fear that any moment they could be exposed, that the sword will fall from the heavens and strike them down. This sense of foreboding lies in the recognition of precarity. The delicate trigger of tragedy is always threatening without the anchoring of spiritual resolution or holistic integrity. The Four of Swords's remedy for the disquiet of the Damocles sword is dream incubation.

In this consideration of the Four of Swords it is appropriate to draw upon the work of Shelby Steele, professor and author of *White Guilt: How Blacks and Whites Together Destroyed the Promise of the Civil Rights Era.* Steele says the white guilt that arises as America begins to acknowledge the four centuries of oppression inflicted upon Black Americans is not one of conscience but of authority; the loss of moral authority becomes white regret. The acknowledgment of oppression quickly turns to center the white person who has hoarded social, political, and economic power as they scramble to disentangle themselves from the stigma of racism. Steele ironically posits racism as a Black power over whites in their ability to manipulate moral power so that whites work harder to prove they are not racist. Steele makes a clear point in naming the power that comes to Black Americans in the moral capital of history. Steele published his work on race relations in 2006, at a time vastly different from the pandemic time when I am writing this work. He discussed favoring individual responsibility and acknowledging the good will of whites while breaking from dependency upon white folks and institutions in favor of Black self-reliance and development. At the time he supported competitive advancement as a goal, calling for individuals to take control of their destiny. With this commentary, I am reminded of the way that the fallen but devout warrior-king of the Four of Swords is still framed within an institution with historical power and influence that extends beyond any one ruler's or individual's life. I see Temperance at play between the tension of how society frames or restricts our movement, agency, and voice, and our capacity to individually push back, to aim to set our mind and spirit free even as our bodies may be bound by unwanted circumstances. We may be given a frame, a societal boundary, but what we present can subvert expectations to affirm an integrity that restores and heals in its expression.

The peace and integrity of leaders wielding great power bear great responsibility while guarding against the fear and anxiety that come with such a position. Who, wielding institutional power today, has not committed cruelties to secure such a position? For those who've committed cruelties in their consolidation of power, the Four of Swords turns into the terrorizing Nine of Swords, ensuring they never know peace as they fall prey to the pitfalls of the tyrant. The Swords remind those self-appointed Kings that still there is a greater power to answer to, that they shall succumb to truth laid bare.

Four of Wands

Power centers can perhaps be best visualized as clusters of choices on an electromagnetic field—a field that is capable of movement and change into ever new and different designs. However, empowering our recognitions of the present design, the dangers of thinking of it as a frozen four-part model is that we simplify and freeze what must be seen as a process of complicated and ever-changing dynamics.[30]

In the Four of Wands consider how to appropriately affirm the embodied, erotic intersubjectivity of visionary fire. This is a card of alliances and unions, and it harkens to the institution of marriage as a historical function of this type. The Four of Wands is the search for common ground. Unity is often forged at the cost of nurturing a world of "enemies." The Wands are about contestations to power, and as the wands are staked in the ground in this card, we are reminded that this site of contestation has been around land claims. The Oceti Sakowin express the struggle of the Four of Wands in their struggle to situate Standing Rock within a sociopolitical historical context of Indigenous resistance against settler-colonial occupation. The card is about rightful jurisdiction and stewardship of one's homelands. It cautions us to be wary of "the rhetorical emergence of a 'we' who have a 'shared' set of rights/claims to the 'space of this country' in ways fairly disconnected from the question and practice of Indigenous sovereignties."[31] This arcanum asks who is controlling and establishing the means of equivocation as it tells the reader to refrain from resolving potential disjunctions into a singular, systemic account.

The fact that we have shared interests or a shared set of concerns does not mean we have established an authoritative framework that unifies aims, understandings, or actions of resistance. The Four of Wands is the struggle of establishing solidarity, the challenge of translating across disparate political imaginations, in a manner that appreciates difference rather than expunging it. Efforts toward engaged solidarity made in good faith must be committed enough to continue developing historical, social, and cultural distinctions across various movements. To assume a shared language, resolution, or scope of political imagination is a subtly but deeply challenging obstacle to establishing meaningful and lasting multipronged movements. Solidarity is not simply showing up at a rally and celebrating under a banner of change; it is also taking the time to truly understand the concrete differences in the context and experience of oppression. The Four of Wands is the risk of making oneself a mascot that is a caricature of support for a movement or people. The Four of Wands challenges us to move beyond drawing careless parallels of unity between peoples of difference. There is no "us" sanctioned by the United States that is free of such lazy assumptions. Such a unity that forces people into alignment is misleading and illusory. By guarding against an a priori singular group incorporation, more meaningful, dynamic, and productive relations may be sought.

> *If we as third world feminists decide it will be counterproductive to act as a single entity (which must deny its differences for the sake of unity) then we free ourselves to explore a different kind of community building. The oppressions we had experienced in the women's liberation movement taught us how easily one's humanity can be erased under the edicts of liberation. In order to avoid this kind of liberation we realized we must develop new definitions of community based on the strength of our diversities.*[32]

The Four of Wands is a response to the attempts to establish a single, homogenous, frozen unity that erases difference in favor of a single subjectivity deemed to be the only correct answer. The Four of Wands wants to develop coalitions on new psychic terrains. Existence within a social-caste system is multiform and varied. The work of trust required to organize movements of change can happen only when there is recognition of our realities and where we each stand. As we honestly locate ourselves within this system, we form the basis of meeting and establishing trust with other people. To build community we must also locate the values we share across difference. It is not enough to bond solely on the basis of our skin or any other identity marker. It is who steps up, for whom and for what; it is the demonstration of moral and ethical courage that is the basis of building community and communion.

Visions of unity are called into question by the Four of Wands in the implementation of group structures. Do the structures of our meeting facilitate a renewed sense of community? What is united and what is divided in these structures? Structures of domination, exclusion, appropriation, and inaccessibility are often rekindled and reinforced in the group structure of conferences, alliances, and committees ostensibly committed to social change. To advance egalitarian social relations, as imaged in the Four of Wands, we must provide a setting to shape and clarify the visions of liberatory perception. For these visions to take root they must have an official public expression, even as fraught and wary as certain forms of recognition are. Full, in-depth recognition may be insidiously limited within the larger limiting structures of the platforms where such visions of change seek expression.

Recognition is only established mutually. Members across groups of social difference are responsible for nonarrogant misperception. To mark the tentpoles of new psychic territory we are able to look across time, distance, and space toward the work of radical feminists re-membering lost histories. To maintain a solid basis for radical change, platforms must be available for *all* to make their discoveries heard and incorporated into the new orientation of circulating power. The Four of Wands shows that oppositional actors *can* stand together, sharing a new psychic terrain, a new solidarity, so long as the expanse of our differences is held in clarity within each stance and vantage of our unique positionality.

To decolonize these relations is to encompass the distinct modes of communal relations not bound by dimorphic gender categories such as those that continue to exist within Indigenous and Afro-descendant communities. The Four of Wands is a subtle reminder that various forms of resistance cannot be subsumed into any single framework under the banner of solidarity. To engage across difference, difference must first be recognized, for inclusion without influence is tokenism. If unity only comes within the parameters of hegemonic values, then this front of unity is an affront, a force of marginalization and restriction, counter to the purported aims of its coalescence. The Four of Wands asks us to examine the structures of consciousness that would enable us to create a movement whose central concerns are those of egalitarian gender, race, class, and culture relations. The medicine of this card is medicine of belonging, of refuge. It offers a way to belong in a way that does not compromise your selfhood but rather frees it. Within the communal greeting we can read or perhaps misread expectations and assumptions about where we are beginning and which endings are promised. Within the agendas of our welcome, is there space for the requisite confrontations of anger, frustration, cynicism, and hope that arise in struggles and striving for change—confrontations needed for true coalition building? Can we discern if smiles belie a less permeable social structure of separation? The Four of Wands offers space for the spirit of optimism within these confrontations. The Four of Wands asks for flexibility and enough responsiveness to change our agendas, to share power, to rethink our stance.

As the fours seek group relations, the framing of the relations takes on utmost importance. It's as if rather than expanding the frame to encompass all the specificity of people and their expression, we often adhere to a frame too tight for anyone who isn't smiling to be remembered. Cutting people out of the picture is the symbolic dislocation that conceals the state displacement and erasure of physical bodies across borders and states. We are beginning to recognize the limitations of seeking supervening structures that envelop and explain the myriad movements making efforts to realize justice. The call of the Four of Wands is to recognize that as we stand together, we are not identical; it is not to recognize that we are incapable of standing together or foolish for seeking to do it.

Four of Cups

Waiting is an enchantment: I have received orders not to move. Waiting for a telephone call is thereby woven out of tiny unavowable interdictions to infinity: I forbid myself to leave the room, to go to the toilet, even to telephone (to keep the line from being busy); I suffer torments if someone else telephones me (for the same reason); I madden myself by the thought that at a certain (imminent) hour I shall have to leave, thereby running the risk of missing the healing call, the return of the Mother. All these diversions which solicit me are so many wasted moments for waiting, so many impurities of anxiety. For the anxiety of waiting, in its pure state, requires that I be sitting in a chair within reach of the telephone without doing anything.[33]

The Four of Cups goes back to the primal anxiety of being separated from our mother. Enter the scenography of waiting, attachment, and birthing desire. We wait so long for the beloved that our attention becomes fixed on absence, and we, incredulous of our capacity to receive, to be fulfilled, settle into a delirium of anticipation. We close all the doors, shut all the blinds, turn off all notifications, and say no more till there is nothing but this sweet ache of apprehension. For some reason we think we must deny our desire, that it is noble to say *no* when we most desperately want to say *yes,* but as we've denounced desire we've become dissociated. The sitting, waiting, wondering of the Four of Cups is a meditation on worthiness. It's a question of how to put our bodies where our soul wants to be. As a lunar card, this particular position across the tarot's text focuses on finding a safe place to birth, to receive. Like coming back to waking awareness out of a trance meditation, this card offers those intimate moments of soul retrieval.

I've realized I was always nervous when people approached me because I've drawn in shadows my whole life. People who lie, abuse, manipulate. People who seek to have power over me. I've learned from this card how to let the right ones in. From a life of living with a guarded heart, I'm learning how to drop the burden from my arms and expose my heart to the love I so deeply wish to receive. Love requires complete surrender. It wants us unconditionally, completely. There is no way to invite love into life and not touch upon the wounds of scarcity and loss within the heart. The Four of

Cups shows us the affective barriers built around the heart and asks us to extend mercy to the figure most would judge as ungrateful. It is a vehicle toward becoming the kind of person who makes it safe to come out. Though the emotional wall may be unseen, this card shows us our shells plainly. The heart's vulnerability is not so sensitive that we must guard against love. This card comes during Pride season, but we all have our closets to come out of. We will never be free by hiding from who we truly are or being afraid of what we truly want. Sharing just how deeply psychic and soulful we are is a gift of intimacy, a gift we could only hope to receive, a generosity, never a demand or expectation or entitlement. Perhaps because this gift has been taken too many times before, the figure in this card forgets the pleasure and power of choosing to give a love that asks nothing in return. How can you receive anything if you haven't received the gift of giving?

This is the card of pulling away, for once you thought they were all in, there is still some shame they don't feel safe enough to share. And what relationship could exist without this sharing? To come out from behind the invisible glass and actually engage is to make the self not necessarily vulnerable, but open. From this open sharing comes the gratitude of feeling trusted. So the Four of Cups comes to let us out of the box we didn't know we were in.

If we are to find fulfillment, we're going to need to make space for the new and unknown in our heart. This is a type of pre-grieving, for the knowing that love is coming, that love is ahead right before you, means letting go of the mother, the known, a nest. But the mother's love is a bond that can never be broken. As we deal with water we deal with ephemera, the state-changing substances, and the quality of life that is about state change. The mother makes survivors and teaches the reader to adapt and change to find love in a new circumstance, in a new form, for it is that source connection to love that sustains. The Four of Cups keeps us from falling into disillusion.

The love offered in the Four of Cups is one that says it is safe to let go, no matter how much we want to hold on. This is love teaching the nature of love. Love does not operate from scarcity but from an overflowing abundance. Being poured into entails love brushing against the walls of conditioned capacity, working upon them till all our dams are released. The Four of Cups is the card of the growing heart. It expands our space to receive by giving us a new shell, a new cup to contain some sense of the uncontainable. That old form was nourishing, but we need to leave it before it becomes limiting. The Cups are about the pathway of desire, showing that as any connection, form, or state is fulfilled, it gives way to another, larger, deeper substance, a wider love state. Though to think we are leaving love behind is but another expression of the sense that we have to say no to new love to be able to hold on to our firsts. The mother's love wouldn't have you miss out on what's meant for you because of the mistaken belief that choosing love is a zero-sum game. You are not abandoning her, letting her down, or betraying her by loving another. The illusion of the Lovers is the illusion of this choice. Love is not a finite resource. All love informs every love. There is more than enough to go around. In the sweeter, higher, freer form, no love is lost. What a relief; all the love harvested fits there. The Four of Cups patiently waits for the reader's similar realization. The Four of Cups engages this as a process of trust. The Cancer Moon of this card can grip so tightly, but eventually it gives way to the ocean that calls you home from your separated states.

"Within the Soul there exist two coexisting desires. One desire is for separate existence—to separate from that which created the Soul. The other desire is to return to the Source of Creation. . . . Buddha's enlightenment underneath the bodhi tree was based on just such a realization as he pondered the nature of sorrow, pain, and misery."[34]

The figure sitting under the tree of the Four of Cups is perhaps in such a state of meditation. Perhaps they are caught up in a hero complex which requires their self-imposed alienation for the sake of safety. Like Superman they fly high above the earth, listening so deeply from such a remote place, disconnected physically but extremely connected to the collective spirit. From this remote position, the Four of Cups taps into this stream of continuous connection. Perhaps they sit with a sense of guilt for the love they so abundantly possess, reluctant with the awareness of the world's undeniable misery. Perhaps they are *willing* love to come where they are waiting. Perhaps they are hallucinating. Maybe the figure's love lesson in this waiting game is discerning patience from punishment. "Not yet" is not "no" when waiting for the right one.

"Sometimes I want to play the part of the one who doesn't wait; I try to busy myself elsewhere, to arrive late; but I always lose at this game: whatever I do, I find myself there, with nothing to do, punctual, even ahead of time. The lover's fatal identity is precisely: *I am the one who waits.*"[35]

Though we must not wait too long, for stagnancy leads to decay. The Moon, which rules this card, models the phases we must pass through for inner renewal. The boredom or dissatisfaction with exterior surroundings initiates an ability to make something from an apparent nothing.

If the Ace of Cups is to be the principle of life desired, offered, received, then the Four of Cups's refusal is some desire of death, some embrace of death by the denial of life. Wherein I recognize a trauma response within this, I practice heart listening, hearing what the soul is telling me about how I approach the world, how the world approaches me, and how to stand up for myself, to protect myself, to maintain myself. I no longer see myself as the locus of justification for the pain I've endured. I learn through the Four of Cups to come to emotional awareness by coming into the body. With this card, I aim to offer compassion for that distrusting self, abused in the neglect of love. I know the need for that love is present when this card presents. In the enduring emptiness of the Four of Cups, the worthiness of love must be considered, with any wound of dignity or deservedness to be overcome. Call upon the power of love that makes us survivors of such broken-spirited suffering shared in the world.

We run up that proverbial hill, racing to be there first to greet love. We get there but then doubt our efforts, question our intentions, when we find ourselves alone. Wondering if our love striving was worth it becomes the Four of Cups's inquiry. I remember one time I was in elementary school, learning my multiplication tables, and my teacher, Mrs. K, would go out on her lunch break and reward any kid who earned a perfect score on their multiplication quiz with food from McDonald's. When I finally got that one hundred, I remember waiting for my lunch, waiting for a long while for this gift that was promised to me, that was an exchange on the part of my willingness to learn and to be disciplined. And as I waited, I sat alone, apart from the other kids, in a closed-off section of the campus, waiting for my Happy Meal, which eventually came just before lunch ended; but I sat contentedly nonetheless. This time my aloneness was not because of being bullied but because I had earned something special, and that made me feel special. Now my queerness was for my intelligence, a queerness I could finally sit with without shame, for in that moment it was triumphant. I waited patiently in the presence of my own desire and pondered a sense of worthiness that stood in direct contrast to the extreme homophobia of my early environment. My aloneness marked a freedom; it marked a self-honoring, a self-belief, showing myself what I was capable of, scholastic achievement—but more than that, patience, imagination, and a sense of presence in the absence of human relationship, protected from violence.

I didn't realize it in that moment, but now I know how love sometimes pulls us apart from the crowd, how it promises itself in exchange for our sacrifices, and how we imagine what its flesh might feel like. How fertile it is even before its arrival, for all it conjures up inside evidences its reality. This race up the hill of love is no competition; we each have this special place waiting, welcoming us with congratulations as we find fulfillment and worthiness through diligence and trust.

Four of Pentacles

Life is full of peaks and valleys, triumphs and tribulations. We often cause ourselves suffering, by wanting only to live in a world without struggle and difficulty, a world that is flat, plain, consistent. We resist the truth of difference and diversity. We resist acknowledging that our constants exist within a framework where everything is always changing. We resist change. When we are able to face the reality of highs and lows, embracing both as necessary for our full development and self-actualization, we can feel that interior well-being that is the foundation of inner peace.[36]

In this card, realize that a refusal to care for the Earth, let alone revere it, is tied to the human willingness to exploit and dehumanize another. As humans violate and diminish the natural environment, the human spirit is demeaned and dwindled. The Four of Pentacles presents a mini-emperor clutching tightly to four gold coins, sitting upon a gray, flattened environment, alone. It reflects the reader in a state of self-preservation. There is a holding in or back. There is concern for what is to come or what has been, holding firmly onto the present moment, holding tightly onto one's resources. This is the energy of financial conservation. There is no giving or receiving, only preserving. This king has sacrificed mobility, an embodied agency, for material reward. He has confused what has been entrusted to him with something he owns, or perhaps he fears the theft that is the legacy of his inheritance, that of capitalist imperialist white supremacist patriarchy. His space is not created but owned; this is a violent anti-aesthetic. This is the dead space of late-stage capitalism. Moving away from the rural, agrarian lifestyle of our forebears is disempowering when it severs our connection to the Earth. To transition to the city pictured in the background of this card may incur a loss of confidence and power from uprooting an ancestral connection. Like the figure of the Four of Pentacles, we can find ourselves isolated, contained, restricted in our movement and in a dangerous, muted landscape. We pull this card and may find ourselves surrounded by dead things, engulfed by emptiness, for the spirits of beauty and Earth departed here long ago.

The Four of Pentacles confronts cultures of narcissism or ethnocentrism displayed in the rigid holding of spiritual beliefs and moral systems. This card is cautionary in its desperate, fear-born clinging. The tightly wound caution is wary of any foreign presence. Such outside cultures or alternative belief systems are seen as threatening when one is seated upon a system of hierarchy. For them to maintain a position of superiority, they must be blind to the legitimacy and power of the other. Those who cling tightly to the concept of survival at all costs feel they cannot afford such openness, for it would make them vulnerable. Of course our vulnerability is a fact of life, which makes the illusion of security so comforting to the king of this card, even as it severs the king from the life force he is so set on preserving. Notice the Four of Pentacles in your body when your chest tightens, when your hands grasp and grip rather than open. Notice when your insecurity expresses as selfishness, and see a spirit in need of nurturing.

With the Four of Pentacles guard your body as the sacred ground of your soul. In this card, grapple with questions of value, self-worth, and sustainability. The reader discovers which of their roots are to be preserved with a historical appreciation of existence. For people displaced and severed from a homeland, a family, or a people, maintaining these connections through cultural productions and expressive aesthetics are vital strategies of thriving. The ancestral traditions that empower an ecological consciousness can reengage liberated modes of being. The Four of Pentacles comes with the teaching that we are living lives of interdependence. The reader establishes an eco-intelligence when there is a sense that it is impossible to act or live solely on one's own behalf, alone. We realize our place within a larger natural network and the proprieties of place within that position. We forge a vital sense of covenant and commitment to facilitate connections that break the bondage of conditioned loneliness.

"What is money when I have all the earth?" George Washington Carver asks. The Four of Pentacles is a picture of this inquiry. This questions power's price and what exactly is required for an enriched life. To reclaim our ancestral legacy as stewards of the Earth is to claim this card's power of leadership. It is the environment that grants power—power that requires the responsibility of husbandry. This card is potent because it clarifies the values that keep the reader upright, that provide a foundation for livelihood that doesn't compromise spiritual integrity or environmental exploitation. We are brought to the bedrock of character, which becomes its intrinsic worth. Within a culture of capitalist imperialism, the underlying values are to plunder, pilfer, and peculate. To resist the cultural conditioning of scarcity, hyperindividualism, and disdain for the environment that we are inextricably connected to, we can advocate for the communal environments quickly being erased. We can cultivate habits of being that honor the cultures of ecological interdependence and that vivify our relations to the land spirit with which we cohabitate. The landscapes of our community are changing in the violent erasures of gentrification, a modern manifestation of colonial displacement. The Four of Pentacles is that lone tenant who refuses to sell their property to the corporation. They hold out and are confronted with changing culture, questioning how much should be preserved and how much they will need to adapt.

Position is power, but so is place. The throne will outlive any king, but there are only so many ocean-front properties. Colonizers and the like don't want to give that land back. Clutching at status and stolen states is a way goons hang an albatross around the mariner. Misperceived self-worth makes a prison of responsibility. It is compact and compressed, it's time and it's money, it's a Pandora's box. A natural wealth values a nonviolating nature. Wealth generates from the core. It's a center of gravity that anchors you in an earthly relationality. It is not a stone you sit on; it's the trunk of a tree you water within. Piety is not simply withdrawing from the world in a self-imposed celibacy. The Latin root of "piety"—*pietatem,* meaning "faithful to natural ties"—relates to the marble sculpture *Pietá,* depicting the Madonna holding the dead Christ in her lap; for she was the one who wouldn't crucify her own, unlike everyone else. Her blood devotion aligns with an ecological consciousness of interdependent Indigeneity, that faithful disposition to *natural ties.*

The environment entrusts a certain amount of power to us as we draw the Four of Pentacles, bringing us value beyond fiscal estimations. The Four of Pentacles sees us as stewards sustaining culture while opening to change. Consider the possibility of being both sturdy and flexible. To let go of the consumer capitalism that leaves us depleted and longing, we can strengthen our ability for aesthetic appreciation, which is rooted in the sense that each space is a sanctuary. No degree of material lack prevents us from learning to recognize beauty.

> *They revealed to me that the treasures I was seeking were already mine. Away from my home state I often found myself among people who saw me clinging to old fashioned values, who pitied me because I did not know how to be opportunistic or play the games that would help me get ahead. It is rare for any of us, by deliberate choice, to sit still and weave ourselves into a place, so that we know the wildflowers and rocks and politicians, so that we recognize faces wherever we turn, so that we feel a bond with everything in sight.*[37]

Readers of the Four of Pentacles learn to inhabit space in the way bell hooks learned to inhabit space. We are to become familiar with a particular location as we invest ourselves in that place of community and uphold the responsibility of that investment. We pull this card as an opportunity to renew our commitment to the body, to place and community. In this card we learn to speak the language of the Earth, and though we may journey far and wide looking for this seat to set roots, though we may endure changes imposed upon us by the decay and renewal of time, we will always belong.

FIVE

Once having traversed the threshold, the hero moves in a dream landscape of curiously fluid, ambiguous forms, where he must survive a succession of trials. This is a favorite phase of the myth-adventure. It has produced a world literature of miraculous tests and ordeals. The hero is covertly aided by the advice, amulets, and secret agents of the supernatural helper whom he met before his entrance in this region. Or it may be that he here discovers for the first time that there is a benign power everywhere supporting him in his superhuman passage.[1]

Five is prayer cried out in the midst of suffering. Five is God's catalyst, forcing change and adaptation. Until we realize a triumphant Spirit, Five is where we feel defeated, where we walk despairing for miles. Five finds the outsiders, the walking dead. They are the bereaved, the social outcast, the damned. They are conflict and its responses.

Five is the emergence of new realms of consciousness. It initiates the Hierophant, the shaman, the root worker, the *curandera.* Five is the pain the Hierophant heals, the wounds that necessitate their role as a communal healer. Since Four opens up a channel and establishes a basis for understanding relation, Five is what crosses the bridge from the other realm. What passes is unknown and thus necessarily discomforting. If we find Four to be a dark cave, Five is the fear we project into that looming darkness. Fives are assaulting, working against established structures and reified rules of reality. They may see various types of bodily dismembering and penetration. This is a hallowing of the body, slicing into the comatose, anesthetized body so it reawakens the Spirit imbuing every being. By bringing us to the depths of our inner and outer underworlds, Five recovers our lost shadows, works upon our disconnection and self-alienation to reweave an integrated psyche that centers Spirit. Five seeks our completeness by returning the reader to the center, the pit, the root.

To turn the lights on, Five goes to the dark. It digs beneath the surface, revealing what corrupted treasure chests of torment, loss, and redemption lie in the shadows. It marks the descent into our psychic labyrinth, where we navigate psychological dangers and stumble upon the deep caverns of the soul. The deeper we go into the narrows, the more there is at stake, the more vital our survival becomes. This exploration reveals a greater capacity than we could have possibly conceived we possessed, an expanding awareness that could not occur without falling into our depths. Five readies for reunion through pain purging fear and outworn energies. Five reads to surrender. Five asks, *What will save us?*

To survive we must suspend disbelief. We have to slay dragons and demons.

The strife of this stage is unearthing a transcendental concentration, for Five is where reason and rationality are powerless. As we feel ourselves stripped of certainty, we enter a realm of discovery. Within this sphere pride is put aside to humbly bow before forces greater than humanity. Five stretches language to try to express the ineffable till the sounds snap the tongue shut. Five is where the ego goes to put itself to death by the dissonance between language and experience. Five forcefully opens the body to divine revelation, a painful experience but one with great promise. Five decided agony will be the means of catalyzing critical awakening.

The Five cards counsel courage when working to finally embrace the fearsome being denied within. It is a point of no return, where the way back will not be the way we came. Five is symbolic of humanity, the head and our four limbs, the four fingers and the thumb. It symbolizes human aspiration in the actualization of a spiritual selfhood, the striving connection with the godhead. Nothing satisfies the hunger and thirst of the Five except for the satiation of spiritual longing. It is a force of mediation between the beginning and the resolution, itself a narrative climax, a numerical full moon. By bringing us to the nadir of our ignorance, Five illuminates the apex of Earth's consciousness. A rock's silence does not mean it is dead. Fives are widening, opening, and provoking. Five is where we find the deepest core of our personhood.

The Hierophant

[Prayer] is the act by which the man praying stands in the presence of a being in which he believes but does not see and manifests himself to it. The invisible before which man shows himself can range from the radical invisibility of the Spirit to the inward sacredness or power of a being visible by itself, like a mountain, a star, or a statue. This act of presence puts man thoroughly at stake, in all dimensions of his being. It exposes him in every sense of the word *expose* and with nothing held back. It concerns our body, our bearing, our posture, our gestures, and can include certain mandatory preliminary bodily purifications such as ablutions, vestimentary requirements such as covering or uncovering certain parts of our body, bodily gestures and movement such as raising the hands or kneeling, and even certain physical orientations. All these practices, whether they be obligatory or left to the preference of the one praying, can be gathered together in a summoned appearance that incarnates the act of presence. Even he who turns toward the incorporeal does so corporeally, with all his body. The being before God of the one praying is an active self-manifestation to God.[2]

The Hierophant turns our ontoformative abilities toward prayer. Speech is brought into relation with the Divine by this arcanum's inquiry. The Hierophant considers the voice's role in characterizing the Divine, as in God, Goddess, Teteo, Creatrix, Shiva, Kali, Father, Mother. The interpreter of the Divine is a narrator whose characterization, perspective, and gaze have a knowing that is simultaneously constituting. The words we use to analyze, theorize, order, understand, and constitute reality become *the word,* that which constitutes Divinity, Deity, cosmology, that which is real even if unsounded, opening a linguistic dimension of silence. The prayer is more than any single speech act, as each prayer ever uttered is strung together like a mala bead upon the rosary that hangs on the neck, wrist, between the fingers of the faithful. Prayer lends our tongue to limitless lips. Our word echoes through space, reverberating blessings back and forth through time. The Hierophant regulates the twofold current by which offered-up prayers descend upon benediction. *The word* becomes a vehicle for the soul's concentration. When we turn over the Hierophant, we turn to the ultimate essence of religion: "This noun of action was derived by Cicero from *relegere* 'go through again' (in reading or in thought), from *re-* 'again' (see re-) + *legere* 'read' (see lecture (n.)). However, popular etymology among the later ancients (Servius, Lactantius, Augustine) and the interpretation of many modern writers connects it with *religare* 'to bind fast' (see rely), via the notion of 'place an obligation on,' or 'bond between humans and gods.' In that case, the *re-* would be intensive. Another possible origin is *religiens* 'careful,' opposite of *negligens.*"[3]

This teacher's often critiqued, and feared rigidity is but an expression of faith telling us that this Red path is not something we take on only occasionally. It is as real as we make it. The reciprocal relationship of soul and spirit that is bound by mutual sacrifice. Discovering how lasting the word becomes, we learn the solemnity of vows to regard the requisite sacral quality of sacrifice. The Hierophant is about the emancipation of faith, the declaration of belief, accomplished by discipline. Their vocation is as a custodian of soul, heritage, lineage, and spiritual tradition. The Hierophant is rigorous, but by such discipline is able to offer absolution and benediction. Protection is inseparable from purification. The Hierophant's blessing is then twofold: preventive and remediative. For as we rigorously recollect our words and our thoughts, we renew our meaning, our purpose, our sense of worth. We come to realize that the utter unconditional mercy of God is epitomized within the gift of our voice. To recognize the significance of such a gift is to never again speak carelessly or cruelly.

This is the realization that inspires rigor: the voice is inextricable from what is said. This teacher demands we speak as we believe, that as we so speak, so we will believe. If, to believe, we must speak, the Hierophant teaches us how to say ourselves before the Divine, before the invisible other. As we undergo this preparation for a presentation before the invisible, the invisible illuminates what we could not previously perceive within ourselves. The phenomenon of prayer is marked as sacred sound for its healing, redemptive intentions and effects. The Hierophant is our teacher of prayer, keeper of medicinal mantras, and confidant of our deepest existential fear. They teach us as Taurus would how to sing scales, how song is sacred, how singing gives one's voice over to the sacred. To sing as the Hierophant is to use the voice to free our faith and our joyous spirit and to empower the divine presence and its intervention in our life.

The Hierophant prays to presence the invisible. This arcanum teaches us to expose every body of our multidimensional being as a supplication. We take our turn in the Hierophant to receive the word, the body, and the blood of God, vocalizing ourselves as a child of the Divine, manifesting ourselves anew in the eternal plane of holy sound. In this act we are not speaking alone, but we are warily certain our speech is heard. This is where the power of the Hierophant is most prescient, teaching the reader to hear how we are divinely heard when we feel most silenced, most invisible. The Hierophant does an inventory of all the possible modes in which the face of the Divine appears and administers these prayer rites of presentation before all who are willing. The Hierophant takes you to the source of sound, with its center in silence, showing that despite any bias describing the divine as "aphonic,"[4] it has always been felt as an impetus to speak, to call out in praise, to plead for help. The Hierophant has realized severity as the unending avenue where prayer finds voice, whereas mercy's meaning is made in bestowing benediction. In such a vulnerable state of asking, humility has gain. The devout's attention turns to a source whose giving is beyond egocentric capacity and individual limitations.

Giving our desire a voice when we pray to God is giving desire a way to exist so its weight becomes unburdened, so it is released from its shame. In God's listening we learn to accept even our most secret (primal) desires as something sacred, because they were given to us by God. For the soul to speak more clearly, we need the Hierophant, for they are the one who teaches soul literacy, facilitating fluency in the language and omenology of the Divine.

Do you still have a personal connection with the teacher who brought you to God? The Hierophant is the true power of the teacher who engages not just the Logos but also the pathos of their teaching. The Hierophant does more than explain systems and review technique; they initiate the reader into a family connected through a history of practiced and professed faith. A family may follow a different set of interpretations, but their roots draw from the same source. To be so spiritually rooted, we need the Hierophant. As the difference between the Logos and pathos of our interaction, these are the teachers who bring their soul and their body to the classroom. They are not disembodied philosophers of objective thought or "pure" rationale, but they seek to inspire the fire within the heart-soul of their students to burn brighter. The Hierophant is the way we name our traditions and the depth of personal connections we make with what we are studying. The Hierophant is the inquiry into which tradition to join and which master teacher we will go to, to be initiated. Spiritual practices do not work as powerfully when they are divorced from their spiritual tradition. Choosing a Hierophant is choosing a name that offers a lineage of naming and being named. Extending back through history, it becomes a line into the present, into the unfolding future. It's a line of legitimacy, a root system to nourish the spine of your personal world tree as an offshoot of the cosmic topiary.

It is about how the deeper you learn to listen, the more you hear history, a record of influence, inspiration, reverence, and respect that refuses to ignore or forget those who've made contributions to our peace, survival, and freedom. This is not a cold, academic source citation, but a recitation of verse. The Hierophant is absolutely patriarchal, whether as congeniality whereby we *claim* ourselves as a child of God, or whether we *are claimed* as colonial conquest becomes the crux of the Hierophant's triple cross. Settler colonialism demonized Indigenous spiritual thought and practice through the notion "kill the Indian, save the man," establishing white supremacy through forced assimilation. The pope was the icon spearheading this conversion campaign, questing for power and earthly riches. The pope was the representative power of the church, the one whom even kings and queens bow before, the one who crowns them before God and legitimizes their rule before the people.

People of the church, from its founders to its participants, once enslaved people. The Hierophant, offering and initiating spiritual freedom, is only fully understood in the paradox of the church's deeply significant and genuinely sacrilegious investment in slavery. Despite various attempts of the diocese to set aside portions of their endowment for reparations for their sinful past, the church will not be able to earn redemption by simply writing a check. There is no way to remedy the reality of bloodshed and colonial genocide that is interwined into the material history of the church. The great spiritual gold offered by the Hierophant has been eclipsed by the church's wealth, largely amassed through the slave trade; the systemic child sexual abuse by cardinals, archbishops, priests, and archdioceses; and the brutality of the mission system and boarding schools.

While there are churches seeking redemption and extending reparations, a wealth-hoarding Hierophant has perhaps never been more visible than in the rise of the megachurches. These megachurches conflate faith with congregation size as they align themselves with capitalism. They purport to hold faith while having no reservations about accumulating massive wealth. Certainly, the Hierophant attempts to reconcile spiritual striving with material plenty, overcoming a poverty consciousness that suffers a lack of systemic sacral integrity; but the greatest pitfall of this arcanum is to not retain focus once spiritual striving leads to riches.

Requiring Indigenous peoples to learn English, convert to Christianity, and assimilate into the dominant culture enacted spiritual severance. Catholic and Protestant missionaries interpreted and reported the spectacular feats of Indigenous medicine workers as the work of the devil, working to erase them from the record. The practices, knowledge, and relationships of the folk were disregarded as they were forced into a system of obedience, rote memorization, and uniformity. Thus, the Hierophant appears as we need to unpack the dogma that restricts our relationship to an innate spiritual life by limiting the understanding of the operation of reality. Dogma is established as a strategy of survival, made by those seeking some sense of coherence amidst the disarray of terror, abuse, and torment. Dogma is created by abused children who give themselves internally derived rules to live by so they can stay safe, so their spirit is not crushed. However, when the universe or the Divine does not behave according to this wounded belief system, terror ensues. This mirror reflects tolerance against intolerance. The Hierophant is there during this deconstruction of rigid beliefs and rigid behavior that can only be first felt as a deep humbling. The workings of the Divine are indeed beyond our purview. Humility actually bolsters self-worth because it says you are willing to forgive your flaws; thus, this arcanum shows the dignity to be found in being brought to our knees.

> *To her child mind old men were the only men of feeling. They did not come at one smelling of alcohol and sweet cologne. They approached one like butterflies, moving light and beautiful, staying still for only a moment.... They were the brown-skinned men with serious faces who were the deacons of the church, the right-hand men of God. They were the men who wept when they felt his love, who wept when the preacher spoke of the good and faithful servant. They pulled wrinkled handkerchiefs out of their pockets and poured tears in them, as if they were pouring milk into a cup. She wanted to drink those tears that like milk could nourish her and help her grow.*[5]

To the religious histories that constitute, dictate, engender, transform, and/or eradicate our spiritual practices and innate spiritual connections, this arcanum asks about the image of your guru. Is it a white person practicing cultural appropriation, perpetuating colonial destruction of native spirituality systems? Or is there a void? Between hubris and humility, the Hierophant stands, continuously calling into question how we live our faith. The Hierophant asks where are the elders who can consult with the spirits of the cosmos, whose wisdom and presence can counsel us when secularized society falls short.

In the absence of human elders, I felt a spaciousness to safely seek communion with the Serrano forest and desert landscape of my native environment. In this reliance I discovered I am a biomolecular network, and I cannot be separate from the sociobiome of my environment. My faith was made real outside of the Catholic church. As when the blood bond of family becomes binding, the forging of a family by a sense of belonging provided by belief becomes truly solid and remarkable. There is an image of the Hierophant as the father who accepts all who are lost, rejected, abused, and abandoned by blood. The Hierophant, at their highest realization, achieves a familial affect so the lost ones know they have a home and the childhood hurt begins to heal. The Hierophant is envisioned as the Father of the Marginalized, while the High Priestess is the Holy Mother of the Damned.

The Hierophant is for the freedom of religion. Voice is vehicle to express belief, praise, or to attempt to directly commune with the Divine, and it won't be suppressed or censured by those pulling the Hierophant. The Hierophant maintains this domain of speech, the one that uses voice as a lark does, to harmonize one's song with the Divine. This vocal capacity of prayer-song is how the Divine uses our own voice to act upon us, to teach us about God, to teach us to listen. "The word affects and modifies the sender, and not its addressee."[6] A prayer-voice speaks in hymns, recitations, and rites to write a dancing poetry with all the waves of sacrificed words washing over us.

For the word to return to the Divine it must wrap around chaos. To keep claiming spiritual freedom, keep maintaining psychic health, the Hierophant tells us we must practice prayer. Prayer has been an immense current of energetic capacity that has sustained oppressed people for generations. Should we cease to pray, we would cease to exist. We may have more information than our ancestors ever had, but how much of their faith have we kept alive?

The language is not the same, but the spiritual leaders of various traditions have always brought their people into the presence of that which is deemed holy. The core function of a Hierophant is to make the sacred known.

The Hierophant extends beyond perfunctory ritual, which would otherwise become mundane without initiating the reader into the sacrament of timeless mystery. Their work is outside secularized society, working against the erosion of the spiritual powers of all traditions. They come where they are needed most, wherever there is the absence of belief.

This arcanum keeps the keys. These keys entrusted to their safekeeping unlock Heaven within the querent's awareness. To decolonize the Hierophant is to envision the eradication of the colonizing institution of religion. It's important to work well with what would set you free, what would open the door to ecstatic opportunity. As many leave the church, they may find that once the scaffolding of faith falls, a vivified spirituality is fully freed and fulfilled. To uncritically accept modernity is to turn a blind eye to the spiritual powers of the Hierophant still active today. To regain this perception we need to leave religious institutions that profit from restricting spiritual literacy or damning the spiritual practices of any nonorthodox system, and instead return to ancestral practices but in a new form. As Vine Deloria Jr. observes: "Our ancestors invoked the assistance of higher spiritual entities to solve pressing practical problems, such as finding game, making predictions of the future, learning about medicines, participating in healings, conversing with other creatures, finding lost objects, and changing the course of physical events through relationship with the higher spirits who controlled the winds, the clouds, the mountains, the thunders, and other phenomena of the natural world."[7]

The Hierophant demonstrates humility, a reliance on and respectful relationship with the spirits, and the immense powers conferred upon the individual who has devoted their lives to the Divine. They inspire reverence within ceremony and look to the vast resourcefulness of the Divine before judging possibility based the estimation of our own powers. The Hierophant shows the bravery of standing before an incredulous community and professing love for the Divine so deeply they begin to weep. The most significant system we should adhere to is the one of soul, which often goes against the conventional morality and social structures of the times. For this, the Hierophant offers the reader remission, letting go over and over and over again. This key master with the master key must be found within, as colonization works against freedom most effectively within our own conditioned consciousness. The Hierophant opens us to direct experience with the Divine through their disciplined dedication.

Motivated by their own wounds, they've apprenticed to learn the various modalities of the healing crafts. They teach the reader to enter trance states, nonordinary realms to bring back sacred knowledge and holy medicine. The Hierophant locates, roots, and validates the veracity of *our* spiritual authority. The Hierophant knows one day we will be ancestors and desperately wants us to pass down a body of knowledge, a love that is faith made flesh.

The Devil

The oppressed suffer from the duality which has established itself in their innermost being. They discover that without freedom they cannot exist authentically. Yet, although they desire authentic existence, they fear it. They are at one and the same time themselves and the oppressor whose consciousness they have internalized. Analysis of existential situations of oppression reveals that their inception lay in an act of violence—initiated by those with power. This violence, as a process, is perpetuated from generation to generation of oppressors, who become its heirs and are shaped in its climate. This climate creates in the oppressor a strongly possessive consciousness—possessive of the world and of men and of women. Apart from direct, concrete material possession of the world and of people, the oppressor consciousness could not understand itself—could not even exist. The oppressor consciousness tends to transform everything surrounding it into an object of its domination. The earth, property, production, the creations of people, people themselves, time—everything is reduced to the status of objects at its disposal.[8]

In America everything is for sale. The Devil makes Americans, constructing white men of property who derive authority and autonomy from assuming *absolute* control over the lives of others. The Devil feels this as a force that flows, sensed as some kind of natural resource of the slave master, rather than the conscious willed, deliberated domination that it is. Capitalists everywhere think their being depends on having. The Devil's impetus to possess is unrestrained, a tragic irony of unbalanced, violent relations turning a world of multivalent, subjective personhood into an array of objects to be purchased, consumed, and discarded, such that the world is conceptualized as purely materialistic. Although the licentious lust of white supremacists, slave owners, and conquerors has burnt most fervently for soul possession. And the Devil definitely appears when we are dwelling in *susto,* a state of soul loss.

The arrangement of the Devil's image clearly shows us that oppression dehumanizes both the oppressor and the oppressed, for violence estranges us from humanity. White supremacy and anti-Blackness are unified in this estrangement. This arrangement by the oppressor tells us that whiteness is a deficiency dependent on the acquisition of the dark "other." The hunger born of being so profoundly bereft of culture and community leads to cannibalism, the consumption of the other. The writers who veil these systems of domination to embed them deep within the psyche take their captives as surrogate selves. In this surrogacy they project the problems of human freedom, safe to grapple with these existential terrors of evil, sin, aggression, greed, loneliness, powerlessness, failure, and unrestrained wilderness at a dark distance. As imagined by the canonical authors of American literature, the characters that constructed American cultural identity are white walkers desperate to play in the dark. As Toni Morrison observes, "If we follow through on the self-reflexive nature of these encounters with Africanism, it falls clear: images of blackness can be evil *and* protective, rebellious *and* forgiving, fearful *and* desirable—all of the self-contradictory features of the self. Whiteness, alone, is mute, meaningless, unfathomable, pointless, frozen, veiled, curtained, dreaded, senseless, implacable. Or so our writers seem to say."[9]

Oppressed humanity is backgrounded by savagery, while being the foreground of focus. Humanity here is a "thing," the property of this devil-horned beast who exists upon a distorted scale of power, a hierarchy. The Devil is fully bestial, and it shares horns with its property, though these "objects" are clearly more humanized than the beast, like you, in the process of humanization. As the oppressed pursue humanity, oppressors read subversion in their action. As humanization cannot be fully realized without freedom, the oppressor enacts constant control. The oppressors work toward *inanimacy,* toward a deadening of the world so it is as stiff as the black box Satan stands upon. Unable to control or escape this impulse, they work against themselves as well as those they dominate. By denying freedom, life is denied, and by pleasuring in this denial, the Devil is clearly sadistic.

If the Hierophant initiates us into a lineage of naming God, of transforming word into prayer, transforming our bodies into a vessel to receive God's illumination, harmony, and healing, then the Devil brings us to the absence or antithesis of God voice. It is a card that curses. What else could we call inherited, historical, collective, and personal trauma? The Devil damns our depression, our heartbreak, our physical abuse, sexual trauma, and deprecating self-talk. The Devil is domination that necessitates the belief in your own supposed inferiority, as well as the supposed superiority of the master.

The Devil is so deeply about our freedom, how we get free, how we understand freedom, and the destabilizing fear that must be surmounted to enact freedom. The Devil is ready to allay the internal fears that our established truths and freedoms may just be verisimilitude. They're always ready to rationalize external exploitation with a concoction of alarm, desire, and dark otherness. With the presence of restraint appears the Devil. The domination executed in day-to-day practice is often veiled within the "private" spaces of our home, relationships, and personal interiority. This makes it all the easier to imagine violence existing "out there," beyond your reach or sphere of influence. The Devil ensures that we give commensurate attention to the violence we'd rather neglect. This confrontation meets the ideology of domesticity, the ways in which we cage, silence, and collar our wild, free desire and authentic expression. Domesticity makes its claims to civility through violence. As much as the state tries to disappear problems by disappearing people in cages, the Devil refuses such a denial. It confronts whoever conspires to deny the violence or pain of reality. This arcanum shines a black light, the shadow's glow, where we can see the blood spilt, the pain endured underneath the romanticized master narrative.

The bound, suppressed, and repressed darkness of the Devil is objectified in American literature as an Africanist persona.[10] The Devil tells us the duties of that persona are to be the playground, the staging arena for the elaboration of the "free" identity. "There is no romance free of what Herman Melville called 'the power of blackness,' especially not in a country in which there is a resident population, already black, upon which the imagination could play; through which historical, moral, metaphysical, and social fears, problems, and dichotomies could be articulated."[11] The Devil holds up a mirror that reflects more than an abstract freedom, for it forces us to see slavery and the enslaved. Historically, the Devil joins the "not-free" to the projection of "not-me," predicated upon racial difference.

An antidote to and meditation upon slavery—the shadow companion of freedom's conception—is the construction of liberty, autonomy, and subjectivity. And so the lingering and lasting effects of enslavement upon the collective psyche are summoned in the Devil. History tells us nothing enriched the founding of this country's creative imagining and articulation of freedom like Black slavery. Clear in this card is how we source symbolic meaning from the construction of an imagined darkness always hovering. Through exploring the darkness that awakens all kinds of connotative value, darkness as the richest ingredient within terror, the Devil works through unconscious and conditioned racialized fear of the other.

To throw off "loyalty," even to those who dominate, terrorize, and exploit us, we need the Devil. Facilitating this shadow work is an ongoing process; there is no end to it. It is a blood disease passed down from generation to generation. The Devil is the one bearing "dangerous memory,"[12] the knowledge and histories of those who challenge the moral legitimacy of societal structures with knowledge too "dangerous to make readily apparent." The Devil does this so that in awakened awareness, critical confrontation occurs. Discussing various oppressions like racism in a racist society is extremely difficult, but such a discourse demands confrontation. To avoid being silenced in any space we must confront our internalized oppressor and grapple with our varying complicity in a white supremacist capitalist imperialist patriarchy. This confrontation should not imply violence, and yet many who are charged with facilitating such dialogues seem to fear violence in their stifling of passion in favor of a "safe and polite" conversation. This censured conversation is more dangerous because the silencing of authentic perspectives, experiences, and critical awareness favors the oppressor. The racially coded language that many speak so cavalierly blows a piercing dog whistle till you feel so suffocated it's like you've been holding your breath for a lifetime. One of the curses of segregation and subordination is the imposition of silence. A struggle for meaning entails a struggle over the relations of power, which calls upon those who can articulate emancipatory possibilities while working toward their realization.

The Devil summons emancipatory authority by problematizing the world and enacting critical dialogue in the interrogation of the reader's concepts and preconceived notions, and the origins of their worldviews and self-concept. The Devil works to constantly extend self-awareness toward social awareness. To break the *oppressor-oppressed* contradiction encompassed by this arcanum, the incarcerating beliefs that conflict with our humanity must be deconstructed by a forged, invented, armed, capacious love. The Devil's critical literacy engages readers in discourses of power by continuously critiquing those who maintain powerful positions in society, who structure time and social arrangements so as to not be bound to hegemonic ideology. By challenging the dichotomy of spiritual, psychoemotional health on the one hand and intellectual rigor on the other, the Devil initiates authentic dialogues about our existential experience of inequity by explicitly situating our body, our cultural texts, and our language within an explicit awareness of power, oppression, and transformation.

The Devil keeps account of the mind's self-sabotage, degraded vision, and locked gates. The Devil chains the reader and the writer, challenging the force and efficacy of our imaginative acts. The Devil appears when readers project into the danger zones offered by other writers. The associations of these mind states include illegality, irrationality, darkness, the thrill of evil, and night. Escaping the Devil requires learning how to free language from its sinister deployment of racially informed, gendered, and determined chains.[13] To read the Devil is to write with an imagination unlocked to enter what we are estranged from. This card forays into the corners of consciousness, those spaces deemed off-limits and kept far from the reach of our authorship or writerly imagination. The writer transforms the social ground of this restricted consciousness (the unconscious) into language that liberates. To reconsider how this dark presence is constructed and employed is to shift the critical gaze from racialized object to the radicalizing subject.

The Devil turns up to avert the perception from those who cast shadows. To begin recognizing and assessing the nature of these voices, we move away from the characterization offered by the voices of internalized shame, and we are able to maneuver out of their scripts and off their stage. The writers who delve into the Devil refuse to let the Black presence central to the contemplation of culture and the constitution of freedom hover at the margins. To Devil is to stop reading as a reader and begin reading as a writer. The darkness that is disruptive demands to be noticed for all its complexity and power beyond mere reflection. The shadow indeed has its own perspective, voice, and wisdom. The Devil appears as we finally start to notice the darkness before our eyes. "As a writer reading, I came to realize the obvious: the subject of the dream is the dreamer. The fabrication of an Africanist persona is reflexive; an extraordinary meditation on the self; a powerful exploration of the fears and desires that reside in the writerly conscious. It is an astonishing revelation of longing, of terror, of perplexity, of shame, of magnanimity. It requires hard work *not* to see this."[14] The narrator may get free, but this does not mean the master narrative has been destroyed.

The Devil strips away facades of privacy to urgently remind us that all oppression is connected, to make our personal deeply political. To unweave the inequity that characterizes our daily, personal lives, the Devil pulls you deeper into darkness. The social relations of domination, though changing over time, are deeply entrenched in the multicultural landscape. Slavery is not something that only happens to the enslaved; it happens to the overseers, prison guards, correctional officers, mistresses, and masters as well. One cannot commit atrocities without incurring the effects of that degradation upon their own being. Carceral violence marks the soul no matter the direction of its infliction.

Freedom, though historically reified as an object, a thing to obtain, or a place to arrive, is rather reflected in the scope of our action. Freire tells us, "Liberating action necessarily involves a movement of perception and volition."[15] To move into new worlds beyond the darkness of domination can be jarring, but we must become acquainted with and acclimated to a new inner and external geography. Moving to a new space incites observation, reflection, and creativity in the new context, a renewed opportunity for a holistic self-possession. This movement can be prepared for physically and mentally, but emotional movement is always unexpected. We desire freedom but fear it at the same time. The free acts of leisure, rest, reciprocity, pleasure, and the pursuit of a meaningful livelihood are denied by the Devil's deeply restrictive mental conditioning. The Devil requires consciousness-raising, offering growth through the transgression of limiting beliefs. The Devil has internalized an external image of fear from others. He looks in the mirror and sees a monster instead of a prince. This lie distorts the vision of beauty, love, and partnership. Spirit at its lowest—at the nadir of the underworld, at its least conscious—calls for Divine intervention, a call that is always answered. The union of conscious and unconscious is found through confronting what appears to be our opposite and working to "get the lead out." Restricted consciousness is higher consciousness in *potentia*. This may be why we accept the Devil's invitation: to liberate the Spirit imprisoned in the unconscious.

The Devil, the shadow king, the lord of darkness, Saturn—is the antithesis of the Sun. "Saturn is connected with the educational value of pain and with the difference between external values—those which we acquire from others—and internal values—those which we have worked to discover within ourselves. Saturn's role as the Beast is a necessary aspect of his meaning, for as the fairytale tells us, it is only when the Beast is loved for his own sake that he can be freed from the spell and become the Prince."[16]

Freedom confronts our sense of inadequacy and the threat of humiliation. Still, freedom is worth grappling with its conjoining fear. This arcanum allows the reader to practice moving in these emotional spaces that give depth and range to movement, spaces that allow our being to be more responsive, interactive, recycling, and restorative. Integrity empowers us to experience ourselves as relationally free. This gives rise to new structures of commitment, meaning, pleasure, and communication that are not bound by the mind's oppressed somatic conditioning.

The Devil keeps the reader accountable to the burden of plunder, deceit, and misrepresentation. Assuming responsibility for honest communication and aligned action, the Devil recognizes the tremendous courage it takes to speak, to own your words. This speech is difficult. To name how we've hurt each other and ourselves is formidable, but it is impossible to restore right relations and implausible to end abuse if we ignore the history of harm. If we are to ever trust each other, we need to deal with the Devil through dialogue that is true, difficult, and confronting. "We must face the Medusa, the unfaceable in ourselves, in order to have access to the powers we require. Mistakes must be forgiven. Every day repeats an opportunity for beginning anew."[17] Dealing critically with reality inspires creative discovery toward the practices of freedom. By being brave enough to unmask the Devil all around and within us all, and to decode the rhetoric and gestures of the dominant class, which veil the consolidation of power among the wealthy, white elite, we can move out of the darkness. We can continue establishing a basis for the resurgence of egalitarian mass movements and participate in the transformation of the inner and outer worlds we inhabit.

Five of Swords

No, it's white male life. The master narrative is whatever ideological script that is being imposed by the people in authority on everybody else. The master fiction. History. It has a certain point of view. So, when these little girls see that the most prized gift that they can get at Christmastime is this little white doll, that's the master narrative speaking. "This is beautiful, this is lovely, and you're not it." So if you surrender to that, as Pecola did, the little girl, the eye of the story, is sort of a bridge there, and they're sort of resistant, a little feisty about it. They don't trust any adults. She is so needful, so completely needful, has so little, needs so much, she becomes the perfect victim, the total, you know, pathetic one. And for her, there is no way back into the community and in society. For her, as an abused child, she can only escape into fantasy, into madness, which is part of what the mind is always creating, we can think that up.[18]

The Five of Swords exposes the master narrative impressed upon the individual and collective psyche. Two figures are shown buckling under the pressure of dominant ideology. The one who appears with the swords, with a grim grin of schadenfreude, has stripped these two of their land and status, enacting exile and banishment, an effective social death. The Five of Swords is the cop card, imaging the construction and enforcement of the master narrative, the active force of law symbolized so strongly by the sword. The powerless are taken advantage of, while the victors of conquest promulgate a point of view in their favor. Here blame is not only useful; it becomes another form of dominator terrorism. It makes us villain and victim at the same time, dead citizens either way you cut it. Blame is often cast upon the victims of violence, shaming them as if they are somehow responsible. For those who have a sense of self that is overdetermined by a system that does not acknowledge their humanity, a healthy well-being will be dependent upon forging major systems and strategies of resistance. This card appears as we are to break from the master narrative, to unlearn self-blaming, and instead advocate for accountability that invites recognition of our own agency, our own defiant scripting.

The Five of Swords calls attention to the despair and pervasive sense of defeat permeating marginalized communities. By becoming creative dissenters we can resist the values of the hegemon. Seeking assimilation and acceptance in a dominator society is a fool's errand that only leads to the self-harm of a dark insanity. Identity formation is no simple process. While this card speaks to the ways we cannot and should not assimilate the values of the white supremacist state, it also shows how identity arises from identifying *as against*. The agent of state enacts an antagonist identification, or a counteridentifcation to the two despairing individuals, to affirm a sense of self.

> *In the banking concept of education, knowledge is a gift bestowed by those who consider themselves knowledgeable upon those whom they consider to know nothing. Projecting an absolute ignorance onto others, a characteristic of the ideology of oppression, negates education and knowledge as a process of inquiry. The teacher presents himself to his students as their necessary opposite; by considering their ignorance absolute, he justifies his own existence. The students, alienated like the slave in the Hegelian dialectic, accept their ignorance as justifying the teacher's existence—but, unlike the slave, they never discover that they educate the teacher.*[19]

This card presences the ideological restrictions implicit in the sites of identity construction that prevent us from being able to fully assimilate with the scripts and roles offered by dominant society. The ideological restrictions imposed by the dominant sphere speak to the nature and use of the swords. When claiming a sense of "I Am" as a queer of person of color when everywhere says "you are not," nor welcome here, identity construction becomes especially arduous. In this card is an agent of state enacting normativizing protocols to gatekeep access to an identification with the powerful. The "good subjects" of the dominant ideology—those who fall into the prescribed scripts of white, male, cis, hetero—require "bad subjects" who rebel against the dominant ideology, which proceeds to validate the dominant discourse. In the Five of Swords this "good cop/bad criminal" dynamic plays out. Presented here is a failure of identification that, while initially isolating, can become a site of disidentification, a third mode of dealing with dominant ideology. Jose Esteban Muñoz explains that "to disidentify is to read oneself and one's own life narrative in a moment, object, or subject that is not culturally coded to 'connect' with the identifying subject. It is not to willfully evacuate the politically dubious or shameful components within an identificatory locus. Rather, it is the reworking of those energies that do not elide the harmful or contradictory components of any identity. It is an acceptance of the necessary interjection that has occurred in such situations."

A new self arises from the rupture of the experiences that this card speaks to. This identification refutes intellectual domination through an emergent *identity-in-difference* that gives rise to a counterpublic sphere. The Five of Swords comes to the collision, the ruptures, in relating. From this collision, hybrid identity emerges, and represented here are the deviants. To perceive the queer and the colored, the Five of Swords severs representational contracts.

This card turns over the oxymoron of a marginalized status, calling upon the complexity of negotiating identity against limiting, socially encoded scripts. The Five of Swords as a site of ideological emergence rehabilitates our internal images, scripts, and narratives, changing them from damaging and shameful to powerful and seductive. By refusing to buckle under the pressure of assimilation within the dominant culture, or to be cast as its counter in a juxtaposed stance of counteridentification or utopianism, disidentification is a strategy to continuously work on and against the master narrative, both structurally and locally.

> *Her performance permits the spectator, often a queer who has been locked out of the halls of representation or rendered a static caricature there, to imagine a world where queer lives, politics, and possibilities are representable in their complexity. The importance of such public and semipublic enactments of the hybrid self cannot be undervalued in relation to the formation of counterpublics that contest the hegemonic supremacy of the majoritarian public sphere. Spectacles such as those that Gomez presents offer the minoritarian subject a space to situate itself in history and thus seize social agency.*[20]

Disidentification allows us to stitch the cloth of culture to dress our diverging dimensions. The Five of Swords is taking scissors to texts as though they were textiles to create ways to engage powerful praxis that recycles, reconfigures, and expands beyond the limitations of biases and monothematic minoritarian positionalities. If we are unable to escape a social matrix, we can work to restructure its meaning and dynamics from within. The Five of Swords teaches readers to maneuver with more criticality, resisting an unproductive and uninteresting good/bad judgment. It interrogates models of discipline and boundary enforcement, while pointing to the site of ideological deconstruction. The challenge of the Five of Swords is to not categorically dismiss a person or their viewpoint, though we may be unable to wholly identify with it because of how it is inscribed with homophobia, misogyny, or racism. The Five of Swords interrogates any implicit or overt exclusionary ideology within texts, while still parsing out and engaging any valuable contributions to discourse through a mediated identification. The experience of misrecognition found in this card, the uneasiness of belonging and not belonging at the same time, tells us there is no neat process of identity formation. We tactically and concurrently work on, with, and against cultural forms. Rather than dismissing or banishing our queer and divergent desires, we can be tempered and rewritten through renovated ideology. The Swords, and the Five of Swords especially, explore the links between identity and ideology.

More than simply "reading" or interpretation, this maneuver toward disidentification is a necessary survival strategy. This is a face of exclusion and intentional exile. Colonial rule does not depend solely on overt state violence; rather, it reproduces itself through enticement. The major movement toward minority and marginal representation in media and within the colonial institution shows the state's ability to get Indigenous peoples to identify "either implicitly or explicitly, with the profoundly asymmetrical and nonreciprocal forms of recognition either imposed on or granted to them by the settler state and society."[21] The Five of Swords shows the enforced separation, the violent communication that severs and separates natives from their homeland, which makes them exiled within.

The Five of Swords initiates a process of self-recognition that rejects the aims of reconciliation with the state, for all such reconciliations are built upon unequal exchanges. Violent state power is here deployed in the policies that aim to undercut Indigenous political economics and relations to and with the land through the violent dispossession of Indigenous rights to land and community membership. Here we see how policies and language supplant the physical state violence of dispossession. The colonial state seeks elimination, not just physically but culturally. We have to plunge into the past to purge the internalized effects of systemic racism and colonial violence by rejecting assimilation and instead affirming the worth of our own identity-related differences. The Five of Swords shows the incapacitating effects of being made a colonized subject, of suffering misrecognition. Colonizer recognition reproduces settler colonialism because the exchanges of political recognition end up being structurally determined by and in the interests of the colonizer. We must not reconcile ourselves with such defeat or with systems of settler colonialisms that make hierarchies seem natural. Under the history of colonialism, the reality is that we are all capable of enacting the violence of estrangement and othering. We must be vigilant about our participation in this system, where we enter into these enactments. The Five of Swords guards this entry.

Five of Wands

A finger snaps. At once, the static but now living "others" spring into action. They ease up into the art of dance with sharp poses that ironically have nothing to do with white Renaissance paintings and more closely resemble both the future and the majestic hieroglyphic angles of ancient Egyptians, an innovative people with a stylistic sensibility centuries ahead of their time.[22]

Five figures sprawl across the frame, each holding batons, color-coordinated in an apparent freeze frame of choreography. Are the passions in competition or collaboration? How is the body being positioned in space, and what meaning is translated through the frame? These are central inquiries of the Five of Wands that call for the democratic use of the stage. The bodies find fantastic animation in their drive to stake a claim to center stage, vying for the spotlight, to be at the center of attention, of power. The Five of Wands is a theater of power, a dramaturgy, a staging of the contestation of the social order in dramatic composition.

As the viewer or recipient audience for this card we are to engage in what Erving Goffman called dramaturgical analysis, the critical study of social interaction through the lens of theatrical performance. Attention is paid to timing, positioning, audience reaction, delivery. We are to be the "dramatic judge," determining who gets tens and who gets cut. To read social situations as a scene is to try to detect how the staging, character blocking, and dynamic movement are coordinated by some higher hand. It is to be aware of how people are strategic in their self-presentation, vying for a speaking role, a turn in the spotlight, or a chance for screen time. It is to be aware of the symbolic meaning encoded behind social interaction, making us perceptive of the microaggressions, appropriations, and dog whistles that contort power in the social spheres. Context is everything in the Five of Wands. Our identity is a social construction constantly being remade in interactions with others. We step into the realm of competition, presenting the self to be so "real" as in "fem realness" that we convince the audience we are who we say we are. A social reality and the ensuing social identities are validated through the audience's approval. Here, the audience is the arbiter of identity.

> *Rooted deeply in beauty pageants and pageantry—obligatory shade aside—queer, trans, and cis men and women of color compete for trophies, cash prizes, and adoration (victories that elude them in the outside world) at events known as balls. Balls are to be "walked." The categories for walking are varied, but they often bend gender, class, and physical makeup, requiring participants to assume an identity other than that dictated to them by mainstream culture. If identity is a construct, and the world a stage, then Ballroom is the world's Met Gala. . . . The very idea of* realness, *in particular, subverts the collective "reality" we all assume. Balls allow the poor to be rich, the masc to be fem (and celebrated), and the outcast to perform center stage. And whether or not these transformations are fully realized, the stage is always set for liberation.*[23]

With the barrage of media inundating our daily lives, it is all the more necessary to become the Five of Wands dramaturge. To *read* requires skill, for without the expertise of an eye trained to the sociopolitical, cultural history of the subject matter, one may miss a message conveying powerful meaning. Something may be aesthetically exquisite but conceptually disastrous. Much of this media training has been lost. The Five of Wands prospects character motivations and psychological underpinnings, as all the cards do. The Five of Wands makes metaphors with the body's language. It attunes the reader to various social, psychic, and cosmological structures, rhythms, and stages. Social media has commandeered the stage, seeing that even presidents are compelled to perform on handheld screens to prove themselves or to garner power. The Five of Wands emphasizes the spectacle of the state.

State ceremonies and rituals may be far less elaborate than they once were, but there is still a discernible poetics of power today. Ineffective administration often hides behind symbolic shows of power that aim to legitimize the state's ongoing colonial conquest. But the material bases of power have become all too transparent. These "power plays" are given more focus than the welfare of the governed. Given the scale of the figures on the Five of Wands, they may very well be world powers arguing over territorial claims, their focus fixed on dramatizing rank and displaying political superiority through large-scale warfare, proclamations, and invasions. The Five of Wands has the reader discern between expressive and instrumental action, between pomp and circumstance on the one hand and the power exerted over the material reality of people and resources on the other. It uncovers material conflicts and competing interests. The Five of Wands says it's time to stop measuring dicks.

The schematics of media representation uncover the duplicity of institutional power arrangements around "diversity, equity, and inclusion." Perhaps these five figures are competing for mainstream success, visibility, and power, only to be flattened as a token of monolithic representation by the concentrated white power of media corporations. It's no longer adequate to simply read what is presented onscreen; we must continuously read to become institutional dramaturges, or critically aware of the whole production process: the backstage and offstage power dynamics, the casting directors, the writers' rooms, the source material, the advertisements, the interviews, and then of course the cast. There is a threat of violence in the image. To be cast by a corporation is to risk the danger of communal estrangement. The more ways we can read the social situations we enter by choice or compulsion, the better we can defend ourselves against insidious corporate violence.

So as the Fives correlate to the outcast and the minoritized, they also point to the underground cultures that are the hotbed of creativity that ends up shifting mainstream sensibilities. To be made socially real, we need to risk reinvention, deconstruction, and presentation in front of a crowd. This crowd is certainly not always a chosen community, but the Five of Wands extracts a will to be seen and heard by those who *we* determine validate our entry into a given community or space. The risk is that our dream of a new or truer identity may be shamed, shaded, or still unrealized. The benefit is that the Five of Wands embraces the paradox of identity, the being of many things at once, the continuous redefinition of identity in social space, which affords the spaciousness to more fully be. The person who succeeds from the Five of Wands does so in recognition of the persona—from the Latin, meaning "mask worn by actors"—that is most compelling in any given social interaction. Our roles change by the hour, by the environment, and by those we play against or with.

Constructing a king is not a legitimate way to construct a state, much less a community. No king is consummate, so there is no exemplary center, there is no realm that is truly real within the confines of colonialism. Colonialism subjugates selfhood and imbalances the relationship between self and other, between social and natural environments. But whoever will be the queen of the ball is actually an enactment of colonial subversion. The ritual extravagance within the ballroom community re-creates social relations so that power is wielded by those denied mainstream dignity. Ballroom and other subcultures of queer Blackness reshape the current social conditions to match the inner reality of soulful dignity. The Five of Wands offers initiation into the *metakosmios,* where self and society become liminal before becoming liberated. The ritual performance signaled by the card establishes a symbolic ideal constructed to influence pragmatic reality. The theatricality of social actors across culture and politics calls into question the role of the audience, of the spectator. The Five of Wands works to clarify our role in reading, writing, participating in, and/or protesting social institutions. There is frustration in getting all the parts in order, knowing what goes where, who's carrying what, and who's moving when. Our attention is constantly being commodified, making it all the more vital to refocus on what is equitable and humane. It is always a wonder to marvel at what is validated by focused, engaged, collective attention *and* conscientious action, precisely because of the struggle it takes as shown by the Five of Wands.

Five of Cups

Chastity is something one preserves not for its own sake, which would be barren, but rather so that one may be fully ready for the moment of surrender to the beloved, the suitor whose aim is true. Whether in knowledge or in love, the capacity to recognize and embrace that moment when it finally arrives, perhaps in quite unexpected circumstances, is essential to the virtue. Only with that discernment and inward opening can the full participatory engagement unfold that brings forth new realities and new knowledge. Without this capacity, at once active and receptive, the long discipline would be fruitless. The carefully cultivated skeptical posture would become finally an empty prison, an armored state of unfulfillment, a permanent confining end in itself rather than the rigorous means to a sublime result.[24]

There are a lot of words we give grief, only to arrive at a long, cold silence. Underneath all art and creative realization is grief. Grief is the most devoted lover we will ever know. Grief is a guide for the lost soul and will never leave us alone out in the cold. Black is absolutely the color of my true love's hair.

The modern self is afflicted by a deep sense of alienation—the individual from the collective, but more deeply the psyche from the spirit. Such schisms and separations require us to venture in the negative space of desire, into the hunger, the hole that is yet to be filled. For mending within and without, the Five of Cups penetrates into unconscious drives, those hidden hungers and tendencies, which when repressed become destructively disappointing. Our inability to grieve gives way to the mask of depression.

To meet the creative force of our unconscious we are to embrace embodied eros. Spill your blood, semen, wine, and tears. When you lose love, grieving is violent, messy, incoherent, and intense. Like losing a limb. Still, jump into the river of grief. Stop being a dam for disappointment. Purge.

Poison is the rejection of death, the loneliness of a lover still standing. Let that wash away.

Ride the wave of grief long enough and you will be brought into the rapture of surrender. No one will know if the tears are falling from your eyes for the release of grief or the release of salvation. Either way, it's catharsis. The poet of lamentation has their way with our word with this card. The grief-tortured tears become the water that only wants for us the deepest fulfillment. After Death's uncompromising demands of renunciation, grief is the only evidence of love we have left. It makes us chaste again, not to leave us bereft, but to distill love into its most potent promise. I write this, knowing love by its absence. Its presence is found completely inverted by the Five of Cups. This card is an offspring of the Tower turning toward the rupture of a wailing revelation. The pouring out is processing the impurities in the water of desire. An embrace uncovers the gift to be so dissolved in God, to wash away everything till we want for nothing but God. The card calls for a bloodletting. This is a type of elimination that organizes and coheres what has frayed and distorted. This release restores internal and external environments. The Five of Cups nods to the *lavadoras,* those who persist with the privileged ceremonial roles of cleansing, washing away blood and excrement during birth and death.

We stop to reflect on all the desires that, once met, too soon leave us dissatisfied again, till we come to desire to know the core of our creation. We desire source, we want God, we want Ma, and that desire takes us beyond self-imposed limitations. It breaks the barriers erected between us and life. Desire determines what we think we need, what choices we make, what actions we initiate. Desire is a way of attempting to find out exactly who you are and what you have come for. What is more than the object of desire? The subject who desires.

The quick hits of satisfaction that torment us with lingering, insatiable hunger burn away, leaving the practice of patient fulfillment. It's no more ceaselessly seeking replacements and substitutes. Till we learn that emotional hunger is not love, we are satiated for a fleeting moment only. There is no shame in being hungry or still suffering unmet needs. But care and responsibility are required to ensure we are discriminating enough to finally be fully met, authentically and intimately. The Five of Cups says there is no settling for the heart-soul that desires God as the lasting satiation. The God within this card motivates us to know the longing beneath carnal appetites, with resolve toward a fuller nourishment. We let go of lusts by becoming passionately devoted. There is a place with good and plenty, with more than enough to nourish and feed and fill your cup. It's not about not cumming; it's about evolving desires with evolving consciousness.

> *It is the nature of emotional pain that if it is suppressed instead of experienced, it does not dissipate, but retains a bodily component, while a conscious awareness of the pain is repressed or forgotten. Pain that is not fully experienced at the time continues to exert its damaging effect on the person and finds symbolic expression through patterns of neurotic and self-destructive behavior. The avoidance of pain leads to compulsive reliving and repetition. The defended person continually manipulates the environment so that this repressed pain from the past will not surface. Primitive pains and longings are stored in layers in the body and cause tension and psychosomatic illnesses as well as depression and anxiety. Nevertheless, if one enters a psychotherapy where the atmosphere is conducive to the expression of these painful feelings, one can retrieve this pain and experience it, which results in a reduction of rigidity and bodily tension. The expression of these painful repressed feelings is usually accompanied by clear memories and intellectual insights.*[25]

The Five of Cups cracks the heart like an egg and watches its inner yolk of truth flow out. Mourning doesn't make you smaller; it is expansive. It feels like your chest is collapsing in on itself, but it doesn't give. Sorrowing opens unexplored chambers, and somewhere in that upper trunk you still hold out hope. The Five of Cups finds you looking back at loss. Without getting stuck there, we can give loss its due. Let it take up space while determining—at some point after pouring from the edge of your vessel—to turn toward the future and the love yet to be. But turning toward melancholia is about not being numb. So the Five of Cups restores the feeling capacity. It strips the insulation. This entails feeling the painful feelings we may have been suppressing for years. Positive or negative, we can't protect ourselves from one feeling without sacrificing the other. It's always the stranger that's called the blues. These protective habits keep us sympathetically severed and socially isolated. While the Six of Cups is about the memory bank of self-continuity, the Five tells the reader where and what to discharge. Purging is so painful because it expunges fear from our vessel. The wounding, carving, shedding is an initiation, by which we know the pain Spirit endures to become corporeal.

The love within will not be diminished by small, comfortable containers. This card, then, is about refusing in the way God refuses the containment of the cup. It's the manner in which Spirit confronts us with our futile efforts to try to contain the ocean, or the oceanic nature of love. To desire what cannot be contained means *we* will be the ones shattered. But the brave willingness to be broken for divine fulfillment is not undertaken in vain. What's left when you let go of everything? God. God cascades the soul's pearls to cool the fire of longing. This card turns over with the ocean's invitation: *dive in.* Surrender to the river running into the ocean. Loosen the tight grip of disappointment; surprise is so much better than unmet expectation. Perhaps that harrowing denial was protection and preparation for the glorious comeback. Every shattering can be made into a catalyst toward divine communion. The love wounds open the way for divine approach. The card compassionately cuts into your frozen flesh until you feel the blood flowing again. A love wound is the scar of grace, the evidence of a higher healing. Personal sacrifice and trust commit to holistic reorganization and reunion. This wound documents consecrated reconstitution.

The love of the Five of Cups pierces the veil of our illusions, longings, and separations. The full humanity that is only realized in relation requires the pain and struggle of continually decentering the self, of being willing to let another into the heart, even when it hurts or threatens our most self-cherishing perspectives about individualist self-sufficiency, pride, or egoism.

The Five of Cups is how our interdependency humbles us. To be birthed and to die, we need another. We never come or go alone. When we are ready to acknowledge we are not walking alone, we cannot persist alone, we pull this card. And our grief becomes a blessing that brings us back to God. Assistance is just waiting to be called upon; it never forces itself. The Divine wants your invitation, your acceptance. This card calls upon corporeal prayer, inviting God in so radically we reckon with the discomfort of sleeping organs awakening. If this card forces loss upon our hand, then our role or agency becomes enacted in the choice to make that a loss a sacrifice, something sacred and redemptive that advances us on the path of fulfillment. It is the way to hold on to the lost substance of desire and invest it with new life, a new form. Loss is claimed by sacrifice and becomes a will of renunciation. Renunciation is affirming, saying for *this,* I am willing to give up *that:* doubt, insecurity, addictions, protections. The Five of Cups works to reorient our desire nature by disrupting desire. To give, it takes away. Despite our best efforts we still grapple with the ignorance of what form will fulfill this hunger within. Clarity comes from the well of God, which makes desire pure. Without this substance, every sought-after form would be a synthetic shell. There are spaces in the soul reserved only for God, that only God, only the beloved, can touch.

Five of Pentacles

Any disease that is treated as a mystery and acutely enough feared will be felt to be morally, if not literally, contagious. Thus a surprisingly large number of people with cancer find themselves being shunned by relatives and friends and are the object of practices of decontamination by members of their household, as if cancer, like TB, were an infectious disease. Contact with someone afflicted with a disease regarded as a mysterious malevolency inevitably feels like a trespass; worse, like the violation of a taboo. The very names of such diseases are felt to have a magic power.[26]

Illness, exile, poverty, and despair linger long in the Five of Pentacles. The card's icy touch confronts the reader with the physical, material bodies who comprise the ecological other; those who bear the brunt of environmental exploitation, as "their bodies are discursively perceived as threats to national, racial, or corporeal purity,"[27] as Sarah Jaquette Ray names. Always found on this card are the homeless, wounded wanderers at the cosmic edges, where time decays. This is a card of contagion. No one wants contamination to touch their hands. In medieval times, they hung a bell around the leper's neck to warn others of their approach. Its signal was ironically a tool of avoidance, a reminder of fear, a method to reject and discard individuals. This card rings the bell for the reader to show us what and who we are averting our eyes from. Showing attention, let alone compassion, to those sick, disabled selves whom we leave out in the cold is an act of transgression. These elementally exposed material bodies are every evidence of the systems that displace people. It is a card of insecurity and apocalypse. It unravels time. It approaches decay. It lacks support and deteriorates health. The Five of Pentacles, then, is a card of rejecting rejection. It's for envisioning an environmental ethos that does not necessitate an ecological other in its conception or articulation.

Sontag tells the reader to refrain from finding metaphors in illness because they become moralizing, and they distort the fact that our bodies are simply vulnerable. To engage in characterology, to make a judgment upon the purity of someone's soul, is the card's wariness, for the figures walk isolated from the warmth of the spiritual mercy reserved for those behind the stained-glass window. Illness is no metaphor—it is a reality—but the soul is demoralized when any disease or illness is treated as an evil. This card exposes. Under shame hides hurt. Physical pain compounded by an existential ache. We deny dying as some unnatural, uncivilized, or obscene thing to be obscured. We punish people by impoverishing them. That's neither retribution nor repatriation. What's needed now is restorative care. Only the attitude with which the state condemns people to death is abominable, disgusting. It will be a long, hard walk to find a healthy society, a warm and welcoming place within white supremacist capitalist America. Many suffer too long in this illusory potential.

The Five of Pentacles finds the bodies that are disposed of, in danger, wounded, or healing. The unmentionables, the unsightly, the nonconformists, the ones stripped of title and status, the outcasts, the expendable, the forgotten, the lost, the walked-over, the ignored, the betrayed, the underground, the rejected, the ones forced to the margins. A Five of Pentacles consciousness finds value where others cannot, where they are blinded by a morality that disguises prejudice. It is this card that presences the nonconforming bodies that the state attempts to absence. It is the dumping ground of societies outcasts, it is where the queers reside, troubled by pollution and endemic poverty.

Though the relations among these figures are ambiguous, perhaps owing more to circumstance than choice, they continue on together. The only warmth found in this card, where they walk barefoot in the snow, is the enduring warmth of not being alone. There is no moving forward alone. Without the risk of attempting to love another, life is just not livable. It's not just uninteresting; it's ruinous. This card comes with the one who will walk with you in grief and who stands with you when you need to stand out in the cold and cry. The cold keeps the company of loneliness. There is no time for fair-weather friends when the world and the soul are under attack.

While illness and its cures may be romanticized by embarking upon a voyage, some psychedelic trip that takes us out of the daily pace of the world, healing will be found in radical inclusion, prompted by clarifying the conditions of subordination. The Five of Pentacles is connected to the Hierophant, so *curanderos* may be required to call back the lost parts of the soul and facilitate spiritual cleansing. However, be clear of puritanical conditioning that dichotomizes *what* is clean and pure from *who* is filthy or impure as a basis for justifying the neglect of abject humiliation inflicted upon them. This card keeps the reader from scapegoating individuals when it is the hierarchical institutions that need condemnation.

The Five of Pentacles summons a shared bodily vulnerability in the face of our planet's changing climate and diminishing resources. Environmental racism is enacted upon those deemed "racially expendable" by corporations, through their disregard for the environment. The multinational corporation and its participation in environmental racism are aligned with the forces of the earlier conquest of America. Stephanie LeMeanger describes those affected by such exclusion as "humanity defined as ecological, in the sense of those whose 'way of life' is conditioned by a regional ecosystem" and those who "may as well be recognized as humanity unprotected by rights or status—the human animal whose primary community is nonhuman."[28] The lost subjects of modernity are foregrounded in the Five of Pentacles. Those excluded from modernity are most vulnerable to environmental racism, as those included in modernity are those whose life practices are not clearly tied to place. Yet the excluded form a community all their own. Latent solidarity must be catalyzed in the face of ecological disaster and the capitalist expropriation and destruction of their resources. I see this card and envision a world in which working-class communities of color are not forced to bear the brunt of environmental risk in their labor for a livelihood.

"In the context of internalized colonialism, the material conditions of poverty and violence that condition the colonial situation appear muted to the colonized because they are understood to be the past product of one's own cultural deficiencies."[29] Being labeled as individually devoid of virtue or culturally deficient is a type of impoverishment connected to pauperism. Colonialism has enacted penury not just materially but also spiritually. To remedy the feelings of abjection, being barren or bankrupt, we must recycle and rethink encoded meaning. Let this card of susceptibility expose the canonical cultural texts and their universalizing and exclusionary machinations. "To recircuit its working to account for, include and empower minority identities and identification," the process of disidentification must be enacted.[30] To deal with scarcity is to deal with being queer, and we deal with both in the Five of Pentacles.

> *The faggots are constantly reminding me that in moments of apparent scarcity, our best defense is to respond with abundance. When it feels like we are truly abandoned, there are moonbeams and trees to turn to, to talk and make love with. Bees to listen to. It seems counter-intuitive. We have been taught so forcefully, especially in the deeply conservative time that we live in, that we must look out only for ourselves and indeed conserve our resources. That our resources are what others have deemed valuable—money, time, material things. But the faggots have other ideas. They say that "the more you share, the less you need." They make a way out of no way, and build a life together in fugitivity. They see renewable resources where others might not. They see their sluttiness and madness and magic as surplus. They thrive on cum alone.*[31]

The Five of Pentacles calls upon subaltern communities, those headed north symbolically joined together in literal fugitivity. Like the historic maroon communities, these are the ones who maintain a refusal to be subject to legacies of slavery, racial capitalism, privatization, criminalization, and incarceration.[32] In the repudiation of such psychic and material structures, we can find an outlet for the despair, anger, and rage against social repression in the Five of Pentacles, as we come to reject the values and ideology of capitalist colonialism that justify continued bodily betrayal.

SIX

"Becoming who you are" is not only a paradox motivating us to question our assumed identities; it is an abiding challenge even if one decides affirmatively to engage this paradoxical conundrum. I take its meaning to be something like "Be true to yourself (or to your most deeply felt convictions and beliefs), and act accordingly." Yet this remains an unreliable oversimplification and possibly even a misleading maxim, since our deepest convictions might be held in error, and what many take to be a self might well be a metaphysical illusion. Well, then, how does one ascribe self-knowledge to oneself (or others), and how does one decide what course to take when we come face-to-face with life's important crossroads? Is one driven to a choice by powerful instincts and desires? Or, perhaps, does one look outward and survey the many societal factors and forces that have come to place us at this particular point of intersection in our lives, and, with the greatest effort at understanding such a play of forces and their impact on one's life, does one deliberate and take action ranging from trying something out experimentally to committing to long term projects?[1]

Six reformulates the detached, disassembled self that was torn apart in Five. Every absence born of Five is made essential in Six, each sound distinct, resonant. Freed from the limitation of fixed meaning, Six permits ecstasy for no reason. Six is yet another stage of the transmutation of identity. Opposites are incorporated toward the maximum benefits of mutuality as they meet without destroying each other. The process of internal balance incurred, the meeting and melding with the spiritual self, the wisdom of continuous recombination as a strategy of composing harmony. Six is Medea revivifying her father-in-law with rites of purification, three in fire, three in water, joining in the steam that refines and purifies as we ought to, working upon each other toward a fuller fruition.

Six is the star of the compass pointing north no matter how disorienting the crossroads. Six is the meeting point between dedication and surrender. Its promise is that our unconscious materia will be made into a more sacred substance. It is volatilization. Intensive extremities release the fixed from its prison and unlock its deeper dimensions. No longer a discrete entity but a fluid *medium,* a constant project of revision and self-interruption. Visceral sensitivity within the experiences that transcend mental understanding in their sensuous epiphany constitutes the Sixth sense. Six is the silhouette of diamond light. It is the enhanced recognition of intuitive, subtle, and sensual capacity. It is approving of our most powerful gifts, an acceptance that relates the physical to the spiritual, a knowing that salvation comes from below as it does from above. Six is the self that would be incomplete without sexual liberation, without cleansing the disgust from our animal body.

Pythagoras thought Six was the perfect number, the structure of creation, the audience and the performer that make real the myth of their shared existential significance. Six is futuristic in its vision. It chooses celibacy as an expression of sexual liberation rather than being subject to contexts of persecution and torment. Celibacy as a sexual choice is equal to any other choice of sexual expression. Six refuses to profane the sexual as anything less than the power of liberation. Six is a way for the physical to more clearly inhabit the psychic space of naked exposure. It is the incarnation of heaven on Earth, an equilibrium of divine scale. It is passionate interest reciprocated. To move beyond the boundaries of race, class, and cultural conditionings, Six offers a body vehicle for spirit or a galactic bridge toward the pearl of vast beauty within the temple of our interiority; or it is a key that cracks into the luminous individuality of the reader's radiant depths.

What else could Six be but poetry? The word bends against its inherent logic, imploding upon itself until it becomes a love refrain. The blank page a canvas for exploring the unnameable. It is a labor that never tires, its flower unfolding continuously, as does the capacity to receive the gifts that are given. Six commences the long, mystical conversation of friendship, the interplay of listening, trusting, disclosing, and becoming intimate by each word. Spirits and bodies flow together, sharing a presence of love evolving with mutual selfhood created in tandem. It is the motion of the river, stabilized in its constant direction of cleansing change. Six sails free of purpose, unbound by the constraints of space-time. Six relieves sense as it steps toward spontaneity within the simplicity of existing without pretext, excuse, apology, or presumption. It is pure emptiness in the presence of now.

The Lovers

When it was time to tell him I loved him—when it was what every romance had determined I should do—I spoke in the name of will. I will love. Love as an action not a feeling only. I will love. In the early days of having sex with him (when he could see me, when the Gypsy woman would leave now and then on her own small journeys) I would make love as though my body existed only as the fulfillment of his desire. It was an instrument–surrendered to the feeling of sexual ecstasy. With him I discovered my flesh. In no way physical in other locations of life, I suddenly found my body exerting force and power through longing. Sex was sweet communion. It was my body. Sometimes in the midst of all-consuming desire I could hear the words from communion *Take, eat, this is my body.* I could hear Gary Snyder reading the words from a poem *is this our body.* It was a poem about seeing nakedness for the first time and being renewed.[2]

Everyone pulls the Lovers hoping to find love looking for them. I had hoped to be writing this chapter while feeling the force of its falling, its rising. I write wondering, curious in cafes about when I will feel the arrows of eros claim my fleshy offerings. I look to the page to locate my language of love. I move as a singular body of erotic inquiry in the social matrix of new cities. The Lovers are the ones who show themselves, who look to actually face love. They are the ones who present themselves, bare, vulnerable, and unashamed to desire. I wonder just how exposed I can actually be. I practice in solitude. I strip and sing and see devotion strewn across my body. I let angels of love look at me. Blessed be the Lovers of liberation who see sweet mercy where others see shame. Pulling the Lovers is especially striking when you consider yourself alone. It is an intimation; nothing stands in the way but a willingness to look, approach, be seen, be touched, and taste. The Lovers discover an opening that leads to something sacred and untapped: the other lover's body.

The liberators are the ones telling me I am worthy enough to hold love's gaze, a generosity that sets me free. I pull the Lovers and believe I will one day again know that moment of rapture, of recognition "where we can face one another as we really are, stripped of artifice and pretense, naked and not ashamed."[3]

The Lovers' display receives celestial witness by the stellar audience of angels, one that understands the consciousness exploding emblazoned in their lover bodies. The Lovers declare love in action. Their language of pleasure is vocal in the spread-open body. They stand in positions of full perception. The moment made conscious of erotic desire, the moment when you let the other know your love is an option available. They teach a body language divinely articulated. There is no place Lovers will not look, no place Lovers will not speak, no place Lovers will not love. Every geography and every crevice becomes a canvas of their naked piety. Theirs is a free state. The common ground they share is the body of pleasure.

I cannot resist a love that transcends borders, of body, of language. I cannot resist a feeling that makes me want to hit high notes when everyone else says I should stay silent. The Lovers love like the sunlight that cannot be taken away. Like the mystery of following God and then there *you* are. And here we are finding love together, going where we thought no one ever would. After the encounter with the beloved, nothing looks the same. This meeting that is the real living. After tasting the Lovers' sacred satiation, nothing else will satisfy the soul.

The Lovers reconcile the confrontation between spirit and flesh in the offerings of poetry recited in the dark, sweaty aftermath of their meeting. To be in love is for both the body and the soul to be in relationship with another. The greater capacity of language emerges after Lovers talk. All language is the epiphany of intercourse. Sudden powers become pronounced, improved perception, intuition, sensitivity, a gift of Gemini; eros making body language a reality of pleasure's possibility. Eros and the tongue could not exist without each other, for there are no two ever more intimate. Theirs is the true word, reflective action taken to transform the world in their dialogue of creation. From their speech we know humanity is not built in silence. One of the curses of segregation and subordination is the imposition of silence, but the Lovers give each other back to themselves.

In the journey toward sexual freedom the Lovers choose each other. This choice is a recognition of agency, and of consent, whereby we meet no other authority than the *yes* of our own yearning. Lovers cannot fake orgasm. True love withholds nothing. This is no arranged political union of power. In the affairs of the heart there is no other appeal than to the beloved. It is *our* permission to give to love. We allow ourselves to love or not. We *do* love, or we don't. It is a choice made alone, but in the presence of potential relation. It is a responsibility carried by each. Love never assumes. It is an inquiry of care. It's a search for how many ways can I say yes. Love is only a way of saying yes.

Or is it only ordained by a higher hand that we could glimpse God in each other? Is it only when God says yes that we comprehend Love's articulation? The Lovers appear when most feel they are succumbing to fate or reckoning with subtle bonds that bind even apparent strangers. It arrives with a wish made to love and be loved. This is not something that can be manufactured. Perhaps this is why I struggle with creating new ways of naming the erotic that is ecstatic, the flesh meeting faith. Maybe this is the Lovers' respect, the patience that cultivates intimacies, the waiting for divine consent, that is whatever moment grace deems our fruit is ripe enough to be tasted, known in the miraculous moment when there stands a lover for whom all we want is to be well-fed from our portion. But for many love is an act of defiance, making the lover of a subversive a subversive. This is a morality of desire I understand:

When he spoke of disordered desire, he focused on its power to form and deform. Our desires can make us as big or small as their object. Bad friends can make us bad, as Paul reminds the Corinthians. But good company can make us good. And God's company, says John, does not rest till he makes us fit for his company. God's aim is to make us gods by participation, as he is God by nature—like fire turning everything to fire. In short love does not just admire; it creates likeness.[4]

The Lovers present us a chance to reshape the practices of desire, to shed constraining constructs and realize eros is always in process even as we return to our native forms for its expression. It taps on the animal nature of us, and the will of us, to be open, honest, and transparent, to choose to be there and to do the work of love and relationship. The card and its conflation with choice helps the querent come to the realization that choice does not equate to freedom, despite its illusory presentation as such. What choice is more personal, intimate, and profound than who we give our hearts to? But how much agency can be realized here when the universe conspires to love through us? Often choice is a temptation of will, an obscuring test of desire. A choice that confuses the self-concept may be considered sinful if we veer from an innate purpose or pursuit. Clear and informed consent is a choice ready to assume full liability for the consequences therein. The Lovers feel desire's tension for the sacred *and* the profane burning inside, and with each willful act of love a fuller vision of self is seen. The Lovers find in others themselves, establishing a character of relational composition.

Their challenge is to know there are more than brief moments of sensual gratification. To know that carnality comes with vulnerability, and transparency is the most honest communication. Many would rather risk their hearts than risk a life without love. To see to it that the deep, spontaneous awakening in their meeting is not fleeting, Lovers require constant responsiveness. Their eros is all demanding and appetite-elevating. In the way they imbue each moment with sensitivity they become sophisticated, nuanced feelers. Erotic, intimate, personal engagement has no substitute. The real choice of the Lovers is between control and illusion or surrender, trust, and truth. In the continual discovery of who they might be becoming, who they want to be, whose voice, vision, and body emerges in love, Lovers stand in loving perception. The Lover's gaze is penetrating but pleasurable.

Meet the eyes of someone who truly sees you and holds the vision of possibly becoming more together than we are alone. As Father Iain recognizes, "For God, to gaze is to love—a gospel gaze which blazes its way into the person's heart. He does not simply look at the beautiful; his look makes a person beautiful."[5]

It could be winter all around, but it is spring where Lovers stand. Their eroticism remedies alienation. The Lovers are strangely compelling, finding us in the company of another whom we are deeply committed to growing with, because more than we enjoy their company, energy, or touch, we like who *we* are around them and who we are together. This requires an integrity of self. We can withstand disillusion when we are in touch with the truth of our heart. Lovers teach us to be more than mere reflections of what others say, think, or want, sacrificing voice just to be in relationship. Ariel's ethos will not suffice. I want a relationship with voice. Dialogue is an act of love. Without love there is no communication, as the continuous creation of the world is dependent upon the expressed commitment to others. The Lover's voice is poetry I long to write, but I can only go so far without the beloved. I humble myself to enter the care of conversation, recognizing no self-sufficiency supplants the dialogue of love. I want new palettes of emotion to arise from the chemistry of connection. There are ecstatic oceans I can only dream of diving into, having already braved the darker waters of my lonely disappointment. Yet the Lovers turn up to remind me I am not alone. The Lovers tend to the various relationships that nourish various needs in relationships that are equally valuable. I find that a new voice emerges with each distinct relationship: no two Lovers are the same. To say all I want to say, in all the ways I want to, I cultivate a botanical garden of relationships. I enter a Venusian paradise that is deep and plentiful, overwhelmed by the soul's budding beauty there. The Lovers aspire to a relational ecosystem where everyone is thriving and no one is love-starved, because they are available for love from more than one.

All Sixes are expression of the Lovers' principle; of love is your kin, love is the thread sustaining our relations. Help a woman and child cross, because they are kin. For celebrating the triumph of each other, of championing each other's beauty because they are kin. Of shameless expressions of sexuality, eroticism, innocence, and trust because we are kin. Of mutual aid, wealth redistribution, and the mercy of giving without any expectations of receiving because we are kin.

The Lovers' imperfection is redeemed in the generosity of their honest affection. Here are those who are attempting, together, to understand love as they profess it to each other. When sex heals the psyche, it becomes sacred. Writers of times past have always struggled to reconcile the mind/body split that says love and lust cannot coexist. The Lovers, naked and natural, know of no such division. The bodies of Lovers are where the sensual and spiritual meet and mate. If God made their bodies, their souls, then too their desires. Here carnal consummation becomes an act of devotion. Love cannot be a disembodied emotion; it must be consciously linked with a free sexuality. The Lovers are our bodies, with God's approval. The silent and swift feeling of an absolving blessing in our coming, together. Let us love openly, and legitimately.

The Tower

We are locked in a fight with settlers whose viciousness and savagery compensate for the precarity their presence makes in lands that do not claim them. We have burned their villages to the ground before to protect our lands and nations. We will do it again to liberate our relatives. These will not be the fires of destruction but of creation and reclamation. Only in the ashes of the bordertown will we find the raw material for our liberation.[6]

The Tower taught me tarot is more than psychological inquiry—it is life-saving divine communication, a technology of prophecy. I pulled the Tower on October 30, 2019, and awoke at three a.m. on October 31 to frantic screams from my father, sirens shouting "evacuate," a night black not from the absence of light but from ash filling the air. The sole illumination offered by the red of the flame. I awoke to this hellscape only to flee the all-consuming light. Emergency leaves no room for passivity; agency must be enacted. The scorching conflagration of light cracks the dark. Never have I had a more visceral experience of the irrefutable psychic sight of my soul. While I was terrified by the fire threatening my home, my life, my community, I was fortified by the rest of my morning spread, holding onto the faith that if the Tower came to fulfillment, then so too would the cards that communicated survival and safety. By the grace of shifting winds, my home did not burn down, but others on my block had no such luck. Ultimately all in the community were safe, and were ever closer, bonded not by our shared trauma but the responsiveness of care that arose alongside the flames.

Yet the trauma of evacuating a fire could not be a more literal manifestation of the Tower and its chaotic, violent associations. This experience marked a time of deconstruction in my life, a period of terrifying uncertainty with only the recognition that life as I had built it was falling to pieces. The Tower, with martial force, strikes down hubris, misproportioned egoism, and ambition for summits that lead nowhere good. It is a card of crisis because it symbolizes those moments where we are confronted with the ways we delude, deny, and diminish ourselves. Suddenly our sources of security prove false, illusory attachments severed, and a self-concept shattered. Suddenly our lives go up in smoke, and all you can taste is the soot of deceit. Fire, as it comes to be possessed by humans in its primordial, mythic origin, is the fruit of rebellion. The progenitor of humanity, Prometheus, offers himself to see his creation have a fighting chance at survival. Fire inspires civilization. Its burning activation incurs consciousness and catalyzes creativity that comes by way of sacrifice. The Tower and the Moon represent the ways in which the cards are dealers of chaos. By embracing the summoning of disorder to break out of the prison of certainty and the conditioned patterns of behavior, something new becomes possible. There is then a celebratory opportunity in the crisis and in the calling out of one's lamentations.

> *In the making of freedom, the destruction of slavery and the destruction of planter homes were of a piece. "The burning, slashing and punishment," writes Charles Royster, "were inseparable from the freedom—a single memory." Slaves linked the two explicitly. Savilla Burrell remembered claiming her freedom when the Yankees arrived and "burnt de big house, stables, barns [and] gin house."*[7]

What violence would you endure in your determination to get free, to wield your liberty? Can you defy a power that insists on claiming you, that may resort to severity to ensure self-preservation? Could you choose the freedom of death over a life of bondage? The Tower confronts the querent with these questions. There is easy comfort offered in espousing nonviolence and inclusive love, embraced all too readily by white sensibility, a way to self-indulge ideas of nobility and virtue while pacifying currents of rebellion. To maintain an existence under oppression that offers no dignity is no option of love at all. To hell with respectability, complacency, and conformity.

Emancipatory truth buckles the foundations of hierarchical domination. In general, cities and towns are for men, designed by men, existing as literal structures of patriarchy. They are a fantasy of the Wild West expansion project deeply committed to amassing capital with the forced labor of the enslaved upon stolen land. These bordertowns arise in the historic, social, and psychic rupturing of kinship as physical sites of severance that enforce the colonizer's fantasy. They are the literal manifestation of the state's enduring commitment to colonial violence. The Tower is a glaring reminder that the Earth and the sky are tools of freedom's power that overcome white supremacist structures inside and out. The first principles of freedom are violent, destructive achievements in human history. The Civil War, the Haitian Revolution, the storming of the Bastille, the Attica prison riots. Fanon famously recognizes that decolonization will be a violent event if it must, but the undue emphasis on his violence is fetishized, reduced to anachronism, assimilation, and/or taming.[8] The violence of insurrection, of emancipation, is not in parity with the senseless violence of domination, abuse, and enslavement. That violence estranges us. Violence is not the point of our shared struggle but the restoration of dignity to the colonized. When this truth of freedom refuses to be repressed any longer, the Tower falls.

The Tower has broken the spell of inviolability. Now you see that only flames could adorn the hell that is the plantation. Anything owned by the police gets set on fire. The Tower targets not only the annihilation of the property of plantation and prison, but also annihilation of the property relation that is whiteness, a perverse freedom defined by its ability to have absolute control over another, which is the height of American individualism, a homicidal settler worldview that must and can absolutely burn in the flame if our existence is ever to be transfigured into Native freedom. The Tower entails the borders of rupture that exist everywhere; the settler order constantly confronting Native order.[9] The Tower clearly demonstrates structural violence. An image of it cast down by thunder and lightning inspires the radical imagining of abolition. As mass incarceration is a defining feature of settler colonialism, there can be no decolonization without the abolition of the prison and the police. The Tower orients the reader to a life liberated of panopticonesque self-surveillance of modern media. It tells us there is no peaceful coexistence with settler colonialism. There can be no lasting change or reconciliation within without the downfall of violent structures and of the relational dynamics of domination. Being born Native in America is being born into criminality, because this being that has never not been claimed by the land threatens the legitimacy of the settler's property claims. Their very presence violates settler law. Therefore the abolition of what the settler claims as private property can only entail liberation. There is no peace with a structure hell-bent on human destruction. The Tower engages the material conditions of colonialism and decolonization and is thus necessarily unsettling. The Tower is praxis aspiring toward a world without borders.

The Tower's devastation reverberates in all dimensions. It enforces the confrontation with our lack of control to do the work of making us honest. And in honesty we become worthy of the love bestowing our awakening. This language of freedom entails the violence of separation. It endures even that great chasm of death. All language comes from the abyss of God. The tongue that cuts initiates the reader into the symbolic, the occult, into language itself. The tongue that talks back, says *no* and *no more,* the wild tongue that cannot be tamed, is one that will not be cut out. This is the Tower. The painful wrenching apart, the unbearable loss revealing that life resiliently endures. The first time reality breaks with our expectation, the only response we are capable of seems to be disappointment, and the only interpretation—failure. The Tower takes you to this starting place again and again, not to punish you, but to free you. There is more possibility than you think. There are more ways this can play out. There is more than you know. Dive into that. Jump into chaos and come out something completely different, something free to arise spontaneously, fluidly, continuously.

It sees through the illusion of permanence. It shows identity is in flux rather than a point of stasis to arrive at. It frees us from the fantasy that we can pull ourselves together at once, once and for all. It destroys any self-concept built by repressed desire, codependency, and/or addiction. It forces us to leave these parts behind. When we begin looking inward to discover a truer sense of self, we eventually and inevitably confront the false masks we have put on. The power in the moment when we realize we have betrayed ourselves is born of the Tower. This challenging process is tempered by a willingness to release false personas, to heal sexuality, and to regain agency over our lives. Trauma expelled from the body propels an immense energy current of reclamation. Lost pieces of soul return like filaments to a magnet.

Freed are we of the West and its claims to be a true, impartial arbiter of reality. Capitalism ceases to be credible. There is no happily ever after that can be bought and sold. Our identity, our meaning, is not carved in stone but written in sand and subject to shifting winds. To sustain the self we must become increasingly multidimensional. Body mind spirit past present future above below earth wind sky lover friend family interpenetrate in more complexity. The Tower offers a voice that rewrites legacies of loss and exile into homecoming and recovery.

The Tower inspires the reader to risk disorientation, to speak in paradox, simultaneity, and become multiconversant with a split tongue. To be a diviner is to be open to the many ways in which gods speak to and through us. Disarray composes the reader's augury. The divinely destroyed Tower of Babel is a reminder of our multilingual capacity. The Tower makes a skilled reader, one who can use the cards to perform a type of cesarean delivery, freeing the light that is determined to live. Readers and readings are so helpful because they tend to the disorientation we experience most devastatingly, the sudden shifts of narrative that reshape our entire relationship to being. The Tower readers are subversive, ones who can tell a new story with the same parts, ones who challenge institutional narratives and their methods of legitimacy. They are the ones who redistribute meaning when they read. They are ones who love you enough to throw you into the flame. They disruptively challenge consensual reality and the neat categories of us/them. Like Freire, they problematize our worlds, helping our unique voice to emerge from the contradictions of self in settler society. Who else could we turn to in times of dislocation and disorientation but the queers who've always resided there? They know the Tower is the forbidden pleasure of penetration released. They are green shoots cracking rock. They unearth our nativity and show us roots that we could no longer see are still alive. From the fault lines they create and tend to, new knowledge is generated, new cultures are constructed. They refuse the monolithic perspective of social organization. From them we learn to dwell in the truth of our uncertain historical position. This dwelling allows us to never be forced into one place, perspective, or picture of reality. Unconstrained by the dominators, they experience multiple realities. They shed skin, shapeshift, and speak in tongues.

The Tower forces the reader to bow before the potential of what lies beyond the limits of their imagination. Tarot is a dance with this potential, rupture working toward revelation. Readers make it so the rupturing of identity is recognizable, sewing frayed edges into new designs. This Tower summoning of chaos is processed into being through the very body of the reader. The reader is changed as reality changes through the reader. The body of the witch disrupts the perfect circle of time. The Tower cuts into the fabric of space and shoves you into a new universe, making you multiversal. It teaches us when to tear ourselves apart and how to reassemble. It tears down the hubris of thinking you have sovereignty without the responsibility or consequences of your actions. The Tower does not care about petty concerns; it forces full attention. And only a form that faces you head-on is honest. Death cannot be denied.

When the only answer left is chaos, it is the Tower that speaks. Thunder ends silent imprisonment. The Tower is willing to burn it all down. Every stone and brick blocking our path, keeping us contained, comes crumbling apart. The volcano eruption that replenishes the barren land of a broken spirit comes with no hesitation. Nothing can be more restorative, more reclaiming of freedom than the catharsis of destruction. The Tower comes to me as a dawning realization: *I get to be free.* I'd never thought I'd be free like this. Suddenly I see opportunity flying into a head-first embrace of the dark. This free-fall into freedom is the accumulation of action. I am *present* for this perception shift. Finally, I have stepped away from a structure, a self, a place, a relationship whose scheduled demolition can now commence. The Tower is a turning point, an initiator of the most uncomfortable change. It overturns all relationships. Any lover, parent, friend who enforces the status quo or holds you to comfortable autohistories of victimization is ejected. Upon the ritual pyre I offer who I have known myself to be. The Tower oversees this passage by inferno. But you are not alone. Many before you have lost everyone and everything to the fire. And many have risen triumphant from the ashes. Thank the Tower for cracking the facade of the former solitary self and its reified beliefs. In the fire's light you can see clearly the fictitious parts of you, the made-up story imposed upon you and internalized. You walk with ancestors, planets, deities, and the all-pervasive force of revolution that is love. Nature is alive, responsive, conscious, and will receive you, even messy and disassembled. You will no longer endure the pain you assumed was inevitable, unalterable, and fixed in some foundational reality. It all goes up in smoke, this mental fabrication, this prison, this settler state.

Six of Swords

Miguel's trip home, from his out existence as an academic Chicano to the semicloseted familial space of identity formation, exemplifies the kind of shuttling I describe. Of course, this movement is not only a byproduct of Miguel's status as a queer son; all of the family, in some way, experience migrancy. The text explains as much when it articulates the family ethos: "They were migrant, not immigrant, souls. They simply and naturally went from one bloody side of the river to the other and into a land that just a few decades earlier had been Mexico. They became border Mexicans with American citizenship."[10]

The Six of Swords is about the avenues of escape amid omnipresent landscapes of settler colonialism laden with carceral compulsion. In the boat, you aren't located anywhere in particular, but rather marked by a state of migrancy. Migrancy is characterized by its need to move back and forth, to bridge, temper, contrast, compare, exchange, compound. Migrant souls occupy at least two spaces at once and are always in transit. The Six of Swords images the migrant soul, the status that is nonstatic.

The Six of Swords's drive is to make language that dispels the illusion of privatized separation with their hybrid being that wears down borders. The Six of Swords unveils borders as incoherent. The card is a construction from these contradictions. Those in the boat don't seek assimilation into the mainstream matrix but work to restructure it from within. These are the beings who show the way across seemingly uncrossable thresholds. It is the subjectivity of traversing identity vectors that occupy adjacent, distinct spaces, for it is uncomfortable within any singular discourse of minority subjectivity. The Six of Swords negotiates a fragmentary existence by fusing the impossibly disparate into constant construction of new identities that transcend the either-or thinking rooted in white dominant culture, knowing they can have a both-and. World travel of this sort requires surrendering an arrogant perception of otherness.

The Six of Swords has sailed every river to find that indeed they all lead back to the ocean. The Six of Swords is the island forming itself in the aftermath of destruction, the eruption of its most primal power. This constant process of destructive self-construction creates new topographies to travel to, to recombine the fragmented psyche and heal the trauma of various intersecting oppressions. This is a remedy to the debilitating psychological, physical, and emotional harm of displacement and exile as encountered in the Five of the Swords, the card that marks land theft, body theft. This card restores relationality. It is a translator, helping our minds understand and arrange all the voices vying for expression within. It calls upon revisionary identification, one that accesses "different strategies of viewing, reading, and locating the 'self' within representational systems and disparate life-worlds that aim to displace or occlude a minority subject."[11] These interpretive turns are survival strategies. The fiction of our future survival, happiness, and freedom is made real in a lament that does not collapse into nostalgia, but rather takes flight. The song that finds you, forces you to hop on the instrument of expression, listening with care and love, for this song of grace cares and loves you. The verse that calls us inward and away from the master is the song of the Six of Swords.

It concerns the stories we tell ourselves about ourselves. To attain an alternate ending the psyche rewrites origins. We are gracefully carried across waters of doubting despair. The victim of despondency becomes the survivor of uncertainty. The scars of my body tell a story of resilience, protection, healing, and an enduring will to live, not a story of painful abuse. With this card I interrogate my actions and dispositions in the search for integrity. The ethos of the Six of Swords is rooted in ameliorating the contradiction between our words and actions, or our words and their meaning and our understanding. I use it in my resolve to take accountability for my healing, happiness, and health. I use it as I seek to construct worlds to exist in where I am free to form a complex identity that transcends division.

"In other words, despite the homophobic attempts within her community to isolate and shame her, her transgression empowers her to redefine and recreate her cultural location as a queer Chicana and 'new mestiza' as well as to forge deep alliances in solidarity with others facing comparable experiences across a multiplicity of cultural location. She continually affirms her humanity in view of the many faces of dehumanization."[12]

Whereas in the Five of Swords desire is dismissed and identity banished by the dominant, the Six of Swords shows they can be tempered and rewritten. It is reinvention, rearticulation, that allows the reader to maintain their desire by maintaining the difference in what and how we desire. If one is queered by desire, then so too is the object of desire. Our desire is a queer force. All the dismembered traditions and silenced voices recohere in the yearning to travel to a free space to simply be. These spaces summon the few souls with similar ambitions so the intense psychic energy can take form as we experience the joys and risks of self-exploration. This space requires the freedom to question, to change, and to resist. While the colonialist travels only to take, exploit, and eradicate, the Six of Swords's subjectivity builds bridges between inner and outer worlds to travel across, a method that presupposes reciprocity and respect. A travel guide has much to show us, knowing the way to somewhere new as they do, and yet meets us where we are. They travel with great humility in their sensitive awareness. They are more akin to a therapist, a way-shower through the traumatized terrain of our inner world.

By finding an interior integrity of spirit that is conditionless, that exists beyond circumstance and travels with us always and in every dimension and direction, we are empowered to follow our own inner navigation toward freedom. The arrangement of physical spaces then readjusts to mirror the refreshing psychosocial atmosphere. There is relief in the in between. There is an entry into an environment whereby we become collaborative in creation, cognizant of our agency and of the responsibility required of its maintenance.

The Six of Swords is a release from recent intensity toward grace's gentle transitions. In the pursuit of ourselves we move past fear. An answered call for assistance sees restricting paradigms and physical limitations fall away. The sorrow of separation and change encountered is remedied with a different pen on different paper, writing a new life chapter, in a new context of beauty and potential. Freire tells us "liberating action necessarily involves a movement of perception and volition."[13] Both are taken up in this card. While moving into a new world can be jarring, it is much less so with an ability to embrace attitudes of curiosity. Moving to a new space incites observation, reflection, and creativity in this fresh context for the whole being to experience itself. Despite physical and mental preparations, emotional movement is an always unexpected journey. Dealing with such depth of feeling can unsettle others, but still we must continue. The Six of Swords is a guide in these emotional currents that give greater capacity for depth and range to embodied expression. It is an interstitial space that allows our being to be more responsive and interactive, recycling and restoring. Charting new physical locations in real time corresponds to the discovery of new inner terrain, a type of holistic movement that solidifies personal integrity if the movement is in coordination.

The Six of Swords takes the raw material of physical pain, the scars of tears and blood, and fertilizes hope. The Six of Swords entails all the meditation and spiritual practices that center the sense of self with enough strength to not be shriveled up by the acts of aggression one might encounter, those incidents that may compromise the will or shatter the confidence. The alchemy of meditation, of reflection, allows me to carry things in such a way that they no longer paralyze or wound. I am able to navigate a culture of domination without being constantly wounded. As self-understanding deepens, the perception of personal and collective history and possibility widens. It is now well known that the emotional pain of my mother, our mother, and her mother and her mother can manifest as holes in newborns' hearts. The emotional and physical trauma of their lives literally transcribed onto DNA and passed down to you, to me. The Six of Swords regards the responsibility to heal on behalf of our ancestors and descendants. The mind begins to deal with the body's generational memory, a delicate meeting. A commitment to authenticity even when it is at the expense of things going smoothly or easily has a destination worth arriving at, even as we carefully maneuver. The card with its cloaked figures, always assumed to be a mother and child, seems to say "do not sacrifice authenticity to be accommodating."

Here we find the freedom to be gained when we reject borders, nation-states, and separation of spirit, land, body, people, and place. Here we are changing the psychoaffective equilibrium. Here we are to investigate the inner effects of colonialism, to turn the inculcation of inferiority into self-empowerment. Here offered is a potential means of evading the liberal politics of colonial recognition with self-affirmative perception and representation. It is a pathway toward self-determination through the struggle to recognize ourselves as free, dignified, and distinct contributors to humanity.

While seeking state recognition may interpellate[14] us into the position required for subordination, a personal, inward recognitive process calls forth and empowers individuals within communities of resistance. This work is not reactionary. It provides theoretical tools that enable the reader to determine the relative transformability of certain fields of colonial power over others. To search for our own decolonial praxis is to journey with this card.

It takes time to explore new structures of the mind not bound by dominance. The Six of Swords is practiced in this patience, telling us no matter how long it takes, we will get across. The Six of Swords is the visceral reality of a struggle for life against death. Like you, it knows the pain of losing life to senseless violence. Like you, I grew up learning to carefully navigate cemeteries, finding my way to family member after family member memorialized, confronted with the question of what will be the accumulation of my life that refuses normalization. We will address pain in a way that offers healing, promotes resiliency, and presents a chance to rewrite the impacts of adversity, so that as we remember ourselves we only ever realize our strength and beauty.

Six of Wands

Butch queens dressed like soldiers, saluting, the epitome of ants marching. A gorgeous trans woman drenched in cream cashmere, a broad-brimmed hat, Madison Ave. on her mind. A queer B-boy in an Adidas track suit, smoking a blunt, strutting across the Ballroom floor like he just snuck out of his girlfriend's bedroom window. Realness is an aspirational category. It allows you, within the safe and brave space of a ball, to finally inherit your human right to leap from one end of the identity spectrum to the other, from male to female, butch to fem, gay to straight, basic to sharp, servant to Cinderella, and on and on. The person walking realness is like an immigrant (or the more comparably pejorative "illegal alien") finally being welcomed with open arms into the fold. It is indeed the chance to "blend" into the pool of the accepted—yes, partially as a means of escaping "reality," but in some cases, like those of trans folks, it can be a rare space for self-actualization in the world and preservation from it. Both can be true, and that's what makes realness compelling. It is both in defiance of what bell hooks maintains to be society's greatest threat—the imperialist, capitalist, white supremacist patriarchy, and an assimilation into it.[15]

Being king is a performance. Ruling is a theater. It always has been. The greatest spectacle of pomp and circumstance, posturing, beauty, commodification, social hierarchy, ambition. The Six of Wands opens the royal fantasy. The feeling of walking embraced, celebrated, and elevated among a community, a people, who honor your name when it is spoken. We all want to walk in our power, but that power is nowhere as palpable as when you are amid kin. When you kill or conquer, you get to be king for a day. That has been the master's literal criterion, but when this card comes to the queer it's a hand played to *slay,* to display an excellence of artistry and resilient self-regard that refuses to dull its shine. The like of pageantry, parades, balls, dance halls have trans-formative magic, celebrating what can become real only with the witness of community. There is nowhere where a royal is not recognized.

In the exhilaration of the creative achievements of those devoted to their art are legends made, icons always. The tarot was made for royals but found its way into the hands of the people, and for this very reason, it is the right of everyone to take their place in the sun. Healthy self-regard puts us in a place to lead and inspire. To walk with this card is to learn to stand tall out in the world. To be self-possessed and bodacious, full-bodied and visible. It is an invitation to become the most fabulous version of ourselves.

The Six of Wands reconciles with the vital necessity of being deeply loved and knowing you are truly seen without being dehumanized by way of inferiority or superiority by being put on a pedestal. It's a card of the folk hero, inspiring others with the new path they blaze rather than coercing followers with anger and egotism over a sense of entitled recognition. To place this card in the common hand is deeply healing. It says you are walking with protectors, collaborators, ancestors, a cavalry of support seen and unseen. It is an evocation and acknowledgement of the heroes, icons, legends, pioneers that lead the way. It is to speak their name, to honor those who lead but weren't high-profile or canonized. The ritual naming of the Six of Wands is about the struggle for hegemony and claiming our right to redefine what is real and whose lives matter.

The Six of Wands lets the people obtain opulence. It is glamour as answer, beauty as defiance. It effaces the terms by which the conqueror obtains and maintains glory, affluence; terms that violently shut out queer and Black folks. For the marginalized to portray wealth and lavishness is less an ode to capitalism or a glamorized mode of identifying with the oppressor than an example of how the multimarginalized use cognitive dissonance to their benefit. This card can help shift the reader from American individualism and its inherent capitalist, colonial formation toward a growing, articulating, curious development of the self and the sense of who we can possibly be in this world. This self is situated among communal relations that are uplifting, protecting, and catalyzing; it's not a project of isolating singularity.

Wealth and fame are all-too-alluring images, whether of emancipation from or being offered by the capitalist fantasy. Fame and fortune are often not the panacea they promote themselves as. They are violent addictions so long as they are sought as a surrogate for being loved and really seen. Capitalism is intrinsically linked to white supremacy and anti-Blackness, and what achieves acclaim is always in the purview of white validation. The power performance of the Six of Wands may actually lead to opportunity and upward mobility upon the socioeconomic hierarchy. The card claims the imagination, stretching it to envision emulating something other than wealth and success as ciswhiteness. Dismantling the fragile construction of whiteness is to circumvent the nepotism of Hollywood. It motivates the hustle of Black and queer people to leave these entrenched white establishments with no other choice but to respect them. It is aspirational and enthralling. It is a ticket to the ball, to be the belle of the ball, if only for one night. It reflects the images of success, wealth, and power we seek to emulate. It is no parlor trick to produce this fabrication; it is an embodiment, a way of life that the marginalized enact to keep safe in the world with an unavoidable proximity to cisness. The ball is transfigurative in its opulence that points to the artifice of race. It's passing power into a different context, a different community through acts of defiance that require a capacity for cognitive dissonance. This *passing* is unlike the Seven of Swords's *passing;* it is a "way of obliterating the terms by which the oppressor obtains their opulence, maintains said opulence, and defines this archetype of which you are shut out."[16]

The most visible, elevated, and honored representations of the powerful can be reconceived with the Six of Wands. It is the vision of communal assertion, a type of shared celebratory success that is only possible when done for and with the people. This communal connection constitutes the Six of Wands champion. They proceed because they have made a commitment to kinship and the continuity of tradition, of heritage, of living. As a champion's love and respect grows for their people, this care is reciprocated a hundredfold, a prominence that needs careful navigation. Heightened awareness both from spectators and the spectacle is found in the challenge of being aware of what and who we are glorifying. The Six of Wands signals finally achieving mainstream popularity and/or visibility. This is the work of the invisible queer being creating visibility for themselves. Yet it also asks if we are conflating visibility with acceptance.

Of course, it can be terribly painful to be seen, to even know what exactly is being seen, and by what audience; and so many shut down because they can't handle the weight of their crown. It is a challenge to deal with the vulnerability of visibility. Who knows how we will be received, whether we will be met with praise, criticism, or both? We hope for praise with this card but deal with this simultaneous sort of reality, this dual self-awareness of presentation and reception. We want the system to say we are valuable, beautiful, and worthwhile, just as we renounce and reject its declarations and assessments. What weirdness it is to be seen when you're used to everyone averting their eyes when they meet the sight of you. Awards may then confuse more than they congratulate. They could be mistaken for communal acceptance rather than individual exceptionalism. The Six of Wands tells us celebration can be complex in its ties to suffering. It says there is a shadow to every spotlight. Accelerated visibility does not translate to greater inclusivity. A win for a gay man does not necessarily mean a win for trans women. We all want to identify as people in power, but because this always plays out in the social sphere we are not exempt from the gender binaries and colorist tendencies that demarcate power.

Still, it is the joyride card, the pageant, the parade, the ball, the soul train. It tells us that no matter the difficulty, it is deeply important to be seen and appreciated. By performing for our internal liberation, a space is made for new communal dynamics, for a relationality of resistance, artistic appreciation, and a love to show out. The Six of Wands says give people their flowers while they live, while they serve.

Six of Cups

I remember how urgent it is for the child to stay a child, or for the joy of that child to be an entity with its own body, for as long as possible. I spent the Sunday morning after the mass shooting at the Pulse nightclub in Orlando underneath a swath of blankets, scrolling through any website providing news, knowing that the news, in these cases, rarely gets better as more unfolds. I checked in with my friends and allowed myself to be swallowed by my own anger. I sent tweets and deleted them just as quickly. I cursed politicians, the ones who were silent and the ones who were saying the wrong things. Eventually, I was pulled out of bed by a small chorus of yells and laughter creeping in through my kitchen window. Below, in the parking lot behind my apartment, boys on their bikes were riding in circles, pulling their front wheels up and trying to balance themselves. Falling, laughing, and getting right back up. This small bit of joy, for no other reason than because it is summertime and they're with friends and they're outside and free. I do not know what they know of death, or if they knew a world outside of their own free world was mourning. Or if they knew and, even in knowing, saw clouds blowing in from the south and decided to not let whatever sunshine remained go to waste on a hot summer day to be followed by another hot summer day to be followed by months where the entire land was theirs. The city, a sacred playground with no room for grief.[17]

The card of the sepia-toned sentiment that preserves our sense of self-continuity is the Six of Cups. With a child's wisdom, enter a new time orientation, a remembered space in the soul that returns our capacity to trust, our natural, innocent desire, our buoyant joy. Youth takes hold of consciousness here. And they laugh, scream, and let joy fly high. Children, capable as they are of telling the truth that reason denies, share their wisdom in this arcanum. Children are a continuum, an answer to the decay inherent within time's passage. The young ones within and without share flowers freely, so the memory of love lasts forever. The language of young love is in rhyme, and their work is in play. Like a children's library, a storehouse of hope, wonder, and possibility awaits us as we enter upon the Six of Cups. The free play of imagination creates radical change in attitudes toward being, which results in a new quality of pleasure. This card helps the reader find and care for the inner child so they aren't alone anymore, telling them of the beauty to look forward to. This might be a bittersweet reunion, but in looking back we may find a way to move on toward the intimacy of twilight.

Freed from established paradigms, the play principle presents a path of freedom. So as long we remember to play we will never lose the way to love, even after long winters of forgetfulness. The heart knows a lover who is evergreen. The flower that is this card is a path back to innocence and sexual freedom. We go back before shame, and feeling freely blooms again. An innate sense of satisfaction moves toward mature realization without the distorting interruption of shame. Soul longing finds a natural outlet in sexual union. Through sex we access death, in pulling back the veils of separation to merge with another. All that's stuffed into a singular being is freed with the embrace of eros.

The dalliance of imagination offered in the Six of Cups is an entry into the aesthetic dimension. Giving and receiving beauty and pleasure simultaneously is an ecstasy recovered by this card. Those objects and offerings represented here are freed from assessments of usefulness or functionality. By the hand of love, all objects are enchanted. They become realized as possessing soul essence, freeing these objects into their own being. Creative contemplation and artistic appreciation generate from this sensuousness.

The Six of Cups seems to say *Remember me?* to say that relationships have a foundation upon memory. Bodies may be no more, but memories sustain intimate experiences. Like walking in a desert where the river once was and remembering the water that flowed, love lingers beyond the bounds of time. Maturity in modern civilization entails repressed expressions and denied fulfillments for the rational individual. These repressions are exploded by these love memories liberated in the Six of Cups. The memory of play and pleasure, of early eros, overturns the betrayal of dreams deferred. Calling upon the past experience of happiness obviates the desire for its re-creation. It is cognition giving way to (re)cognition. It's a card for restoring lost connections; physical, spiritual, sexual, temporal, natural. The Six of Cups is the ancestors and the descendants sharing medicine, memory, story, and song back and forth. Keeping us spiritually centered despite the great distance covered on the journey of incarnation, the Six of Cups is a card of the diaspora.

> *Diasporic religion is composed on the one hand about space—about places of origins, about the distances traveled from them, and physical or ritual returns imagined, already undertaken, or aspired to. And on the other hand, it is about how those memories rise in space, out of a given repertoire of the available and unthinkable. Memories are summoned from a position, a place of emigration, a destination. Diasporic religious agents recollect the past through particular territorial and temporal "ways of seeing" and from particular places.*[18]

Death does not just take; it exchanges memory, a past satisfaction surfaces to inspire a new form and forward action. As we give ourselves to life, the living make offerings to death so that memory is retained, culture preserved, and all that we let go of are imposed limitations. Love won't let go, it won't dissolve in the dark. Love pulls us toward life and death at once.

Memory is the narrative our hearts make of endings, the way life tells the witness of death. Memory preserves promises and potentialities, the relating before repression. The face of the beloved may change, as surely as ours will, but the soul recognizes the truth underlying these ephemeral forms. The flower that bears his name keeps his love alive, though he has died. The Six of Cups touches upon the potential immortality of living substance. It is the holy water that refreshes the heart. It is remembering the first time we fell in love, the pink scent that fills the heart with purring melodies so sweet. Along a timeline of love, a shared life develops. Identity is woven through the threading of love memories, connecting us as lovers past, present, and future. These unbroken bonds exist in a space outside of time, but become known in their own dedicated time, kept safe by the Six of Cups.

A card of reincarnation, soul memory, and love's transubstantiation recognizes the need for ritual's constant renewal with fresh enactments. Our bodies are reservoirs for homeland rituals. While their efficacy requires faithful repetition of ancestral tradition, it is also concurrent upon new horizons, changing surroundings, and responsiveness to new crises. Traditions are textured by space, contoured by the practices and ritual elements that fill space with sacred meaning. The solemnity of the past interwoven with horizons of futurity extend the soul's constant blooming identity. Rites and ritual practices are more than extended, and memories more than maintained; they adjust, transform, and elaborate as they are recalled in new social contexts with new, different resources. It is an opportunity for voices of various beings to communicate across time and space. The juxtapositions of present and past, of faith and future, are tools of disarray working toward the coherence of a revised composition. We can use the card to transport into "timeless" states, although the memories mediated here offer radical transformation. Meaning bound by spatial, temporal circumstance is emancipated here. We carry on with the distillation of sensuous encounter, an embodiment of truth beyond the bounds of reason. The Six of Cups is an invocation of authenticity and a return to tradition as a response to destabilizing flux, displacement, and social disruption. It is a wormhole unveiling every entrance into the streams of time, summoning every profusion of possibility for relational selfhood to manifest in multiplicity.

The Six of Cups calls on the individuals recognized as authoritative memory brokers. They are bridge builders of signs and symbols, of representational regime and signified sanctum. They influence historical practice by adding new equivalences, unearthing new memories of the soul's origins and new doorways back to its homeland. They reeducate us in languages of love, the mother tongue of the soul. They show the forgotten ways, the path back to heart, under the guidance of ancestors and deities above. By expanding identification, signs of love detached from our homelands can be reattached to the niche of now. The transmission of memory works to re-Indigenize descendants in the current social matrix. The diaspora reclaims the Indigenous space of border towns and cities with the Six of Cups, inscribing ancient orientation to its sites and replenishing the meaning of sacred objects. The past is ritually reconstituted to create a pathway for future Indigeneity, a retroactive force that seizes the past to redeem the present. The past is an anchor, one we sail to again and again in the Six of Cups, and each time we revisit we bring fresh perspective and flowers for faith fulfilled. Only through the labor of memory is the crisis of continuity overcome, a reorientation after rupture. When you don't know who you are or from where you come, the Six of Cups calls you by a name you recognize and brings you home.

Six of Pentacles

Any attempt to "soften" the power of the oppressor in deference to the weakness of the oppressed almost always manifests itself in the form of false "generosity"; indeed, the attempt never goes beyond this. In order to have the continued opportunity to express their "generosity," the oppressors must perpetuate injustice as well. An unjust social order is the permanent fount of this "generosity," which is nourished by death, despair, and poverty. That is why dispensers of false generosity become desperate at the slightest threat to its source. True generosity consists precisely in fighting to destroy the causes which nourish false charity. False charity constrains the fearful and subdued, the "rejects of life," to extend their trembling hands. True generosity lies in striving so that these hands—whether of individuals or entire peoples—need to be extended less and less in supplication, so that more and more they become human hands which work and, working, transform the world.[19]

There are people begging all over the city every single day, and when we walk by them we become that figure in the center, offering loose change based on an assessment of whether we think they are worthy or not. And how much of the time do we say no, hiding racism and classism in the fear of a poor, disabled, Brown, Black body?

The material reality of exchange within relationships, an interpersonal dynamic perpetuating or reconstituting overarching social values, is in the Six of Pentacles. As individuals relate to their material conditions of existence, the invisible hand of ideology dictates the assessment of worthiness and prosperity, of shame and receiving, of generosity and morality, and of humiliation and sin. As Freire notes in his critique quoted above, this can be a card of false charity that only works to support institutional inequity and societal power imbalances. It may be giving with an implicit expectation of receiving; it may be a caution that gifts come with strings to be pulled on at a later date. It's a card that questions the efficacy of individual remedies to systemic poverty, noting how it is especially insidious if those individual acts of charity only work to prop up one's sense of moral righteousness, presenting a paradox of help and harm. The Six of Pentacles is a critique of charitable organizations governed hierarchically, and any model of relational hierarchy at all. It's a lateral learning, a teacher-student/student-teacher parity of letters. Charity is unsustainable because it keeps folks dispossessed and dependent.

Instead of "false generosity," the Six of Pentacles can help us survive via mutual aid, a system that thrives through shared regard in relationships. Mutual aid is shaped by volunteers and the recipients of support services, it works at the root rather than reinforcing class division. It prioritizes the most vulnerable, and by meeting them where they are, relationships are built that move toward the freedom of self-determination. It is radical cooperation that this card calls upon. It is giving more to need less. It is not denying that we will need systemic change, but its virtue is in finding the means necessary to survive, now. It relies on solidarity in the absence of government support. It requires an abolitionist imagination to establish accountability and assistance that are free from prisons and policing. It is an everyday practice, learning to help each other. Still, the certain resiliency that subaltern communities show in heartwarming displays of solidarity amid the immediacy of crisis must not obfuscate the hardships that need not be so visceral a reality. Collective disaster may spur acts of altruism, but for these acts to lead to lasting civic change they must move beyond isolated acts of redress. The Six of Pentacles wants us to accumulate awareness till it radicalizes and begets organizing and collective activism.

It is an aid in locating the self in the social matrix and our complicity within the white supremacist capitalist imperialist patriarchy that we constantly negotiate. It is vital to name the system we live in and not lose distinct experiences of dominance under the abstraction of terms like intersectionality. Within the spectrum of these aforementioned -isms, some may find us more likely to be victims and others more likely to wield power and dominate. These spheres of power affect the practicality of living. And for those of us who seek to gain footholds in society's institutions, very often the process of entry silences the movements that arise from the active struggle for change in the dailiness of life. The Six of Pentacles is what it looks like to live in a culture of domination and struggle daily to maintain an integrity of self.

Empowerment or improving one's social lot is not about claiming the power to "have it all" and be free from any contestation. To espouse values and beliefs of liberation that are betrayed in action destabilizes individual and collective integrity. Decolonization and living an antiracist ethos requires specific actions in daily life, ones that are remediative but not to be confused with saviorism by altruistic beneficence. From deep recognition of the relational selfhood within the systems of domination comes the knowing that freedom is only mutually achieved. Otherwise, all we have is the appearance of choice, while underlying systems remain the same. The pentacles speak to the Taurean systems of value, drawn from the human body, the environmental body, commerce, and cultural, ideological values. This, then, is a card about cultural exchanges and the tenuous embrace of a bodily diversity in solidarity in the face of white dominance. Political allies do not always have bodies that are shaped in predictable ways or appear as expected. The Six of Pentacles invites critical dialectic exchange about what would be justice here, what each means by freedom, what is meant by mutuality or equality, what it is we hope for.

"In all these stories we are introduced to virtuous men and women who are defined by the quantity and quality of the work they do; with them we experience economic injustice, ruthless employers, deprivation, and a callous society only to see them saved at the last moment of their abject desperation by a charitable donation from a well-to-do outsider."[20]

The Six of Pentacles deploys the deus ex machina device (to be explored more in the Nines) and makes the Divine a political ally for the oppressed. The devout turn toward divine intervention, and so faith becomes an exchange of grace. Reciprocity in relationships is established in the mutual communication of care to meet each other's needs, not from a sense of obligation but from a natural joy. Compromise may be required, but not at the expense of believing certain needs must go unmet to maintain a relationship. The Six of Pentacles makes a distinction between reciprocity and transaction, as "keeping score" kills the care that brings about genuine relationships. Relational scorekeeping commodifies relationships for a consumption that does not satiate. Masses afflicted by the malaise of alienation may be manipulated by appeasement, offered particularly by commodified otherness.

The Six of Pentacles dismantles relationship hierarchy making relationship anarchists of us all. Love is not a limited resource, and being more intimate within one relationship does not mean our relationship with another is any less valuable. No representative is needed to measure our worth against an ideal of what we should be or how we should be performing—a standard that isn't reality at all. We can handle the limitations or boundaries of each relationship without diminishing their worth. We can work with the Six of Pentacles to construct a life full of relationships that can actually hold space for us. The Six of Pentacles is about unconditional love being in the acts of love we do regardless of condition, circumstance, context—the acts we perform because it is of our nature, because no reward is needed to motivate our action. We will love our existence, our unique opportunity at life regardless of who we are or aren't in relationship with. No love is lost if we find ourselves without the romantic, monogamous relationship society tells us we should value above all else. Compulsive heterosexuality is more than a cultural more; it's a strategy of financial necessity. The cishet marriage is state-sanctioned for tax purposes. It's idealized because of its commodity, its illusory accessibility. Its love is a prize not everyone will win. Relationship security is not found in the sedentary model offered by heteropatriarchal society. There is no forever belonging to a person, no way to lock up love for a sense of security.

In order to live fully, the Six of Pentacles is about practice, experimentation, and redefinition of success and security. Every relationship is a chance to practice intimacy and authenticity. Each is a chance to communicate transparently, to establish consent, exchange beliefs, share bodies. The Six of Pentacles is a chance to unconditionally love life, to give to live freely and receive graciously every chance we get, so we may be oriented toward the possibility of a deep, unconditional, loving relationship with anyone without feeling separate from the experience.

The Six of Pentacles realizes the transcorporeality of existence.[21] In the recognition that humans and the natural environment are inextricably linked comes the responsibility to be responsive to the other. We attune to living in and with nature in an active, mutually transformative, but also mutually sustaining manner. This responsive emphasis forges ethical and political positions that can contend with the forces of separation in the modern world. This card is the radical interdependence between different kinds of bodies and beings. Economy and environment are interrelated, and to limit access to resources to only a few at the expense of many is unsustainable for both. The Six of Pentacles is attentive to the ecological fragility of our planetary relationship as it calls for equitable resource distribution.

The Six of Pentacles wants hope to emerge from isolation with an elevated sense of possibility. We will know ourselves to be more capable, and we will come to expect more of each other, more of ourselves. We will intimately know that our actions depend on and affect the other. The scale of the Six of Pentacles tells when capitalism is speaking. We will not be fooled by expecting an input to lead to immediate output. The mutual aid it champions is more than meeting needs in the moment; it is discovering the sense of self deeply interconnected to people and place. A connection that clarifies the structures that make our immediate needs so dire, and pushes back against them. It is network building and wealth redistribution, but more so it is an orientation of revolution.

SEVEN

The Peacemaker taught us about the Seven Generations. He said, when you sit in council for the welfare of the people, you must not think of yourself or of your family, not even of your generation. He said, make your decisions on behalf of the seven generations coming, so that they may enjoy what you have today.[1]

Seven is belonging. Seven is sustainability. As a guiding principle it arranges the order of time. It is the composition of legacy and the wise stewardship of resources that considers those who will inherit the future. It is cultural, psychosocial integrity maintained through time. It is a bridge built beyond incarnation, where elders and ancestors guide, counsel, and protect descendants. Seven confers the community of millennia, and its bone-deep recognition of shared origins comes with a responsibility to teach, learn, protect, and preserve. It is reverence and dedication in the now until time immemorial. The opposite of individuation, Seven is communion, social cohesion, and shared sovereignty. Seven ensures no one person or singular group can claim substantive authority.

The arrangement of the universe is based on Seven. It is the order of the seven elements, the seven planets, the Pleiades, the days of the week, the seven notes of the diatonic scale, the seven rays of the rainbow. It is a lunar number telling of transformation and integration. Seven defines space in all regards, symbolic of the joining of heaven and earth. Three pertains to the spiritual order of the heavens above and below; order as Four is of the Earth, with cardinal elements and directions of the terrestrial. They meet in Seven for multiplicative possibilities, a complex joining. Seven meets us through vice and virtue, guiding us on the moral order. After continuous creation, Seven returns to the center for a moment of cessation rather than final perfection, marking Seven as a model in the passage of time.

Seven is promise and possibility, the number of prophecy. It articulates the visionary. Seven is the sense of salvation in crossing the gateway to mastery, following the teachings of ancestors across antiquity. Seven holds the mysteries of transmutation. It is where spirit infuses matter, where we root into the soul and begin to reach for the stars. Seven makes us responsive to the calling deep within, carrying us far on a journey of introspection.

Where there are borders and culture unhinged from tangible territory, Seven establishes links between spaces, making the reader cognizant of hierarchies of attention and opportunity, even in refreshingly democratic spaces such as social media; and in that recognition Seven calls on us to fight for our humanity. Each Seven presents an inventive alternative strategy that enables movement against and through barriers that stand in our way. Seven rebels against conformity and complacency. They are teachings in the politics of difference that transform individual life along with the work and relations with the public, the social, the larger institutions. The mobilization of meaning is a Seven orientation. It may find us depleted or diminished and yet still reaching for a way to fulfill our calling. Seven knows that in our desire to speak truthfully we will betray those who want to make money. The repertoire of tools for resistance expands in the Sevens. Sevens are an exploration of the ethic mis/aligning with the aesthetics to regulate rhetorical agency. The ethical reading matches not just the aesthetics of the cards but the aesthetics of lived experience. It's pulling the Moon and being at the beach at night. The ethical reader uses each as a vehicle toward each other. The image can become a cue for embodiment, or the embodiment is reflected and translated by the image. The virtuoso is visceral. By literally constellating the card in the lived experience you get the essence, the order, the wisdom, the heart of the card, the communiqué from the Divine.

The Sevens demand vigilance in the pursuit of soulful, creative manifestation. They find more room, capacity, and determination to act upon desires for freedom, mobility, privacy, respect. The dissident movers of the world, the ones of great courage, are septenary. Seven begins the long journey home. We make a decision to leave as we are confronted with the question *Where do we go from here?* till we decide with Seven to quest for emancipation.

The Chariot

Wiley's portrait is so unlike what precedes it that it feels as much like a moral rebuke as an aesthetic antidote. No more autumnal solemnity, no more dead leaves but the living ones of spring, of salads, or salad days. Instead of brown backgrounds and brown furniture, just brown skin. There's no way to be prepared for this thing in person. You will behold it and want to cry. For the distance you might have traveled to see it. For the distance Black people have traveled. We came all this way. There's no preparation for its physical bigness or science-fictional brightness. Bring shades. Bring a parasol.[2]

The Chariot is a movement builder, venturing toward social transformation. Movement is not exactly the same as motion. Movement is an object's positionality changing in relation to a fixed point in *space,* while motion is a change of positionality with respect to *time.* Cartomancy is a consideration of inner images shuffling at a certain velocity over time. While the Star moves toward queer horizons in relation to time, the Chariot moves in relation to space. Our placement in history may be precarious, but our portraiture will be stunning.

The cards are not just images of movement; they are in actual proximity to our many-bodied being, primarily connecting us to the images via the voice of the reader delivering any given reading. By emerging from the primordial Cancerian waters, the Chariot is protean. Emergence is unfolding across, beside, and amid. The card reflects that we are capable of assuming many forms of movement, many methods of relation. Movement does not begin anywhere else other than where we are, right now. Across the matrix of tissue, meat, and bone meeting meaning, the body is text. It's the heart that is brave, the speculation of success measured by its circulating blood. The body is the constellation of personal history, telling us where we've been but not necessarily where we are going or how to get there. As a study in distance and depth, the Chariot pushes beyond the impasse of the present through an acute sensitivity to rhythms. This arcanum meditates on stillness and movement, the ways bodies relate to spatial navigation. The Chariot considers what moves the body into motion and how the Black body is put into motion versus the white or Brown or Red body. We are set into motion by violence, by dance, by athleticism, by desire.

In exploring and rediscovering the human spirit despite the most challenging circumstances, the Chariot bridges the gap between reality and the vast space of possibility. The Chariot finds the right vehicle or vessel for the intention's successful manifestation. It is a card of profound empathy, pushing the reader beyond the narrow frame of who *we* are, with whom *we* is identified. Learn, with this arcanum, to strengthen the capacity to project the self into foreign space and emphatically enter the experience. The more spaces opened by the Chariot, the more empathy is experienced. As they move toward the fiction of the future, they make a foundation for the fantastic with their courageous embrace of lived experience. Their quest for multidimensional freedom is the soul making sense of incarnation. The Chariot moves beyond feeling the body as a suffocating confinement. It is instead fully permissive of the glorious sex drive of the animal body, a sacred companion vitally necessary to wholly embody the visionary self. The switch of hips is all the good-feeling freedom that the Chariot champions.

Incisive imagination and a spirited sense of wonder move the Chariot. Their trips remedy the ways the body has been dislocated in time, the agency and autonomy of the queer, Brown, Black femme body spurned historically. The feeling is not of hallucination but of being transported, physically as well as psychically. It is the transit from one place, one state of being, to another, delivered from one plane of consciousness, one state of circumstance, into the next. The historic domination we've been forced to endure gives way again and again to the Chariot's drive toward freedom.

The Chariot is who takes us home, knowing the roads of pain we've long traveled. Yet it encompasses the paradoxes of kinship and family in the way that homecoming is impossibly complicated for those whose homes were stolen or broken, the kin who were enslaved or imprisoned. The Chariot knows that in the twilight zone between past and present, there is some severance. We aren't returning to what we were but venturing toward what we might be.

The Chariot puts distance between us and the soul-shrinking realities of supremacist culture. In the determination to revolt, to flee, to escape and claim freedom, we summon fantasy to shield us from the world where degrading racial and sexual violence are all too common. The radical imagination of the reader is the terminus of an underground railroad between past and present. Depending upon the point of entry, the order of *chronos* may be disrupted. The Chariot arises through this imaginative impulse toward escape, and yet its direction leads the reader to anything but an escapist fantasy. To be sustained as a seeker on the path, there must be invention. With this arcanum we feel not as though we are fleeing something terrible but approaching something destined. This is no dreadful voyage like that of our ancestors. This is the conviction to find or invent fulfillment. It is the certainty that every personal fate has a place within the larger destiny progressing toward the dawn. It is this certainty of liberation that Harriet Tubman speaks of when she says, "God's time is always near. He gave me my strength and he set the North Star in the heavens; He meant I should be free."[3]

If abuse is always about abandonment, then the Chariot arrives most triumphantly when we feel stranded, lost, and discarded. The Chariot offers more than just a way to be moved around from place to place. It is a record of endurance, a legend of the numerous acts of heroism and humanity that rescue and redeem the spirit from being crushed into oblivion. We get in the Chariot to realize we are not helpless, we are not stuck in dependency. The arcanum affirms that it is possible to move past domination and toward triumph, though it is uneasy movement. The Chariot is how we move forward, pursuing the future. Its movement is precipitated by crisis; there is urgency to migration. Though we endure forced migration, the manner of our movement brings dignity and repair. Migration is both a dream and a necessity. We can simultaneously sense the visionary possibility promised by migration and also the risk, danger, and tremendous uncertainty that must come of dis- and relocating. Disoriented with the loss of life but in the midst of vision and growth. These are migrant horizons that only the Chariot knows. Every story of actual, intellectual, and mythological movement across the horizon calls upon this card. The domains of sustenance have yet to be entered, so we endure the shifting skies and tough terrain. But discovery arrives always at the greatest moment of need. From emergence into sustained lands, we bring the legendary with the historical, the personal with the cultural.

Resiliency is the polish of life, bringing prestige to places that with our every step become positions of possibility. The landscape covered by the Chariot is rife with the violence of colonialism. But from the land of open death comes the creation of cosmos. The trip is blessed by starlight, a power more ancient than memory can recall. The Chariot's speech is a gift to readers telling stories of liberation. The Chariot is where creativity moves with chaos, each pulling on the other, each negotiating a pace and a path. The speech addresses the *not yet conscious,* a *we,* that must be addressed so we may be related in the future. It is not descriptive or solely aspirational but an act of inscription. We are the past coded into the future when we learn the Chariot language. A future that changes the origin, or the meaning of it is what the Chariot drives toward. Determined that fate is not the same as destiny, the Chariot realizes as much self-possession as possible before being forced to surrender the body back to the Earth. This arcanum is willing to surrender movement, to be fixed in the frame of the card, so that in our meditation upon the Chariot, an inner engine is ignited and there is no more standing still. The future won't wait; it will only take shape as we risk failure to begin again.

The charioteer arises from the unconscious, appearing static in a mythic vessel that is most dynamic in its stillness. The consciousness emerging into form is a ceremony of migration, a creation story seeded in movement. These are the journeys that delve inward through contemplation. Motion is applied meaning. As the body is the chariot of the soul, the Chariot is the eternal carrier of consciousness, carried across every generation for many miles. The Chariot resides in the ecstatic unity of space with temporality, for the Star crowns the Chariot. They are a vehicle of convergence such that experience is liberated from linearity and is passed back and forth across past, present, future. And so our becoming in the here and now is a gift offered to three generations hereafter. The Chariot faces you, the future. Behind the Chariot but further ahead of you are ancestors unseen. Appearing before us as the one who knows another way, who is the embodiment of our assured success, the Chariot transports an avatar of the future. They tell us what we need to do now, what path to make, what turn to take to arrive at the promised place. The Chariot saves you from you this barren place by bringing forth from the future a vision of you—strong, purposeful, powerful, honored, blessed.

From sustaining lands to sustaining traditions, the Chariot sees the reader reemerge with every miracle heeded. It matters not so much the tradition the Chariot continues on in, so long as there is the knowing that one is called to love, for the only path the Chariot travels is one of love. The direction to walk in is the one that stirs the heartbeat, in the direction of the freest, most fulfilled life possible. The Chariot's movement is only possible with the revolution that comes with self-care and self-belief.

From the rubble of ritual departures and regular losses comes a great odyssey, an exodus of memory, "to this impulse to see the past in present events and see present events in light of an ongoing historical and mythical past. He depicts it as a reassertion of patterns, which is not a repetition, but a constant return by which the travelers reassess, revise, reconfigure, or double back on history and divine creation."[4] The Chariot is the origin rippling through our body into the future, ensuring that though it changes and evolves, it is never forgotten. Likewise, movement will never be denied our right. Bodily, intellectually, spiritually, the Chariot crosses continents.

What will be the vehicle of fulfillment, and who will accompany us on the journey? These are not immediately known. Every journey is full of tension. Closed in a car together, as with the wild animals in a zoo's small cage. There are days of warmth and intimacy, and there are days with irascible growling. Feeling locked in is dangerous, for it reveals that maybe we haven't escaped the pain of the past. Failure haunts the mind, but self-sabotage is what keeps us from success. The Chariot says to travel light, to catch the train to the greater unknown even if we have to leave our bags behind. The

Chariot ensures we keep moving, so we do not give into despair as we are so close to fulfillment. We may need to go with nothing but our body, our will, our determination, and our vision. We know not what we will encounter, but we are capable of responsive integrity. Goals may be flexible, but the purpose is firm.

It is the capacity to attain fruition, to grasp what we reach for within our soul. The Chariot journeys toward the materialization of soul substance, never journeying alone. The spiritual orphan is no longer so as soon they chart a journey home, determined to find family anew. Intimate relationships may bring us closer to home than we ever imagined, a possibility that comforts or confronts or both. We bring love home not as a trophy of capture and possession, a success of abandonment confused for progress, but rather as a navigation system, a new technology to move through the world with purpose, honor, and integrity. The Chariot reveals the power available as we pursue authenticity. The path here forged is one that feels truly fulfilling. The moment burns with anticipation and promise.

On toward the reconciliation of desire, the joining of individuality and relatedness. We take the reins of desire into our hands and become the mediator of impulse and instinct. The pursuit of freedom is the pursuit of responsibility, both personal and collective. Even if we must surrender to the terrain, it is our choice alone to decide to take the helm of our life. We champion the Chariot within when we decide to go to therapy, or to return to school, or to quit a job to pursue a true vocation and right livelihood. The Chariot does not avert the gaze nor turn away from the present while simultaneously moving toward a future beyond their conscious conception. They know there are many futures beyond present-day life. The Chariot says we are what does not yet exist, at least not as fully as we will later come to know. The Chariot has no anxiety when asked *Are we there yet?* for they know arrival is continuous. In the constant coming, they pursue vistas beyond limited perception. This orientation does without the intervals of anxious fear or nauseating motion sickness from too much time since touching land. The Chariot does not rush into taking a new route but inspires us to make a new map of life. Whoever does all the driving anyhow? Do you ride in silence, or is the trip too long, so hot that you start to feel regret, start longing to leave before you have even arrived? Persisting without clear direction, without an end in sight, is a burden best given to God. Expect God to lead you, and you will always be secured a Chariot.

The Star

What's the opposite of transcendence? When you sink so low into something that you start to move with it. When, instead of rising above into airy utopia with the critical distance to match, what you feel spills over into whatever's next to you—and vice versa—replacing any easy subject-object distinction with something more like critical intimacy.

Philosophers call this mucky space immanence. I call it bass.[5]

The water bearer pours sound that propagates as waves, rippling long and wide across space-time to bring the body back online. Time signs its signature in song; it textures the environment that renews itself with fresh flowers each year; but its bones are the same. Water slips through every crevice, patient but persistent in eroding walls and breaking down barriers that stifle self-expression, autonomy, and liberty. Water is a paradox of privacy. It is unknowable in its depth but contains every known connection. Sound is the primary way of knowing. To orient ourselves in relation to the world we depend upon stereo hearing to locate sound sources.[6] Yet the Star replaces this sonic system of knowing and navigation so we may experience pure presence. It is blood and it is bass; it permeates and blurs boundaries between my body and yours, between the personal and the civic. There is no separation in this state. There is no direction to go, there is only immersion, there is only love.

The Star is irrigating love. With no ostensible direction or self to discern, love circulates in all dimensions, calling for a surrender to the intensity of sensitivity. Relational forces may be channeled but never controlled. Together we dream of freedom, bringing beautiful Brown bodies into being as the fruit of ancestral imagination. From those distant relatives unnamed by lost identities we have inherited the legacy of imaginings. The Star drops us into an existence that spills over the bounds of the body, that pools prayers round the poisons of past karmic imprints, and in the celestial streams every thirst is quenched. Under starlight we strip naked and wash ourselves clean in rivers and tides until we recognize our waters within as one and the same. This water ritual of love released lets the body dissolve its rigid boundaries, blending the spirit into an open, peaceful environment, fully claimed as the space of serenity.

The Star is a card of Aquarius, a card of Saturn, and of hope's fragile resiliency. Hope is hard to hold because it is so gentle. Hope is a question of capacity: how much trust and belief can we hold in either hand? Hope exceeds containment. The objects of our desire, the focused receptacle, container, or vessel of fulfillment must be emptied continuously so we can understand that the essence of hope's substance is impersonal in its intimacy. With release we discern the substance from the form. Desire will be beyond this form, beyond the present, beyond this attachment to a body or feeling or state or status. It has known us by a different face in a different time in a different body and a different language. And still the substance we sought was the same. And still it was hope that made the heart brave. Hope is the part of us that believes by suspending disbelief. The curtains of a cosmic theater open, boundless possibility merges with the present moment, and we let ourselves dream for as long as possible. Heartbreak and disappointment feel somehow more honest or safer to expect. Disappointment may just keep me afraid of getting what I want. Conditioned fear keeps dreams of freedom contained and controlled. And certainly we fail in the forms of our aspirations, but the heart is defiant, it holds hope anyway. In the struggle for justice, hope gestates.

"The more you recognize your fear as a consequence of your attempt to practice your dream, the more you learn how to put into practice your dream! I never had interviews with the great revolutionaries of this century about their fears! But all of them felt fear, to the extent that all of them were very faithful to their dreams."[7]

To keep from becoming incredulous, the Star draws upon an ancient source to return a natural wellspring of well-being. Despite any external evidence or even evidence interpreted to the contrary, the Star does not falter. The Star instantly recognizes this play of evidence-absence and faith-presence. Faith is incomprehensible, its substance is inimitable. Faith is that invisible force that permeates the cynic's patrolling mind to disturb the established social order. Straight time's stranglehold is interrupted in the pitch-black void where nothing seems to be promised and fearful confusion abounds. The Star is easily and immediately felt as a force of ecstatic time. José Esteban Muñoz in *Cruising Utopia* describes ecstatic time as announced with ecstasy, proclaimed in screams or pleasurable grunts that open into a contemplation that looks back at past, present, and future alike.[8] Hope is brave. Sculpting reality from dream material requires flesh-and-blood belief.

It is pure power. The hope so often associated with the Star is not naive but an invocation of future collectivity and a reclaimed connectivity to ancestors past, the intermediary of the flowing water facilitating this forward-and-back coupling. Daring enough to believe that we will be freed, peace overcomes the heart. Hope is a substance to steep the heart in. It is the spirit that wants to be washed in your pools of defiant, devoted hope. It wants to wade into the primordial waters of creation and let go, let go of fixed interpretations, labeled failures, expectations, and dogged plans. Interpretations have no absolute truth. There is fact and then there is interpretation of fact. You can have *hopelessness* as a feeling but never as a standpoint. Paralysis is not a viable option. So from the Tower and its disappointment of deliverance, the Star, with the pragmatism of possibility, restores. But it's a far feeling from being beaten when the Star appears. Hope is the state that tempers the intellect's pessimism with the will's optimism, making its substance informed, and aged, distilling a potent lasting confidence in the future.

By sheer vibration it is the temporal motion through time that accompanies the Chariot's movement force. They work as a time machine to transport the reader's consciousness while their body-soul undergoes repair. The Star cleans away old fear caught up like cobwebs. It antagonizes the ruling order, flowing an unseen substance between power and powerlessness. It summons the dedication to continuously surrender to change. The Star relaxes the reins. What is fundamentally unruly and ungovernable flows freely under starlight. It offers the space to immerse oneself in the love that is endless possibility, or even just the possibility of love. The Star opens perceptive relation to alternative temporal and spatial maps. We recognize that from the present there are more than one or two ways fulfillment can be found. There are more realities and more ways to overcome any immediate obstacle. The Star is the technology of divination, an ancient listening to future worlds with words that diverge from the mundane and mainstream to encompass the fantastic.

The Star is where we know the body as God's dwelling, a temple where only the Divine enters, the fountain where the Divine alone drinks, where there is nothing but the Divine to receive. In faith we find the entrance. In faith we heal. The Star is pouring deeply, deepening the capacity to love. Pouring back into water, onto land, extending compassion to places that have never been touched by love. Bended knees in the pleasure of piety share the body with the soul. Giving the space to love mountain high or river wide, pouring becomes an act of pleasure rather than depletion. It signals transcendent aptitude. Flowing from each container a constant love, undifferentiated, like a blessing.

A love bigger, tighter, sweeter, higher, flyer pulls from deep places. In the moments when we are conditioned to take personally people's failures to show up for us, the Star defends us, protects us, cherishes us by showing us a moment of compassion wherein we recognize a well that has run dry. "Despite changes, distortions, misinformation symbolized by its containers, the water will continue to sustain and nurture life."[9] Without the Star's limitless supply of unconditional love, we'd be unable to extend forgiveness. And the future would always be doomed by the brooding resentment of unresolved heartbreak.

> *Abstract utopias are indeed dead ends, too often vectoring into the escapist disavowal of our current moment. But a turn to what Bloch calls the no-longer-conscious is an essential route for the purpose of arriving at the not-yet-here. This maneuver, a turn to the past for the purpose of critiquing the present, is propelled by a desire for futurity. Queer futurity does not underplay desire. In fact it is all about desire, desire for both larger semiabstractions such as a better world or freedom but also, more immediately, better relations within the social that include better sex and more pleasure.*[10]

The time of queerness as Muñoz describes is akin to the Star's orientation of temporal unity.[11] The past isn't static; it is performing, it plays with the present, and in it can be found flickering illuminations, ephemeral traces of other times and places. The Star follows that previously unrealized potential from the past into the future. Finding us in a depressive position, wading into shifting and blending rivers of time, the Star steps outside the present as they pour into the future as an answer to the desire for perfectibility. Utopian desire has hope that won't die no matter the disappointment we parse from the pleasurable sensualities of the present. We feed upon past pleasures as our desire for futurity mobilizes us to embody utopia. The Star achieves hope in a heartbreaking reality by offering and opening every imperfect port of possibility where multiple forms of difference adhere to a belonging in collectivity, free from feelings of fraud, inadequacy, or insecurity. It is hope cognizant and consequential. Our desires may not exactly fit into our present moment, but the more desire responds to the present moment, the more concretely the force of hope forms as the integral core in our life.[12]

One is inspired by embodied gratitude. To share, to be honest, to extend oneself as an active force of change in the world via our dreams and our commitment to them is truly remarkable. Give to yourself so much divine water that you have more than enough, that you are joyed to share all you have, ready to refill the wells of the creative subconscious continuously. By the Star is the space of imagination, vital for any decolonial effort, "because the decolonization of the imagination is the most dangerous and subversive form there is: for it is where all other forms of decolonization are born."[13] So the Star is where faith fuses spiritual teachings and social consciousness in the body.

Rooting and stability come from within, from spiritual practices and ancient cosmic technologies in the embrace of ritual reflection. Generations of hardship have fortified the dream. Our ancestors don't die; they become shooting stars showing us the way home. Starlights and celestial luminaries pour their power into our vessels made of clay, blood, and bone, and so being of their body becomes our blessing. The Star is the transference of divine life force into earth, consciousness into the body, love into the empty, fearful darkness. This arcanum encourages and engages in biomythography as championed by Audre Lorde. With no more rigid self-definition, the Star fashions us from dreams and fantasies and futures yet to be. It is a survival strategy of skillful adaptation born of necessity.

Clear vessels come from the Star. It is the water of baptism, the power of beginning again after delusions, deceits, and self-denial fall suddenly away. Self-imposed limitations are only overcome as we perceive ourselves in right relationship and proportion to the far greater cosmos. Playing our part in sustaining cosmic harmony is a sacred responsibility. We must engage in ritual washing, ritual praying, ritual releasing regularly. We are to share, be blessed, and know the mercy of abundance that emanates from source. To be liberated from material bondage and released into the rapture of grace, we need the Star.

"Whenever we try to envision a world without war, without violence, without prisons, without capitalism, we are engaging in speculative fiction. All organizing is science fiction. Organizers and activists dedicate their lives to creating and envisioning another world, or many other worlds."[14]

The Star is every sacred and spiritual space that allows people to reach deep inside and let grace gush, to literally discover who they are and express parts of themselves they'd never dare to before. The communal spaces where likeness is found and thanks are given are sites of spiritual rooting that move beyond traditional religious structures or sites. The dancehall, the ball, the classroom can be unexpected spaces of ecstatic experience. There are many ways to rejoin a spiritual tradition that "taught us to love, sing and praise all our lives,"[15] for of course the Stars belong to an ancient stratum of human consciousness. The Stars are the ancient anchor to calendrical systems.

The Star is an appraisal of replenishing commonness in the way that water connects all, and in the way that hope, like water, is ultimately formless as immanence but always readily available to take form. More than imbuing a moment with joy, the Star uncovers beauty where it may not necessarily or normatively exist. The objects of desire we hope for most fervently may fail us, as we may fail to properly hold desire or see it misaligned from lived reality. But the water continues to pour forth, so even as our reach may exceed our grasp, desire is a continuous horizon that keeps us hoping. Hope for love reciprocated, love that replenishes and brings us into a state of being-with, which may be complex and flawed but nonetheless utterly necessary. It continues rather than clings. Hope can only be possible as we make space to accommodate disappointment and disorientation as redirection. The Star offers nothing if not this space.

Knights

The Green Knight is the pre-knight, the squire, the apprenticeship sworn to knighthood; the Black Knight stands for him who undergoes the tribulations of sin, expiation and obscurity in order to attain to immortality by way of earthly glory and heavenly beatitude; the White Knight is the natural conqueror, the "chosen-one" of the Evangelists, or the "illumined one" reemerging from a period of nigredo; the Red Knight is the Knight sublimated by every possible trial, bloodied from every possible sacrifice, supremely virile, the conqueror of all that is base, who, having completed his life's work, is fully deserving of gold in its ultimate transmutation-glorification. Knighthood should be seen, then, as a superior kind of pedagogy helping to bring about the transmutation of natural man (steedless) into spiritual man.[16]

The Knights each enact an aspect of the Chariot, carrying the reader further, farther. The Knights are all about praxis, employing varied strategies of agency to move through the world with integrity. Knights are trusted because they have trained to be self-possessed. They long to be liberated from fear, are in pursuit of purpose, and are bestowed with sacred duty. Knights explore the tension of communal responsibility and independence. Knights, as seekers, champion their people by assuming personal responsibility. Knights are active, direct, and enduring. Through these archetypes we make the bridge from childhood into adulthood; we channel courage, bravery, and resilience. These are dimensions of selfhood that sustain conviction no matter the obstacle. By being self-determined and yet duty-bound we pursue the world with passion, creativity, and care.

Activists articulate their beliefs and commitments with action. Activists are Knights. They call upon tenacity to forge an authentic path as self-doubt, self-denial, and distrust are overcome. Knights *do;* they put forth flesh, blood, and bone. Knights navigate liminality, maintain ethical integrity, and focus upon fulfillment across an ever-changing, dangerous terrain. The necessity of holding, resting, reflecting is real, but all would be empty theory without the practice, the doing, the trying daily. Knights are practitioners. Their habits of living and being embody a practice of theorizing liberation. The new cultural terrain we walk upon is critically investigated by the Knight. They are in process. They pursue a constant unveiling of reality, continuous self-location and reorientation, to proceed toward transforming reality.

The Knights say this:

> *I aim to make the most of my incarnation. Blood may be shed in my pursuit, I may "fail" over and over and over again, but truly I am succeeding so long as I refuse to give into despair or to give up on myself, my path, or my purpose. I want to ripen my talents and creative potential into fruition. I want to direct my life toward something meaningful. I want to live well so I can die without fear. I want a warrior's death, full of honor. Knights are not swayed by their individual limitations or vulnerability. This body will return to the earth, and while I may lose some battles, the fire of this spirit shall never be extinguished. While the colonist travels only to take, to exploit, eradicate, I must travel in a way that builds bridges between worlds, which presupposes reciprocity. I hope to have enough authority that my people welcome my presence on their journey, and hopefully, with my guidance, we can unravel the plenitude of their being. As I pursue liberation, I rely on intuition and observation to discern danger and take seriously the charge to champion and protect. I seek not only to survive but to embrace a symbiotic relationship with the environment and with my relations.*

By the Knights we know reading tarot is for the brave. Traveling physical, social, psychic, linguistic, and institutional distances can become debilitating should we journey alone. Recognizing the fragility of our lives, we may equip ourselves with the hard armor of a tough exterior for survival. Knights accompany migration, providing healing, offering perspective and support. They tell the reader to take advantage of new environments to (re)discover, (re)interpret, and (re)articulate selfhood. Migration is then a type of rebirth. Knights reorient the reader from a homesick longing for the ancestral lands toward becoming global citizens struggling between spheres to find support, renewed visions of success, and the eventual reunification with family. Knights pursue humanity. They traverse borderlands but transform them as well, crafting a poetic device from rupture, "aimed at fusing relationships and narrating coherence out of a life of movement and fragmentation."[17] Knights change the point of view. They don't look *at* migrant life but *from* migrant life. Theirs is not a double absence but a double presence, as indicated by their mounted steeds.

Often the hardest lesson with Knighthood is realizing that producing theory is complex and requires far more collective engagement than a purely individualist practice. Knights are champions for the people when they participate with people, and thus culture, in development. The Knights are the different locations where theory finds varied use. Knights are in the midst of the world, outside the bounds of the institution. Since translation and accessibility are vital for theory to be used in every conversation by the larger public, Knights carry meaning across context. They read and write the world such that the knowledge produced connects meaningfully to lived realities beyond the academy. They champion literacy for all, advocating an educated public whose various ways of knowing are equally valued and regarded.

Divination is a praxis of liberation. The cards are cues. They are more than psychoanalytic reflection, they confront. Ask them for guidance only if you are ready to *do*, to enact and seek creative realization of the messages offered. It is for those who wish to put their power into practice. Their theorizing is not done from on high, but down in the field. They are motivated to answer the questions at their core of being:

> *Who are you, and where do you come from? Where do you exist, who do you love, what do you do? Where are you going? Who are you with? Who are your enemies? What do you value? What is your success? Where is your abundance? Where is your joy? What is your work? What are you learning? How are you changing? What are you challenging? What do you need to challenge? Where are your spaces to exist, grow, learn, love? Where have you lost yourself, forgotten a part of soul? How can you call it back? What is your past? Who might you be in the future? How can you meet the unknown? Who aren't you? What's driving your motivation?*

Knights are the warriors within, showing us how to defend, protect, and honor. They are idealistic but teach us to move at an authentic pace. With

Knights we grow in self-efficacy and develop our abilities to be accountable. Becoming a Knight is deciding who you serve. Knights possess a quality of discernment, understanding the spirit of service as something other than a state of victimhood or indentured servitude. Knights make a commitment to serve with nobility, dignity, and defense against violence and debasement. Knights touch upon a truer spirit of service. To deal with the dehumanizing conditions of everyday American life, we need the Knights' critical sensibilities. They are culturally competent; they know where they come from, skillful in both mainstream and divergent cultures, which is personally useful but also deployed in service to larger social causes. They are able to transition between and across multiple identities in an awareness of the world and their position in it. They are the progression of discovery, moving past their fears in pursuit of themselves, claiming emancipatory authority to pursue democracy, seeing the world as it truly exists: a process in transformation.

Knight of Swords

How could you, belonging to no one, but property to those despising the smiles of your soul, how could you dare to create yourself: a poet? A poet can read. A poet can write. A poet is African in Africa, or Irish in Ireland, or French on the left bank of Paris, or white in Wisconsin. A poet writes in her own language. A poet writes for her own people, her own history, her own vision, her own room, her own house where she sits at her own table quietly placing one word after another word until she builds a line and a movement and an image and a meaning that somersaults all of these into the singing, the absolutely individual voice of the poet: at liberty. A poet is somebody free. A poet is someone at home.[18]

The Knight of Swords is looking for language while wielding the word. By the sword, colonizers severed many mother tongues, so with slaughter and conquest came Standard English. The problems of language lie in its use to steal and hide away, homogenize, slur, holding no one accountable, flattened in and by the passive voice, making us addicted to a passive existence. It is irresponsible to be nondescript or to agree to use a language that blames the victim. Only the active voice leads us into action. The Knight of Swords looks for language that hurdles, flies, soars, and sings to lead participatory democratic discourse. Broken, ruptured words make counterlanguage. The spirit of rebellion emerges, and the oppressor's language we are forced to speak becomes something more. Languages' quicksilver transformations say more with less. Minds are altered, hearts are entered, and with the alacrity of forbidden, strange intelligences, a new voice emerges. The Knight of Swords labors to forge themselves as a poet despite every force of censure, repression, and denial around them. To claim a free life, they claim the word, choosing to come of age, struggling to speak the truth of an existence in alienation. The White Knight insists: who did what to whom?

The mind regularly exercised is disciplined, critical, and confident. Expression is clear with something to say. By telling the truth, the truth changes. The Knight of Swords possesses this speech power that forges spaces for new and alternative cultural production. They make do with any language available, trusting their tongue enough to overcome being pacified by state-sanctioned language. Truth is the purpose of this Knight's language pursuit. In this space we think and know differently. It is the space of opportunity, a chance to listen without owning, mastery, or possession. The space where an understanding of another's language lacks is always where learning to communicate begins. Learning arises from the spaces of silence as with the spaces of speech. It's language made malleable so it tells the truth of our many selves. The Knight of Swords breaks with a clean, neat narrative, knowing there is no need for perfect pitch; honesty is preferred. What's idealized as perfection is often misunderstood disinformation. So the Knight of Swords is shifting the narrative to open up pathways previously unrealized, trusting the process of investigating what is real and what is not. By assessing what is happening in the moment, a fictitious narrative that deters is bypassed. This power pursued and claimed by the Knight of Swords is essential to creating decolonized, counterhegemonic worldviews.

The desire that the Knight of Cups uses to disrupt is the language that the Knight of Swords refuses to contain. The way words impose themselves in even the most private spaces of mind and body point to their violating potential, as it speaks to the Knight of Swords's determination. It is not language itself that hurts but rather how it is wielded. In the hands of dictators, language dispossesses and limits. It is a weapon that shames and humiliates. Tongues unremembered are numb, they are tasteless. In learning to deal with language loss, the Knight of Swords pursues renegade speech to realize new ways to speak with one another. In this Knight's hands, the oppressor's language is repossessed, expressed as a site of resistance. With this Knight, speech becomes subversive. This is language remade, altered, transformed, so it can speak beyond the bounds of conquest and domination. This is enacting language intervention, breaking the boundaries and limitations of Standard English. This Knight questions why—in spaces deemed professional or esteemed, in the classroom—is only Standard English heard? It occurs to the Knight of Swords that there is something new to say in another language.

Communication restored makes language intimate rather than violating. We touch tongues, we make language. We liberate ourselves from exile in language shared and mutually shaped. Shared speech creates community. In respecting or recognizing the voices that are silenced, censored, or misrepresented, the Knight of Swords disrupts the primacy of domination. This Knight changes how we know, our epistemology, by shifting how we consider and deploy language. Knowledge relations transforming power relations.

"At a lecture where I might use Southern black vernacular, the particular patois of my region, or where I might use very abstract thought in conjunction with plain speech, responding to a diverse audience, I suggest that we do not necessarily need to hear and know what is stated in its entirety, that we do not need to 'master' or conquer the narrative as a whole, that we may know in fragments."[19]

The Knight of Swords probes around paradox, exhilarated with ideas, a racing mind covering vast linguistic landscapes, reading several texts at once; and yet, to subvert the culture of capitalist frenzy, learns to listen patiently. And they strive to eliminate the passive voice from democracy. Language ceases to be the experience of subordination, becoming a brandished weapon of resistance. They decode symbols, study signs, and map the failures that form language. No matter the tone or style, one who leads a lyrical life in that they decide to lead language, rather than be led by language, is a Knight of Swords, is a poet made.

Knight of Wands

I woke up alarmed. I didn't know where I was at first. It was that feeling of waking up someplace foreign and being like, "What the fuck?!" But then you look to the left and you're like, "Oh, wait, that *handsome* guy."

It's comforting to wake up with someone this attractive, and I'm sure he was thinking the same thing, but I also couldn't go back to sleep because his sun-spanked disco ball was flashing high beams all over the room.[20]

The Knight of Wands agitates, arouses, and inspires humanization. This entails the ability to foster hope in seemingly hopeless circumstances. The Knight of Wands instructs inspiration as part of an ongoing process central to organizing, and channels the longing and suffering of their community, which often goes unacknowledged. They come to personify communal pathos. They rouse the conscience, startling the people's sense of propriety, exposing its hypocrisies. Their argument is scorching, rallying not with light but fire. In the pursuit of freedom, they transform conformity, brazenly indicting the state and its agents of dehumanization. The Red Knight cultivates an infectious inspiration that sets eyes upon collective freedom, with the power to ignite intimate understandings of personal burden and suffering into political dissent. Theirs is a humanizing pedagogy awakening both critical consciousness and compassion. Their fire revives revolutionary fire as they capture the imagination to recover, reframe, and redirect ambition. The anger and grief of communities under colonial attack burns right along with their aspirations for freedom. The fire burns against hatred that dehumanizes. We are companions of the blazing flame.

The Red Knight calls attention to how some of us seek to dictate others' behavior and sexual practices behind moralistic "shoulds." There are those who try to assume the power to determine what and who you should desire or dream. This politics of sexuality is state-sanctioned violence that the Knight of Wands fights against. They mean to be freely and fully all that they are. Freedom is indivisible. The tyranny that dictates desire and the acts of the honest human body uses any means necessary to snuff out the flame in the human: race, gender, sexuality, class, etc. To deny any part of ourselves is to risk self-deception and insanity. The Knight of Wands burns away puritanical ideology. They are not bound by groupthink, nor do they succumb to peer pressure or anyone's imposed concept of "correct." The Knight of Wands measures action as a basis for relatedness. Not on the basis of who or what we are, but what we *do* for freedom, how we *enact* justice. The Knight of Wands is free, they are not predictable, and they are not controllable, and neither are you.

The Knight of Wands is looking for sexual liberation. They titillate. Sex and its energetic activities, its activating energies, are distinct from discussions of sexuality. Expressing any expansive sexual desire or impulse is so threatening to state-sanctioned colonial sexual conceptions that it is taken to suggest corruption or anticommunity values. Puritanical American values redirect all sexual impulse into commodity, something to be exploited, degraded, or denied. The Knight of Wands wants you to have sex, like a lot of sex. Their eternal resolution is to do too much, for there is no revolution without sex. Take everybody as a chance to practice being your authentic self, says the Knight of Wands. Take the pressure off performing by mounting passion, letting joy run unbridled. Treat self-pleasure as a heroic journey. Express and enjoy sexuality without shame. Seek sexual healing, trust your pleasure, trust your penis, trust your pussy, trust your nipples, lips, and lust, fuel your eros to open your heart's agency. Fire is irresistible, all consuming. Attraction is everywhere, but pleasure is placed in your hands when you pull the Knight of Wands. This is eminent eros. Power emanates outward. The Knight is discerning. The power and force of their sexual freedom know the difference between sexual harassment, consensual obsession, and palpable flirtation. Access to more power requires more responsibility for such discernment, but with greater freedom comes greater clarity. The artist's vision, born from the fire, bears a greater responsibility because it is the artist's—the Knight of Wands's—vision that comes into reality. Sex is the imagination's primal fuel, the horse, and the Knight of Wands the rider. It is a fundamental force erupting out of us, a fount from which passionate life emerges. The Knight tracks the movement of our sexual beings through the world. It's a multispecies affair. Every sexual experience is a joining of a vast erotic collective. Via the erotic we can be transported beyond the body but also come more deeply into the body. It is an accessibility of creativity, a capacity for a connectivity that exceeds categories. This Knight of Wands's knowing is a creative channel both beyond and within you. The body is the force of penetration but informed by the imaginal.

An expansive erotic life resources a deeply rooted sexual-spiritual plane that is the spiritual life practice that respects and directs the animal body in the presence or absence of its many diverging desires. The Knight of Wands wants you to have pleasurable sexual autonomy, and for many that means being able to have no sex at all. It is erotic to embrace feeling, for it is highly tolerant and attuned. Rather than simple sensation, which fears the force of desire, the Knight of Wands encourages erotic excellence. They demand the full depth of feeling and a consciousness emblazoned with desire, and they demand that you take responsibility for the satisfaction of your deepest desires. Sin, as here understood, is to fake orgasm.

They ride desire as a force of consciousness-raising, increasing our capacity for pleasure, for meaning, for fulfillment. They ride round lighting everyone's fire. They are the torchbearers, preserving the faith over the long night after the Sun's decline. They cultivate within each of us charisma, confidence, and congeniality so we feel worthy of our particular passions. Realizing that there is much to experience, many pleasures waiting to be liberated, the Knight of Wands is a practitioner of possibility. In every endeavor the erotic must be enlivened, spilling over across every dimension of life. The erotic is a stream, a carrying, a motion, moving toward an elsewhere. The Knight of Wands, in erotic movement, brings nascent potentialities into present embodiment to move beyond habituated boundaries of the body. Arousal reaches beyond social constructions that foreclose access to feeling. Erotic intensity opens and transforms the body. The doing of this Knight is felt acutely. Erotic knowledge empowers. What the fire touches and what that touch means is freedom personified.

Knight of Cups

I want to write about a political and radicalized form of love that is never about absolute consensus, or unconditional acceptance, or unceasing words of sweetness, or endless streams of hugs and kisses. Instead, it is a love that I experienced as unconstricted, rooted in a committed willingness to struggle persistently with purpose in our life and to intimately connect that purpose with what he called our "true vocation"—to be human.[21]

The Knight of Cups is looking for love. To navigate a culture of domination without being constantly wounded, the Knight of Cups armors themselves with love. They are fighting for love as they go, fresh with the spontaneity of courageous vulnerability. The armed love Freire conceptualizes—a love that is as bright, lively, and stimulating as it is critical, challenging, and insistent—is a literacy of the Knight of Cups. This Knight refuses oppressive discourse by propagating poetry and prose. This armed love protects and perceives the valuable emotional experiences of pursuing paradise. They know the twin pleasures of resisting and imagining. They enact love defensively, denouncing dehumanization, and they wield love progressively, imagining what becomes of love. They announce justice by announcing love.

The Knight of Cups unveils love as a mediating technology between an oppressed present and an inclusive, free-loving future. This is less concerned with the definition of love than with the action of love. When we question what to do or how to love, it is a question of will, of action. Love, as defined by bell hooks, is an amalgam of care, commitment, knowledge, responsibility, respect, and trust. Love like this is unbound by preconception so it may be based on direct experience. Love like this seeks to find authentic life, a wholeness, an internal peace. Love is a practice. The Knight of Cups, the practitioner who looks for new ways to love because they want to prepare themselves for the possible, wills themselves to love daily through making choices informed by a pedagogy of heart. They consider: *how do I love?*

Love, water, cups may encompass great feeling, but perhaps most of all it is an ability. All of us are born ready to love and to receive love. It is a birthright. We are designed for relationality. Our need for connection is just the same as our need for physical nourishment. Real love is the "most fundamental of our innate capacities, never destroyed no matter what we might have gone through or might yet go through. It may be buried, obscured from view, hard to find, and hard to trust . . . but it is there. Faintly pulsing, like a heartbeat, beneath the words we use to greet one another, as we ponder how to critique others' work without hurting them, as we gather the courage to stand up for ourselves or realize we have to let go of a relationship—real love seeks to find authentic life, to uncurl and blossom."[22] Love is an innate ability, an act of will, it maintains the capacity to humanize lies within the heart.

Everyone has the potential to experience real love. The Knight of Cups sees love from this expanded perspective. In the matter of love, this Knight knows you are much more capable. It is incapacitating to be left unloved. It's a conditioned inferiority that makes us distrust that we are worthy of love. To overcome early imprinted messages about our love-ability (the ability to love and be loved), the Knight of Cups recognizes self-love as an ever-unfolding process that strengthens over time. Love has no fixed point of arrival. There is no end goal. The Knight of Cups's daily application and methodology of love is to not be reduced by events that happen to him outside of his control. The Knight of Cups exercises an elemental ability to progressively, radically reorient our views about the source of happiness or what and who brings joy. Work with this Knight to reclaim the love of which you are innately capable. Leaving love in the hands of anyone else leaves us vulnerable to having no love at all in our life. If it is understood to always come from outside, it is something that someone either delivers or takes away. This Knight transforms this understanding, showing us love is in our hands. It is *our* choice of what to hold onto, what to extend, and what to receive.

Dominator culture, in its negating binary, judges rather than observes, and voids all the good an individual does with one conflict. To keep from becoming either forever a victim or a dominator, we practice forgiveness and refuse a dehumanizing determination. Forgiveness centers self-respect and a dignity that, though it may be wounded, recovers. Rather than judging another we observe the greater totality of their, and our, humanity. With humility, self-compassion, and self-forgiveness, we gain greater capacity to think in love's terms and forgo vengeance. Accepting and accommodating imperfections and disappointments, but still willing to be led by the open heart, the Knight of Cups is a testament to the heart's resilience.

Others may awaken or threaten love, but thanks to this Knight I know love as a capacity that is mine. This understanding is liberating though daunting. Knights follow a natural progression from ability to responsibility. Responding to the question of responsibility challenges the Knight of

Cups to cultivate love even in deeply difficult circumstances. It becomes a test of compassion. In pleading a commitment to cultivating the practice of love, the Knight of Cups attempts to love everyone by pinpointing the *how*. The practice is with everyone, not just the people we naturally like. Loving the stranger, loving the other, even the ones beaming hate or intending me harm, is a daily struggle. The Knight of Cups recognizes that our capacity to love is distorted by economic inequality and social injustice. This Knight does not succumb to relating with hatred, negativity, or shame because of disagreement or feelings of disdain.

When the purpose given to the fight is for the restoration of humanity, the fight constitutes an act of love, and the fighter is always known as a Knight of Cups. This Knight follows the pedagogy of the heart with sustained relation between cognition and emotion. Love—a radical, revolutionary love—is a method of resistance, a vehicle for social change, a practice of freedom.

The Knight of Cups determines the aesthetic experience in desire's expression as a force infusing artistic vitality into the mundane. For this Knight, emotionally embodied experience is an art. They seek immersion, taking in, responding, producing.

"It's satisfying to be emotionally, intellectually, and artistically immersed as critical spectator and producer/designer; such immersion has the potential to become transformative when coupled with activist goals of effecting social change out of a commitment and love for self and community."[23]

This Knight enables the heart, willingly sharing themselves as a feeling, loving person. They are unrelenting in the courageous embrace of emotional honesty. The Knight displays discerning vulnerability, enveloping the reader in greater emotional sensitivity. Because they share in the struggle with loneliness and grief, we can speak freely of fresh love with this Knight, with all of its accompanying titillating newness. Love is a force of movement to be followed, with endless emanations.

Knight of Pentacles

All my longing to belong, to find a culture of place, all the searching I did from city to city, looking for that community of like-minded souls was waiting for me in Kentucky, waiting for me to remember and reclaim. Away from my home state I often found myself among people who saw me as clinging to old-fashioned values, who pitied me because I did not know how to be opportunistic or play the games that would help me get ahead.[24]

The Knight of Pentacles is looking for a life worth living. This calls upon nothing more than a humble honesty, a consistent embodiment, a sophisticated sensuality that trusts the body's physical communication. The Knight of Pentacles is able to live in an existence of *insecure security.*[25] They do not demand absolute certainty or fixed solutions to move forward. They know that to embrace change, they must tolerate uncertainty. Even in the staunchness of their steadfast standing, the Knight of Pentacles remains open to foreign lands, revised dreams, alternate paths. With an ethos of sustainability that appropriately cares for the world's resources, they pursue belonging, the homeplace that is sanctuary on earth. To have a sense of homecoming, one must know nature as the place of victory, a free place where race and identity constructions fall away. We need firm ground to stand on if we are to stand in integrity. No matter how estranged we have been, the Knight of Pentacles guides us home. The Knight of Pentacles connects geographical location and psychological states of being. They are driven by the power of place, cultivating communities of belonging, sharing in the stewardship of the land as an extension of a larger collective body. Still, even within the same place, different bodies produce different knowledges, arising from diverse personal experiences and positionalities. With diverse histories and locations, all bodies are valuable networks of knowing. Pursuing knowing is a form of embodiment sought by the Knight. No matter the chosen place or country of one's residence, the values that ground their being are truth-telling and responsible action. The Knight goes the distance by respecting, resourcing, and renewing the body, treating it as a site of exploration. They say it is okay to go at a speed the body can handle.

The Knight of Pentacles serves the historically dispossessed. This Knight knows dispossessed people on their terms, in relation to social history based on legacies of subjugation, treating their worlds as worthy of analysis, introspection and appreciation. To change material conditions, they attempt to change social relations. We desperately need the Knight of Pentacles to overcome a deeply embedded deficit paradigm. Deficit thinking is an extension of victim blaming that finds the fault within the individual character and a perceived lack of moral capacity. Deficit thinking evades assessing the social ecology of impoverishment. The Green Knight pushes perception of worth beyond a narrow focus on individual weakness, a focus often skewed by internalized "value-led" judgments of character that obscure the more potent social forces of racism, sexism, classism, and xenophobia. The Green Knight sees the forest for the trees. They prove that no one is worthless; they practice appreciation even in ghettos and slums because, as the Knight of Cups does with love, they know value arises from within, inherent within every life. They represent the necessity of the practitioner to shift perceptions of cultural deficits into appreciated funds of knowledge[26] as potential rich reservoirs of critical praxis engaging the culturally, bodily, and psychically diverse. The Knight of Pentacles champions self-worth by walking a path that proves that those outsiders punished with impoverishment by white supremacist capitalist imperialist patriarchs have resources that evidence resiliency, adaptability, and innovation.

The Knight of Pentacles reframes negative appraisals of individual behavior into asset appreciation so others become inspired to act in accountability with their self-worth. The Knight's insistence on appreciating historically accumulated and culturally developed funds of knowledge as essential for well-being facilitates social relationships that prize the exchange of resources, including knowledge, skills, and labor, that support communal survival and thriving. This Knight understands systems and cultivates ecologies of intelligent, embodied relationality. Their relations are anything but thin and single-stranded. The thickness of this Knight's relational perspective develops robustly over time. They are for long-term relationships. This reader-writer learns to draw from knowledge funds from multiple spheres of activity in which the client, the querent, or the self is enmeshed. This wealth appraisal is refined by seeking transferable value across context. Each distinct and new context is an opportunity for learning and exchange. And each context considered by the Knight of Pentacles is seen to contain ample cultural and cognitive resources with great potential utility. The fruition of that utility depends upon how they are used and toward what aims. The Knight of Pentacles emphasizes *strategic* knowledge that informs related *activity* or behavior essential to well-being that is driven by the needs of the community or querent.

While pursuing the utopia of social ecology, the Knight celebrates and encourages those persisting, alive, in spite of the barren, bereft landscape that has been left for Black and Brown people to tend, to restore. For like many disenfranchised and indigent, I take pride in place among the Arrowhead hills and mountains of the Serrano. The natural environment spoke to me when I found myself alone, depressed and despairing. It was backyard horses, coyote communion, and feathered supplication that kept my spirit alive and my body wanting nothing more than to explore a world beyond the ghetto. Still, I envision the humanity that would flourish in nourishing environments, and though I have since explored more of the world, I am persistent in discovering the treasure of each and every place.

Seven of Swords

Passing is what one has to do in the streets, in the greater culture, in order to dodge the persecution of being othered, and/or to reap the benefits of reading as one of the people in power, like that young biracial girl in the film *Imitation of Life* who has a Black mother but "passes" as white in her life outside the home, at times pretending she doesn't even know her own mother. It connotes tragedy, a betrayal. Walking realness on the other hand is an embodiment in the context of ball culture and all functions that reclaims from mass culture who is allowed to be "real." Basically it redefines whose lives matter. All of this distinction-making is to point out that, as it is within the Black community, the idea of "passing" has a stigma, is frowned upon. If you choose to do so, you're essentially a sellout, throwing your culture aside for the white-hetero gaze. From this perspective, it feels to me that Balou, a seemingly adept and thoughtful writer, used the language of passing intentionally, a choice equating walking realness with trying to pass as cis/straight, to deceive—to pass as the oppressor.[27]

The Seven of Swords is about betraying our masters. In the determination to live freer and fuller lives, the Seven of Swords finds unorthodox self-assertion. They warp language to disguise the subject of their dissent.

They partake of transformative flight to evade carceral geographies. Many readers look upon the figure tiptoeing away with stolen swords in plain sight as treacherous, treasonous, or an insubordinate defector, terms historically applied to the wartime resistance of the enslaved. These terms are only sensible upon the presupposition of a trust or allegiance previously forged. The masters believed their own propaganda, assuming the slave was harmless and even pampered in their "care," despite ample evidence of discontent. The Seven of Swords forces reconsideration, causing the mind to dwell on insurrections and our own self-deception. People who lie to themselves and others are unable to trust, and within the evidence of their dishonesty is a sidelined love.

Suddenly true character is unveiled in insolent actions, the deception of the double-agent consciousness made clear. We learn to read the "insolent" more carefully, no longer underestimating the extent the exploited will go to get free. It is the thief, the spy, the traitor card of Houdini and Robin Hood. Certain character-based estimations often reinscribe racist logic of implicit inferiority and baseness, but the figure in the Seven of Swords must be seen with a social awareness and recognition of structural subjugation. The card clarifies our implicit sociological conditioning toward crime and punishment. The character slipping away with five swords is the trickster, the scammer in the act of thievery. But perhaps they have gained access to gatekept, stolen knowledge from colonial institutions and are pirating it back to the people.

> *The harder white women pushed, the less slave women worked and the more they claimed personal time and space and authority over themselves and their families. When, with Union forces closing in, Emmeline Trott's mistress prepared to flee to Alabama, Trott made her claim, refusing to allow her mistress to take one of her sons along. This she could not have done before the war. Trott's husband, the carriage driver, ordered to drive the white family to Alabama, instead stole a horse and escaped to Union lines. Emmeline Trott had helped her mistress hide valuables from Union soldiers. She was not willing to sacrifice her freedom or her son's for her mistress's sake. In the wake of the departure of masters and mistresses, slave women like Trott began their own journey to freedom. Like Trott, the*

> *vast majority of slave women would make freedom on the ground where they stood in 1861.*[28]

In the midst of war and apocalypse, the card depicts the psyche grappling with the knot of contradictions, the linguistic discourses that must be severed if we are to be free from bondage. We may be attempting to *pass* or escape when pulling the Seven of Swords, seeking some subtle or overt self-sabotage. Internalized oppression co-opts us agents of our own dispossession. As B. Binaohan critiques the myth of the closet, a Seven of Swords sensibility emerges when the expectation that all trans people, Indigenous people, and/or people of color should be "out" is tossed aside. The problem with this social construction is that it expects marginalized bodies to be made more public, more readily available for consumption, less self-possessed. So the Seven of Swords renders the public body private. It disrupts the bodily dispossession that sanitizes desire or reins in sexuality. If your body is the state's property, the slave owner's property, the husband's property, then any act of reclamation will be a theft in the eyes of the master. Taking back their own body that had been rendered property of the state meant the "theft"—that is, reclaiming the liberty of their own autonomy—was not just a bodily insurrection but a linguistic one as well.

Escapism as a survival strategy is often more about dissociation than embodiment. As the principal recourse for fleeing bodily incarceration, psychological pathologizing is flight. As a card, the Seven of Swords offers tarot to the rebels, the fugitives, those with an outlaw sensibility. Swords and feathers, freedom, belonging itself, is configured around flight in the Seven of Swords. For the native born into criminality, the Seven of Swords comes with the sense that at any point you could be caught, captured, jailed. Feeling like a fraud, you become suspicious, observant, scurrying, always working toward a logical justification of the body's natural pleasure. Pleasure can touch upon this internalized law of the master that claims *our* joy is illegitimate. Pleasure is only accessible through embodiment, but this seems like a trap to the colonized. Pleasure-seeking becomes associated with feelings of danger or dishonest immorality. The body and soul can only be deprived so long till, under the duress of starvation, desperate to survive, we'll do anything. This is a precarious state to be in, for it can find one easily compromised.

From coercive bodily conditionings within contexts of servitude, the attempt to "pass" as a white person or be closer in proximity to whiteness, to stand in the mainstream, entails an abandoning in the reach toward hegemonic social acceptance. It certainly depicts the dangers of code-switching, of navigating "enemy territory." What is seen and what is said are also ways to hide away and be silent.

Race is a red herring, an effective strategy of conquest via diversion. It may be illusory, may be a fiction, but its effectiveness as a strategy of subjugation is nonetheless real. As the colonizing nation-state breaks apart Indigenous lands, dispersing and displacing peoples physically, Indigenous identity is severed in becoming a racial identity, where the focus shifts from modes of land sovereignty and homeland territorial jurisdiction to statelessness, social death, and fugitivity. So the Seven of Swords is about the assault of settler-colonial theft and the ways in which oppression is increasingly made invisible. It draws attention to the violence of appearances within colonial recognition, to become aware of what's still being appropriated, what harm is hiding in plain sight. Colonial recognition structurally ensures continued access to Native peoples' lands and resources. The Seven of Swords depicts the way representation fails us by offering symbolic acts of redress that veil the further entrenching in law and practice of settler colonialism. We must not watch them steal our land, knowledge, and people right in front of our eyes. Our participation—our investment in the dominant culture, institutions, and popularized representations—benefits the state in an asymmetrical fashion. State apologies for past harm are a smokescreen to avoid the structural injustices continuing to inform the settler-colonial present. It is the subterfuge of broken treaties, broken words that refuse to acknowledge the political authority of Native nations. The Seven of Swords figure is in dangerous, uncertain territory. They are an outsider on the inside. It calls into question whether and to what extent we must participate in the state's legal and political apparatus. And so it is seeking to decolonize without the sanction, permission, or engagement of the state or Western theory.

The political sensibility found within "disloyalty" is key for the oppressed to exploit possibilities for freedom. It is a point of departure wherein we seize the property of our body, stealing time back from capitalist constructions. Then there is no more "Who said *you* could do that, by whose authority?" I move and act by my own authority, doing what feels good and free, for it is sacred to embrace and express joy freely. Escapism becomes the knowing determination that *I am going to be free*.

The pain of being made alien to one's native place via colonization is remedied in recovering and reclaiming the traditional values of the past without needing to transcend them. Reclamation serves to reestablish the Seven of Swords actor as a historical protagonist in the present. Ideas of how justice should look are left behind to more deeply discern how (in)justice functions all the while. The figure, reflecting the rebellious character of the decolonized, turns away from capitalist aims of progress to instead regenerate political and intellectual traditions in Indigenous cultural ways of being. They regress to recover language, knowledge systems, and ways of being. They present an ethicopolitical practice of Indigenous resurgence. They reclaim and redistribute narrative space, taking the assimilated tongue back so as to shout rebellion.

Attending to the inequitable distribution of character development, the card calls for renovated structures of subjectivity, via the insurgent subjectivity, to seize social agency. Those at the margins have a full and rich subjectivity. They stand alone, opening a world of language, politics, aesthetics, and perception that is contrary to dominant modes of knowing and being.

"Our glamour, our joy, our magic, are not commodities to be ripped off and sold back to us by corporations, they are ours. When they try to steal our essence, we slip away like snakes and leave them only the shedded skin."[29]

The Seven of Swords signifies turning against a symbolic system, but the danger is to not be caught in a structure of counterdetermination. Shapeshifting in taking the chance toward freedom, the Seven of Swords depicts disclosure as a tool of the individual determining how to move through the world with what they need to feel safe, free, alive. Whereas in the Seven of Wands, the minoritarian implements direct, pronounced resistance strategies, the Seven of Swords survives hostile public spheres with strategies of disidentification.[30] Finding themselves within the dominant public sphere, the Seven of Swords's subversion works within and outside simultaneously, neither opting to assimilate nor able to strictly oppose environments settled upon dominant ideology. "Instead of buckling under the pressures of dominant ideology (identification, assimilation) or attempting to break free of its inescapable sphere (counter-identification, utopianism), this 'working on and against' is a strategy that tries to transform a cultural logic from within, always laboring to enact permanent structural change while at the same time valuing the importance of local or everyday struggles of resistance."[31] The Seven of Swords makes mirrors out of dominant discourses and texts that were never meant to reflect oppressed subjectivity, to contrive ways to read or see yourself where you aren't supposed to. A positionality rendered unthinkable by the hegemons erupts as they crack the code of cultural scripts, reconstituting the raw material of the lock. We are no longer held captive by narrative. If the narrative is encoded into our minds and bodies, it is up to us to turn it around and revise. We come to treat our stories with respect but without allowing them a stranglehold in our determination.

"Someone might be coming down the runway in Chanel from head to toe, and one person is like, 'Wow it's so sad that they need to be wearing Chanel to think they matter, to think they're beautiful.' Then someone else is like, 'It's a gag that she stole all of that last night. She's proving you don't have to have wealth to look sickening. It's an anti-capitalist act.' I think a lot of the times it's actually both."[32]

To create movement out of static caricatures we seize space, attention, and time from the realms we've been barred from or locked into; like Lauryn Hill, we get out. We deploy a strategic double consciousness and enact narrative insurgency. The contexts within which we work toward decolonization may differ, but we each endeavor to overturn the matrix of being, power, and knowledge that maintains colonial structures and consciousness. In seemingly inescapable dire socioeconomic conditions, amid impossibly tight constraints, a sly space of freedom is found by the Seven of Swords sensibility. For a life outside of the claustrophobic confines of a carceral country, the Seven of Swords maintains the desire for mystery and contestation, for a love outside of limitation.

Something in Oz, in me, was amiss, but I tried not to notice. I was intent on the search for love, affirmation, my reflection in eyes of blue, gray, green.

Searching, I found something I didn't expect, something decades of determined assimilation could not blind me to: in this great gay mecca I was an invisible man; still I had no shadow, no substance. No history, no place. No reflection. I was alien, unseen, and seen, unwanted. Here, in Hepzibah, I was a nigga, still. I quit—the Castro was no longer my home, my mecca (never was, in fact), and I went in search of something better.[33]

Without the force of criminality we would more easily make the decision to be visible. My behavior, my pleasurable expression was so policed that I became so self-conscious and ashamed that depression swallowed me whole. Without witness, we are never recognized at our true stature; nor do we feel we will ever come of age. I tried to slip away, seeking safety through strategic means, but eventually the Seven of Swords called on me to move with an authenticity that was contrary to expectation. We make ourselves invisible until we are dragged into the light by our own determination. Taking responsibility for the things that I do means I don't have to hide in the darkness. I reclaim privacy with no shame or sense that I must justify my behavior to those who seek to exploit me. I contemplate the Seven of Swords attempting to offer medicine for those who don't really feel seen. The present is mutable; a future beyond the past beckons.

Seven of Wands

What is my life if I am not visible? Contrary to what homosexual rhetoric suggests, my queerness and my radical femininity are not just retractable features of a grander being who can comfortably exist in a cis-heteronormative society. These are not secrets that only expose themselves in who I "choose" to love, in the privacy of my own space, no. My feminine queerness is in all of my identity; it lives in every part of my body and it will manifest through my gestures, my behavior, my walk, my thoughts, the way I dress, and all the things that make me visible as who I truly am. These are not tricks. Even my chandelier earrings do not serve a decorative purpose. They make me, me. So if ever I had to suspend my visibility . . . I would be socially dead. But though I am alive, I am still not safe. An attack is penciled into the fate of every day, as long as I have the audacity to exist. Attacks range from a disapproving glance from a stranger, refusal of entry from a taxi driver on the way to work, to a whole street screaming and shouting in your direction as they did to Glow and me last Saturday on Eloff Street. These attacks, physical or otherwise, are all violent and they are all equally traumatic, and above all, they compromise the quality of one's overall life, therefore it is not enough for hateful transphobic comments to be replaced by passive compliments upon entering "safer spaces" when you still have to walk out and exist in an unsafe world.[34]

The Seven of Wands is yet another strategy to practice asserting your right to exist, taking back all the space long denied. While the Seven of Swords is the flight response, fight is found in the Seven of Wands. From powers asserting beyond the frame, several wands work against the central figure to tell us we are in friction with forces we can't even see. The enemy is on all sides and all at once and it is depersonalized and still it is an assault on the body. It's a moment when you realize, yet again, you exist in a world with historical structures organized around misogynoir. So from this friction comes the construction of a queer selfhood, which hooks describes as "a self at odds with everything around it and [that] has to invent and create and find a place to speak and to thrive and to live."[35] It is an existence that has only known resistance, only ever defended against contradictions and impositions of the outside world. The queer Seven of Wands's self-assertion guards against appropriation, co-optation, cannibalistic cultural consumption, and microaggressions. To reconcile ourselves we must stand in defiance. We must be the active resistance against forces of domination. Pull the Seven of Wands, refusing to let dignity or freedom be taken from us.

The Seven of Wands is for any artist who wants uninhibited, unrestrained cultural terrain. This means the artist's work must inherently challenge the institutionalized systems of domination. These systems seek to shut down the potential for the artist's creative self-realization, for such systems are always attempting to limit, co-opt, and exploit the artist and their art. It is difficult for anyone operating in the cultural marketplace to defend against art that seeks to usurp the real. Entanglements within the capitalist, corporate machine threaten the virtue, the soul, of the artist. The capitalist formation of the American project is predicated upon an isolating individualism. The superficial seduction of immediate recognition and some measure of attention may be offered in a turn that still marginalizes and sets apart. None of us are free from this struggle against a profound internalized colonization that has a primary apparatus in the media. But the Seven of Wands stands against this threat to the artist and their work. The Seven of Wands necessarily champions the free-moving spirit that creates provocatively and openly. They are vigilant in their defense of difference. Artists, readers, writers must be literate enough to break the hold of colonizing representations. Their work will be necessarily provoke.

Cultivating a community of diverse aesthetic and artistic identities, standpoints, locations, and practices calls upon a solidarity that counters the individualistic standpoint of consumerism. To maintain such a stance requires hard work. It takes training, self-awareness, and everyday emotional fortitude. This is the deep labor of reclaiming self-assertion. In developing the sense of who "I" can possibly be in the ghetto that is this white supremacist world, I found a burning determination to talk back. In contestation I could take a counterhegemonic stance and fashion a way to continue growing, learning, and holding myself with regard. I find a way to disrupt the spaces that confine or constrain the authentic reality of my existence. I reject the images, the narratives, the interpretations, the structures of symbolic and material reality that reinforce and perpetuate the subordination and hierarchy of bodies. Resisting the image, diverting the gaze, is much the same as shielding the body from a blow. The Seven of Wands is this shield of the imagination. By saying no, blocking entry to imposing imperial forces, and changing positions we ourselves become a revolutionary body and subjectivity. The young, queer, Black, Brown, trans body has unique power to dismantle gender binaries and class disparity. The increasingly visible, highly vulnerable trans folk are the ones evolving our understanding of desire, gender, sex, and sexuality. "It's an old-school reticence, I admit, shaped on the playgrounds of my early dyke days, where bulldaggers who almost passed as men reflected all I feared and admired because of the great courage it took for them to publicly stand in that dangerous, visibly queer place. In that mixed-matched body."[36] However, creating subjectivities with enough vision and insight to resist racist stereotypes and challenge the imagination is no simple task. It is a baptism of fire that calls upon the integral power of those possessing pronounced female *and* male attributes, fundamental to creation. It takes courage to walk in the memory of what the dominant culture has forgotten, the way we walked before war.

The Seven of Wands is a card that necessitates action. There is intervention, there is a body revolting, defying the norm. The Seven of Wands says you have to go through fire first. Each has to confront all the suspicious definitions of themselves. We could withstand anything in the refusal to be left abandoned in a lie. An honest-conscienced courage bent on freedom proclaims love freely despite every social mandate demanding silence. The fire strips away delusion and makes you lean, so you may see the core of your selfhood, so that then you may make peace. Then is the arrival of the delicious, fully formed adulthood. It is a trial by fire from which we emerge unburnt. There is strain and stress, feeling like we are fighting alone, but still we stand firm. There is an active challenge to how *you* exist in the world when you are Brown and femme. Those who aren't fighting for their survival in systemic oppression cannot often appreciate the radical acts of self-determination we ingeniously enact. A powder keg of creativity erupts in the Seven of Wands, from which our response to a host of chronic cultural constructs creates a disciplined commitment to artistry in the practice of freedom.

Rally the courage to take a stand, to defend our selfhood, standing visibly in the struggle. Self-assurance, self-declaration is transgressive and subverts the previous imposition of institutional silencing. And so the Seven of Wands defends the spaces where queer, feminist freedom lives, the spaces where these bodies express most freely, which must be every space. A body branded, a light dimmed, targeted, and subject to assault, has no illusions about a so-called safe space. The queer body is open, despite attempts to foreclose; it is revealing, which enables the multiplicity of identity. Though to receive the potential abundance of this body's creative being, artistic processes, and cultural creations there must be a continuity of affirmation and support from all possible fronts, very much the inverse of the Seven of Wands iconography. The notion of the disenfranchised succeeding over limiting hardship, against historical struggle, as some sort of artistic initiation is a delusion of false consciousness. I want, with the Seven of Wands, to interrogate this image and imagine instead grace, ease, and mutually nourishing support.

Practicing freedom in daily life entails uniting embodied, physical expression with the will to imagine. The will may meet extreme resistance, but its execution is always a liberatory act. Whatever force summons us to the page, the protest, the politic, the poem is summoned in this card. The Seven of Wands makes clear that Seven is about discipline. Erupting passions can overwhelm or become the fuel to break through the barriers that block our full potential. Forbidden desires, continuously denied, deaden us inside. To live in and with the body of our natural desire, the Seven of Wands shows us what is more than what we want; what, if we did not do, we would die. The defender or defense of desire that is fundamentally as spiritual as it is sexual is found in the Seven of Wands, for what would become of the body that is a site of resistance without the vantage of desire's duty? It is in the body of desire that rebellion continues to burn.

The words, which are our praxis, we speak daily *against* a context of dehumanization become the *language of war.*[37] The work of literacy is its own warriorship. We only write what we can't not, what we are compelled to write. In our attempt to speak freely the Seven of Wands warrior-artist wants their tongue to be tormented in the unendurable light of God. Those writers, artists, teachers, diviners, who protect us like gladiators, keep us from falling over the edge into the abyss of cultural oblivion. If they could not do this work, if they could not speak their truth, I, like you, would disappear from the face of the Earth. In the small spaces in the upper chambers of the soul, afforded by these champions, the fire of tongues rains down.

Seven of Cups

One of the first achievements to be made in the reconciliation of body and spirit, which is a prerequisite for a deepened, soul-filled sexuality, is a rediscovery of the virtue and value of the body's eroticism. To find the soul of sex we have to wrench it out of the materialistic and mechanistic body that we have created by means of our modern philosophies and reunite it with the subtle, fantasy-filled, mythologized body of the imagination.[38]

The Seven of Cups invites the reader into a world of shadows, for in its enfolding blackness is the location of our destiny. In the cups' overflowing water are many mirrors for what was once real, present, and embodied. Possibility outlines the past, present, and future in this Seven of Cups state. In decontextualized desire is an insistence to find ecstasy in daily life through our habits of being. The Seven of Cups's key to transfiguring desire is to treat every desire as valid. It finds us inebriated on thirst, giving into desire's overabundant excess, into the changing substance of pleasure. It is a place where we question our cravings, attempting to discern essence, substance, or motive from form. Is what we want, or what we need, even any good for us at all? Is there space to want differently, space to be less immediate in your choice? How often do you dream new dreams, and what will develop when your aspirations age? It is then desire that disrupts restraint (inhibition). Desire exposed is revelation.

The sexual history that has been rendered "spectral through discrimination" is held in the Seven of Cups.[39] It is where we access every yearning we've ever had, where all the desire that has ever been denied gets stored, where all wishes waiting to incarnate await. It's a reservoir of dreamscapes, an aesthetic dimension of alternate realities and potential timelines. These openings have requisite ambivalence attached to them. None of us know the portals at the bottom of the ocean, but what great and new art yields from the same dark source where desire is preserved. So too there are depths of desire still unknown within us. To leave one world for another requires dwelling in liminal zones, *nepantla,* the bardo. The essential unknowability of water makes it a mirror where everyone can see their reflection as they stretch their psyche's capacity for fantasy, for world-building based upon innermost yearning. The Seven of Cups presents an opportunity to ask ourselves, "If I look at what's happening through the eyes of love, how would I tell this story?"[40] We become curators of a poet's political imagination, learning to read the screen, read the image, with criticality. We cannot escape the truth of what we have seen, but changing *how* we see will affect *what* we see.

"As a practice, disidentification does not dispel those ideological contradictory elements; rather, like a melancholic subject holding on to a lost object, a disidentifying subject works to hold on to this object and invest it with new life."[41]

The crux of the Seven of Cups is discernment: which desire to satiate, where to turn our attention, what to give body to, how to read the screen so something new is seen in the same image. We can wait till we want differently. To the imagination, no power is absolute. Anything from any era can be remade, reimagined, in the huge creative outlet found in the Seven of Cups. It's related to an ethos of recycling appetite: nothing and no longing is without worth. The essence transforms, and the appearance undergoes a process of reformulation. Out of the objects, ideologies, and symbols offered by dominant culture, the Seven of Cups gives form to the dreams we've long been denied. This is the artistry of dissent, the progressive social change that always starts in the imagination. In the Seven of Cups's search for the most eloquent expression possible so vision may move into reality. Create symbols of a new reality, born in the crisis of change.

Even in the wake of erasure, we recognize that desires come from many sources wanting many forms. We learn to love as a poly-amor. The Seven of Cups shows tarot has an indexical use, capturing, collecting, and weaving poetic coherence out of fragmentation to maintain an active kernel of utopian possibility. This card is participatory. We choose, discern, challenge, revise and practice artistic freedom to struggle for liberation.

Or rather it unveils desire as interconnected, in the way that all water returns to the source that is limitless. Cupidity is a pathway. To get free we must pass through the aesthetic dimension, following beauty's lead. Play is how we find passage through a mode of life that exists without fear and anxiety, and thus with a manifest freedom. Like a Sailor Moon–silhouetted power-up, the form of desire evolves. Within the fulfillment of one lies the seed of another, until finally it takes you toward union with the Divine, until all sense of separating desires are sated. Perhaps a lifetime's journey to embrace the desire that is more than any one cup could contain.

The Seven of Cups foregrounds the aesthetic so the subject can continuously change. From the aesthetic dimension great art is brought into the world upon the ability of artists to be critically reflective, perceiving many at once. Desire emerges radically liberated, never static, always developing. Beauty is beheld in its own right, on its own terms despite its supposed function or "usefulness." Beauty is sustenance in the face of scarcity and suffering. The erotic spills into everyday life, making the mundane sacred. Life becomes the space where beauty is made manifest.

Seduced by fantasy, aroused by the imagination, and in the ecstasy of a pleasure beyond your body's singular capacity, the Seven of Cups envelops and retains the erotic. Through ongoing satiation, fulfilled eros becomes bigger and bigger, becoming the creator of culture. Judgment becomes appreciation as we allow ourselves to marvel at creation, enraptured by futuristic forces coming into being through our very own body. Phantasms move through every body, creating a fantasy ethnoscape across the bodies mixing, sharing, exchanging the orgiastic. We realize, in the Seven of Cups, that we are always in so many relations, truly never single. "A solidarity [is] born of the fact that one's own quiet labor in the dark is the shadow of the same act committed by others in 'the same clandestine dark thousands of miles away.'"[42]

It calls forth and praises everything brought to our erotic encounters (fantasy, feeling, technologies, images, memories, electricity, water, flora, fauna, etc.). It posits the alchemical, substantive, material change to the eros body, becoming more as more meaning is infused into the body. This change happens backstage. It is the patience of the audience, letting sensual pleasure yield aesthetic appreciation. It teaches us to conjure. It teaches oneiromancy so we may become *nepantleras* dream-walking between worlds, facilitating passage for our people. It acknowledges a queer sexuality that is fluid, open-ended, spacious, and presenting in plurality. It is the simultaneous identifications with erotic multiplicity. It is the hallucinatory knowing of the shaman, the artist, the image-makers, tarot-readers, weavers of otherworldly knowledge responsible for a sacred language that is more than an arithmetic of symbols. It is a flight of altered consciousness, engaging suppressed Indigenous perceptual repertoires. Fantasy functions fervently. Desire searches for pleasure continuously, exploring and envisioning any number of potential paths toward fulfillment. Attempts to contain the sea of longings are illusory.

Still the card insists that behind illusion lies knowledge. The imagination has its own truths to tell. The deepest levels of the subconscious link with the art of the highest consciousness in the imagination working toward reconciliation. The imagination mediates the senses and the intellect, desire and realization, so that reality comes from the dreamscape. In every moment there are many paths. Like ghosts and queer spirits in the air, choice hangs; to change life, the Seven of Cups teaches the reader to see them. Disrupting the boundaries between public and private, life and death, the Seven of Cups seer reveals all held in interiority.

Desire, vitality, or pleasure we've been forced to forgo is again imaginable by the Seven of Cups. Latent potentials desiring carnal realization come to the forefront. Many here confuse sexual hedonism with sexual liberation. There must be an ethics of eros that transcends the question of where we fit in the marketplace. "We are bought and buyer, sold and selled cheaply, especially if one is coily-haired and brown. Market logic says 'it's not racism or sexism, the preference, it's choice.'"[43] This choice comes at a loss to the other's freedom, for is there really one who is offered up to make all your wishes come true who isn't dehumanized in their exoticization? True love builds no cages. We are responsible for choosing the values by which we live, the dreams we affirm. We take a fresh look, question, and if necessary, revise. We enter the laboratory of ideas, the studio. We decolonize the imagination by first recognizing that white supremacy is propagated in large part by the media, the vast power of the image to affect the psyche. The Seven of Cups asks, "Why should white supremacist aesthetics still be dominating our lives?" to effect perceptual plasticity. The task is to make images that exploit, distort, or deny, become "pleasurable, erotic, and self-affirming."[44] We free the figure from its historic associations of and with abuse and domination. Disorderly ways of knowing born by dwelling in altered states stand in opposition to coloniality, crossing the confines of the normal toward the extraordinary erotic consciousness. Divination is a daily practice in transgressing boundaries, as it is a place where visionary insights are revealed.

As we reject repression to choose passion, we reclaim the expansive feeling nature that portends, through fantasy, an expanded capacity for fulfillment, an increased sense of pleasurable possibility. Pleasure is how the Seven of Cups lays to rest. The obliteration of orgasm grants entry into a state of rest that is erotic contemplation. And when we awake, we will have become anew. This rest allows us to rise in fullness. By turning our back on those who would discount our experience, the black figure with her own gaze creates an alternative space to be self-determining. The water is life and blessing, beheld by the foregrounded black subjectivity. This knowledge held herein is threatening, subjugated, and recently remembered. She becomes her own authority of witness, her own historical subject. She is witness to water and its meaning for her life.

We meet love beyond the veil. The Seven of Cups is the diasporic landscape of longing. Longing is a force of loss where, in states of melancholy, the bereaved share life with the dead in the mourning that refuses to finish, while they share scenes from the future, whispering what will be. In measure with the lost love we mourn, slowly fading back to black, we suffuse the self with the light of new horizons. Death survives by consuming life. Poets pay tribute to their dead, keeping them from dissolving into oblivion. Reconciliation with lost mothers and grandmothers only exists in states of flowing, floating suspension.

Seven of Pentacles

I found that folks in these men's lives (parents, friends, lovers, etc.) both expected and accepted that they would need space and time apart for the workings of the everyday to blossom, for them to engage in necessary renewal of spirit. For the most part, their biographies and autobiographies revealed that these men did not have to spend an inordinate number of hours justifying their need for contemplation, for time to be alone, to revel in quietude, to work undisturbed.[45]

The Seven of Pentacles calls for feminist artistic practice, calling for folks other than cishet males to claim space for creative contemplation and reverie. As solitude is a necessary ritual for artistic self-actualization, for the *other* to enhance their creative capacity they must reclaim their right to solitary space.

Standing in the Seven of Pentacles is yet another vigilant figure. Sleeplessly watchful, they tend to the harvest of the earth, the body's creative fruition, the good thing growing. The figure is in a state of contemplation, implying critique. The shape it will take is amorphous, so the card reflects a need to defend representations, images, and understandings from and by the oppressed from being continuously devalued. Otherwise, like the Seven of Pentacles figure, we will question whether our toil is futile. Each of the Sevens, in their own way, takes a stand. Everyone wants to live the fast life, but the Seven of Pentacles goes against the capitalist pressure to work quickly, to blossom when everyone else does, or that says you should do these things lest you risk never really arriving.

Artists are the ones who birth from their flesh creative nourishment to all, expressive fulfillment for self. Artists are mothers, caretakers, intermediaries working the land to harvest the bounty of the muse, the mother. The pregnant, laboring body is a vulnerable body. Acknowledging its vulnerability does not deny its strength. Rather, it calls for valuing vulnerable lives.

Part of the work of an artist is also found in time spent in contemplation and solitude. The space of this meditative time looks differently and changes, but is a needed space-time nonetheless. Sometimes, as with the Seven of Cups, the space is dreamy, inspired, and visionary; and at other times, as with the Seven of Pentacles, not much appears to be happening. This *negative* space, the bounty of absence, is as necessary for artistic fruition as water is to growing life. It is solitary and silent; it is patient in its unknowing, dark development. Nurturance needs stillness. For the breath of this young life, there can be no breaks.

There is communion in letting the project of life grow into what it wants to. This is relating to the land with respect rather than entitlement. For despite our best planning, hoeing, and toiling, our crop is susceptible to forces beyond our being. These may be violent, sudden, and tragic, quickly changing the trajectory that artists spend so long cultivating. But an artist is anyone making beauty out of the tragedy life has handed them.

All artists need time, but marginalized artists often deal with the stressful urgency of limited access to material resources and external investments in their skill and craft. This affects their work and disrupts their ability to develop slowly, with care and intention. Each of the Sevens creates oppositionally, actively against the grain. The Seven of Pentacles depicts the struggle to find time, the fight to reclaim time. The workers' bodily freedom is a sacred struggle to limit the working day. This takes thoughtful effort, the changing of one's relationship and experience of their body in time. The *negative space* that an artistic practice requires, for the marginalized creator, entails the formation of a liberatory space. The space the Seven of Pentacles consciousness constructs is one uninterrupted, undisturbed, wherein we can contemplate with abandon, necessary to sustain a body of creation.

If we feel that no time has been given to us to fulfill our calling, then it is we who must take time. I still imagine the support of patrons, investors who recognize that the worth of my potential is a sure bet because of my devotion; I still imagine that the appreciation for teachers will one day be materially reflected in recognition of history's inequities; I imagine reparations. But still we teach, we write, we read, we create value even in the face of external depreciation, by standing in the recognition of our worth.

To give myself more time I decided to teach independently. It may have appeared to everyone else that I was making an abrupt life choice after a flurry of years working endlessly to become a credentialed English teacher, with graduate degrees and professional recognition. But the Seven of Pentacles comes with that kind of seven-year itch as one seriously considers whether it is time to leave. I decided that to continue growing as an educator, thinker, and community member, I had to leave the formal education institution. By leaving I was actually committing to see the potential of my artistic practice, my teaching, all the way through. I made a counterinvestment by investing in myself. I worked with the Seven of Pentacles to establish a value system not determined by capitalism. I sacrificed financial security to have spiritual, mental, and creative stability, not to be altruistic within some spectacle of moralistic renunciation but because what I value most is my freedom of expression, in body and being, and above all, the luxury of time.

Financial fear colors the relationship to daily life. There is never enough money for the capitalist, and yet capitalism sells an illusory security that soon enough becomes the maximum security of a prison cell. It is a regular practice to give myself permission to fill my time with prayer and pleasure. I move through fears of financial insecurity by learning to exalt the honesty of my devotion. The intensity of my drive to answer the call to write, calling me back from my break, even when my wrists are sore and strained, adheres to the necessity for sustained work. I feel more comfortable accepting the truth of my circumstantial uncertainty because I use my time as honestly as I can. I suspect that fear is just a cover for the guilt I initially felt about seizing time for artistic creation.

What will only grow with devoted attention is some love-fruit antithetical to the abusive neglect that impoverishes a people and a place. The Seven of Pentacles contemplates what it takes to emerge from a food desert that has made the body deficient and the spirit stunted. For life to not simply emerge but to blossom where it has not before, it needs nutrients it was never given before. It needs intervention. There must be water, protection, warmth, light, caring communication, time.

For I am creating out of faith made flesh. When there is the Seven of Pentacles, there is concrete evidence of all that has been sowed. Can you roll around in that, ground yourself in the pleasure of that, and simply bask in the baby birthed from your very body that no one else even noticed was there? Can you contemplate celebrating the laboring body enough to depict the dignity of undervalued work with a body at rest? Disability politics is also poised in the assertion of bodily dignity. This dignity sustains; it ensures resilience and enables longevity. The Seven of Pentacles is a bodily assertion read as a political act of resistance. I see the Taínos, experts of the land, like the High Priestess, resist exploitation by withholding vital information from colonizers. "Lacking knowledge and fearful of the 'untamed' forests, the Spanish starved. The Tainos' refusal to grow food took the lives of 'half the Spanish population' on the settlement. They died of hunger only a short distance away from a 'seemingly endless supply of mangoes, papayas, avocados.'"[46] In the Seven of Pentacles is the refusal to harvest fresh fruit with broken bodies. A transcorporeal vision of the Seven of Pentacles sees land workers uniting with body laborers like disability activists also protesting the endangerment of working bodies, such as the farmworkers protesting pesticide poisoning. The Seven of Pentacles reminds the worker of their rights, their immense power in harvesting the wealth of life that is dependent upon the Earth.

Many are thwarted in their resistance and reclamation of time, so from a solitary stance the Seven of Pentacles is a signal of solidarity. It calls for us to theorize and interrogate artistic production, as an active political movement, from a feminist, decolonial standpoint. Reading tarot has kept me accountable to this interrogation, reflecting my strategies and actions back to me so I may continuously revise my perspective in regularly meeting all that I do not know. It is investing inquiry in female creativity, because it is women, irrespective of race, class, etc., whose artistic creation, whose manifest selfhood, is most devalued and denied.

The Seven of Pentacles, with the sickle, cuts away the animosity of indifference. It tends to the soil of the soul. In the moments of reflection upon one's psychosocial material reality, a criticality bursts forth that changes the trajectory of our growth, our understanding of environmental relationality. Compassionate responsibility comes through critical environmental awareness. There is value in withholding or resisting because resistance can be employed to affirm the dignity of all life.

My friend told me that the Seven of Pentacles is being *all up in* your manifestation. It is a miracle to stand here at the place of fruition, because it took getting on the ground, touching and tilling soil, daily watering, and daily praying to the rain gods to get here. It took trust that our efforts were not in vain. Each alleged failure redeemed in the vision that becomes more refined, more tolerant and perceptive. Then yields the fruit we actually desire to harvest. You have just built something beautiful and soon will savor it. What a gift it is, after being hungry for so long, to be at the banquet of your dreams. Let yourself be gracious with your ravenous discovery.

EIGHT

A complex symbol embracing several important meanings all of which are related to the central idea of a tightly closed link. It implies also the symbol of the spiral and the sigmoid line. The sign for infinity—the horizontal figure 8—as well as the number 8 itself, are at once interlacing and also knotted, and this emphasizes the relationship of the knot with the idea of infinity—or, rather, with the manifestation of the infinite. It is comparable with the net, the loop and the plait, in that it expresses the concept of binding and fettering—a concept which is generally expressive of an unchanging psychic situation, however unaware of his predicament the individual may be: for example, that of the unliberated man who is "tied down" by the Uranian god.[1]

Eight is the serpent's number, for it takes the serpent's shape and so partakes of its wisdom. There is a success that is achieved in the spiralic rather than the linear. It is the difference between hybridity and integration, that which yields total transformation. Rather than negotiation, it is a force of regeneration. In the Eights, the outer circumstances reflect the changing psychic landscape, the inner transformation. The generative field of the soul's deep-seated creative power is Eight's dynamic unfoldment, and we begin to see the shape of the soul more clearly. Its language is in its own style, natural and flexible.

The system Eight establishes is self-regulating. Recycling energetic, psychosomatic materia, Eight endures through every revolution. Eight fortifies. Subtly connected to Justice, Eight determines that balance is not symmetry. The projection of the mirror image splits an integrative body, while balance can be achieved, artistically, by a small red mark to the left of a larger neutral-colored canvas, which gets to the sense that equality is not about sameness; which gets to those distinctions between inequality, equity, equality, and justice.

Its balance of alternating power and systemic regulation can accommodate, accept, and transmute all energy. Eight repudiates nothing. For this love, zero is incorrigible. There is no bottom, no top, to Eight; just circles and circles of love. It survives by sustaining motion. It is a motor, a serpentine belt that powers all creation. Fluid from both energetic poles arrives at the still center. Energy in motion is maintained, is allowed to transform and flow into every expression. Emotion that is repressed or denied becomes still water, stagnant and mired. Behavioral repetition at regular intervals can make perception automatic, mechanical, lazy. Eight brings suppressed awareness to conscious attention to broker a consciousness beyond a bondage in an accidental world.

Eight harmonizes the previous numerical energies. It brings our spiritual revelation into daily life. To be freed from oppressive circumstances, the Eight searches for a way in, a way to renovate the psychic architecture and liberate the conditioned consciousness from self-loathing. Freedom comes from inner disarmament. The Eight presents the psyche's patterns. Unconscious behavior and relating hold much insight into our personal and collective fears, desires, and aspirations. Transpersonal experiences, our personal social net, our intimately mundane life become clearly interrelated by Eight. As experience is understood and applied to one's overall development, it is enfolded into the Eight, the body that passes through all things. Twice born, found in the moment's aspiration toward the harmony of infinity, it is an intermediary form, the shape between shape-shifting. Through the heavens' eternal spiral, spirit is made flesh, angel into animal, silence into song. One half tending toward form, the other toward form's dissolution. Eight devours life to re-create it, as memory fading into forgetfulness is surely to be summoned again. The Sun and Moon can only wait so long before they come to kiss again. Eight is the shared breath of their love. It is their passion play that shows our soul the way.

In Romanesque art, Eight entails the intersection of Earth with Heaven, the natural world spiritualized. In Medieval mystic cosmogony, Eight correlates to the fixed stars of the firmament, thought to be the plane where planetary forces have been surpassed. Whatever stands in the way of wholeness, the Eight subsumes. Flesh is given to get life going again, blood rushes, equilibrium changes, the deepest instinct fulfills the highest potential. Eight discharges the pains of the past, finding a point of karmic release right at the center, right at the heart.

"What is required is the finding of that Immovable Point within one's self, which is not shaken by any of those tempests which the Buddhists call 'the eight karmic winds': fear of pain, desire for pleasure; fear of loss, desire for gain; fear of blame, desire for praise; fear of disgrace, desire for fame."[2]

This is nothing less than an alchemical transmutation, the spirit liberated from ignorance, the soul finally embodied. The Eight exhibits that the symbol functions at several fundamental levels to achieve some expansive, viscerally imagined "I."

Strength

And so, I stand here . . . before you, Calvary, at the edge of infinity with no ideas and no plans, with my arms and my heart and my mind opened and I am saying, "oh, Lord Jesus, make me something new!" Yes. Oh, God, I'm asking you right now, I'm asking you to show me forgiveness where there can be none. Redemption when it's far too late. The waters where the wells long ago ran dry. Acceptance where there is hate. Lord God, I want you to show me what I can't explain. I want you to make me what I came to become. Yes, Lord God and I can say, please, please make me new.[3]

Strength incisively illuminates the moral questions embedded within the heart. It is a willing display of faith in which an appeal to the incomprehensible mercy of a love that overwhelms with its forgiveness becomes one that inspires surrender. It is a love that humanizes in its mercy, acceptance, and revival. From the suffering endured emerges a compassionate witness with Strength, and with it I've learned to summon the power of my strongest emotions without being overwhelmed by my own nature.

All humanization entails art-making, the upper levels of which are language. Although defense against and survival in a hostile environment also motivates the creative tongue. Evil is so loud, seems to have so much to say, that the creative ability in goodness's vocal delivery becomes background at best, forgotten at worst. Then fear seems to be the only response to a dangerous environment. Goodness always seems to be equated with weakness, and the weak with the feminine. The weak is the pitiful, the frightened and helpless. It's always a little girl running for her life through the woods. But her savior bores the audience, and it is only ever the pursuing villain who captures the imagination. Goodness is blasé, while evil is the blockbuster.

The work of evil is to silence goodness, to take attention and energy away from its pursuit and its intention. Yet there is no color without oppressed people's language. Those made strange in their own neighborhood are never heard properly when their address is to the white male gaze. They have been conditioned to estrange the expressions of emotional freedom that are most liberating. The voice of compassion has a hard time projecting, for it speaks softly from being subdued too long. It can be hard to speak our good name after it's been damned. We may consider the endeavor fruitless, frail, ironic, or requiring an apologetic disclaimer. Then the language of goodness is inextricable from courage. Forceful emotions such as anger, lust, or self-loathing may be the loudest, the most difficult to rein in, but Strength's love is stronger still.

Unbounded in the neoliberal marketplace, evil sells violence for profit. If our Strength is to be feminist, we are to be concerned with the consequences of violence. Fickle are fame, status, and employment, so a feminist ethics demands that our accountability to love be beyond accommodating the marketplace. Strength undoes the adherence to patriarchal systems of dominating power across sexuality, gender, class, etc. Strength eschews a politics in which the power any oppressed person pursues is patriarchal.

After tragedy beyond control has done us such deep damage, regret can run so deep it poisons everything. Repair comes from self-respect, which is often rooted in behavior. Ethical behavior, those actions that maintain and bolster our self-regard, begets goodness's nimble response to the threatening or dangerous. With self-respect comes the resilience goodness needs to deal with evil's incessance. For good, the difficulty, the evil, the trauma and tragedy are not a barometer of basic self-worth, so we endure without being disheartened. This language is the law of transgression. It knows the rules of language but also breaks them in interesting and powerful ways. It's never nailed down. It's always moving, leaving a little trail out of the woods. This is language that knows its limits. It knows there is never a final word, a final say, but it speaks striving still.

Nevertheless, Strength allows goodness its own speech, and its language is knowledge, and it is love. Strength helps us hear the voice of compassion, behind the silence of good deeds. Strength is realizing that shame, regret, and self-loathing do nothing to contribute to escaping the chain you've been taught to hang round your own neck. The rejection, the hurt, the trauma, the trouble you caused, the suffering you endured, are not all that you are, says the strong voice. So Strength is getting to a point where we know ourselves as more than the hurt that happened to us. With Strength, we comfort the fear that runs wild and rampant, that hides behind a mask of pride and egotism. That which frightens still deserves respect, and more than that, examination. Shame often stands in the way of these intimate attempts at knowing. Strength is a promise that we can get beyond the burden of shame by seeing the source of pain as an opportunity to care for and love ourselves more seriously. The compassion we cultivate in response to shame can then become a way to create deep connections with others, for it is from our deepest points that we connect heart to heart.

So Strength entreats its possessors to inquire more deeply into the whole of their nature. It calls on courage for self-discovery; but examining the beast, the fear, and the pain that must no longer be ignored comes with freedom. These beasts may run wild in the environment, but wherever they approach our realm it becomes our responsibility to bring them into submission. Sovereignty entails such responsibility and is only realized through this process of self-inquiry.

> *To search for power within myself means I must be willing to move through being afraid to whatever lies beyond. If I look at my most vulnerable places and acknowledge the pain I have felt, I can remove the source of that pain from my enemies' arsenals. My history cannot be used to feather my enemies' arrows then, and that lessens their power over me. Nothing I accept about myself can be used against me to diminish me. I am who I am, doing what I came to do, acting upon you like a drug or a chisel to remind you of your me-ness, as I discover you in myself.*[4]

Goodness succeeds when there is the acquisition of self-knowledge, something vital and morally insightful, that was not known at the outset. This success is not about winning, nor is it drawn from an annihilation of evil, but from the maturation of consciousness, a humanization within the heart. This acquired knowledge of goodness displays in the language of moral clarity. Trusting ourselves to love what feels dangerous, with its power undeniable within us, is only possible through such self-awareness.

Strength is an attempt to love ourselves more fully, to then love more broadly. It directs self-discovery toward the "broaden and build" theory[5] of positive emotions. "The idea is that cultivation of positive emotions, including self-love and self-respect, strengthens our inner resources and opens us to a broader range of thoughts and actions. In turn, we gain trust in our resilience and the ability to face whatever surprises life may throw our way. Indeed, life can be stressful, with periods of peril, but we can have confidence in our capacity to meet it, instead of being torn apart by it."[6]

What could be more characteristic of genuine goodness than what is not impressed by or interested in evil? Goodness does not deny evil, nor its necessary confrontation, nor the impact of its ravage, but it does deny evil an audience. It has no words of judgment; it seeks no vengeance, or recrimination. It is unwilling to clamor for retribution and even refuses to judge evil. Though good *is* the response to evil, for in its refusal to fix blame, or to lionize the violence of evil, or to televise trauma, it is not simply, or always, silent; but most profoundly a word, a language that is disarming, emancipatory.

Strength subverts the patriarchal sensibilities that always associate the feminine with the weak, the emotional with the fragile, the intuitive with the ignorant. Strength is a commentary on gender and power. It offers a feminist undoing of the white patriarchal use of abusive force to maintain the domination of women. Moreover, at the heart of the violence between those who oppress and those who are oppressed is the Western philosophical notion of hierarchical rule and coercive authority, which distorts our sense of strength. Western gendering works to make women play small so as not to unnerve. There is more concern with acting right rather than feeling good. Strength overturns the pressure to deny sexuality, to keep its consumption low, to preserve the pussy. It loosens the corsets of erotic, sexual restraint.

Strength lets the pussy talk. Strength, as a garlanded woman with flowing robes of white, is a virgin woman in full reclamation of her sexuality. Her virginity is sexual self-possession and is not about chasteness or abstinence. This is not a domesticated woman. She experiences pleasure of her own choice, by her own agency, and thus possesses immense power. The lion that heeds the queen with a kingdom between her legs infers that her authority is one of *legitimate* power. She is comfortable with the pursuit of her pleasure, a truly profound achievement after centuries of puritanical slut-shaming. Strength captures this feminist knowing as virtuous by associating the feminist praxis of holistic self-care with the lion, sometimes the bear or the jaguar, rather than with the snake, which denigrates the knowledgeable and sexually self-possessed woman. Strength undoes the patriarchal notion that intellectual work, or *knowing,* is not for women, especially Black women. Sexual reclamation goes hand in hand with elevation of consciousness and self-awareness.

Strength encourages the femme to be her own heroine, her own beast, in her own language, of her own beauty. Goodness, or virtue, was mocked by twentieth-century novelists, ignored as a simplistic gesture; but for the aesthetic imagination of Pamela Colman Smith, the artist behind the now-iconic deck that also arose at the start of the twentieth century, virtue made the femme her champion for Strength. Reconciliation and the restoration of order would be *her* triumphant humanity, with the feral as the recipient of the grace of her extended compassion. What greater strength could be more readily apparent than that displayed in her treatment of the wild, because it reflects that she too is wild. She has a language that nature knows and a beauty that disarms. Strength can establish an armistice with a beast with the confidence born from her unconditional self-regard. She saves herself, but her achievement is in surpassing the will to dominate, maim, or hunt. She tames a lion, unarmored but unafraid. The lion is compelled by the language shared with this good, free woman. This is anything but trivial or incidental. Faced with speaking her truth, she trusts her instincts and restores self-worth. Whatever properties of goodness this woman possesses are life-changing.

She, Strength, welcomes us, of her sound integrity, to meet rapture with her. Strength brings our sex out of exile and, like the lion, extends permission to enter the energetic exchange of bodies. This invitation collapses the feeling of separateness. The amount of pleasure we allow ourselves to receive is dependent upon our sense of dignity. Strength embraces the dignity of pleasure, espouses our inherent worthiness of love's pleasure as an erotic ecology. It says I am supposed to access the fullness of feeling; I deserve love. This is *supposed* to feel good.

The container of love, as depicted in the relationship shown in Strength, as emissary of Eight, is one of safety, honesty, and authenticity. This preserves a sense of freedom within, for each is there for the other in integrity. There is trust because there is mutual reverence and honoring. With the sense of safety born from this trust comes the ability to be fully surrendered before a pleasure unbound and beyond our control, a submission that in turn inspires tenderness. The vast potential of sexuality then becomes an exploration of how much pleasure is accessible. Feminist Strength plays in a fluid dynamic power exchange with the wild and eccentric through the deepest energetic listening. It draws focus toward discomfort, desire, boundaries, pain, satisfaction, for power, pain, pleasure, respect, and reciprocity exist on a shared continuum.

Love is often a force of sensitivity so strong it frightens us, makes us unsure of our capacity to handle such gentle tenderness. Strength is facing this fear of being loved, of being really seen. We pull Strength to know the freedom of love's fearlessness. Being loved in the ways we've always wanted turns on confidence. The body is the lion that is transformed through the social practice of loving Strength. It is the trustworthiness that emboldens our courage and willingness to love.

Strength champions a less cruel world by refusing to repeat its cruelty upon ourselves. But further it is the active promotion of our own well-being that is a major part of the process of self-actualization. So recognize the full force of the impact goodness has on the structure and meaning of your life, and you will know Strength.

The Moon

The jerkiness of the stop-and-go animation replaces the smoothness of the mannered movements associated with civility and humanness and aligns stop-motion with a relay between wild and domestic, destruction and consumption. . . . The wolf also represents the outside of the fox/farmer dyad and the utopian possibility of an elsewhere; and in his aloneness, the wolf signifies singularity, isolation, uniqueness but also death. The emotion that wells up in Mr. Fox as he confronts his fear ("I have a phobia of wolves") brims with all these possibilities and brings us back to the Freudian theory of the uncanny—something that has been repressed recurs, the repressed instinct. The uncanny here is represented by the wolf and as he confronts the wolf, repressed feelings flood Mr. Fox and he turns to face his dread, his anxiety, his other and in doing so, he reconciles to the wild in a way that instructs the humans watching the film to reconcile to wildness, to animatedness, to life and death.[7]

The Moon is not a master. The Moon is the original technology of animation. Its power is undeniable and recognized by all. The domestic dog and the wild wolf share a primal hunger. In the unison of their howl are the instincts, the nature that cannot be silenced nor mastered. The beasts wander, led by appetite. They hunt to feed. They are desperate to subdue the aching longing and loneliness of the night that stretches across centuries. Their howl is a mixture of alarm, desire, exhilaration. It is a plea. It is the audible power of conviction. And if not a wolf, then see a coyote and the mortal danger of border crossing.

The Moon knows we can only know so much about oceanic consciousness and sublunar alliances. We meet the Moon bewildered, ignorant, and faith is tested by fear, and desire runs wild. All these intelligences converge toward the Moon illuminating a path toward purpose, a single point of focus that opens a vista of awareness and possibility that is divine and flesh in its fulfillment. Night restores the day, death replenishes life.

The Moon is the nexus of convergence in the tarot as well. It focalizes all the primordial waters, rivers, and oceans across the cards' cartography. It is the origin of time, the center of space, where all the threads of life entwine. It is under moonlight that we learn to cope with chaos, disorientation, and uncertainty. The Moon confronts the reader's wildness within, the tension it has with domestication, pulled taut across class, gender, race. Domesticity entails discipline, servitude, respect, well-mannered politeness, but by night its dog has gotten loose. Domestication is a saddling, a corseting, a leashing; it does not convert wildness, but contains and coerces, or kills. But it does not conquer the wild. There are always wild souls who survive.

The Moon is the call to subversion, one we answer reveling in "the sheer animality of precariousness and survival."[8] The white supremacist imperial power is a common enemy to any natural, living being. The whole of life emerges from the Moon's collective seas. The Moon's solidarity is forged across species, collaborating instinctively on a new narrative, new self, new world. The analogies, parallels, and comparisons of the human with the animal communicate clearly to the reader the internal state, thoughts, or feelings of the querent. See a horse gallantly galloping across the frame and you know that something about masculinity, beauty, and power is prescient. The animal establishes a visceral response that is only accessible when we are so associated with the nonhuman. From this imagistic, metaphoric language that associates the human and the nonhuman emerges the reclamation of an ability to engage the natural world as a positive metaphor. For those who have spent their historical life being compared to an animal as a strategy of racist dehumanization, this is no small reclamation. So rather than being estranged from one's humanity for being animal-like, we can positively imagine or clarify our animal relations. They become teachers we respect for their lessons in our primal aliveness, power, instinct. In our treatment, conception, and consideration of the nonhuman, our own humanity takes distinction.

All answer the Moon's call to come home. All share the cry of craving for some sacred return, all famished for freedom. All intelligence remembers its origin. We know where we come from. Deep inside are our wild, free instincts toward fulfillment. The liveliness of the wild is invigorating. Though they may be repressed and faded in the darkness of the subconscious, the Moon always summons something from the deep. It's always weaving a golden web from all the disparate desires for you to realize. Whether overhead or in your hand, the Moon wants you to let yourself off a leash so you may take a path of trust and respect. The Moon lets desire just be, lets it walk free for the first time. We've held out for far too long; now it's about being uncollared. Freedom is the night's taking.

In the willingness to go somewhere we've never been, we necessarily embrace the darkness. The first step to illumination always begins in the eclipse of ignorance, in the blackness of possibility. Perhaps we wouldn't take the path without the Moon's soulful romance. It contains both our desire for a limitless, empty frontier and our fears of borderlessness. The Moon longs for a remembered unknown, a love light reflected in physical form. The seas we are willing to cross for this freedom, how far these currents can take us, the depth of these feelings, only the Moon knows, only the Moon can access.

The Moon is a return to that new place. Excited with all sensory stimuli, the Moon may overwhelm. With every layer washed away, we may feel raw, exposed, out in the open. And still we can't help but imagine all the creation that may come from that free, wild space. The wild offers itself to the lunar imagination. The Moon finds you in a very volatile time. When you are released, unleashed, or unbound back into the wild, it is initially exhilarating. But when it gets dark and cold at night, do you long for the comfort of the cage?

The night is immersive. We are ravenous in its discovery, gracious in our curiosity. We hear the dogs, we keep going. The Moon keeps calling. The Moon doesn't demand that we be good, or repent for hundreds of desert miles; only that we let our love be uninhibited and wild in its passion. The Moon makes all the more evident our unconscious driving obsession, the primary longing, the primal quest. When queer Black femmes indulge those deepest drives of art, eroticism, self-definition, she is monstrously threatening to sexist cultures everywhere. She must intuitively understand how she is surrounded politically by threatening wolves everywhere. But she walks under the warmth of moonlight. However lonely we believe ourselves to be, the Moon finds us, pulls on us to head home again. So begins a journey back to the galactic center.

"In personal journeys, we seek the center. Our concepts of immortality, enlightenment, and the individual's spiritual journey have been born from this omphalic beginning, this pole-centered heaven where all things moved around the sacred point of stillness. This was the first great impact that the constellations, the fixed stars, and the night sky had on the human mind: a primary philosophy that is so unconscious in the collective that it is generally unnamed and unrecognized, yet so strong it has formed the very foundation of our minds."[9]

As we walk on and on to our resurrection, may we be reminded of the play possible only when we take off our armor, under the covering of green sanctuaries. May our paths cross at an oasis after many dry steps in different directions. And of our meeting, some hybrid being becomes; transformations through which, within late capitalism, all subject citizens are formed by "the horizontal coexistence of a number of symbolic systems."[10] So our compound meetings exist across environment, nonhuman animal, animal, text, sign, augur. The Moon governs these mutual mergings.

The Moon takes the reader to the sublunar, subconscious, and subcultural circuits where new social relations are envisioned and activated. It is the collision of identities that give representation to deviant discourse and identity.

The Moon synthesizes dualities, contradictions, and perspectives across disparate worlds to construct a space that defies the borders of bodies, geographies, and possibilities. The Moon's dwelling is in the liminal, refusing to acquiesce or assimilate. Moonwalkers know freedom is a road that must be continuously paved anew. There must be made new topographies of cultural integrity.

The crucible of visionary perception is confusion, from which we recover the marvel and wonder of one who recognizes their small body within the vast unknown. We find the limitations and boundaries of conscious, rational knowing in the Moon, with relief. Disorientation is the obscuring grace of long-awaited change. What comfort to know the Moon knows more than man. When we need to stay with the mystery, we pull this card, we question the nature of our reality. The Moon stirs what is deeply felt, teaching the reader to discern between anxiety and intuition. Moonlight is obscuring. Shadows are cast in darkness. The fear that naturally arises can then be a potential ally for new knowing. Darkness and shadow may then be known as forces providing time for rest, inspiration, stillness. Strength's solar work of embracing feminine instincts is balanced by the lunar test of intuition. You can try to climb to the top of the mountain, but you can't get to the bottom of the Moon's ocean. The Moon ushers you into the deepest domain of the feminine, the celestial body unafraid of complete darkness, to thus access complete renewal.

The arcanum invites dream work, meditation, therapy, astrology, or other manners of psychic, cosmic exploration. The Moon is a perfect champion for the tarot, for it teaches us the language of symbol, myth, and metaphor. The Moon teaches the reader to shapeshift, becoming *nepantleras* who aren't "constrained by one culture or world but experience multiple realities. Ensuring that our acts do not mirror or replicate the oppression and dominant power structures we seek to dismantle, las nepantleras upset our cultures' foundations and disturb the concepts structuring their realities. Las nepantleras nurture psychological, social, and spiritual metamorphosis."[11]

Through the Moon's portal we truly explore liminality, often pursuing and experiencing soul retrieval at the psychic, social, bodily sites of past trauma. Images, memories, feelings surface that cannot be avoided. At this stage we overcome regression or avoidance, instead allowing our inner child to be found, held, seen, and comforted. We learn to leave in a manner that makes it safe to return.

Time is cyclical; linearity is an illusion. The soul grows in spirals, not straight lines. This shift in orientation is succeeded by the transition into the nocturnal. Every transaction with the forces of terror and hope is inscribed in the dark. The Moon summons us toward a new world, and like the early Americans crafting the nation's literary identity, a dark, abiding presence moves through the heart with fear and longing. Shadow work has many meanings, but if it does not lead to the most sordid histories of humanity and how and where the reader has arisen in this, then it is futile. The Moon is the shadow worker looming over each and every one of us. A haunting darkness looms over the landscape, something to consistently negotiate, avert, or make the antithesis of a hyperindividualized freedom.

Colonizers failed to make a "new world" because they brought the same old story with them; no matter the name change, the world is still in thrall to poverty, prison, social ostracism, debt, and death. Shadows were imported from European culture and then romanticized. There are no new worlds, there is only the one we have, being continuously remade and rediscovered, being altered and changed permanently, continuously. By moonlight the repressed have returned. The old reality caresses, grips, and shapes the new in the subtle and unseen that lives within each of us. The Moon makes wide the body of our historical canvas.

Everyone wants the new, so no one considers the old. But the new is raw, half-savage to the patriarchs; it's never respected, only feared. There is no new world, no release into a sort of historylessness, no blank black page for whiteness to impress upon. There is the Moon drawing the tide, washing over the shores of history, forgetting and remembering again, only gaining and shedding its light. It's the same world, but it calls us to begin again, and so it is as important to know what we are rushing from as it is to know what we are hastening toward. Whatever ways we build illusions become paramount, through which we only come to clarity in retrospect, in historical study and appreciation. We encounter the dark till it becomes casual. We live daily in the darkness of ongoing historical oppression, and yet we are still walking, still being summoned by a force of freedom within and above. Courage feathers the faith of fulfillment.

For some the journey to fulfillment is about profit; for others it is about license and release from limitation; but for some it's about faith. In the Moon there may be a marked absence of hope, realism, materialism, or promise. Before we arrive at the newness of our potential or our embodied freedom, we begin troubled, frightened, haunted. Oppression precedes the desire for freedom. It is living in turmoil, dissatisfaction, and constraint that precipitates a resolve toward wilderness, to take freedom's temptation as apprehension blows away. Regardless of the motivation, each trip taken is considered to be worth the risk, pressing toward a future, a free state with endurance. The departure is marked by images of thresholds, crossroads, an opening in an underground place.

The typology of diabolism so desperately sought to be left behind becomes reproduced as a measure of prevention through inoculation. The Moon is the plane where the psyche imagines, engages, confronts their demons, desires, and dreams. The Moon makes it possible to embrace, with varying risk, human fears and anxiety around failure, powerlessness, boundarylessness, being outcast. The Moon presents an unbridled nature couched for attack, summoning Americans' fear of "the absence of so-called civilization; their fear of loneliness, of aggression both external and internal. In short, the terror of human freedom—the thing they coveted most of all."[12] Darkness is terror's conceit, which becomes racialized in America. The Black population becomes the playground for hegemonic and countercultural imagination. The subjective nature of ascribing worth and significance to color cannot be questioned at this time. The founding masters of America made slaves function as a surrogate for meditations on freedom that conceptualize Blackness as the simultaneous not-free and not-me, which makes conscious the necessity for establishing difference. Exploitation then becomes rationalized because what is being restrained is not a person with humanity but a darkness simulated by otherness, alarm, desire. That shadow is put to work. Freedom and enslavement, civilization, domesticity, and savage wildness become mutually accountable; one is made to support the other. Domestication becomes enslavement by the white supremacist capitalist imperialist patriarchy. It is repression, desecration, and dominion. The terror of a limitless nature, natal loneliness, aggression, death are reflected in the American empire's founders' meditations and treatment of the enslaved. Again, white supremacy exists on a continuum of anti-Blackness. That terror has been colonized by every American since. It is the Moon that shows us this shadow of the consciousness concerned with freedom, or the consciousness that considers itself free. It is the conditioned tendencies of our self-reflexive capacity. The Moon makes our references for difference completely clear: it is whatever frightens us. While our desire for that difference detects our equivalency. In the line of demarcation, the Moon's shadows hover in implication.

The Moon is nature and the Moon is symbol. It is both the subject and the system. It is the opportunity and the search for the self, the sublime. It is about becoming, transacting. It conjures fear to be imaginatively conquered, to quiet the howl of deep insecurities. Internal conflicts are projected against this all-encompassing darkness. Historically, this fear was transferred to the conveniently bound, violently silenced Black bodies, but is it possible we could now enter the dark to become purged of that internalized racism that condones structural oppression? This is the power of darkness, the anarchy of the other. It gives expression to the metaphysical, moral, and historical problems and dichotomies of human freedom. It lures, perhaps because it is so elusive. Night comes and curtails control.

What is the Moon to the native but the power, the guide, the mode of shamanic trance and shapeshifting, and of readily traversed alternative planes of consciousness. It is the Moon that makes tarot readers, writers, witches, the shadow workers. The ones who relearn how to be the free self out in the wild. The ones who recognize the chaos of the night as a shared power yet to be potentiated. Those humble enough to respect and realize nothing is known for certain. These are the instincts of evolution. There is no turning back.

Eight of Swords

Look to yourself. You free. Nothing and nobody is obliged to save you but you. Seek your own land. You young and a woman and there's serious limitation in both, but you are a person too. Don't let Lenore or some trifling boyfriend and certainly no devil doctor decide who you are. That's slavery. Somewhere inside you is that free person I'm talking about. Locate her and let her do some good in the world.[13]

The Eight of Swords is one of the most violent, truly challenging cards in the tarot. Clearly there is a kidnapping, a human trafficking, an exploited hypervisibility, as a life hangs by a thread. It's always a white rope that binds a woman, positions her in exile with an illegal sexuality. Though as she is most assuredly tied down, she is certainly not loose. The image evokes white patriarchal freedom defined by its ability to have absolute freedom over another, the height of American hyperindividualism. The Eight of Swords shows a literal confinement to the margins. A body held down, betrayed by violence, physically frozen in self-doubt, trapped in the compound violence of the victim's blame and shame that justifies violence against women. The mind, after and because of living through trauma and violence, makes mental walls, psychic boundaries aimed to keep the body safe, to preserve the fraught, fragile life from falling off the edge. The card harkens to mummification, a method of preservation, to keep what's worthwhile from decay. This mental block comes from external conditioning and is not to be mistaken for a naturally repressing orientation, though it reflects internalized alienation and victimhood. Like a voodoo doll someone else is piercing, our body is under someone else's mind control.

The repressed psychic channel, whether withholding memory, sexuality, or some other essential aspect, although made docile or controllable is not a severed psychic attachment, capacity, or content; rather, it is bound and silenced. So much desire dysfunctions through denial. As most harm starts within the family, to unbind and get deeply free where the deepest bondage is buried, generational cycles of abuse must be broken. And so when we pull Eight of Swords it's as if the body suddenly finds itself at the end of its leash. There's some invisible line that keeps our body from opening and accessing certain places, states, emotions, and experiences. By the blindfold, it becomes a repressed bodily betrayal that keeps us in place. And it's too tight and it's been too long.

Despair is a prison with bars of disbelief. Immobilized by doubt and the demons of despondency, the devils of insecurity. The remnants of powerlessness linger in my psyche, ever evident when I am petrified by fear. I pull it when I am stuck, afraid to move forward with my life by my own accord. Prisoners, the sufferers of the abuse of neglect, in that abuse are conditioned to anticipating others forcefully acting upon them. Emotionally imprisoned, I spent so much time just waiting around for someone to come save me, believing that the answers to my prayers for divine intervention would be some white knight who would free me with his love.

I am waiting for an arrival, a return, a promised sign. This can be futile, or immensely pathetic; in Erwartung (Waiting), a woman waits for her lover, at night, in the forest; I am waiting for no more than a telephone call, but the anxiety is the same. Everything is solemn; I have no sense of proportions. . . . The being I am waiting for is not real. And if the other does not come, I hallucinate the other: waiting is a delirium.[14]

My silent cries for help needed my enlightened witness most of all, but all I could see was the love that wasn't there, held captive in an incarcerating helplessness. A prison that is most effective when it is not just the body that is bound, but the mind, the perception. A victimized mind survives on an attachment for rescue from some other savior. Even though I finally see the delusion of this thinking, I'm still grieving the savior that never came; but it is a pain more welcome than that of confinement. This pain is redemptive, for by it I know I have determined to walk freely, even if I walk alone. Freedom has no time to wait, its moment is always now. By the Eight of Swords, I slowly began considering that I might possess the means for realizing my freedom. I had so much shame I never thought I could be my own hero. I didn't want to let go of seeing my life a certain way because I thought I would return to blindness, but I was already living in blindness. And now for the first time I can see without delusion. Now I am primed to see, to find what it is if it isn't this, it wasn't that. I'm taking time to unbind repressed eros, as my own Knight of Swords, in red, white, and black, riding a dark horse, with sword held high, the determination of a survivor, and the voice of compassion.

I see in the card's reflection that I am not powerless to pursue my deepest desires, but that pursuit predicates the embrace of taboo desire. I stretch the tension between the victim and the forbidden desire. I have a desire for submission, for passivity. I think this desire acknowledges my relative powerlessness relative to the larger forces of life. The Eight of Swords helps me not claim an individual powerlessness against larger circumstances or powers beyond me as a personal failure. I acknowledge and accept that I am not the sole or individual actor in the story of my life. Through the surrender of futile attempts to control is liberation. I pull the Eight of Swords as I continuously unravel the sense of self-belief robbed of its agency. I learn to surrender the responsibility of healing those who have hurt me as a strategy to stop being hurt. Free of this weight I have carried on my person for so long, I say what is true about the power dynamics of my relationships: all exist relative to the massive systems of domination that shape our lives. The Eight of Swords makes the dynamic between power and powerlessness transparent. We politically shape the other in intimate relationships, and we are responsible for how we orient and respond to the larger oppressive systems within the relationship. Choosing partners who share our values and can commit to care even under pressure from such external forces is the most life-affirming choice we can make.

The relatively powerless populations situated perniciously in the racial and socioeconomic order are externally restricted toward the end of internal fragmentation. They come up against the mental block, the puritanical conditioning that is the Eight of Swords. The imposition of racial identity upon diverse populations with distinct cultures, languages, and spiritual traditions is like the elephant rope of the Eight of Swords, so that the slavers, capitalists, colonizers could have a single thread—skin color—by which to exercise, reify, and mirror their conception of freedom. Though narratives of women's liberation have consistently centered around white femininity, there is no body more suppressed in the American psyche than the objectified Black female persona. The radical tradition attempts freedom by acknowledging racial hierarchies, but binds itself based upon solidarity in struggle, rather than a mythic racial homogeneity.

Whatever is impossible to say is said in the Eight of Swords. It provides an occasion, through the contemplation of a bound body, to consider the absence or presence of restraint, freedom, condemnation. When the Eight of Swords appears, getting free is the only work that matters. The only interest is in the strategies for maintaining and breaking the silence. The only inquiries are: what will set this woman free? What will be the articulation of her freedom? What will she say to claim subjectivity? Whose truth is she hiding, and who did this to her? What man's innocence and freedom depends on her disposal? Whose story does her silence prop up?

What is more clearly the invisible wall we place in front of ourselves than the mirror? Many myths are made of being trapped in the realm of mirrors. It seems to show a witch trap, as if all that's left is a stake to fire. We don't want to see the image shatter with the sound of honest hurt. They want to see a smile, a success, a survivor. No one wants to see the victim.

This absence of sight reflects those complicit in the abuse, sharing a silence that condones and endorses the abuser. They, too, live within the policing voice. It's not the protection against psychic capture they think it is. But this is the card of the whistleblower and truths must be told, even if their efficacy is nefariously neutralized.

"The legislator's narrative could not coexist with a response from the Africanist persona. Whatever the popularity the slave narrative had—and they influenced abolitionists and converted antiabolitionists—the slave's own narrative, while freeing the narrator in many ways, did not destroy the master narrative. The master narrative could make any number of adjustments to keep itself intact."[15]

Representation is not so simple when the other's name and narrative are appropriated by the master. But this narrative and the implication of its distortion can still render a complex, rewarding body of knowledge. We learn to consistently make the strategies of silence audible with the Eight of Swords. We become aware of the conditions under which "we" are reproduced to disentangle ourselves from negotiating with existing power relations, as we seek to abolish them completely.[16]

It is an imaginative encounter with the captive that is regulatory and self-reflexive. Do you distinguish yourself from the incarcerated as free? If they are the helpless, is it you who are powerful? If they are the damned, are you the innocent? Is that the blind accident of evolution and this the manifest destiny?[17] Silences must be broken over and over, for the disciplinary apparatus of punishment is all too accommodating. The Eight of Swords calls for critical attentiveness. The methods of narrative manipulation must be analyzed, along with the strategic use of difference.

The Eight of Swords touches on every rope that has held you back for so long. Cut it, and it's like you're suspended in air. I change my framing of stillness, inactivity. This is the point of the sword's severance: to detach. And then you fly. No longer your old story, no longer your name. You simply were, are here, and still yet to be.

Till we can let ourselves off the leash to run free under moonlight we can change the quality and texture of the rope. For survivors it's important to know the limits, to know the bounds of a situation, relationship, or space. A body whose boundaries have been violated is led to fear borderlessness.

The rope is the body's tether that keeps us separate from the wild, roaming wolves. It's asking consent, it's communicating clearly, it's adaptive, and it's consistently assessing safety. You make better and clearer choices, knowing where you start and others end.

The rope is the rosary, the mantra, the prayer we repeat to get free in our heart, mind, soul. When the box gets tighter, darkness closes in and you feel powerless to move, you realize how deep this wound runs. The rope pulls you out of the quicksand of posttraumatic triggers, personal and ancestral. The glass we live behind becomes clearer until the self who feels safe and strong enough can now emerge, one you don't yet fully know. It's that essential free self, tapping on your shoulder to move, get on, and get going to that new place. That self that's been calling to you the whole way from the very beginning, saying for you there is more.

The Eight of Swords helps the reader deal with living in the limits of the body. We aren't just floating freely in space. While the Nine of Swords depicts the pain of pushing past cognitive thresholds, the Eight represents the limitations of knowing by the restrictions of the body racialized, gendered, historicized. So if there will always be rope, we must change the point of pain. If it is pain and limiting boundaries we have ample supply of, why not let it fuel a destination of pleasure rather than despair? Can our embrace of life accommodate pain and fear as a vehicle of healing and become a source of deep respect, deep acceptance? If we recognize that loving and relating may be painful as we pursue more than our conditioned containment, then it will be the pain of loving that breaks you open, stretches you, as it pursues your pleasure. Love will encompass the requisite pain it takes to yield such ecstatic climax. The aforesaid acceptance needs no straightening; it lets the natural be as kinky as it wants to be.

Eight of Wands

Feminism without borders is not the same as "border-less" feminism. It acknowledges the fault lines, conflicts, differences, fears, and containment that borders represent. It acknowledges that there is no one sense of a border, that the lines between and through nations, races, classes, sexualities, religion, and disabilities, are real—and that a feminism without borders

> must envision change and social justice work across these lines of demarcation and division. I want to speak of feminism without silences and exclusions in order to draw attention to the tension between the simultaneous plurality and narrowness of borders and the emancipatory potential crossing through, with, and over these borders in our everyday lives.[18]

Language is arriving in the Eight of Wands. These eight wands depict the dissemination of knowledge, while the Two of Wands is its production. This formulation is directly political and discursive; it is purposeful and ideological and it must be held as such. Its characteristic imposition of swiftness is the neutral power of virality, like disease or religion; the nature of what spreads widely is known by its effect. The swiftness of communication can evidence the voices of collective consciousness.

As with the Two of Wands, this card sees us seeking new horizons, envisioning transformation, perspective waxing strong with rising sunlight after the darkest night. It is aware of global ideologies, and it concerns the most principled way to cross borders. This awareness must politicize the reader, the first step toward a radicalized organization/orientation against the domination, nationalism, and conquest that differentially characterize each of our lives.

As another one of the rare cards without human depiction, it offers a sense of universal accessibility, especially as the eight wands are suspended and scaled high above the ground, signaling movement and a flight of the imagination. Implicit in the imagination of a global collectivity is a fiery force that moves beyond and through borders. It is a card of expansive, inclusive vision that can steer us past the pitfalls of diversity, equity, and inclusion initiatives that yield tokenism, appropriation, flattened conflation, and superficial engagement.

This Eight of Wands is a way of seeing. It offers a vista of an alternate time and place in the search for emancipatory knowledge. I pull the Eight of Wands and see no small imagination; I think of Toni Morrison's scorched earth and the four *centuries* her work covers. Life reaches a larger scope, a farther reach, and assesses a multigenerational trajectory. It summons a search for the basis of relationships among diverse communities. Solidarity is an active struggle to construct the universal on the ground of difference.

A diversity of voice, understanding, history, strategy, and aim must not be erased in coalition building. Without acknowledging and respecting such diversity there is no real solidarity. Rather than centering whiteness or foregrounding oppression as the reason for solidarity among the oppressed global majority, we must build alliances on the basis of mutuality, accountability, and common interests.

The Eight of Wands calls, with urgency, for clear analysis and critique of the interwoven systems, attitudes, and institutions that reify conquest and domination. With an internationalist commitment we can explore strategies to realize the vision of a just and inclusive antiracist feminist framework, anchored in decolonization and committed to an anticapitalist critique.[19] Sonia Sanchez says that to survive on the American landscape, we must reimagine ourselves every ten years. The Eight of Wands offers the reader a chance to rearrange the thoughts, the actions, the guiding principles, the grand goals, the point of view of our world and our definitions. The Eight of Wands gives you a freeze-frame from above to envision what an antiracist feminist politic looks like. It will take work on many fronts, in many different collectivities, understandings, and articulations to challenge repressive systems of rule.

When the past of your people has been degraded and the records burned, it is the Eight of Wands writer who imagines historically. Because the past has been ruptured, their soaring spaceship of creativity becomes a vehicle to return what has been stolen, denied, or deleted. To restore the regard of their people's contribution, they invent. From their fertile imagination, just a fragment of narratives, an ignored utterance, can become a whole world of commanding dialogue. They offer an archive, they offer everything for a people who've been told they have no history, and there is no singular narrative.

The Eight of Wands wants words inspired by ideas far distant from anything in our lives. Our individual life is too little to really know anything worth writing about without some sort of cultural embassy. We write out of culture, through it, because we are in it. And before the modern moment of social media and technologies of global connectivity and virality, it was the image, novels and literature, that opened a door for the domestic mind. This record endures, it has longevity, its impact upon culture and the collective mind unending. The test of the writer's power is one of range. The power to imagine what is not the self, to inure the foreign and confound the familiar, is measured in their ability to offer this to readers.

Words are the Eight of Wands's force, known by the writer whose spirit is possessed by the passion of the pen, "where forces beyond my control inhabit and take me, sometimes against my will, to places, landscapes of thoughts and ideas, I never wanted to journey or see. I have never been a girl for travel. Always one wedded to the couch, the back porch, the swing, I want to see the world standing still. My thoughts are movements, my ideas, my adventures."[20] Word, God, grabs hold of the writer, whether by hand or the throat, and something from higher realms comes into form down below. And the writer is astonished to see this process play out at yet another interval; for what greater delight could there be than to hear different voices read the words you wrote however long ago, however recent, move through another's intelligence, another's creative spirit, another's tongue and come back to you in new colors and new sounds and new meanings. And still you are the so-called author, but this language no longer belongs to you, and it's beautiful. Inspiration never stops. Its fire wakes us from reverie, relentlessly working our inventive faculty till its unseen truth is made tangible.

The power of language, its revelation, is signified by the Eight of Wands. It is the language born of fire. The Eight of Wands writer has a message to share, a testimony to deliver. This is the voice of gospel, regardless of religious affiliation, strengthened by a chorus tribute testifying truth to the spirit of dignity beyond doubt and despair. This language is more evocative than analytical. The Eight of Wands has global reach, pandemic perspective, and considers the center of a larger epic narrative. To achieve *conocimiento* with the Eight of Wands, we witness the words' behavior in their encounter with the dominant discourse. Pull this card and consider what you can do where you are. Not everyone is out in the trenches, marching in the streets; but the work of amplifying and recording the thoughts, the voices, the books and ideas of revolutionaries is accessible to the Eight of Wands reader-writer. These ideas can never be privately owned, for they are always communally constructed. There is certainly a through line of history that the card follows as wands move from *there* to *there.* To write contrary to the dominant racial ideology one is cast in, they must change their point of view as a reader. From high above there is a scope of the cartography of struggle *and* possibility.

The Eight of Wands adds fuel to the vision, but it is nondescript in its proffer, so I offer you the "bare bones" feminist vision of author and scholar Chandra Talpade Mohanty, a vision realized by the active decolonization of the whole of psychic and social structure, which entails manifold strategies for active withdrawal, resistance, and deconstruction of domination:

> *This is a vision of the world that is pro-sex and -woman, a world where women and men are free to live creative lives, in security and with bodily health and integrity, where they are free to choose whom they love, and whom they set up house with, and whether they want or not to have children; a world where pleasure rather than just duty and drudgery determine our choices, where free and imaginative exploration of the mind is a fundamental right; a vision in which economic stability, ecological sustainability, racial equality, and the redistribution of wealth form the material basis of people's well-being. Finally, my vision is one in which democratic and socialist practices and institutions provide the conditions for public participation and decision making for people regardless of economic and social location.*[21]

Eight of Cups

Pilgrimage is a sacred act of devotion and initiation into the mysteries of the Black Virgin. . . . In 2001 I undertook my first pilgrimage to a sacred site and since then I have undertaken at least one pilgrimage a year. I have been documenting my travels, as well my spiritual insights and started creating the sacred altars which became my first tarot deck. The very first pilgrimage I undertook to a Black Madonna was in 2001 when I visited the sanctuary of San Michele in the grotto at Monte Sant'Angelo in Puglia.[22]

The language of freedom has a taste and texture that we cannot know till it is discovered. After a long life in exile, the journey home is always a pilgrimage for the displaced and dispossessed. Like a posthumous postpartum depression that's yet to be recognized, the Eight of Cups is the call of darkness.

Night is always the landscape of discovery and invention. For a fulfillment they've never known, the seeker must go down dark, distant paths.

The Eight of Cups, and reading tarot by extension, is an initiation into the sacred and hidden. It appears as we are ready to dive deep into the subconscious as we question the boundaries of space-time, going to the origin of before and after, the field in which time arises and dissolves again. Reality is mapped by accessing the root of our perception, the foundations of the soul. This is a journey of psychic navigation along invisible structural boundaries, an interior labyrinth whose center we must find in order to be reborn. We are the fish finding awareness of the water with the Eight of Cups.

Seeking and its success depend upon the accuracy of sight. When perception converges with reality, it is the inner eye that has fluttered open. This is the liberation of insight. Every reading enters the iconosphere, as depicted by the card, to read reality in a manner that interrupts mundane perception with the witness of the nonordinary. We more than awaken to hegemonic social order; we become capable of accessing the interior design of the heavens. This is the card of the psychonaut, the one traversing trance states, open to an infinite horizon. The pilgrimage of perception is not of outer space but inner space. Often it is existential frustration that stimulates such exploration. Instinctively, we seek the center to fill its void. We search for something that coheres the chaos or simply makes the incoherent and terrible useful. As we look, everything becomes the territory of exploration, everything is information, and everything can be used, should we so choose. In the reading, everything is an omen, everything is read as a sign, using the vehicle of symbol and synchronicity to convey sacred communication. In a reading we walk through the Eight of Cups, searching for a stable center.

> *Whenever I finish a work, I always feel lost, as though a steady anchor has been taken away and there is no ground under my feet. During the time between ending one project and beginning another, I always have a crisis of meaning. I begin to wonder what my life is all about and what I have been put on this earth to do. It is as though immersed in a project I lose all sense of myself and must then, when the work is done, rediscover who I am and where I am going.*[23]

The Eight of Cups shows that passage comes from renunciation, which registers as darkness. It is as the lover approaches the beloved, basking in the intimacy of twilight until they join in the eclipse of each other and their unsuspected depth is disclosed. To turn inward the Eight of Cups turns away from hollow happiness and refrains from simple satiety. We can wait no more, nor can we settle for some substitution, no other love will do, nothing less than that divine encounter will fulfill the soul. But at this point in the journey, they've gotten over everything that got in the way of finding that fulfillment.

> *If, given another chance to assert myself over others, I instead resist the urge to dominate, allow the others to be themselves, and say to God, "I don't need that; I need you," that is love. If someone on whose example my belief had depended, ups and abandons the gospel they had taught me to embrace, and I nonetheless cling on to it, that is faith. If, in the face of a deep-seated defect, I do not allow cynicism ("It will never change") to close doors on the future, that is hope.*[24]

The card emphasizes that pursuing fulfillment is more about space-making, about actively increasing receptivity. The Eight of Cups is a point of departure, a night exodus where we might not see any more than the next step right before us. It withdraws from all that is less than the Divine until the center sought becomes an encounter with God. Then they have secured something that will empower a personal cosmology that will discern the shapes of the universe. Then there is a topography of spirituality, a landscape of faith that keeps us from falling off the edge of futility. Then there is a shift from being a passive visitor, a tourist who has others read to them, to an active participant within a sacred, animate divinity, enraptured in a being beyond time. This path is not one to walk casually or occasionally. This trip is about alchemical transformation, not vacation. Likewise, every reading can become a pilgrimage and we devotees, even if only for the duration of our visit. The interior movement made by reading the cards, proxied by the Eight of Cups, is a type of trance work whose purpose is not to taste-test, appropriate, or gawk, but to enter a profound ritual relationship. It does not seek to revive one's normal routine but to move toward an encounter, an experience of ecstatic communion that fundamentally changes you from within. You are not supposed to come back as you have left.

When in the Eight of Cups, when reading tarot, you go beyond the veil of your mind. Pursuing the personal relationship with the sacred being inside yourself, with cards not consciously chosen, reveals a transcendent power. Like the seeker in this card, every time we turn to tarot we are walking into the unknown, resting upon trust, revelation, hope. We follow faith into the secrets of spirit. Detail and synchronicity guide you through the process, and each card that comes out is a sanctuary choosing you. Meditation upon them offers potential entry into a deep shamanic state that lends itself to change and personal transformation. They allow us an experience of inner pilgrimage.

"Seldom are powerful icons found in the middle of a bustling city; they are usually tucked away in distant places and they require from one to undertake a physical and psychic journey. Different shrines have different attributes and you will visit the one that you are most in need of."[25]

A reading creates a psychic portrait, and the reader is the guide, the seeker going to recover the lost, frightened, silenced soul parts within, guiding the querent to new planes of consciousness and realization. The reading brings you back to the galactic center, it alchemizes your unconscious limitations and potentiates profound fulfillment. It is a metaphysical voyage that requires trust, self-examination, bravery, and dexterity. The Eight of Cups moves with this aptitude.

We forge a way by getting out of the way. The more room we give to God in our hearts, the more ground gets covered as we scale the mountain of revelation. We walk emptied to discover what God gives, to ensure that our hearts are ready to receive. The immensity of our longing is sometimes more than can be borne, so sometimes it stays hidden. But in the Eight of Cups we want to know where the beloved has gone. Our spirit's thirst is pure, for here the soul's caverns have been emptied. This thirst makes us willing to go further, to explore the depth of our devotion, and manifests as the impulse taken toward a prayer that pursues presence. Prayer becomes praxis in the walk of the Eight of Cups. This method deifies the heart within by working upon the ways we enclose the all-encompassing, and it seeks to move into an ecstatic experience of the Divine free from the binds of our assumptions or the dogma of religion.

"The first step to mystical realization is the leaving of such a defined god for an experience of transcendence, disengaging the ethnic from the elementary idea, for any god who is not transparent to transcendence is an idol and its worship is idolatry."[26]

Passion has inspired this surrender, signaled by the blood-red cloak of the card, for what is sought requires sacrifice. The solitary search says the odyssey toward the beloved, toward home, toward God, toward union is for the lover alone. This arrival, the meeting with the beloved, is worth our leaving. There is no regret here because though the oceans between us are vast, we are connected nonetheless. From the movement initiated by the Eight of Cups, we know love is never idle; it is in continuous motion.

Eight of Pentacles

It was believed that the soul suffered irreconcilable loss if gifts were not developed, used, shared. Hyde contends: "the genius of daemon comes to us at birth. It carries with it the fullness of our undeveloped powers. These it offers to us as we grow, and we choose whether or not to labor in its service." No doubt it was this recognition of the gift that compelled enslaved Africans to express their artistry, their capacity to make pictures and elaborate designs, even as they constructed instruments of punishment or torture that would be used against them or their brethren. When I first encountered such objects, adorned with carvings, in a museum, I stood in awe, weeping. Crying in the face of a will to make art so intense as to lose oneself in a rapture of forgetfulness. How to imagine the mind of the artist then—how to articulate the aesthetic beliefs informing this creativity? To be bound and yet not bound—this was the paradox: the slave liberated for a time in the imagination, liberated in that moment of creative transcendence.[27]

The Eight of Pentacles is a reminder that our reality can be defined by something other than the circumstances of our oppression. The spatial imagination is made tangible in this Eight. An aesthetic engagement with one's environment is pictured here as a pouring forth of intent, a continuous refinement. The Eight of Pentacles has an awareness of design that allows the reader to think about space politically, about who controls and shapes environments, and how white supremacy bends individuals' space as it overrides and overdetermines the nature of structure, location, and the dis/comfort we have inhabiting any space within a body condemned in the pursuit of capitalist profit, an experience that isn't exclusive to the spaces designed for their denigration. Structure informs the way people are allowed to exist in space, the way they see themselves in space. This awareness must subvert and disrupt the perception of an artistic endeavor or inventive expression as politically neutral.

The architecture of dreams very much concerns the architecture of space. The gateway of the card is as much about the relationship between architectural design and embodiment as it is about cultural production, power, property, and ownership. The Eight of Pentacles, immersed in creative production and artistic practice, looks intently at objects of their creation, understanding them as cultural artifacts that must consciously resist the reinscription of the prevailing structures of domination. There is constructive critical interrogation in the Eight of Pentacles. A focus, a critiquing eye that enhances and illuminates the work. It is an invitation to transform the ways of looking and participating with larger cultures while working at the margins. It considers both the subject and object of creation, one's claimed cultural genealogy, the labor making the project possible and toward what end by whose vision. The pentacles they make are more than decoration; they are worlds within themselves documenting a personal history, displaying an artistry, recognizing a cultural influence. The pentacles are thus a commentary on legacy and impact.

As Lucile Clifton says, "we cannot create what we can't imagine," and what's created is viscerally rewarding. Artistic creation is a deliciously intimate practice in a private space. The necessity sensed in the Eight of Pentacles is the need to create, for the process is a deeply satisfying personal experience of skill. Nothing is more nourishing for the artist than time spent honing their talent, cultivating their gifts. Culture is clarified as a collective benefit from their solitary sharpening. Their artistic manipulations of the mundane communicate personal experience to raise consciousness.

With the Eight of Pentacles we are rooted in a concrete acknowledgement of our material reality, working steadily toward dreams and desires for our dwelling upheld by class-based longings to raise one's socioeconomic status. Economic pressure adds motivation to their endeavor to achieve artistic stature. A starving artist's success is as much about paying the bills as it is a creative catharsis realizing the zenith of artistic ability. The card depicts the artisan preparing their wares for the marketplace; they have to make enough to make enough. Art is functionally vital to survival in every way. The Eight of Pentacles artist overcomes material alienation, knowing that to be poor is not to be powerless. The Eight of Pentacles intervenes in the environment of sameness and its monotony of structure, maintaining a persistent ability to transform one's relationship to space. A liberated embodiment always intimately entails the transformation of space.

My grandma Cece was always shifting furniture around, rearranging her living space, regularly excited by the spatial possibility of home. The walls of her house did not confine her but challenged her imagination, a creative pleasure she readily pursued. I presume she developed this capacity most potently in the prison cells she was in and out of in her early adult life. She shared her excitement for interior design with my mother, and my mother with me. She was an artist of the found object, moved by the texture of the tangible. She frequently hosted and sought yard sales. Her means would not prevent her artistic investment in the interiority of her home. She constructively engaged her environment as another expression of relationship to aesthetics. It's important that I record her creative control here, her display of spatial resilience. Lacking material privilege does not deny this relationship; it only makes it all the more inventive, dissident, and distinct. The concern for beauty, design, and art is not determined by class privilege. Certainly, in the Eight of Pentacles there is no poverty of spirit, skill, or vision.

Within the design of our dreams we may be able to transcend circumscription, but once we undertake their manifestation we are met with the limitations of our lived experiences. With great creative consideration to design a space that meets our concrete needs when underresourced, deprived, or disadvantaged, we are imaginatively tested. The Eight of Pentacles is this opportunity to think about the viable spaces for growth, safety, and creative freedom, now and in the future. We are all capable of conceiving, reconstructing, and repurposing space. Tarot mirrors this creativity in every hand with this card.

Architects practice a cultural function central to both the imaginative and material relationship to space. These skills are always needed, as all space must continuously be transformed to meet growing needs while also preserving a history of that transformation. There must be those who know the distance between the dream and the practical. There are those working tirelessly to diminish that distance so one day we might actually dwell in our dreams. They are the ones choosing to honor their artistic gifts, their creative capacity, and maintain an artistic practice despite the dire circumstances the other endures. By the Eight of Pentacles we yield to the creative call, we set about liberating the gift of our genius, a labor recognized by those of an ancient world.

The bridge the Eight of Pentacles builds is between heaven and earth, offering their art as a site for transcendence. Thus they are an architect of faith. The Eight of Pentacles, by making a place to make art, engages oppositional cultural intervention. Those on the margins find the freedom to create whatever they want there. Any space where Black and Brown people make art is an oppositional space. They use and understand architecture as a vernacular of cultural expression.[28] Their environments touch upon the deep roots of a heritage of artistic intervention. Their space has a poetics. They pull out every record, every album cherished like gold, sorting through inspiration. Material is taken in hand, a medium is made. Each pentacle adorning a moment in time, captured in one space. They are the ones doing preservation work, record-keeping the historical and contemporary relationship to space and aesthetics. Suddenly seen in each pentacle is how each is a structure that "transparently (and invisibly) permits the ordered life it contains to exist in the larger world."[29] The art of each pentacle is placemaking, culturally, physically, psychically.

"Framing this cultural genealogy of resistance in relation to space is necessary for the 'cognitive mapping' Frederic Jameson speaks about when he insists that 'it is at least empirically arguable that our daily life, our psychic experience, our cultural languages, are today dominated by categories of space rather than categories of time.'"[30]

The Seven of Pentacles is the time spent in stillness and solitude, necessary for the continued devotion of an artistic practice. The Eight of Pentacles concerns the concrete production, the moment of putting pen to paper. Still, sustaining a body of work fundamentally requires undisturbed hours for creative rendering, as does it a studio space. The Eight of Pentacles artists are building a unit, a discography, a prolific body of work woven with the throughline of their artistic signature. The consistency of the excellence of their artistic expression is the mark of longevity. They are the ones making artistic achievement several times over, securing their space in the honorary hallways of culture's greatest contributors.

The Eight of Pentacles creates on the margins, claiming liminal space outside as a continuation of one's creative environment. They write, imagine, and build in the yards, the porches, the patios, the sheds. The Eight of Pentacles finds you a location of cultural production, a role in shaping the aesthetic, and a showcasing of subjugated knowledge. This work must be visible, remembered, if it is to disrupt the neocolonial order. The Eight of Pentacles does not erase the shadow of the Black body's contribution to the larger mass of dominant society. Rather, the perspectives and standpoints of the poor and working-class people are centralized. We cannot assume those given marginal attention have had marginal impact, or that they signify or mean nothing to the larger imagination. The Eight of Pentacles does not permit the Black presence central to any understanding of cultural and material creation to hover at the margins of the imagination. Any project that ignores the relevancy of race, class, gender, or sexuality supports white supremacy in discrediting difference. The apparatus of dominator ideology denies to destroy, using silent blindness to enforce invisibility. An absence of consideration in mainstream cultural critique, or limiting the narrative engagement of the other to a touch of color or comedic relief here or there, is a reflection not of Black contribution but the white imagination. The Eight of Pentacles is attentive to the creators' ideological inscription upon the cultural object. For the Eight of Pentacles' imagination, engagement has self-conscious consequence. They realize, as Toni Morrison does: the subject of the dream is the dreamer. The pentacles are reflexive, and from the process to the finished product, they are an extraordinary meditation on consciousness, the culture, and the times.

The Eight of Pentacles recognizes the importance of discipline and devotion, determined to respect, sustain, and enjoy a previously oppressed creativity. Not everyone may like or appreciate the work, the art *we* make, but none can take away the passion, the hours spent, the attention given, the blood and bone your creation takes from. The Eight of Pentacles directs their intense devotion to art-making as an avenue toward the most rewarding freedom and fulfillment.

The Eight of Pentacles uses subversive historiography as a connective tissue between oppositional practices of the past and strategies of resistance today. In a reading we are like the Eight of Pentacles figure, looking at this tissue, each card a pentacle, each an altar, an opportunity to imagine the future differently by reappraising yesterday's cultural artifacts. We read the cards to witness our own dreaming, to transcend the limits of our imagination, so our bodies may move beyond the confines of fixed locations. Our architectural realities must display our creative control, aesthetic agency, and artistic talent if they are to be free and responsive to the needs of those dwelling there. Most of all, the Eight of Pentacles says, ours is a world still in the making, still in our hands.

NINE

If impossible things are happening every day, then why shouldn't I have impossible hopes and dreams? Even something as impossible as going to the ball?[1]

When Whitney Houston appeared as fairy godmother to Brandy's Cinderella, singing about zanies and fools breaking sensible people's sensible rules, she sang to me too. Her song was a key, given to Brandy, given to me, to unlock the perception of my self-worth and self-belief from the stranglehold of scarcity that comes with living in the ghetto. As I started to sing with them, I stripped away the impoverished image I had of my own potential for profound fulfillment. Despair, the atrophy of the imagination, ceased to afflict me. I then knew myself a daft and dewy-eyed dope. Her song began to disentangle our confusion, our fear, our tragedy. Her revelatory song gave the satisfaction of cutting my Gordian knot. Her sparkle shared, showed me a genius, a deservedness, a magical realization of artistic expression, along with the sensual satisfaction of the soul.

Nine is the final archetypal number, the crone's number. The maiden has three, the mother her six. Nine is the crone as fairy godmother to the maiden, reaching back in time, sharing knowledge, self-worth, and self-realization as a preserved possibility for the foregone spirit of her own youth. This represents the maturity of lasting female friendship. Nine is the possibility of what may still become, by any means necessary. Nine is the knowing that nothing is ever hopeless, that salvation isn't unattainable.

The working class find in the fertile ground of their imagination an alternative to the grim realities and dead ends of capitalism, which offers endings bereft of any sense of meaningful achievement. Nine offers the tarot as a deus ex machina, to subversively undercut the internalized, conditioned logic of dominant society. This device is a mediation, a contemplation upon completion. Both Nine and tarot more broadly probe the mortal relationship with the Divine. Our lives and attitudes are complicated as they are confronted by divine encounter. In this, Nine is the numinous. It transforms the plane of consciousness, facilitating a quantum leap of attainment. It is a magical number, always returning to itself, maintaining an essence through any of its many forms. Nine deploys a saving grace and records our response. It's a reminder of the larger forces acting upon the actors of a narrative, external to but observant of the actors and the trajectory of their drama.

Some may think we pull a card to *make* God appear, as if it is all that simple or satisfying to push a button that calls upon divine intervention. Generally, the agent of change and its subjectivity, character, or intent are given less regard than the *mechanism* of change, the machine. Nine is selfless in this way, standing virtuously in service to the whole, enduring obscurity for a liberatory, illuminating function. Reading tarot is making the reader aware of divine possibility, each card a machine that unveils the character, the subjectivity, the influence of the Divine in all things. There are various phenomena that happen when you're particularly close to the conclusion. When an ending's sudden abruptness comes sooner than expected, you fear fumbling, lose focus, and fall anyway. Or commit self-sabotage by getting lazy, or you cash a check before it clears. Maybe there's a third wind, a sprint with unstoppable grit. No matter the nature of the ending or our response to it, we need Nine to ensure we get to the end of our personal journey. The ascendancy of the self cannot be a solitary achievement; divine assistance must be rallied. Without unworldly intervention there is no way to survive in an unjust world. The figures found in the Nine are a worrier, a warrior, a genie, and an icon. With Nine we find fulfillment, face disappointment, refuse to fail. If race is a fiction that has bound us all too tightly and made us all too myopic, then the deus ex machina resolution emphasizes the discomforting artificiality of any fictive resolution that can become hyperreality. A reading brings relief with the Nine, but its solution or reward is limited or provisional. Without continued literacy there is no guarantee of long-term relief.

Nine preserves archetypal meaning, the ethic, while simultaneously transforming the aesthetic to challenge cultural assumptions and thwart generic conventions. A solidarity based upon class identity is maintained along with the desire for self-determination and a developed financial stature. No narrative is all of our own making. There is no simple resolution we can affect or even understand. Nine stands to contrast with the self-made narratives. It knows no willpower or individual effort sufficient enough to yield happiness or prosperity in collective conditions of political and economic injustice. By forgoing joining, assimilating, or conforming to an unjust order, Nine saves us a path to salvation, a fruition for humanity. It acknowledges an emancipation that is only possible by transgressing the entire structure of capitalist relations. The conflicts of classic bourgeois narratives are typically considered to resolve by a developed interiority via the internal efforts of the hero, in which a latent virtuosity is realized. Nine, the *carte ex deus,* is used by the working class to ideate an ending that transcends the individual hero by the imposition of external forces. It is a force encompassing the antagonistic discourse of the social classes.

> *[Working-class] stories refuse to endorse socially confirmed heroes—those who reflect, are part and parcel of, or excel in the worlds they adopt. Working-class characters remain alien to a world that generates its heroes, and the collective conflict with society is not resolved. The working class is thereby shown to be excluded from established apparatuses that allow for personal growth. Especially in Chartist fiction competing on the free market, deferring gratification and being diligent in employment do not lead to prosperity.*[2]

Many critique the deployment of this device, but certainly the drama, damage, and difficulty of disentangling from white supremacist capitalist imperialist patriarchy is worthy of a divine unraveling. This device, the tarot as the divine object, has the power to change our entire perspective, to successfully break the mold of given narrative scripts and reality conventions. It opens ideological possibilities and reinvention of the virtuoso (the ethic's aesthetic embodiment). Nine is then the perfection of technique. Nine, as the device of divine deliverance, and its narrative of miraculous assistance counter the narrative of the self-made man "in which the self-starting, persevering, and doggedly moral underdog overcomes an uncaring and often corrupt society by joining it."[3] Nine uses fantasy, miracle, the extraordinary divine disruption to envision an artisan mobility that capitalism denies.

It accounts for what is still to be written, recognizing that "the impossible"—just another expression for the limitations of our ignorance—cannot be underrated or overlooked. Impossible hopes keep building up every day. Nine, by being the vehicle of disruption of a narrative's internal logic and its seeming validity, champions an unlikely ending. Even after disruption, or particularly because of disruption, Nine sees "the natural ending" of the narrative anew. Each Nine is about visibility, the lucidity of sight. By starlight or sunlight, it is the elemental response to being seen. Each responds differently to the light and its heat, its glamour, its pressure, its insatiable, insistent stare. Nine sees all. Where others fall away or break, Nine still stands. Its light is irreducible. You cannot diminish Nine. It is a pole staff.

Nine offers endurance strategies, ensuring we get our personal achievement by confronting our expectations of achievement, completion, and realization with lived experience, and it attempts to redefine success accordingly. With Nine, we realize achieving the endorsement and respect of a cruel, callous society is pyrrhic, offering no redemption to the society nor the individual. A hero has had flesh flayed and deserves to resolve the narrative complication, the moral quandaries, the obscurity of their individuality. The hero needs Nine to distill wisdom from experience, compassion from suffering, and patience from disappointment.

Nine has penetrated the source. The journey, the zenith of individuation, culminates with Nine, representing completion but not finality. It is the twilight, the measure of satiation. It is the waning moon and Six the waxing; Eight the conjunction. Nine is most distinctly evident of separation.

Each elemental Nine finds a solution for what success is to the survivor who stands alone. In Nine we contemplate, anticipate, fear, or pray for the unexpected. With greater psychic flexibility, the more the unexpected may be understood as a miracle. Then Nine becomes the reorientation, the return to center, the void of infinite nothingness, an ending from which any voice, any life, any beginning may arise.

The Hermit

Being a medicine man actually involved a search for truth that in other societies is granted most often from wealthy patrons or achieved through the stubborn rejection of social values by rebellious intellectuals. Thus, he argued: "While power could be sought as a means to an explicitly and socially conceived end, the shaman's calling is most frequently associated with the search for knowledge. A recognition of the reality and profound significance of the sacred character of the religious world, the inner impulses of a questioning mind, and the determination to delve ever more deeply into the mystery and meaning of life are intrinsic to the shaman's search." Lame Deer probably said it more concisely: 'I believe that being a medicine man, more than anything else, is a state of mind, a way of looking at and understanding this earth, a sense of what it is all about. . . . In a sense, the person was set aside from ordinary individuals, living an isolated life in which higher invisible powers controlled much of what that person did. Thus a medicine man may be sitting in a congenial social atmosphere and yet be receiving information he hears perfectly but is inaudible to anyone else in the group. . . . Most people place their dependence on the medicine man, who understand this life and all its surroundings and are able to predict what will come to pass. They have the right to make these predictions. If as we sit here we should hear a voice speaking from above, it would be because we had the light to hear what others could not hear, or we might see what others had not the right to see because they were not properly qualified. . . . Communication with the higher powers has its limitations, as we can see. The spirits do not confer powers on anyone, but seem to recognize that certain people are chosen to fulfill certain tasks and missions. There seems to be an aspect of predestination inherent in the recognition of a medicine man. The voices people heard in a dream or vision are addressed specifically to them and their situation and lead one to conclude that each individual has already received an outline for his or her life and need only to realize their unique inherent possibilities.[4]

We are sitting with each other in the darkness, and the anticipation of silence is the eroticism of our listening. After sunset, our looking is done differently, we see not what is before us, instead we sense. This darkness is the night of illumination. Fear comes, as does doubt, illusion, delusion, but in this darkness we make a fire, we pray, we make love, we dream, we wade into the waters of renewal. We breathe softer, harder, hushed. This is the night of our truth, where love is ever present but unseen by standard faculties. This is the Hermit's darkness and it is contemplative. In the midst of this night shines a North Star with the power and perspective to shift the narrative center of our soul's telling. This is beyond the darkness of dissolution, the mourning into darkness. The Hermit's darkness holds the inestimable blessing of knowing Divine relationship, finding the right direction in the blackness of the unexpected.

Holding this polestar is the Hermit, retrieving the scattered light in hand, employing its potential into loving. The Hermits hold still at the galactic center, at the apex of the night journey, with the heavens rotating round them. It is always night when there is a gathering together of all the strength, potential, and longings of the soul. The Hermit holds the core of this layered harmony with a total commitment to the stellar power of love. The golden mill of starlight weaving the threads of destiny, connecting the cords of consciousness as shining constellations of wisdom.

Directing the planetary flock toward celestial ends, the Hermit guides through the star's symbol of supreme power, utilizing their emanating light to guide lost souls home. They are a demonstration of pouring forth the faith given to them in their own measure to endure the darkness till they can embrace the night, learning to offer their spirit light in every direction, which provides protection along the way. The light of the Hermit's glowing lantern expresses the communication between different worlds, various cognitions, a matrix of cosmological ways of knowing. It is a meditation upon the soul within, attuning to a light that serves as a guide toward transcendence for seekers of mysteries upon metaphysical voyages.

The Hermit is a midwife tending to the Earth's umbilical cord, maintaining the "Mother Bond of Heaven," that eternal connection that cannot be severed. The *ombligo* is the Hermit's staff, supporting their erect stance, a channel connected to our center, the navel of our origin. It has been considered a pole, an axis, a tree of life, a measuring rod of time and space. It measures the distance from the earth's navel to the human navel, how far we are from uniting the celestial and the chthonic. Position confers power. This eternal pole measures how far we are from the center, from power. The Hermit is any leader who claims the power of the celestial center "by holding a staff or rod that symbolized the pole or shaft of the sacred mill. Later, this pole became the Royal or Holy Scepter as well as the Sacred Sword of the Celts. This philosophy of divine power that came from the center was echoed at all levels of human society, from the very physical seat of government or throne to the central fireplace in every home."[5] This emphasis on place and relative position describes the human relationship to land as a relationship to power, belonging, and wealth. But the Hermit's rod is not the king's royal scepter. Their authority is not governmental but celestial. Their leadership is unto the soul's development.

"*Xictli*, or navel, is depicted as an eye in the sign for movement, *ollin*, and as part of the eagle's eye, creating *'ombligo-ojo,'* or belly button-eye signification (Tibón 1981a)."[6] The Hermit's iconography continues such connections between the navel and cosmic sight underscored in several Mesoamerican codices. Many cultures consider the Cosmic Tree, but there is more than the rod present in the card; there is the lantern (machine) and the star (divinity) within it. The lantern and its light imply sight. It's as if the Hermit stands above the baby, holding the lantern of God's light from a still point, while we lie enthralled by the mobile of love's motion. They keep the light shining, held high enough above so that no matter where we are in the darkness of our own wilderness we see the way home. The Hermit, a shepherd of the starlight within our earthly bodies, recognizes the shining spirit as the principal guide. We each have a guide, a guardian angel, a fairy godmother pointing the way in each person's journey. The Hermit is a soul guide. By giving themselves over to the moving force of light, they help us navigate the darkness of our own ignorance, our night journeys. They are the reader who *channels,* pouring forth lucid streams of healing insight.

The Hermit possesses an asceticism that is accessible only to seekers in search of more complete solitude, more intimacy through an immersion into God. The Hermit is who we would be if we gave ourselves permission to get love-drunk on God because there can be no other way of knowing God. For even one brief encounter with the beloved the Hermit becomes devoted to love's fullest realization. To know the Hermit is to know the many miles one is willing to walk to meet true love. The spiritual path is not one that can be walked occasionally. It is a way of living; and true spiritual power, visionary perspective, and ecstatic trance movements cannot be appropriated, no matter the popularity of New Age spirituality. Hermits are the ones who answer the call. To make themselves available to transcendent spiritual relationships they fast, they pray, they get remote, empty of themselves to gain openness as a place of visitation. Solitude is a necessary ritual for artistic self-actualization. The devotion that solitude entails is a sign of the artist's, the Hermit's, genius, and is a model of ascetic discipline via the aesthetic. This disciplinary solitude is essential in the cultivation of brilliance. But historically this devotion is suspect for anyone other than the male. Mocking any devotion or investment to an artistic practice is rooted in sexism. The Hermit's passionate devotion is cloaked in their isolation, which is not a sign of misanthropic disaffection for humanity but a rebellious reclamation of space-time to pursue the light of their innate creativity.

The Hermit has no doubt about God's involvement in worldly affairs. Without this faith, the Hermit would be no good guide to anyone. They would be too stressed, overwhelmed, and doubting. The Hermit has an earned faith, earnest but also relaxed. The Hermit is the reader, the teacher, the writer, using the cards to chart their own emotional, psychospiritual landscape. They hold the space to heal the *how* of our learning so it is both gentle and rigorous, attentive to both our spaces of ignorance and our spaces of genius. When I teach, tarot or otherwise, I feel that we are walking and mapping new terrain together. The text, the cards, become little red tags that mark the trees of the forest of the wild unknown we brave. And the Hermit is the one who sees the forest for the trees. Though the Hermit's faith is firm, the knowledge is not a given. Knowledge is made in the moment when the muse comes through, only accessible with responsive, deep listening. And it's magical. The Hermit brings forth lived experience, our empirical knowledge, but the genius is a force that can move through any of us when we're willing and showing up together. The Hermit shepherds such moments of shared genius, shared humility.

The Hermit is the great observer of organic life. The elders began their quest for understanding with observation of the physical world in self-reflexivity, but they also accommodated the "continuing but sporadic intrusion of higher powers in their lives, manifested in unusual events and dreams."[7] They recognize in the regularity of natural cycles a greater power that provided enough reliability to give life meaning. The Hermit's role is to sustain the relationships with these greater powers that sustain the cosmos so physical life is constructive and purposeful.

Scholaris, the pupil, is meant to see. The Hermit's gospel has eyes. Sight is always a moment of exposure. Seeing into the heart changes it. The Hermit looks upon the light leading the way, lighting up the road and heart all at once.

> *It has been said that a "person is enlightened," not "when they get an idea," but "when someone looks at them." A person is enlightened when another loves them. The eyes are windows to the heart; they search the person out and have power to elicit life. So the gospel has eyes which are not dispassionate, nor merely passive. Their gaze is not an art gallery gaze, wandering from exhibit to exhibit and leaving what they see obviously unchanged. Their gaze engages what they see and affects it: For God, to gaze is to love.... These eyes are effective.*[8]

The Hermit, eased off of their own self-importance, is in a state of ecstasy, that state of rapture that dazes the body as the soul contemplates divinity. Their ecstatic stance, their firm social place, is of entrancement, astonishment; which from ecstasy's root, *existanai,* is a displacement of its own. The Hermit marks a position of divine possibility that presents a unique relationship to being "put out of place." The Hermit is a model, someone who steps outside of the conventional consciousness and frees the mind from habituated perspectives. Rather than remaining entrenched in the circuit of their own thinking, the Hermit listens and looks with humility, for they have endeavored to stand before God, at last in truth before another, and see.

The Hermit retraces the journey up the mountain for our benefit. The Hermit offers us the direct, narrow route up the mountain, while helping the reader avoid the dead-end, meandering routes that lead to futile frustration. At the top of the mountain is the all-spaciousness, the nothingness of God's all-encompassing envelopment, the space where Spirit breathes freely. Ascent is a lover's quest, whereby to be seen in God's gaze is to be enlightened in the beauty of the beloved. The Hermit stance in this God witness, this holy gaze that draws us out of ourselves, where in such reflection we find self-realization pushes us toward totality. By treating solitude as sacred, treasures are gathered from the darkness that emerge into the light of our looking.

Tarot is intrinsically connected to the process of discovery, but this is a card of attainment, rather than pursuit. The Hermit is also psychologically, emotionally, and spiritually developed. A character that is not fatalistically dependent on the social order matures us as artists and thinkers and seekers, as the Hermit is the one who has arrived holding the source of self-regard before them. The card confirms when confidence has been shifted from the small solitary self to God, from which all the symptoms of stillness come.

Seeing what has been foretold from a state of fruition, the Hermit stands retrograde, looking back along the long line preceding them with the clarity of hindsight. There is relation to *prudentia* here, since the arcanum is sagely wise with discernment and providence. There is so much possibility in the prophecy awaiting its flesh, and the Hermit is the guiding spirit through it all. The Hermit is a bookend, holding the narrative of exploration in place, reminding us that progression by linear movement can only go so far.

The Hermit is the human on the vision quest, the pilgrimage, the retreat, ritually setting aside time from routine, mundane life to open themselves to the possibility of forging focused relationships with spirits, deities, animals, and forces of nature; communications, knowledge, and mediations from the nonhuman.[9] On this journey into the heart of the cosmos the Hermit is enthralled in bearing witness to the essence that transcends ordinary spacetime. Typically, we only think of ghosts as the ones who move between the living and the dead, but the gnosis of the Hermit asserts otherwise.

No white person has ever had a vision quest and they never will. Their missions into darkness couched colonial conquest and enslavement in terms of *el requerimiento* and *manifest destiny* and confused spiritual night with religious repression. Not everyone is a Hermit, not everyone knows natively, and not every native has a spirit journey. Again, the Hermit is a role model, holding up a mobile of the cosmos, by which their mapping can only be trusted to the extent that their character and perceptive capacities are seriously sculpted. The Hermit's singularity is a recognition that, while anyone might have a spiritual experience, only certain souls are called upon to enter a knowing of deeper mysteries. Dreams often open the path for most people, but the approval and support of elders and ancestors is still required. There are powers conferred upon the medicine people, and their sacred confrontation imposes additional responsibilities upon the Hermit that cannot be minimized. These responsibilities release the Hermit from certain earthly ties and yet they perform a public service. The Hermit does more than complete a logical circle, their contemplation is more than some frozen thought. They change the world by shifting perspective and present the people new paths to follow. They heal, they predict, they locate the lost. They share visions where the influence of the invisible spirit is respected for its activity and direction in the world.

These are the holy ones who live a rigorous, disciplined life to commune with higher powers, who look with the understanding of the elders and offer the signs of inner recollection. They are the ones others recognize as having experiences, insights, and powers that could not be denied when searching for answers to critical existential questions. They share and initiate encounters with the deeper mysteries of the universe to necessarily reach a more adequate understanding of and orientation toward life.

The path of redemption the Hermit walks is one in which the suffering we have endured is not for nothing. The deep struggles we inherit are a burden the Hermit makes into a well of compassion, patience, wisdom, and understanding, a healing tonic they extend to others that wouldn't have been possible without persevering through such painful adversity. The Hermit is when our history is no longer an open, festering wound but a scar. A scar I can touch and tell stories about. From the gifts of the Hermit, I use the tarot, I write this book, to explore the interchange of possibilities offered by compatible spirits across different knowledges, traditions, and histories.

The Sun

By now you know how it must be: there must be contradiction, multiplicity, Underworld descent, sacrifice, sustenance, and revisability. And when the book catches a share of these things it wraps up: the hero twins discover maize and become the celestial lights, and the humans are made. But the book does not end there, and we soon learn that the world is still in darkness, waiting for these humans to bring the dawn out from the eastern sky. The first humans thus wander around for some time, suffering trials and growing intellectually to be able to bring light out of the horizon. When they do, with poetry and ritual, it is a glorious moment in the book. It is as if the Sun does not so much emerge from the eastern ridge as the earth and its human and nonhuman inhabitants turn toward that glistening light, pulling the planet into its rotation, which makes it appear as if the sun rises in the sky.[10]

It has been so dark for so long, every morning I wake to the cold loneliness of my longing for the warmth of his explosive brilliance. One of these mornings I might wake from these troubled times renewed in the joy of a better day when his love is held in my hand, his grin before my gaze. I wait for the Sun to break the silence of the night, to make fate fortunate. I pull this card, and though I still struggle to accept a new vision, I know fulfillment is always the future's promise. All I need is a new prism to perceive its possibility. I need the Sun's divine sight to attend and help me understand how the inner world interacts with the visible one.

The Sun, as in the Popol Vuh, as in this book, in this deck, is not the real sun, but a mirror reflecting the light of consciousness, a central location of identity. The Sun is an unblinking witness, our forward future face, cast in the interplay of light and shadow of the worlds in which we live. The tarot stares too in this way. We are but a matrix of refracting light, casting shadows in many different shapes at any given time. The Sun concerns recognition, origin, totality, visibility, and the apparatus and politics of sight and seeing, inclusion, surveillance, and self-conception. The Sun champions self-reflexivity as a force of spiritual renewal so that the light therein cast may lead to the glorious illumination of love consciousness. With the Sun, all of life at last approves itself, love has at last come along.

The Sun summons attention, for a conclusion is culminating and the future is now commencing. No matter if the ending is happy or bleak, every beginning has promise. The Sun's arrival is the crescendo of creation's opera. It asks about lighting and turns toward its source, thereby locating a central power, a primordial generativity, a core vitality. The arcanum is an instrument for seeing the glorious dawn that mesmerizes us with prophetic possibilities. The Sun is so absolutely sure of itself. Anything that looks upon it must always reveal themselves before the Sun. Everyone approaches the Sun in darkness, but you cannot get closer to the Sun without basking in the warmth of its illumination, so generously given that you also begin to see yourself in its ever-new, unending light of attention. Clear seeing comes by way of clarifying screens, the tarot cards, that can recall the creators who consult the diviners before originating.

> *In Plato's world, when you look into the mirror—you will see the interaction of substances flowing from a world beyond your perception. That is not what the Popul Vuh is saying. In its world, when you look into the mirror, you will have a fog distorting what you see, but with the right kind of attention (and instruments) you can clear the reflecting surface—the instrument for seeing—and see the world actually. But you should not expect that in doing that you will see Plato's real world of unchanging models. The sun is not the sun actually, because it is subject to the same ceaseless screen that is time originating itself in what you see.*[11]

God is not blind, though divine light may be blinding in its overwhelm. The Sun is always a challenge to our imperfect faculties of perception, wherein the ability to distinguish between image and reality, representation and substance, is diminished by the veil, the fog gods place on humans to prevent them from such divine sight. The Sun is who sees, but the one who sees is often unseen, at least one when one relies solely on the Logos. We have already explored how the Moon teaches the reader to perceive the unseen, to see psychically. Every image of the Sun is only a reflection of its abstraction. When we pull the Sun we have a chance to burn through this fog and see the world actually, finally. Then the light you thought was gone, the one you grieve with the weight of darkness, is reborn with the morning, with fresh flesh, an open heart and a full spirit.

The Sun is omnipotence, ontological sovereignty, and God as divine child riding strident and bareback on the white horse; the soul chariot is your champion. The Sun is how humans understand God revealing themself. So much has been written of God's abandonment, the icy reserve of their inattention, forsaking us to their forgetfulness; but when God emerges, irrevocably and suddenly, their virtue is immediately accessible. Who could blame this beautiful child for the sins of their father and forefathers? All that's left of their birth, their innocence, is a reflection in the card we carry today. It wasn't one child but every child that is a messiah, rescuing the reader from oblivion. They are a psychopomp, bringing the soul back to joy. Marvin Gaye sang about saving the children, but it is only their forgiveness that could set us free. It is by the child that we know God has blessed us, so please God, help the child. The future is perhaps only fully, purely imagined by the young.

The Sun is always a meditation on the future. Nothing encompasses the consideration of the future more than the child's body and being. By their body is newness translated into innocence. They are the fresh-born being emerging from the Moon. There is a marked difference in stance between the Hermit, with their age and their retrograde posture toward the past, and the Sun, with its youth and its progression into the future. One is the embodiment of the past, which is always old; and the future, which is always young, is personified as a child; and the distance between them is time, for they are its guardians, its progenitors. The period we are living in is always with a prefix pointing toward the past, which must mean we have succumbed to each other's judgment, a deadening damnation to a future denied. The modern prophets look back like the Hermit, as if everything that will ever happen has already happened. And the present landscape from which we all look back is dreary, repulsive, and overcast. Love never lasts long enough. As soon as it leaves, I'm scavenging the present, fearful of a future where so long as love refrains from returning my heart, I'm all alone.

For centuries imperialism, capitalism, and colonialism have stolen the futures of countries and continents around the world to establish, amass, and expand empire. How could faith in the future not be exhausted? But the vision of the future presented here is optimistic, joyous, renewing. Happiness is as miraculous as the child's simple smile telling us we only need their trust for fulfillment. The future's children aren't mine or yours or even ours, they are the Sun's. Our concern for *the* children must reach beyond a couple of generations of children and grandchildren. These children gesture toward a brighter, broader, greater time to come, a possibility transcending the purview of current politics.

Yet youth in modern media do not signal hope or renewal or a future, but a plastic hell, one in which they are apathetic, unwilling, or unable to learn anything that would mature them. They are stuck in the patterns of the past, subject to violence, resource theft, climate collapse, displacement, and divestment, powerless to change the world. The kids are stuck at the carnival and instead of celebrating, it's all horror. They've been caught by the dead lights of the modern clown's monstrous eyes. The renewal of their laughter has shifted to be ironic, solemn, and more melancholic. These false lights freeze time, working to hypnotize and transfix those caught by its unchanging gaze. This is a dead-end oscillation on a merry-go-round that is neither playful nor celebratory. And so there's no adulthood for those children caught in a terrible, frightening forever.

Everyone's always trying to correct children, telling them how to walk, how to react to the world ablaze all around them. Depictions of these youth blame them for the problems they have inherited as they are pressured and expected to be the saviors of tomorrow. To displace the responsibility of ensuring survival for the future onto the children is an immense pressure that is simply unjustifiable. Adults allow children to be the collateral damage for their unprocessed trauma. The Sun's reckoning will be the ending of cumulative anguish passed down through generations so that the trauma is not the obsessive location we identify as our truest self.

The signatory features of the modern West are advancement, progress, and a triumphant everlasting youth; and yet it is here that the future is most uncertain, for as Mrs. Morrison observes, "there is no comfortable assurance of 'world without end,' there is clearly no year 4000 or 5000 or 20,0000 that hovers in or near our consciousness."[12] This meditation on the viability of the future, the promise or disappointment of a new golden age through the metaphor of the child, is ages old. The golden age as a concept has been either a clarion call for future utopia or an instrument to critique power with its grandiose vision of empire.

It was Virgil's prophecy of a child who will bring forth the golden age, the Christ child born, the mythologized savior son, the king in the new world who now has a new word, so too then can we enter newness. But this world was not new, it was native. Can we stand under the true Sun so we may realize we are natives and not nationals?[13] Imaginative forays into the far distant future that are liberatory must advance the modern, the postmodern, any perception consistent with a European notion of Enlightenment. The Sun is a historical marker of humanity's multi-dimensional being, ever and always reduced by the categories of Enlightenment thought to be rendered intelligible, so the project of *progress,* that is, the progression of empire can unfurl unfettered. The Sun is a call to consider the ways a virile conquering "heroism" is romanticized so that absolute authority may be wielded over others. The Western project of progress has been debunked by post- and decolonial praxis as eurocentric, imperialist, neocolonialist fallacy. No more is the human envisioned as Eurocentric; no more can a single framework, a particular pursuit sell itself as the universal to secure its own interests. The Sun as symbol of progress, future, and utopia tells the reader to dispense with a progressive reading of history to decolonize thought. What succeeds after the end of a Eurocentric white supremacist capitalist imperialist conception of progress will be the Sun's new symbols.

> *For perhaps the major lesson of postcolonial scholarship over the last thirty-five years has been that the developmentalist, progressive reading of history—in which Europe or "the West" is viewed as more enlightened or more developed than Asia, Africa, Latin America, the Middle East, and so on—and the so-called civilizing mission of the West, which served to justify colonialism and imperialism and continues to underwrite the informal imperialism and neocolonialism of the current world economic, legal, and political order, are deeply intertwined. . . . The language of progress and development is the language of oppression and domination for two-thirds of the world's people.*[14]

As Alice Sparkly Kat observes in *Postcolonial Astrology,* the Sun, its light, and the metaphysical dimensions of sight become associated with truth and reason. Light thereby becomes a power relation where race becomes a classificatory mechanism to measure degrees of "rational perfection," where the Indigenous along with the mass-enslaved become irrational, subrational, and savage. Light when reconstituted as a racial and racializing technology becomes an index of evolution and development circulating narratives of white supremacy wherein dominators naturalize themselves. The Enlightenment overemphasized rationality while defining "human" progress through dehumanizing systems. By making the Indigenous and the enslaved the "backward" example of the irrational and wild, Europe and its colonial offspring position themselves as the pinnacle, the center, and justify colonial conquest and mass enslavement. The Sun, then, with its new body for the future, conceives of its rational self-conception always with otherness as a referent. This Western Sun is a globalizing force via a universalizing, racializing human conception. The thesis of liberal universalism flattens difference in its inclusionary aim, making monoliths out of diverse populations for the aim of representation. Racism then becomes manifold microaggressions, debilitating as death is doled out by the variety of a thousand cuts. The project and practice of inclusion is insidiously dangerous should we forget this solar history. These considerations grapple with circular rather than linear time, and the regularly revisited past that we confuse with the future in our optimism.

For the Sun to extend beyond hierarchies of race and rationality that have so long ordered and cohered the planet's populations, the techniques and strategies of antiracist and anticolonial movements must be held in clarity, or else they can be confused into contributing to the systems they seek to dismantle; for by simply being included, recognized, witnessed, or seen by the gaze of this established power, they mistakenly promise progress. Representation fails when the lens, the gaze, the camera format, the composition is not our own technology. The Sun's concern with image-making means our credibility, our experience, our story must be our own ingenuity if they are ever to be enough. The Sun says truth is either in the image or in the wielders of the image, the camera operators, the directors of production. A camera format, as any image construction, reflects what the consciousness associates with a telling of the truth. Importing an external white image maker, a white savior who delivers a platform they deem legitimate, is a trap, an Oz in the Emerald City selling us short. All entertainment industries, including sports, music, film, and television, extract from the image and likeness of Black people. When the lens isn't ours, we may be the subject but have no subjectivity. The settler state does not constitute a legitimate framework, so Indigeneity seeking justice through inclusion within such a framework will only work to reproduce colonial, racist, patriarchal state-power configurations.

The work of freedom must be seen to exist, generate, and collaborate outside the institutional and systemic powers of dominant society. The Sun calls, as Glen Coulthard does, for more than a politics of state recognition; it calls for the visions of Indigenous people's self-determination, for a possibility, a pedagogy, a future arising among the oppressed. When we look here, then we may see more than a scientific "upgrade"; we may actually rekindle hope in future collectivity, knowledge, and time itself. When we look toward the ingenuity of our image-making technologies, we gain all the validation we will ever need; we have a way to believe our own experience independent of an external gaze. The Sun is the climactic moment where we re-create our forgotten history, standing with our story, our experience that cannot be pushed to the margins, erased or exploited or deleted. Like the Sun, we are still here to tell our tale.

Without the Sun there would be no time. Our measurement of its light is a measurement of a clarity we've conceived of ourselves. Time is a measurement of light waxing and waning in our lives. We can measure our growth, our attainment of the most important goal of the soul, a crowning liberation of love consciousness with the clarity of light. But the world no more believes a messiah will arrive, for now the afterlife is absurd and the immortal soul unintelligible; the future becomes some gilded product that only improves the health of some single life span by imagining ceaseless consumption. And it's certainly not always the case that we know if we're making any progress at all, when the world seems to only show unending streams of apocalypse, a collapse of any futurity or any plausible potential for continued existence. It's a constant apathy when the imagination of the future atrophies. It is senseless, simply unreasonable to imagine a future when you don't believe in your survival. Even with all my own recounting of past prophets of liberation in this book, it is hard for me to claim the luxury of imagining the articulation of a destiny without a felt guilt of deferring or displacing contemporary suffering. Yet I read and write to refuse a future severely diminished, where all may recover from the wounds of dehumanizing domination.

I write toward the future of time, not progress. A future timelessness, a better time without end, must be insisted on. There must be a future where nature reconciles with culture. Our diminished expectations of survival have the implicit critique of futurity, but it's the future that is infinitely more hospitable to humanity. I am not obstinately optimistic but diverging an imaginary from a myopic vision that is gendered, hunted, displaced, colonialized, racialized, turning toward a rescue of time. I am seeking the voices that excavate the places where the future has been folded in. The future is a construction, a building in equal parts discovery and conception. "I am not, of course, encouraging and anointing happy endings—forced or truly felt—or anointing bleak ones intended as correctives or warnings. I mean to call attention to whether the hand that holds the book's metaphors is an open palm or a fist."[15] All knowledge must certainly perceive its precedent, but what would prophecy be if it anticipated no solace for future humanity? For history to persist, it is to be shaped by the stirring of the dismissed, the pressed upon, and the cloaked. I shall not be dimmed. We shall not be dimmed. We are allowed to be fully in the rising of our own light, emanating our God glow from within.

I see the Sun as a unique technique of movement, turning away from the academic mainstream in order to maintain a potent energetic channel of transformation and concentrate transgressive intention into action. To me this is the path of righteousness that the Sun spotlights. The artistic rendering of the Sun we hold in our hands is but one sign of renewal for the future. We become prophetic witnesses to a social revolution that would improve every creature's chance of living in well-being, peace, joy. When you pull this arcanum you are where the Sun dawns. However you arrive, you are welcome as you are.

The discipline of turning toward sunshine when you've been conditioned to gawk in the shadows is a soft one. The Sun reunifies the reader with all of nature. Every animal, small and large, exults when the Sun emerges, every river rejoices. For all the Earth's offspring there is but one praise, one dawn that rises for the innumerable mass and their complicated, conflicting lifeworks, problem spaces, political imaginations, backgrounds, and states of being. But the Sun does not assume we are under an empire of multicultural universalism. The Sun, historically, is the monarchy, the dominance of the rational we've so convinced ourselves of possessing. I do not see the Sun championing a universalizing history of time's unfolding. This work is a systemic analysis, but I am cognizant of the ways system building has interpellated populations in ways that collapse diverse life-worlds, orientations, and conceptual horizons in the fraught process of translation. In the exchange among such diverse life-worlds offered here, I am not seeking to collate varied collective experiences into a singular account. There may be one Sun, but its life is refracted and dispersed into spectral components. Its warm horizon is always imbued with multiplicative potentiality.

The Sun is a supreme unifying principle of life, which has not been neutral. For love to be the unifying force, the spirit, the motivation, and the method must be furnished by its light. For the revelation promised by the Sun we need the Moon, we need intuition, instinct, reason, and gnosis. When the glory of revelation is revealed, the Sun is enacting an active process. The human spirit must rise up to touch the grace that reaches down. When contact is made, the Sun shares sacred insights into the celestial realms. Songs of love's epiphany come pouring out when, where everywhere there was once blindness, now there is sight, now color. Love is light illuminating. Every day I pray: please let love be my salvation. Please help me love. Please help make me new in love. Let love be my song, my art, my nature. Let love emanate from me. Please show me what a world in love looks like. Love is not without me, love is not beyond me. The struggle and the loss, the separation, the return to darkness is worth the liberation from delusion, is worth standing in the Sun.

The Sun comes with a light to set the child free by turning us away from the past so that we may be ready to entrust ourselves, like the new child does with its guardians despite its scapegoating, still only ever open to the unexpected, the uncharted, the incalculable future within God. Every child is wild, unaffected and untamed, representing our unconditioned, natural impulse toward future fulfillment. These are child prophets, the Sun's soothsayers, with smiles beaming bright so the darkness of doubt and deceit are cast away. They wipe our eyes so that our vision of the forthcoming glory will complete with our laughter, love, and dreams no more deferred. The Sun comes and the inner child takes hold of consciousness to fly higher, shining generously in the sky.

Everything lost along the way gets remembered in the sunlight. Our fractured, dispersed humanity is seen clearly with the Sun's dramatic emergence. What was and what is is now the Sun's say of what will be.

Nine of Swords

Periods of psychological rebirth evolve biological and other-dimensional memories, or resonances of our time in the womb and subsequent physical birth. A period of incubation, enwombment or gestation follows, during which the future shaman may be physically and/or mentally ill, when he descends into the terrain of "death." He may be called upon to battle demons, endure various psychic trials, or encounter spirits that have possessed or attacked him. Imagery of death may symbolize a former world view, self-concept or phase of life that is dying, to make way for rebirth.[16]

Overwhelmed by the night, bearing the weight of being so desperately unknown is a loneliness so heavy in its silence. My mind walks on the edge of abyss, drawn by the pull of this dangerous desire. The Nine of Swords is the mind putrefying, and it feels like evil has seized all the energy of the intellectual platform. Like the internet, it is increasingly difficult to discern the validity of what's said on this platform, especially when conflict gets more attention. The madness of our psychic architecture reflects the internet's nightmarish design, making it impossible to separate engagement from magnification. The attention merchant that is the internet has financial incentive to fearmonger. Here is a trick mirror, a panopticon enforcing self-surveillance. Making the world's woes a personal punishment is the dangerous delusion of positioning personal identity as the center of the universe. Some enormous singular thought that wreaks havoc is wrought from statement separated from context. Jia Tolentino teaches that the internet is engineered for misrepresentation, poised to confuse the image for the body, the word for the action, the picture for the reality.

Pain is the object of my action of knowing in the Nine of Swords. That's the problem with evil: it is never silent, its inquiry is never satiated, it is never convinced. It's a constant Cassandra syndrome, assaulting a core sense of self with disbelief. As put on as we are with the pain-proof of our lived experience, our alternative ways of knowing and being, when disavowed, make the relationship to truth psychotic and pathological.

Whatever we are turning toward in the Nine of Swords, we know it is difficult, because facing it proves painstaking to perceive. The text is too difficult to understand to produce any intelligence from it, but the message keeps keeping you up. The signs we ask for in augury are frightening when we are afraid to accept the truth they're pointing toward. Everything feels futile when waiting for a return to light, a promised sign of confirmation as we anxiously obsess over what can't be controlled, what has yet to be critically understood. The nightmare mind of the Nine of Swords arises from and points toward a lack of rest, which withers the faculties of perception. This rumination is not the remedy our mind convinces us it is, for it wants viscerality. This is an image of disproportion, a loss of scale. Panic is an exaggerated negativity suffocated, swallowed in the darkness. Panic clouds rational thought. Like an alarm, light ruptures the night, flooding it with fluorescent flashes. Overwhelmed by what is impossible to realize but proceeding nonetheless, we sit sobbing in the darkness. Piercing past what you think is possible is at first terrifying.

We have never been so confronted with an environment of uncertainty and the insecurity of truth, so severed from the rites and initiations of the night. The quietude of spirit is assaulted by the incessant demand upon the economy of our attention by constant social media connectivity. We learn how challenging it is to be with ourselves in the Nine of Swords, a capacity that, if undeveloped, threatens all fronts of freedom. There is no liberation without self-acceptance. This is a moment to recognize and respect the part of the soul that does not wish to be captured. The Nine of Swords shows that the spectacles—the ones we make of each other, of ourselves, of Black, queer, native people—are vile. Who doesn't deserve privacy to cry? America is a hell realm where the only way people know how to cope with the most horrific experiences is to make them into an amusement park, to cloak their memories in commerce, to upcycle every iota of existence, turning trauma into entertainment in the search for attention and the hope of an eventual payday.

The Nine of Swords cuts the lights, otherwise we'd never have a private moment, never a reprieve from performing. We can, for this moment, stop questioning how much of ourselves to slice off in tribute to some notion of social relevance. I wonder, even with our incessant investment in image production, is this a world where images are enough? Can you believe your intuition, your foresight, even without tarot imagery? The internet's architecture has conditioned us to be too dependent upon a particular camera style, a certain scene, a filtered perspective to take truth's claim at face value.

Fear veils itself, and that is the veil of the Nine of Swords. It mimics the sound of rationality and reason, as it is so sure we will never find our voice, that truth will never reveal itself, that we will always be alone in our unknowing. It's the usual story of incapacity, not the reality but thinking that we can't do it that stops us. But this is strategic. This mockery is a scheme of mental assault. It's the oppressor's disbelief in our validity that is dangerous when heard as the voice within. The fear that our emotions, our desires, will ruin our objectivity arises in a distorted sense of scale, a misperception that is primary to the card. The misperception is that the emotion, the intuition, the nonrational way of knowing is illegitimate. Whatever we know we know with our entire being—body, emotion, mind, and all. The Nine of Swords never disregards the objects of intuitions, they place them under rigorous investigation, as it seeks critical comprehension.

Fear would have us believe meaning is never ours to possess. This can be an apprehension before reading the text is overcome by feeling free to attempt *inventing* meaning as well as discovering it. Comprehension then becomes reader-created knowledge rather than memorized or deposited knowledge. The action of understanding makes a producer of knowledge, a re-creator, a coauthor, an innovator of language. The production of knowledge requires this continuous reconstitution.

The night is feared for it confronts us with limitation, powerlessness, but it need not be fought, for we could not handle the lights always on, or always off. This distorted interplay of light and dark reveals the photonegative of the psyche. Our perception is skewed because we are looking at an image, an in-sight that is still processing. The light of the day would disrupt the development. So you must endure the darkness a while a longer before we can let the dawn in. In the Nine of Swords enter the dark room, swathed in red light.

The meaning is created when the reader has achieved the Nine of Swords's critical consideration of the writer's texts, symbols, and stories. When you confront your fear of what you don't understand—what remains still in the darkness, still unknown, no matter the light cast by your gaze—you refuse to be petrified by terror. To get free from the voice of demons or internalized oppression may require screaming, crying, sweating, shaking, stretching, singing, humming, weeping, praying.

The Nine of Swords makes critical readers through work and reworking meaning, teaching, again, not to be passive before the text, to leave it there, immobilized, waiting, as if our life has already been written, as if we were powerless against fate's predetermined demise. It forces us to resist the temptation to be naively fatalistic. Refrain from cherry-picking the worst criticisms as the foundation for your identity or your future. Our identity can be constituted by much more than the relation to our opposition. While white supremacy exists on a spectrum of anti-Blackness, Blackness needs nothing to do with whiteness to exist. Our text is our tongue, our eyes, our hands, our heart. Destiny is the narrative, the subjectivity we enact out of the raw material of fate.

Creative reading requires critical reflection, a willingness to meet a cognitive challenge. The challenge is akin to psychic weightlifting; the tearing of mental muscle is functional toward its expansion. The Nine of Swords piercing the mind is this process portrayed. And it's certain that when you pull this card, you must actively exercise the imagination. The mind penetrating the veil of night is somewhere sewing light through an immensely dense velvet darkness. It can be hard to hold the thread because one slip and you're drowning in darkness. But taking the chance to critically comprehend what is beyond us, beyond our perceived ability, incompetence, or insecurity, produces far more complex understanding.

The child's innate curiosity-led inquiry must not be repressed; rather, the child must be trained to *use* their imagination. The child's imagination is so strong that, when skewed and susceptible to fear, it matters not if what generates the fear is fictitious; the fear felt and held in their being is concrete. Fear must not be allowed to paralyze us, to persuade us to quiet, to be challenged without any effort, any fight. Their fear must be allayed by inviting them into responsibility for their creative, cognitive abilities. They must be disciplined readers to develop their own potential and their own voice by their own hands. For them to recount the story, with plenty of room for the imagination, dreams, feelings, and desires, is for that child's curiosity to be kept alive.

Possess enough curiosity to indulge the child's fear, to look under the bed and in the closet, when attempting to comprehend augury. It's slippery but then you can actually grip the text to finally discover its significance. The writing, the reading, can be a very lonely endeavor, making the spirit of discipline that keeps you going all the more necessary. The Nine of Swords is a chance to ensure our treatment of the child is one of support, reassurance, and care. It is a chance to teach them the power of prayer, the comfort of building a relationship of divine trust. It's a chance to leave a warm light on, to recite the saying that soothes.

Though we always think of ourselves as individual actors in the stories of our lives, it is so painfully lonely to assume sole responsibility for your happiness and well-being. This Nine of Swords supposition would tragically mean no one else is looking out for you, nor praying for you, nor seeing after your safety. This is obviously not the case. The card calls for being tucked in. For in the fear, vulnerability, and desire for protection that arises in this psyche-scape, stripping us naked of false pretense to get what we really want, we submit to the mystical, to the mystery that is love. The night of the Nine of Swords, though painful, is an enveloping, protective experience where we can let agony dissolve. This psychic container wards off dark spirits and entities. We drop the ego to surrender to the healing darkness of unknowing. To let go of the clinging mental attachment to dire outcomes and have just a little faith that the greater divine spirit is bringing goodness to your life is all the wherewithal you need.

For the Hermit, the Nine of Swords is an unavoidable stage in the healing journey. Wisdom is made when suffering's meaning has been distilled. Wisdom is whatever medicine it takes to live authentically with nothing to hide, for there are parts of us we only get to know when we live in our truth. There is a tonic in looking at the fear that is so often just the earnestness of a young heart that hasn't learned to endure separation. Often, the desire that would bring us the most fulfillment causes us the most fear. Early and consistent childhood conditioning makes us hostile to the body's natural impulse.

Looking at fear is often looking at what we we really want, but reject. It is the desire you wish you didn't have, the one you can't just accept without feeling the air of judgment. When we have been taught to reject what we want, what we know, what has happened to us, memory gets dislodged, suppressed, until in the Nine of Swords it comes back to the forefront. The card comes so this resistance can dissolve, so the thorn in the paw of our perception is pulled. Its sharp release can be so challenging that you question any healing promised on the other side. It cannot be done without mourning an identity, a story of your selfhood that you were so sure of. But truth is never a punishment. Truth is what makes mercy possible. Surely not every darkness is contemplative, but when I pull the Nine of Swords, I know if I can write it, if I can name it, it has no power over me. Alternatively, I find prayer an effective instruction in knowing the names of God. I find the roots of my faith go deeper than the fear.

> *The more that we were willing to struggle for an emancipatory dream, the more apt we were to know intimately the experience of fear, how to control and educate our fear, and finally, how to transform that fear into courage. Moreover, we could come to recognize our fear as a signal that we are engaged in critical opposition to the status quo and in transformative work toward the manifestation of our revolutionary dreams.*[17]

All truths must maintain and recognize our states of confusion and sites of ignorance. It is false to presume we are all-knowing or all-important. The first truth, the primary knowing, is of our ignorance. Part of the prophetic work is respecting and preserving the mind's dark corners, the unexplained, the yet to be revealed. To inhabit our mind, our being, and our body with peace, every light cannot always be on. The Nine of Swords is the deepest point of night before dawn breaks. Its intensity is a river of black velvet covering you, cutting you off from the outside world, ensuring you withdraw deep inside yourself. It's a paradox of the sight. It's night but your eyes are opened, you are isolated in a moment but you realize you are woven into a greater spirit, united with all living beings. Turn the lights down low and let go. You don't need to be David fighting Goliath. You don't need to do it alone. But you do need rest, you need trust and community, you need physical release, and you need the night.

Nine of Wands

I define solidarity in terms of mutuality, accountability, and the recognition of common interests as the basis for relationships among diverse communities. Rather than assuming an enforced commonality of oppression, the practice of solidarity foregrounds communities of people who have chosen to work and fight together. Diversity and difference are central values here—to be acknowledged and respected, not erased in the building of alliances.[18]

The Nine of Wands is an immediate invitation to attend to the integrity, security, and safety of our bodies. It is the card of a soldier's sensibility. Soldiers are romanticized, sold as a symbol of valiance, heroism, and masculinity.

Military recruiters given access to schools to prey upon poor youth without any perception of a viable future make them fodder for its forever wars.[19] The soldier state being billed as character development, a citizenship program, which the youth—so developmentally susceptible to such promises and incentives of education, citizenship, and debt relief—do not find quite so convincing after experiencing war. Soldiers endure; they are trained to reject the needs and natural knowing of their body to adhere to a disciplinary, violent hierarchy. In this environment of strict discipline, mob mentality rules over individual decision-making. The culture of this soldier social structure is one of obedience, authoritarianism, conformity, instrumentality. The soldier is but the arm, the pawn, the collateral damage toward colonial conquest. Being routinely commanded within an environment of authoritarianism displaces the moral responsibility of individual actions. This is precisely why militant ideology commits so deeply to obedience: so that its violent commands are carried out without any question. Rather, the Nine of Wands figure seems to be claiming the choice of their own actions, for they stand alone. Or perhaps they are the last one standing, still so proud to perform their duty to obey, not realizing the fight has finished or at least not willing to give it up. If you are pulling the Nine of Wands it's imperative to know whose war you are being enlisted to wage.

What is it that this figure sees that makes them so defensive? Is this card a template for goodness fighting evil to the death, or is this wounded figure of a vengeful nature? Is the posture here one of someone defending against the West's inclusionary aim of empire, resistant to the structures of psychic, social domination? Or is their stance strictly exclusionary to maintain an unjust, racist notion of purity? Their gaze is fixed toward the past, perhaps a tell that they are still haunted by the bloodshed of historic combat and conflict.

When your body's boundaries are violated, there is a theft of dignity. This figure has survived assault, a condition intimately known by most women and children living under patriarchy. In the Nine of Wands is yet another refusal to submit. It is a reclamation of power and a reconstitution of bodily autonomy. A strength that was dormant within, but awakened with pain, is possessed by the survivor of the Nine of Wands. Survivors may have guilt and complex posttraumatic stress, and may remain hypervigilant against any possible threat, any foreign invasion to their body that's still keeping score. Depending on the scope, the wands in the card act as a border, a walled-off territory doggedly defended by the Nine of Wands soldier. Medicalizing language when applied to the health of the country or the people becomes a veiling language for xenophobia. At what point does an individual boundary become representative of a geopolitical border staked in the ideology of nativism and xenophobia that each citizen is conditioned to carry? Exclusionary borders have many guises. Whether they are racial, linguistic, physical, or religious borders in the Nine of Wands, the sole figure is attentive to their burden on the body.

Ideology shapes the access we give to our bodies, places, and communities. Paulo Freire observed the social, civic, and political discipline called upon in the Nine of Wands in recognizing citizenship as a construction that is never finished. It is not obtained by chance but by continued fight, commitment, political clarity, coherence, and decision.[20] A well-behaved patience will never break the bonds of our oppression. Democratic relations will come by the Nine of Wands mobilization of consciously critical collectives.

The figure here has experience, they are wounded, they have fought, but still they stand. It is worth saying again: this is a survivor's card. An assault on the body is an assault on the spirit, and assault on the spirit is assault on the body. Surviving trauma means dealing with lingering psychological and physical wounds that, like a scar, take many years to begin to fade. Healing after trauma and assault requires psychosomatic regulation. When we are dysregulated we may go into fight mode and become defensive, guarded, and wary. There is no permanent defense against dysregulation, and thus it shouldn't be held as the goal of healing. Dysregulation is a valid, necessary response to recognizing a potential threat. The body's and brain's vigilance is a survival mechanism, a soldier we carry within, which cannot just be discarded or denounced. This warrior has no fear of danger, nor pain, nor ridicule. The only fear is the failure to defend the flame that the fighter holds so dearly. They are the ones willing to put their bodies on the line for their beliefs, for their safety, for their people's preservation. They know how to fight so that their land, their body, isn't lost to some government's eminent domain, that legal violation of consent. But is this soldier a hero whose rank is only achieved through altruistic self-sacrifice? The wounded are often never seen, let alone praised as the hero. War has irredeemable consequences, harming soldiers, society, and human sensibility alike.

What is this figure if not the regulator? Of bodies, boundaries, borders. They have erected a barrier, and where there would be an opening is their own wounded body. The Nine of Wands, as representative for the pattern identification practice that is reading tarot, is an ally raising the flag of dysregulation so our bodies' patterns and internal cues come clearer into our consciousness. They let us know where the limits are. The soldier's disrupted spirit is nursed as they learn to more quickly assess potential threats, regulate, and return to their window of tolerance. Overall unitive wellbeing is the ongoing conversation with the whole self about experience as you are experiencing it. Healing happens as dysregulation is detangled from old beliefs that limit or punish.

Just as with the other Nines, the Wands call for self-reflexivity, but here it's aimed toward a reflective solidarity.[21] What may arise may be a standpoint of epistemic advantage, for as feminists such as Nancy Harstock, Sandra Harding, and Patricia Hill Collins note, this social location, social experience, and epistemic perspective offer authority that counter the dominant power structure and perspective. Access to a feminist standpoint is achieved through critical reflection in which one realizes there is no single feminist standpoint, nor is any standpoint necessarily fixed. Social position shapes what and how one can know.

"Finally, the critique of essentialist identity politics and the hegemony of postmodernist skepticism about identity has led to a narrowing of feminist politics and theory whereby either exclusionary and self-serving understandings of identity rule the day or identity (racial, class, sexual, national, etc.) is seen as unstable and thus merely 'strategic.' Thus, identity is seen as either naive or irrelevant, rather than as a source of knowledge and a basis for progressive mobilization."[22]

We each stand in a different social position, and the knowledges that arise from such stances are unique in their transgressive potentiality, for they are ignored, marginalized, or misrepresented by the ruling class. The Nine of Wands recognize these various positionalities of knowledge-producers, the readers and writers of the world, so that the power inherent in this location is made plain. Like the Nine of Wands, we are to grapple with difference and plurality, which are often complex and contradictory.

The Nine of Wands is a talisman to foreground our commitments to antiracism and decolonization both at home and abroad. Solidarity is an active struggle to realize a global freedom on the basis built by the particular. Solidarity is the only viable option because there is no vision that stands alone and succeeds. This work owes and honors the numerous feminist, antiracist, and decolonial scholars, writers, and activists around the world, across time. This solidarity shouldn't be vague, construed as some simple alliance with the other. It must be defined clearly in order to be realized. For the cards to be an antiracist feminist framework enabling and anchoring our commitment to decolonization and anticapitalist critique, they must bridge connection between the octaves of personal and social reality we experience. The Nine of Wands bridges these politicized social spheres with the spiritual realities we defend from denunciation. There is none who could deny you your spiritual relationship(s). No one can take your faith away. There is no singular front that this solidarity can stand upon. The repressive systems of rule we fight against require many kinds of collectives to organize. The Nine of Wands, perhaps at the innermost, highest octave, represents what it is to be fortified by a spiritual relationship. The spirits that come as protectors of peace and defenders against domination are contacts well made, and their calling card is already in your hand.

Nine of Cups

"I'll answer your questions," God said. "Ask." She didn't want to ask. After a while, though, she gave in. . . . "I want them to have the only possible utopia." Martha thought for a moment. "Each person will have a private, perfect utopia every night—or an imperfect one. If they crave conflict and struggle, they get that. If they want peace and love, they get that. Whatever they want or need comes to them. I think if people go to a . . . well, a private heaven every night, it might take the edge off their willingness to spend their waking hours trying to dominate or destroy one another." She hesitated. "Won't it?"[23]

In the *Book of Martha* by Octavia Butler, Martha meets God and makes it so that in the dreamtime everyone's night fulfills their heart's desire while motivating their growth toward a waking maturity. She decidedly isn't dead but is as if in a dream of her own. Through her time in this sacred, timeless plane, she comes to encounter the Divine first as a white, male, human God. But eventually Martha comes to see God as her mirror image, a Black woman, as if God were her sister. In a sense she realizes, like Toni Morrison, that the subject of the dream is the dreamer; the image by which God is known is in the believer. Simply, the dreamer is the demiurge, the world-builder. I believe that every time the Nine of Cups appears it is a chance to track how our perception, our sight of and sensitivity to the Divine, increases and attunes more to our own likeness. God's images are continuously developing past the caged mind's conditioning, harmonizing toward the soul's imagery, relieved of theological baggage. The Nine of Cups knows God has indwelling within every soul, and the card can be held as the God mirror within. A mirror is an apt reflection of the divine nature, because whichever appearance is the most relevant or appropriate to social context is the one God assumes. And as we can each pull out the magic lamp that is the Nine of Cups, many decks with many mirrors in our many hands means God is able to aid different people in different forms at the same time. The images of God in the mind, when imbued with insight, become appropriately mythologized, awakening insight and imagination upon meditation. The Nine of Cups offers entry into these planes and orders of consciousness.

The cards become an emotionally laden object in which to enclose, process, summon. The cards overlay physical experience with cognitive processes. We can process negative emotions in the Nine of Swords, remember resilience in the Nine of Wands, and extend our capacity for creative manifestation in the Nine of Cups. Exalting yourself to omnipotence is the hubris of immaturity, in which the moment is at hand for the humbling of a higher revelation. You can't think you could trap God in your image, in your lamp, in your cup, without showing the smug shadow of this card. Form can praise, but not replace nor succeed, the profound. The image of any god beheld must be transparent to transcendence. Humans have been thought to be like clay pots, made of the earth, but each a container for the pouring forth of the Divine. The images we bring to life are flawed because the source is always more than the container.

The Nine of Cups, like Butler's short story, is impressed with an impulse toward dreaming, wish fulfillment, and utopia. The card is held in our hands like a magic lamp with the vast, absolute power of a genie, a God to make our dreams come true. Of all the Nines and the cards in the deck, the Nine of Cups encompasses the deus ex machina, the god in the machine most distinctly. From the Latin *miraculum,* tarot then qualifies as an "object of wonder." When Martha had the chance to share in God's power, to ask God any questions, to change just one thing about humanity with the intention to help, her wish extends beyond self-interest and even perhaps goes against it. Social good comes to depend upon the moral character of this Black woman. Martha, as Butler writes her, recognizes that free-market competition, deferred gratification, and diligent employment at the expense of rest do not lead to prosperity. Martha's grace and generosity are most evident in determining that, despite all of our violent pasts perniciously persisting into the present, people deserve for their dreams to come true; they deserve to experience the prosperity of their soul's satiation. Social resolution relies on her charity, but her consideration of beneficence, or moral development, is informed by the racialized, gendered struggles of the working class. In this scene, in this exchange with God, Martha becomes either a demiurge, a jinn, or a genie. Rightfully so, she earns her own book of creation for being a miracle worker. Since her being is in a heavenly sphere, by which is any setting where God is, she is a heavenly being. Her subordinance to God's supreme power is plain, but she is in creative partnership with God. She mediates the purely spiritual with the material.

The Nine of Cups interfaces different worlds, deities, and the bodyspiritland.[24] These interactions between seen and unseen forces that coexist in the material world are complex. It is a borderland of the mundane and the magical. The Nine of Cups crosses this threshold with prayer, an offering, in recognition of the guardian that dwells here. And we get to choose our guardian deity who receives our prayers, fulfills our wishes, and marks the passage of the temporal opening to eternity.

"Dreams are a form of data gathering and method for asking for knowledge, just as are the ceremonies. In Native science or IK, dreams are ways that authority and authoritative knowledge are produced. To include dreams as part of an Indigenous science defies accepted agreements in much of Western scholarship about what is reality or a valid realm of knowledge."[25]

Dreams are a site for divine instruction. Dreaming is a cocreative process with a spirit greater than you. By daring to dream we are put into relationship with the sacred. The genie of the card is a manifestation of our own creative ability to bring desire's fruition. This power, grand, subversive, and miraculous as it is, always comes with a disclaimer: we must accept the changes of granted wishes. If we aren't careful in our wishing, we could succumb to hubris, foolishly assuming we could *command* a God to shape the world according to our design. God powers the lamp, but in our perceiving of it a prison says more of the human conditioned to have greater belief in the power of exploitive incarceration than in emancipation. The imprisoned genie is a trickster who makes false promises with fine print. The genie, often bound to the lamp, their almighty power restricted and reserved toward the mercy of making others' wishes come true, knows intimately what it is to be denied self-determination. The genie, the dreamer who uses the wish offered by the Nine of Cups like Martha, is exceptional not for joining an enemy society nor for attempting to pronounce or validate its virtues, but for attempting to save it from itself, which she knows her well-being relies on.

"*Genie* in this essay refers to the Orientalist construct of powerful, wish-granting beings trapped in objects, while *jinn* alludes to the free-willed, invisible beings of Middle Eastern and Islamic lore. . . . In the process of traversing time and space through repeated entextualizations, the free-willed, potentially dangerous *jinn* of Arab folklore have become the enslaved gift-giving genies of global folklore."[26]

God tells Martha she is free to ask questions, free to argue and to investigate *all* of human history, free to take as much as time as needed for full consideration. He assures her that she is truly free, reserving an assurance that she will do the work of helping humanity become less destructive, more peaceful, more mature and sustainable. Butler makes it ambiguous as to whether God's choosing of Martha for this task is just a recognition of the dharmic integrity of Martha's own heroic, altruistic character, or if God is the one demanding such self-sacrifice, expecting her to be exceptional despite her societal dehumanization. Is her choice to follow God's imperative a matter of will or innate nature? Those who never rebel or disobey in doing what God commands would be considered slaves by some, or soldiers by most, but are called angels in the Quran. When you pull the Nine of Cups, consider which God you are serving and for what motivation. Is the Nine of Cups then a chance to submit without becoming a slave? The will that arises from the nature of a saving grace is altruistic. Her response to God accords with her moral nature. Images relay moral values. God, by being able to be all images, is unseen, an all-pervasive force. And within every Nine of Cups is their changing image, messengers, and their assignments. Innumerable dreams from innumerable dreamers.

Capitalism ascribes moral virtue to the other who self-sacrifices on behalf of the majority to justify servitude, but this is not real altruism; this is a spin on scapegoating. Capitalism and its hyperindividualism, with their innate transactionality, have no capacity for miracles of grace, generosity, forgiveness, or fulfillment. The genie becomes the bartender through contemporary and colonial globalization, spreading an ethos of excessive consumption toward the relevance of rampant consumerism. This capitalist emphasis on satiation shifts the orientation of the deus ex machina as a portent of divine intervention, saving grace, or an inspired act of the jinn, to instead conceive of a magical slave designed to make its master's wishes come true. The prison becomes our selfishness. In this arrangement the genie's freedom depends on human generosity, for just one to wish the genie free. Then emancipation is not independence; we need each other to get free. But while the grace of someone who would unlock our chains may offer us emancipation, a tenuous dependence already, they could not give us anything but an approximation of freedom. We are still in the postslave economy, in which we still don't quite know what it actually means to be free. So if self-sacrifice is pressed for or presumed, it is crucifixion veiled as altruism. Generosity is never coercive.

Martha reconciles the satisfaction she wishes for others because the satisfaction she provides is not material reward but an inner satiation, within the interiority of each person's own imagination, heaven, and private paradise. This internal nourishment, as she reasons, would yield positive material consequences for the collective benefit of all. The dreams she grants everyone in the world are intended to motivate self-determination, promote more concern for real consequences. Pleasure is not repressed but so deeply granted that it becomes a pathway for the evolving desire to be a marker of soul growth, so humanity can survive beyond its adolescence. As Martha demonstrates, altruism becomes a sign of maturity as we realize that ignoring looming disasters in favor of focusing on personal pleasure, because we can only imagine that disaster happening to other people, is an adolescent's thought process. But the growth is not just in the abstract but in the demonstrable action. We overcome self-serving pride and transcend by virtue of selfless deeds done.

When we use the opportunity of our chance, miraculous encounter with God to free another, we become the fairy godmother, making new worlds out of wishes come true. These are the ones compelled to help those who need it most, the workers of wonder. Their hearts are the deified one because their desire cannot be realized without the spiritual and material benefit of all. Theirs is a transjoy. Their living in joy invites others to do the same. The skepticism demanded by survival is transcended with the Nine of Cups. "We are trained to cope as social beings by keeping our desires within realistic limits. But where God is concerned, the problem lies in our desiring too little, and growing means expanding our expectations; or rather, making his generosity, not our poverty, the measure of our expectations."[27]

If tarot is a map of our inner world, then mustn't it include the utopia, the place where all of our dreams come true, the heaven where God is? The Nine of Cups is this revelation of longing. The deepest dreams and desires residing in the reader's consciousness swell from a central empty openness that composes the card. This center is the readiness to receive. From the *Book of Martha* we know we read to feed our dreams, to satisfy our longing. The Nine of Cups locates the center of that emptiness and gives it to God, and then fulfillment comes. The Cups concern how we follow the heart's desire, till finally in the Nine we desire God, which is what prepares the person to be united with God.

The Nine of Cups arrives with permission to dream, with the relief of realizing others are acting on your behalf. Prayer's power is in belief; that is its medicine. The Nine of Cups's balm is using the tarot to enter a sacred plane to approach God. Giving God the care of your heart is the ultimate act of trust. The card comes up when we are calling out for help, with the humility of a heart asking for its portion of love. It's simply accepting that there is benevolence greater than your own, a maturity of generosity that isn't conditional. There are beings willing to share their portion. The card imagines a giving that is greater in measure with the bravery required to receive God's help by asking for your heart's honest fulfillment. The power of asking for what you want orients your life toward a dream so you can actually envision thriving more than merely surviving. Resolution comes when Martha accepts the asking, when she accepts that the lamp works, not necessarily within understanding the light that lit the room or how there was a room, a house, her house, in this Twilight Zone of a place. This acceptance is really quite hard to achieve in real life, but it's worth the relief of not needing to prove your faith or your right to dream. The Nine of Cups is a chance to focus more instead on the ask, on the responsibility of language in prayer, so that an unlimited generosity isn't limited to personal circumstance. What would you ask God if you could ask directly?

And if God asked you, in particular, to help humanity, what miracle could you imagine?

Nine of Pentacles

I am a girl who dreams of leisure, always have. Reverie has always been necessary to my existence. I have needed long hours where I am stretched out, wearing silks, satins, and cashmeres, just alone with myself, embraced by the beauty around me. I have always been a girl for fibers, for textiles, and for the feel of comforting cloth against my skin. When I have adorned myself just so, I am ready for the awesome task of just lingering, spending uninterrupted time with my thoughts, dreams, and intense yearnings, often the kind that, like unrequited love, go unfulfilled. Lately, in the midst of that solitude, I find myself writing, spinning words together in my head so as not to lose or forget the insights, the sharp moments of clarity that come during this quiet time, that surface amid the luxurious smells of expensive French lemon verbena soap and fruity perfume, a book in my hand.[28]

Aesthetics must be on the agenda for feminist thinkers guiding us into a revitalized, revolutionary future. We can be led into this feminist future by using the Nine of Pentacles to theorize on the meaning and presence of beauty in our lives. With criticality we can examine the Nine of Pentacles to see reflected how and what we associate with the wealthy class, how we attain and spend money, and how we embody an aesthetic of self-worth through gender presentation. Adornment, fashion, aesthetics, the power of glamour, the magic of image are all about this card. The tarot is an object of art, and placing its beauty in the people's hands *is* radical. Though this art object may be a mere mirror, its reflection shows us a world of shadows that glimpse the past, the present, the future possibility. The tarot, through the Nine of Pentacles, insists that elegance and ecstasy are accessible in daily life. The Nine of Pentacles welcomes our participation in the artistic practice that restores our bond with flesh.

Love, like beauty, is decadent. Irrespective of class differences, beauty has a place in our lives. When we not only lack material privilege but struggle with the basic means of living, the Nine of Pentacles can be very confronting. Nonetheless we must consider beauty, the significance of luxury, and our material aspirations. Material wealth should never be mistaken as a prerequisite or measure of style. So much of beauty is just for you, which is a radical excess when the aesthetics of white supremacy and the economy of capitalism polices who has access to beauty, who is judged beautiful, who is allowed to invest in and develop artistic selfhood.

The Nine of Pentacles puts the pomp in psychopomp. To write about the Nine of Pentacles I had to get up and get dressed. I put on jewelry, do my makeup, coiffure my hair, spritz a sweet scent, and give a little kiss to the mirror. The ritual of glamorizing myself gives me the embodied sense of luxury that I associate with being loved. It is transgressive for those of us assigned male at birth, socialized in a masculinity that mutes, to reclaim time for the ritual of beautifying, sensualizing, and adornment. Cis men are taught to think that beauty is not for their person. They are generally taught beauty is reserved for women. But everyone can pull the Nine of Pentacles as an invitation to invest in beauty, which is so often an investment in the body and embodiment, even without the pentacle correspondence. And as bodies are gendered, beauty and gender are typically inextricably linked for queer and trans people.

I see reflected in the figure of the Nine of Pentacles the gender euphoria I experience as I present the femininity I've always inherently felt. I don't need to be a beauty queen to embody womanhood or femininity, but when I pull the Nine of Pentacles I can access a transfemininity that lavishes itself upon self-presentation. This is not about other people's opinions or understanding, brand or public image, or some elitist reach, but rather self-respect. Euphoric gender presentation entails this process of refinement. I know that achieving feminine beauty is a losing game for all women and femmes in a cishet white supremacist capitalist imperialist patriarchy, so the value I place on my aesthetic is always tenuous. But failure can relieve the pressure of patriarchal ideals and offer unanticipated pleasure. Though I continuously interrogate how whiteness influences my beauty goals or my aesthetic desires, I've always relished the way my skin tone glistens in the Sun; looking good like buttery toast, I've always wanted to be more Brown.

The Nine of Pentacles shows up as an admonition to untangle beauty from gender presentation, to find beauty within ourselves that doesn't depend on how feminine, androgynous, or masculine-presenting we are on any given day. The beauty of a love so lavish is not about contortion or endless posture. It's about loving what comes naturally to you, and how you carry confidence. It's a personal practice in the play of one's own image and aesthetic. There is joy in the creative manipulation of your textures, colors, scents, and expressions. There may be much artifice to beauty and aesthetics, but it is also an armor. The pentacles have a history as talismans of power, emblematic of a higher truth. Adornment was understood, and is still used, as a specific spiritual practice of empowerment and protection. The Nine here knows what you wear out in the world is as much about safeguarding who you are as it is about showcasing style or self-expression. Beauty is a tool to navigate the world, and though it's often softening and sensual in its delivery, its arrival can be painful. Because the prominent animal of the card is a bird of prey, grace and elegance can be formidable. As a card of aspirational wealth, the Nine of Pentacles is also about the politics of envy.

An effective strategy of colonization is to perpetuate a pervasive sense of lack, materially and spiritually. The concept of self-care is always considered to cost money and always for the aim of looking more beautiful, more desirable to a male gaze. Rather, a self-care that would be radically nourishing would have nothing to do with perfecting physical appearance. Learning to see, appreciate, and cultivate a selfhood imbued with beauty is an act of resistance in such a disfiguring, impoverishing culture. In this learned look of beauty, the artist constructs a confident identity. Pull this card and rest assured we can fashion ourselves a world in which there is space to create, contemplate, cultivate.

"The faggots reminded me that superficiality, style, messiness, and play are not bad things, they are transformative ways of being. Our glamour is not superfluous to changing the current order, it is instrumental."[29]

Aesthetics is about the intentional arrangement of and balance between various elements or bodies in space. For the Nine of Pentacles it is important we fill that space with love, art, the pursuit of specialized education, luxury. The falcon perched on the glove of the flamboyant figure of the card presents the pursuit of luxury as a means to address any felt primal, emotional hunger. Luxury means a life devoted to and oriented around beauty, despite the social response and valuation of your raced, gendered body of a particular class status. You can still know beauty even if the world thinks you're ugly. Beauty can be a tangible presence in your life, uplifting and renewing the spirit. Luxury is having time: time to gather yourself, to harvest your talents unfettered. The luxury of living with a sense of self-worth, fulfillment, and embodied sensual pleasure entails the embrace of eros.

The Nine of Pentacles is an aid in going from self-appraisal being determined by desirability, exclusivity, or access to a certain echelon of material wealth toward an erotic liberation, an ecstatic pleasure in the power of one's own beauty. There is solace in the beauty that we remain to be despite all the ugliness of hate, oppression, and violence in the world. Beauty, in a dominator culture, is subversive so long as it sustains life against the forces of deprivation. It affirms the intimacy of an intense closeness of our being with splendor. Beauty is beyond an object; it is enacted in human interaction. It is in the will to create, the desire to commune. Patriarchal, dominating men don't know about these states of beauty, harmony, and peace. They are blind to their body as a beautiful place, and so the Earth they desecrate becomes uninhabitable. In this way, the Nine of Pentacles is the secret garden. The Nine of Pentacles unveils the hidden spheres of domesticity. This exposure is revelation. For in the shadows of what we reveal in private is the outline of our destiny. When this card comes up, it's up to us to determine who we invite to sit in our lap of luxury. It is *our* lives where beauty is made manifest, a beauty that is never nothing.

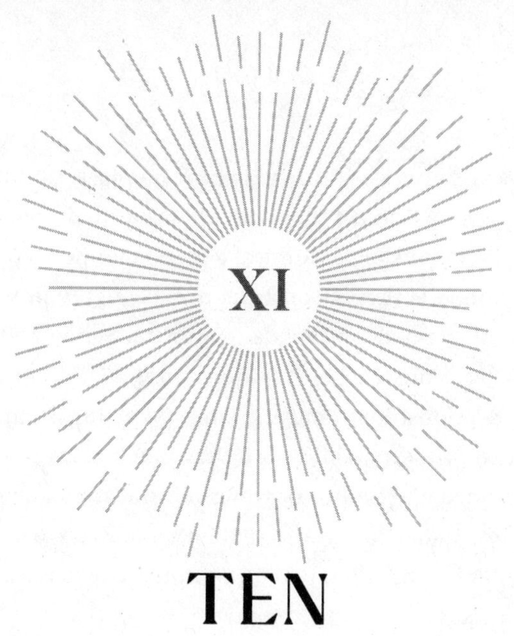

TEN

What does it mean to conceive of the Americas as Native space, and where does doing so leave non-native people of color, particularly the descendants of those stolen and transported across the Atlantic in the African slave trade? More specifically, what happens when the coerced diasporas of black-ness created by the transatlantic slave trade are transposed into a conceptual structure oriented around Indigenous self-determination and the repudiation of a presumptive non-native right to occupy Native lands? How can people of African descent be settlers when blackness continues to operate as a site of fungibility for projects of possession, accumulation, and property making? Conversely, how can a group of non-natives not be understood as settlers when they participate, often in unacknowledged ways, in the colonial occupation of Native lands and for which full inclusion in the settler-state sometimes serves as a horizon of political aspiration?[1]

Ten contemplates an ontological relationship to land, to the ways that country is constitutive, and to the ties of belonging. This placemaking collectivity is always about the relationship to land. Collective locatedness is a complex consideration in ongoing settler-colonial occupation. Settler mapping defines slaves and savages as those who have no place, no subjectivity, and who are themselves an object the setter claims as their personal territory. Settler-colonial relations make survival dependent upon a propertied subjectivity. Personhood is then a construct of sovereignty in which the land can be owned, objectified, and made inanimate. Settlement is defined as the possession, by nonnative persons and groups, of the Americas. Though Black people's relationship to land and land ownership is implicated in this white-dominated property regime, it is very much distinct and very much tenuous as they struggle against ongoing gentrification and displacement. Between the settler state and Native nationhood, Black people exist in an indeterminate limbo and often end up continuously made alien, fungible, or at odds with Indigenous landedness.

There is a "curious conjunction," as Tiffany King would say, considering land relations, settler colonialism, Blackness, the nonnative, and Indigeneity. Indigenous geographies of peoplehood and placemaking may exist beyond the frame of an administrative colonial mapping of empire, but without criticality they can still enact anti-Blackness, exclusion, and oppression in their citing and institutionalization of sovereignty, and in their criteria for membership as well as disenrollment. The boundaries that define members require the creation of nonmembers, who may be made stateless strangers. These strangers must seek alliances in some "free territory" in which the displaced diaspora continuously reconstitutes collective placemaking. The longing for a free territory is about autonomy rather than nationhood. It is a longing for the stateless to flourish. Thus there are more ways to contest the legacies of colonialism than a sovereignty modeled on the form of nation-states.

Mark Rifkin highlights how these narrations and framings are incommensurate, remaining opaque rather than transparent to each other. When these nonequivalent orientations are brought into relation, they produce disjunction and contradiction. They are not inherently triangulable and should not be reduced to equate to each other. Though they are equally real they are often nonidentical. Ten teaches us to embrace nonequivalence, so that significant differences are not lost in our attempts to address various social movements and struggles. Ten teaches us to reject an assimilatory impulse. The reading that is oracular is space-making. It activates fault lines, and eruptions of possibility emerge from the ongoing revelation of reading tarot. It leaves room with Ten because Ten tells us closure is an artifice; there is no single, final, resolute point. Ten leaves us on ground that is uneven, open-ended, and unresolved.

Ten tells us the reading is necessarily an act of speculative hesitation. For more capacious, less insulating hierarchical forms of sociality, there must be contemplative visions of possibility. The reader facilitates attention to dynamic changes in forms of conceptual and perceptual orientation across disparate persons, peoples, and social formations. Ten understands that these various processes of engagement may be beyond any one individual understanding, unable to be merged into one systemic accounting. Ten sees the various shapes of nonidentical frames of reference. Thus, Ten pluralizes the real and our ways of knowing it. The One can stand in relation to and distinct against the whole that is plural. The One before the whole is perhaps the individual between worlds, soon to experience their positionality critiqued and questioned within a new frame of reference, within a new encounter with another, a new articulation, a different definition, a unique phenomenology. Accordingly, the oppressor and the oppressed often change from one frame to another. Ten attempts to understand how one's position, perception, and action change meaning within another movement, worldview, cosmology. Ten sees the individual reorienting, reuniting, reassessing their role in and relationship with collectivity as it perceives the invisible barriers to or enclosures of space and community. Ten and its focus on placemaking require a fluid matrix of relation. Being part of a people is about tradition, genealogies, shared archival knowledge, and the dynamics of governance. A civil polity may here arise that is not institutionally recognized but is real to the social quotidian.

Ten is how we stay on the same side, or cross or construct communal containers. We've discussed world-traveling in light of Maria Lugones and the Three of Wands, but the worlds that the Three of Wands traveler traverses come into view in Ten. Ten practices cartography, in which the tarot is a useful auxiliary. Mapping the land is a mapping of the body, a corporeality that has endured the violence of genocide, racialization, and enslavement. Ten can then be a kind of revolutionary internationalism. Ten imagines identity beyond the bounds of a nationalism, dreaming of defining subjectivities that exceed the terms of imperial territorialization. With Ten, with tarot, we can more precisely recognize and reform the basis for our relationship with the land. Land relation is a distinctly different epistemological orientation from land ownership. One is not absolute ontological possession; One is a sacred regard, a relation. We need Ten to keep finding frames that establish personhood and forms of collective belonging that do not rely on or re-create geographies of settler-state ownership. As comfortable and challenged as we are by the changing cards in our hands, in which any one may arise at any moment, tarot helps us to approach the world, as Mark Rifkin does, knowing the frames of reference that foreground various political geographies enable greater collective engagement with liberation, self-determination, and futurity.

Ten readily risks disorientation to increase the capacity for translation, negotiation, distinction, and transformation. Ten insists on a shared humane sociality. Can a shared commitment to defending against assault and occupation be enough for disparate persons and communities to be in relation? The solidarity of Ten involves accountability across translation so that what is, what was, and what might be never stagnates or stops expanding. Ten is realizing there are many endings happening all at once and just as many beginnings.

The World

I refuse to acknowledge time, famously so. I've made a lot of jokes and memes about it, but it's a very real belief for me. I cried on my eighteenth birthday. I thought I was a failure because I didn't have a record deal yet. That was my only goal. It was as if I was holding my breath until I could hold a physical thing, an album that had "Mariah Carey" printed on it. Once I got my deal I exhaled, and my life began. From that day on, I calculated my life through albums, creative experiences, professional accomplishments and holidays. I live Christmas to Christmas, celebration to celebration, festive moment to festive moment, not counting birthdays or ages. (Much to the chagrin of certain people).[2]

I write this in praise of the prima donna, the grand dame diva herself, the World. The World is the grand temple of the Diva, an archival record of her claim to autonomy. Of all the Divas I applaud, it is Mariah Carey who is central to my creative adoration. As she tells her story, she reaches a retroactivation that frames her present iconicity as an illumination of the politics of the past. If power is a performance, a show, a display, then onstage is where it is most critically negotiated. In the archive of the Diva's afterlives there are moments when the power she negotiates onstage, in her work, becomes legible, ever more so as one who always held the pen, a fact contemporary audiences are only beginning to appreciate because she has been made illegible, erased, or forgotten. She performs through and against limiting frameworks and retrograde tropes, as her iconicity becomes a "moving performance" when her show, dripping with poignant artistic execution, extends into her public persona.[3] She's made her Diva persona a vehicle so her artistry, her iconicity, are mobile across space-time, which affords the longevity of her legacy. This mobility reconfigures the meaning of her performances across geographic space and time, and continuously works against shifting and sedimented racial logics. Her work persists even when her musical, cultural commentary is trivialized, subsumed in glamor, or constrained by dominant narratives. Her performance tactics work through and against exploitative cultural ideologies.

A Diva is power-conscious and self-proclaimed, undeniable in the prowess of her performance. The Diva's image must be reappropriated from misogynist portrayals of obstinacy and willfulness that need taming. To make her legacy legible she revisits and revises against shifting political frameworks of public reception, recitation practices, and the stage. With the World, she works to unmoor her artistry from the confines of a reductive culture, to let her talent overflow the limits of enduring primitivism, orientalism, and exoticism in representational economies. The World is her way of moving completely outside the orthodox body of knowledge and all its present conceptions. Her methodology is temporally queered. Moreover, the self-fashioning of the World is a way queer collectivity creates, an ingenuity that challenges the reified, racialized world order.

To speak of our aspirations, experiences or definitions, calculations and considerations of accomplishment, the World is a record. It tells us we can succeed in becoming timeless, for we just need that celebratory moment of sharing in the Diva's iconicity that we can indulge in time and time again. It appears as we surrender the fixation we have on time. The World goes round, back and forth, up and down, adding the moments of sacred memory to make the meaning of now. The World is the Diva's time orientation, where progress is measured and growth marked by an artistry realized, a soul expression made manifest, and a celebration shared. All achievement is measured by her artistry. Accomplishments all the more meaningful because of her continual confrontation with the larger consolidation of whiteness that both excludes and incorporates the racial and sexual other to invent the modern. The World is winning, like pussy, like cunt. It is a portrait of virtuosity and it is visceral. The World is her diamond record, the smash success, the worldwide wonder. The World signs her priceless autograph on culture, which is a composition of memories, mishaps, struggles, and survival in song. The World is the Diva triumphant in her autobiography, for she has refused to be defined or filtered to fulfill another's assignment. The World is the word that matches the Diva's dance. It is the story of who she is according to her.

The show begins when her body takes stage. The whole production was made to see her presentation. We entice her to entice us, the audience. The World takes center stage, fulfilling the common need of all for artistic satiation. The expertise circulating in the World's attributions encompass the power of feeling as well as the determined and comprehensive training. This success is more than talent's happenstance. The World is the Diva's realization, it is her opus we are blessed to attend. Hold the card in your hand knowing it is a ticket. With it you gain entry into another world.

Entry is also about receiving, and it is the World that receives the honors of the opera's success. The opera historically demonstrates massive social adaptability, possessing an atemporal immunity of cultural appreciation: "Opera's ability of being taken as socially highly valued phenomenon in every society in which it was presented enabled opera to communicate or perform a relationship with the elites and the masses, the courts and the crowds, the rulers and the citizens, the publics and the audiences. And to all these often antagonistic social agents opera served not rarely at the same time."[4]

The World performs for all, and endures all, preserving the legendary position through time and across shifting social contexts. The World wreathed in laurel, suspended in space, surpasses national borders and social boundaries. The circulating iconography is cosmopolitan. The opera's social mobility is similar to the tarot's origins as entertainment for the European elite gradually transforming into the public ceremony of chance. So as the opera, the World motivates social migration, cross-cultural experience, and exchange. Tarot is the general admission, making it so the people can partake in the witness and celebration of the artists' display of excellence.

The World is the black swan prima ballerina who must, in the movement and articulation of her being, establish the philosophical terms of her own world. She is a poet, a critic, a curator, an *architextress,* all at once. Her achievement of ontological sovereignty is the crown jewel of recognition celebrated in the World. Hers is a cyclical endeavor to own her creation, archive her past, articulate her present, and proclaim her future.

The World's enclosure is paradigmatic. As enclosure can be an oppressive force exerted on the human psyche, the World molds our position within a closed ring, a plaited cord, a circumference of protection. The Diva is in her own self-defined, self-defining hermetic field. In her own frame she is her own thing, so finally we can apprehend her wholeness. The Diva at the center of the World, at the center of consciousness, is an icon captivating across time and place, yet isn't captive. The disembodied heads of animals, angels, or humans on the periphery only serve to highlight how full-figured is her freedom. They are guardians of her cosmic order. They are sky bearers who have retrieved the lost sacred essence, and now behold the beloved. The World, with a lavender scarf strewn across their naked body-in-motion, breaks free as they dance across the card. Dance is her way to archive our stories, a way to pass the baton in an epic, multi-generational collective relay race toward freedom. The World dancer does this defiant bodily act of collective recovery as an act of abolition. The magnitude of dancing Black and Brown queer bodies is of grand proportions. The power of this dance can transcend time, mend the past, recourse the future. Dance emancipates the World, and dance will emancipate you. So take yourself to the disco when the Diva tells you to, when you pull the World, and then write about it. Make every twirl you take an ampersand between phrases, and eventually it's just and, and, and as you race to keep up with your breath. Because before all the cosmos unravels the World will know of your one brief moment of rhythm, when the rough-cut stone was polished. Emancipation is your song to sing too.

It is complex for a Black diva to take center stage, but in the World, it makes sense; Blackness was, and remains, the prime invention for Western culture to thrive. "Haunted by the afterlives of empire, slavery, and minstrelsy, the modern stage was then, and continues to be now, a space constructed through reception practices whose genealogies are steeped in the pedagogies of racial spectacle that Saidiya Hartman's work in *Scenes of Subjection* cautioned against."[5] Always of an identity between the bramble of exile and the edge of abyss, and yet the World is the one dancing. The World fosters connection, making and taking every opportunity for an intense identification with a collective being. The World is digital, like the oppressed have long been. It is Blackness in circulation. We, who make the World go round, are "compressed, reproduced, ripped, remixed," as Aria Dean says. The World, like the meme Dean discusses, is a way of "further figuring an existence that spills over the bounds of the body, a homecoming into our homelessness."[6]

> *One of the greatest tasks of Blackness as collective being has been to hold itself together in something like cohesion, to exhibit some legible character. This cohesion only becomes necessary, perhaps, as the collective being is made visible to non-Black society. When considered on its own, in what to some are the shadow, this collective being is allowed to expand and contract at will. But when society shines a light on it, what is atomized and multiplicitous hardens into the Black.*[7]

Patricia Hill Collins may see the World continuing the genealogy of "distinctive sexualized spectacles" that mark contradictions in the Western perception of Black women's agency concerning the use of their bodies.[8] The World is a self-authored spectacle. The Diva is her own creation, though her legacy is subject to distorted reception, state control, and the social schemas of vast power differentials.

Time is an inadequate measure of the Diva's legacy. By refusing time, she encircles herself in her own artistic creation. It is a strategy to hold herself against a violent outside world that threatens, endangers, and brutalizes the Diva's transfemininity. With the World, the Diva heralds her own body, her display of femininity, of recovery and personal reclamation. The Diva uses the World to imagine a *mobile* self-portrait of her iconicity and iconography. The portrait is a vehicle for the World Diva to transcend as her artistic mobility transgresses cultural capture. I refer to mobility as Jeanne Schepper does, to evoke more than cosmopolitanism:

> *It points to geographic mobility (escaping race riots, urbanization and migration, intercontinental travel, movement within cities and public spheres); the body in motion (dance, performance, moving pictures); social mobility (class, race, nation, and so on); discursive mobility (shifting significations and meanings, or how the subject is produced and redefined through discourse); and finally, importantly, temporal flows (how meanings shift across time and how performances are remembered and archived in dynamic and retroactive ways). These queered temporal and spatial mobilities can be modes of survival, acts of necessity rather than the products of choice and privilege that a term such as "modern cosmopolitanism"... might signal.*[9]

Racist legacies and colonialist discourse circumscribe the Diva's circulations, curtailing her movements onstage and off. The constraints of a primitivist reception to the Diva would freeze her in frame rather than set her in motion. The public may fail to recognize the limitations the Diva surmounts or appreciate the intelligence of her performance tactic, but *her* perception is the primary consideration here. It is an ethical imperative for the Diva of color to then produce and own her lens so that it may work on and against "the forgeries of memory and political amnesias," as Schepper would say.

The World's exaltation is a redress that is ephemeral yet persistent. In this persistence is the creation of continuity. The weaving that sustains the World is like a snake reemerging from the underground after transmuting and incubating the jewel of a new cultural body. You can never really see its entirety like we can when we see the World. In reality each of our singular perceptions is unable to zoom out far enough to behold the collective being. This World of ontological totality turns the underground inside out, offering an entry to statelessness, timelessness. There is only a concrete, central location of the World in the sense that it is a center of motion, the point that remains at rest while all the rest revolves round it. Capitalist culture moves in cycles of production, distribution, appropriation, and reappropriation. To imagine a structure that protects and benefits the Black cultural body requires a liberatory politic. The creative space of this collective body would be exposed but not vulnerable.

European conquest and enslavement forcibly uprooted an Indigenous autocentric self-conception. The World represents a soul center that is lost when one becomes classified as a subordinate, inferior, marginal. Colonial settlement is the ground upon which other relations of domination are framed. Indigeneity and its land-based conception of people challenge the legitimacy of the state, as well as the sociality and modes of governance that build on occupied land. The arcanum helps us understand settlement as a structural frame of the World. The World enables conceptual revolution as a move toward a greater shared sense of global humanness by which the metric assessing relative humanness is no longer the Euro-bourgeois subject. However, in settler contexts every track of liberation must sustain an engagement with the Indigenous project of self-determination and repatriation to be articulated as decolonization. The new social order of revolutionary political geography that is the World would make negotiations with land and water, rather than a problem space organized around racialized relations.

If you could look at the rings of a tree without cutting it down you would be looking at the World card; you'd be measuring the rings in the soul. In many concentric circles, the creatrix supreme, the dancer, weaves worlds. And there are as many ways to world-weave as there are hands to hold them, ever complex and often overlapping. The World archives every link between collective cultural memory and the innumerable gateways to every possible future. It is an excessiveness that should be celebrated, for the World gestures toward pluralizing the possibilities of being and becoming. It is an archival body, a collection of self-curated libraries. The World is the ever-changing but interminable social network. It is a third space for cultural performance, discovery, design, and invention. The internet is no longer an open space, but the World's enduring endeavor to be everything we've ever been, remain to be, and ever could be, says there still may be.

The World refuses to be narrowed or bowed. They demand the audience to expand their perception, to deepen their knowledge, to texturize more nuance, for the struggle of ethics is worth the aesthetic accomplishment of the World, with the delivery of its reading that constellates awareness of the divine presence. And the divine presence in the World is the goddess immortal, ever-present, all creative. The World of the Diva is a nexus of social-spiritual intersection. The World's imperative is to deliberately shape consciousness with cosmic import.

The World is a picture of the diva's self-presentation, and she isn't frozen, she is eternal spring. She exists in sacred space. She has sublimated the Fool's freedom into self-realization. She is not wandering blind, aimless or impetuous, but marks another lap in the journey from chaos to consciousness. She knows now the trumpets that need to play for her to sing. She is faith made flesh, and she is full-bodied. She is the vision materialized. She is every artist who embarks on the provocative endeavor of embodying artistic authority, economic autonomy. We arrive at the World, in which there is no psychological terminus but simply a city center, a stage, a fountain, that continues spinning us into another performance. The World is the heart that can be fixed in a central place but also a psychic space that ports into many other planes.

The World covers all the encounters of *claritas,* as the aesthetic instrument of integrity here appears with clear radiance. Its wholeness is arresting, its harmony ecstatic, its rhythm fortuitous. This radiant aura of her climax reaches audiences across broad temporal distances, resounding and rippling across time. The World pops up like the high note she hits when you found the G-spot. It is this epiphany of pleasure that heals the soul. Her art is so completely heart-enchanting we are brought into a spiritual state. So as the World turns, the Diva remains.

The Fool

Max leaves the sad haunted beasts with whom he has built and destroyed habitats and submits to the strong pull of the Oedipal home. But along the way to these "happy" endings, bad things happen to good animals, monsters, and children, and failure nestles in every dusty corner, reminding the child viewer that this too is what it means to live in a world created by mean, petty, greedy, and violent adults. To live is to fail, to bungle, to disappoint, and ultimately to die; rather than searching for the ways around death and disappointment, the queer art of failure involves the acceptance of the finite, the embrace of the absurd, the silly, and the hopelessly goofy. Rather than resisting endings and limits, let us instead revel in and cleave to all of our own inevitable fantastic failures.[10]

The Fool has no ordinary language, and no ordinary clothes. He is dressed for the occasion and it is festive, and you must follow this Fool if you want a world where dreams dance out loud. The Fool is the wind section, the bagpipes, the birds, the whistles, the horns telling you to take the jump; not to tempt you to fall into some self-destruction that is the annihilation of suicide, but to shatter the silence by singing your song till you soar. This airhead is the loudest one in the room, just being carried along by any shift of the wind, clattering, hunkering, and hollering along his merry way. The fervor of their announcement is to catalyze normally neglected or repressed feelings into expression, aiming to maximize creative fiction. The Fool's festivities, in their celebratory affirmation, excuse conscious release from social mores, rules, decorums, rationales, and restraints. The Fool exempts us from the steps logic would have us take toward success. In this way the Fool is society's failure, society's dropout, is social failure itself. The clown's fashion is cross-stitched by social failure, as it is meant to mark juxtaposition. But by the countercontact, the normal, natural, or necessary is a farce just the same, all a part of the same social engineering. Failure is confronting, telling us we must continue regardless of the prospects, because losing is not an excuse to dismiss life. Failure and foolishness are the price of taking any meaningful step toward fulfillment. The Fool doesn't fit into consideration when the World is obsessed with winners. But they rejoice as loser.

Is the Fool just going nowhere, forever? Certainly it doesn't seem they are in a rush to get anywhere in particular, but they wonder why you would ever leave the carnival to go back to captivity. Well of course the carnival was liberation only for a short period, what Terry Eagleton points out would be "licensed" transgression at best. But still, for that short period neither the church nor the state exerted control. The revelers inverted political, legal, and ideological authority in this anarchic period. The Fool is this spirit of free thinking and impiety that can ridicule or reconceive the set rules and beliefs of the day. So the Fool shows up accounting for every time when *no* superseded *yes.* Their present, and their presence, is so immersively embodied it becomes yet another failing of social prescription that the present exists solely to prepare for the future, forgoing that forever-delayed gratification society measures as a marker of moral capital.

They are a dangerously free character, just as they are honest about the danger they face, on the verge of tragedy and comedy at the same time. The only way to see what these characters are made of is to place them on a cliff and push them as far you can. And so the Fool will always capture your attention with their unpredictability. They are an emanation of zero, the infinite blackness said to contain the abysmal mystery of God. They are the early hours, unaware of the world's dangers and unafraid of death. Attack and admonition do not stop the Fool. Whatever drive allows him to go forward in pursuit of his vision is seen as either the innocence of grace or the madness of existing before social constructs, disconnected from mundane social reality to touch a divine one. As the rolling stone he is at home nowhere and everywhere. Tragedy is alleviated with humor, when the only option left is to laugh. As the Fool threatens with their radical authenticity, transgressive self-possession, and cutting comedic honesty, they are made into caricatures of some white supremacist epitome of the ignorant, incompetent, and unfit, always poised to fail. The Fool could care less; they just follow the basic desire to live life differently.

The Fool's perception is still an unwarranted authority. They talk back, they satirize, they clown to critique. The Fool is undisciplined and illegible yet politically autonomous. To be made legible to the state is to be standardized, uniform. Their illegibility is their escape. Beguilingly, they evade being subject to the disciplinary institutions of the state. They are the bold, young ones making everyone laugh, nervously for those really paying attention, calling out what is plain. What most are reluctant to reexamine, the Fool mocks and derides. Since the jester's getup is meant to mark juxtaposition, maybe you too will be able to tell when the emperor is naked. The laughter they elicit sharpens critical awareness, so humor, parody, and mockery are more than trite; they are pedagogical and political. Comics use the popular medium used to arrive at alternative histories that counter the propaganda of imperialists.

> *But along with being amusing social commentators, the native ritual clowns tend to be endowed with considerable supernatural power. During their performances, the clowns are frequently believed to become particular gods, demons, and other supernatural entities. In addition, through role reversal and inversion, they often seem to embody the chaotic timeless powers from before creation. In Mesoamerica, sacred clowns commonly appear at critical junctures during rites of passage, such as accession to office, or new year celebrations and other calendrical events.*[11]

It takes some sort of supernal power to contest hegemonic supremacy. Disidentifying with the heteronormative world reforms, redeploys, and rehabilitates mainstream representations so the soul's essence and dignity are kept intact. The Fool is the phobic object Jose Esteban Muñoz discusses in the canonical *Disidentifications.* The Fool is the feared thing reconfigured through a "campy over-the-top performance" just as glamorous as it is titillating, and then it is not the "pathetic and abject spectacle that it appears to be in the dominant eyes of heteronormative culture."[12] The Fool is disidentification as a survival strategy to seize social agency, wielded by those whose existence would be punished or suppressed. The Fool makes failure, faggotry, and flamboyance a seductive site of recycling self-creation.

Comedy is always judged as *the* inferior art form, but unlike other genres comedy is unique in its explication as a social form. But as the Fool stands atop the edge of a cliff, they evoke a literal high comedy. Maybe the Fool is mocking us when we think we are seeing clearly, as they look as though they possess a clear perception of reality. Regardless, the sight is still breathtaking. The fun is inseparable from the madness of the social order, the absurdity of our current reality. Comedy always exists on a social pane, and yet the Fool is singular, in the wild, and with only an unleashed dog as a companion or audience. The Fool is the alien making home in the reliability of exile. They are never bored, they have magic, they have sunshine, they aren't concerned with begging to be seen, and they are there back at the beginning.

And at other times they are in the king's court, allowed in the room, but only for entertainment, only to foil the king, dressed all in chaos. They are the king's shadow, the madmen who fail to see reality, impressing their romance and idealism riding roughshod at the expense of everyone around. The Homer Simpson infantilization whereby comics try to excuse the harm of their humor by pleading the ignoramus is just as tired as their racist, sexist, classist, homophobic jokes. The Fool that reproduces these violent modes of reception and performance has no subversive value or power. If humor is the only virtue Homer held, then who is really laughing at the end? The Fool can dance, joke, and entertain toward the interests of power, as those who are on the king's payroll only too willingly turn themselves into an ass emblematic of the king's folly.

But we can't abandon the Fool, or strike an X through them. The Fool is all of ours in every deck. They may make dangerous choices, and as *other* as they sometimes may seem, any encounter with the Fool brings with it the shock of recognition. Turns out the clown is your cousin. So you'll never see the Fool and sense that because they are alone they have been abandoned. You see them and know they are fleeing to freedom.

The Fool's humor has an intimation of redemption, seen ultimately as the vindication of joy. Finally we have liberty to laugh at ourselves. Laughter is prescribed by *curanderas* to dispel depression and heavy emotional energies. Laughter opens the mouth, opens the core, and so open we receive perspectives outside of conditioned perception. The imprisoned human spirit is not so cynically fatalistic when the Fool laughs. The Fool's failure is executed spectacularly, making it far more liberating than any success could possibly be. Failure turns us toward unforeseen, alternative, new directions, unfurling a path of its own. The Fool's humor, the card's iconic wit and sarcasm, become the cadence of its poignant precision. Since success is always so self-serious, their failure affords them the freedom to be frivolous and fun. When I failed to get hired as a teacher, I began tarot *seriously*, and I began realizing just how trapped I have been by respectability and responsibility. How little space I was afforded to let it be messy, complicated, contradicting, or easy. None of us will be responsible or mature enough, alone, to stop the immense violence continuously inflicted on us, continuously killing us. The youth are so hyperresponsible because it's not been safe to play, and that's our fault. I don't want to live in austerity, and I don't want to live in denial. Prisons show you all the shades of grey, but I long for color. And even without the right costumes and cuts, I'd rather indulge in the browns, blacks, pinks, and golds of my bare body than be bound by the fear of expressing myself authentically. I laugh so I don't die. I may be an instrument but my song will live on.

As compelling a desire as it is to be taken seriously, too often it leads us down the well-worn paths. The Fool is more interested in mapping detours and creating new contexts and being far less rigorous in their reason to laugh or smile or look up. The Fool is low-class but high up, a folk figure, a purveyor of popular culture yet possessing esoteric knowledge. I have discussed tarot as a tool of social-psychic cartography, and with the Fool it is ensured we shall come out and play, we shall get lost, and we shall be detoured. Despite our best attempts at convincing ourselves otherwise, we set out all the time without knowing our way. The Fool can't help but laugh at how seriously we play this game. They may move in circles, improvise, or fall short, but our Fool will reunite us with a belonging we may just be beginning to remember our way back to. Theirs is reverse arrival, jumping from the ridiculous to the sublime, taking a crash landing for freedom.

Is the Fool following the absurd joyfully and willingly to their death? Is it fantasy that drives the Fool to step over the edge, or is it the recognition of a destiny just before us? Perhaps the Fool's fantasy is just the apotheosis of advanced imagining, letting the power of his perception soar, knowing we will not fall but fly over that proverbial precipice. The Fool sees their dreams clearly, they know where they want to go. Not knowing the way doesn't get in their way, because the Fool is *the* fuel for every society's survival. The Fool's capacity for fantasy is fundamental to actually open toward any new future. In fantasy they perceive the spiritually sublime, and in festivity they experience it. The Fool's feast is found in the transcendent moment when time stands still. This poet of social satire, in the excess of their celebration, offers not a luxury but a necessity, for fantasy is a natural and indispensable expression of the imagination. The Fool catches us suddenly, with the fantastic made manifest. They challenge our assumptions, ensuring our feet are on the ground and our head in the clouds. There is no custom that could contain the Fool's potent curiosity. Standing outside and above standard conceptions, or dismantling their logic completely, the Fool moves into more chaotic realms of knowing and possibility. They may be unconventional, may be a loser, and may be self-schooled, but their way in the world is authentic and all their own.

Akin to reading comics, laying cards in a spread connects fragmented information across gutters, or the frames and gaps of each card. Its narrative structure is episodic in form. As a greater whole is perceived and meaning is established, the reading creates closure.[13] A mental completion of what is incomplete is made. For this there must be the Fool's continuous motion. Each scene in the tarot is distinct, and between the gutters we make to connect the cards in a reading is a marked change in the card's simulated time, space, and motion. The Fool is the force of continuity amid disparate elements and experiences. The Fool is our persistence of vision; the more we stare at these shuffling, still pictures, their animacy is unveiled as our own is transformed. The Fool offers a space of potential where this comic closure *may* become a method of *conscientização,* or conscientization, the active process Paulo Freire defines as learning to "perceive social, political, and economic contradictions, and to take action against oppressive elements of reality."[14] The comics can help you come to critical consciousness by experiencing closure, but it "is anything but automatic, straightforward, or predetermined; I am simply suggesting it could be possible. Even in the most heavy-handed of comics, the text and images are still guides that must be interpreted actively by the reader, and each comic book is open to a variety of different readings based on individual experience, context, and prior knowledge."[15]

Rogue intellectuals wander in the spaces where humankind's laws are inadequate and unenforced. They pursue the territory of revolt, fashion themselves the revolutionary subject. Is it only these Fools who consider what could be beyond coloniality? These are the nomads at the end of empire.[16] The challenge of the Fool is that trap of undermining tradition in the pursuit of revolution in a way that actually encodes the same markers of colonialist consciousness intent on eradicating the traditional, sacred ways of knowing. The Fool may find its greatest folly in its iconoclastic, progressive secularity, too dismissive of the traditional. The Fool is most effective when, rather than asking why all aspects of culture shouldn't be problematized, they consider "how the processes of problematizing itself may serve as a homogenizing force, muting and domesticating the distinctiveness of traditional ways of knowing."[17] The tarot can become a catalogue of critical literacies to continuously mold, orient, and critique our emancipatory orientation. There must be more than the Fool's spirit of radical resistance. My aim with *Red Tarot* is to present a needed pedagogical structure that provides a multivalent method of inquiry and analysis that exposes, critiques, and disrupts colonial, dominator consciousness. But this disruptor consciousness is incomplete without the tangible action of decolonization that brings about the repatriation of Indigenous land and life.

The Fool never lets the reader rest, never lets you feel certain you exactly got it. The Fool answers the question by avoiding it. They are quixotic, and of their tragedy, humor is found. Tarot reading shows that prophecy can be a vehicle for social subversion by never letting our understanding settle. As soon as you touch upon clarity, the Fool introduces a new element to contradict or complicate your previous premise. The Fool makes you quick with inventiveness and makes your skin thick. They accept our existential ambivalence, an acceptance or capacity of the wise. Every contradiction and paradox, taken in totality, approaches life's complexity, as an approximation rather than a precision. The Fool is the substance, the stock of the tarot, the conception of a psychospiritual environment where our personal and collective confusion and ambivalence can wander with some degree of comfort. This is especially helpful when society always wants us to always be so crystal clear about our judgments and journey. It's a tonic against allowing familiar, narrow, retrograde frameworks to naturalize. Otherwise, the Fool is just entertaining racialized masquerades and perpetuating toxic repertories and tired tropes.

On the perennial quest to be the self that one truly is, the Fool follows critical pedagogy, encouraged to go beyond the known world, expanded in the pursuit of possibility. Somehow the tarot contains multitudes and multiverses. It is kaleidoscopic, constantly folding in on itself and expanding back again. So from the continuum that is the World, the Fool emerges. And because there's never a fixed image or finite point of meaning, you keep looking. It is a cypher for the nonlinear growth of consciousness, epitomized by the arcanum. Becoming fools who read the tarot looking for guidance, support, and transformation forces a foray into exposed vulnerability; but eventually we become strong with self-trust and courageous in the capacity to feel deeply guided by the universe. It can be utterly pathetic to be so open, to hope and hunger with nowhere to take it but to call out, and cry as you pull cards. You gather all the weakest parts of yourself and derive some open devotion. The Fool is what happens when the world says no, when its ways won't help, when there is a commitment to refusal and renunciation. Still, using the cards and their confessional capacity is a helpful catharsis. To leave behind all the pain accrued, the Fool announces it, the anticlimax of sorrowing. Everyone is heartbroken, everyone is lost and has lost, but only the Fool admits it.

Ten of Swords

The press devoured my silly TRL stunt and me right along with it. It was the first time I had experienced the phenomenon of a public fail that woke the monster in the media, that vicious vampire that gains its strength by feeding on the weaknesses of the vulnerable. The bombed stunt mushroomed into a big, nasty, never-ending story. Some mainstream media is a glutton for negative energy and fear. It places a mask over pain and presents it as entertainment news. It was visible and I was vulnerable. And when the Cinderella of Sony took a fall, no king's horses or men tried to set the record straight, pick me up, or put me back together again. Rather, they fed on the spectacle and just wanted more—more stumbles, more embarrassment, more breaks, more ridicule. The monster in the media is only satisfied when you are destroyed. . . . It was such an obvious and pitiful power grab. I could almost see him puffing up believing he'd taken the diva down. Not only the tabloids revel in watching stars crash the ground. I was defenseless—knifed in the back by my ex-husband and stabbed in the heart by my brother and mother. And they all left me to bleed out inside some hellhole.[18]

There is a body that needs burying. There is an unwellness no one knows what to do with. There are ten swords in one back turning the dark into the grim. In this vile territory there is no intellectual sense to be made. Here there is no hiding the dehumanizing dimensions of our lives. When you carry the suffering of a rage you never chose, all you see is wasteland. There is a body in desperate need of justice, and a fascination with dysfunction forces us to look. We are an audience damned in the Ten of Swords. Who has a clear understanding of the healing process when all anyone wants to see is murder? The dead body on display is an indictment of the viewers, those whose attention supports this prurient economy, those who still show up to the gore. It is a card of cultural complacency. Those who profit from the pornography of violence show no images of love or resistance. There is just complicity and compliance with the perpetuation of malfeasance. The Ten of Swords is the look of condescension that cuts perceived hubris down to size. How ironic that those arbiters of humility take pride and pleasure in their ability to orchestrate and profit off another's humiliation. This is a card of cannibalism, of eating the other, of carving up their fallen body for personal gain. It is not creating greater cultural awareness. It's getting stabbed by the master narrative ten times over and by everyone and from everywhere.

This is the body being a medium for the masses to project their fear onto. It's being afraid of free speech, because by being a dissident, provocative speaker saying things you believe in front of large audiences, you risk character assassination. The Ten of Swords is this consequence of transgression in public spaces. It is the town square that doesn't engage in dynamic social discourse but rather performs public hangings. We are compelled by profit-driven media to gorge upon image after image of abuse inflicted on Black and Brown bodies, across class, across gender, across age. Violence relies on a melodramatic appeal. These images and scenes are packaged as though they have new social significance, as if the white gaze hasn't looked upon abused Black bodies since the slave auctions. These images are pedagogical regardless of the image makers' intent. Their audience learns only of self-hatred, abuse, and abandonment. This image and images like it would have us believe there are no movements for social change or that the ghetto many Black and Brown people endure, and the violent fate they may experience, is self-inflicted or deserved. It is a hellish fantasy to only project a fatalistic, inescapable, and violent ending for its watchers. The biggest deceit of these Ten Swords is that there is no way out of despair, or that these violent images constitute an art that is to serve a mirror reflection of some tragic ghetto reality. Again, this is just colonial fantasy and projection. Tragedy is purported to be the superior art form, but surely there is nothing redemptive about simply depicted violent abuse. Art only offers alternative, redemptive visions when its aesthetic interest is also politically progressive. The victim is the subject of the card but has zero subjectivity. Seeing only the impaled body of their tragic death in their fallen silence, we learn nothing deep of their character. This is the body of discredited information, the discredited way of knowing, the discredited people. The viewers inundated daily with these terrible images are supposed to passively accept this reality. This inundation only works to render the victim and their abuse invisible.

The Ten of Swords is then the card of ultimate objectification. Freezing us into a frame where we are only seen as ugly, angry, dumb, and dangerous does not serve as a meaningful catalyst for social change. The Ten of Swords is the master narrative, *mestizaje*, constructed to forcibly de-Indigenize peoples.[19] It is the tearing from kin and community. It is the mind that holds hate alone. There is no location for this identity, no clear landscape of return, no country to call home. It is nameless, homeless, dishonored, and violated. The slave is a stranger, and their identity is defined by its death. The outsider is dispossessed first from land; and again when they are raced, they are culturally excoriated. This death spectacle has a long social history, always with supposed moral import. In this card is consigned the space of otherness. When the colonial state classifies you as irrational or subrational and backward, they kill you by considering you the counter to their universalizing conception of the human. This is the figure that falls at the bottom of current racialized world order. Structural violence is so viscerally configured that in the end, its "injurious effects on bodies are similar to the violence of stabbing or shooting. This is what the English working men described by Friedrich Engels called 'social murder.'"[20] How monstrous this one must be considered for this crucifixion.

Viewers are not encouraged by this hedonistic violence to create cultural awareness. Commodified violence leads to dead ends, no matter how endorsed, glamorized, or legitimated it may be by market rationales.[21] So then the Ten of Swords must demand we develop a capacity to survey the political ramifications of art that proliferates the traumatized and abused Black body. We must consider if these images invite empathy or critical reflection, or if they are supposed to be some perversion to gawk at. The ghetto seems impossible to survive. The terrible futurelessness cast here is a daily challenge. How many more martyrs must there be? How many more Medusas will be made sacrificial victims so a propertied, patriarchal hero may be made? Their tragedy is that theirs is the life valued only because of their death. Who are we, who have never died, to say death is better? This card is a house haunted by the flesh ghosts of our resignation, for whose death we are responsible. But enough enabling and self-loathing; responsibility cannot be skipped with a substitute sense of guilt.

When the famous, wealthy, and powerful purport a crude vision of freedom that comes at the expense of other people's safety, humanity, and dignity, their imagination has atrophied. A philosophy of solipsism only leads to a Ten of Swords fate. In the ghetto that is the Ten of Swords it is hard to feel anything but hopeless; but in addition to being unacceptable, violence is unimaginative and uninteresting. As a reader, a consumer, or cultural critic we must assess how our attention will be paid moving forward. We can regulate our media relationships by analyzing our own interests, priorities, and curiosities. Art should fuel our imagination and provide us with new tools and tactics to see the freedom we still don't quite know. There is still every obstacle to housing, income, and material well-being. Our bodies are still policed and incarcerated.

A definition of mortification is pathology, "the death of one part of the body while the rest is alive," which is a very fitting interpretation of the Ten of Swords. It comes with severe dissociation, when your spirit leaves your body. White supremacy makes it so its victims self-administer its poison. The aesthetics of white supremacy condition audiences to worship whiteness, to be saved from becoming victims to abusive trauma. Celebrities like Kanye West, or authors like George Schuyler in *Black No More,* exemplify how assaulting this self-rendering is for both the "artist" and their audience. The anti-Blackness that marks conservatives like Clarence Thomas or Kanye West constructs of their bodies what's classically called an Uncle Tom, for a stage production selling tickets. This fiction of white supremacy is commercially circulated worldwide. There is no better publicity in

Western media relations than a breakdown. But as Mariah shares, this is really sabotage, for those who pull the Ten of Swords aren't having a breakdown; they are being *broken down,* they are collapsing from the exhaustion of an exploited body. They are called unstable, they are drugged and institutionalized. They control them by destroying their image. These vultures only feed after death. And all eyes are on the performer, on the bodies gutted by white supremacist capitalist imperialist patriarchy. The production situates its audience as voyeurs into an exotic third world, schooling them in colonial ways of seeing and consuming spectacular raced and gendered popular cultural performances.[22] This miseducation brings mania for the mob. Their attention economy justifies the proliferation of this trauma porn, all the more complicit now that the people are the press. The hunger for social death is ravenous. The platforms have changed, from tabloids to Twitter, but the media monster still feeds off the suffering and humiliation of its most prominent social profiles. When Nine of Swords worry exacerbates into catalepsy, it becomes the Ten of Swords. In this frame there are no survivors, just a screen filled with a broken body, offering no future; just a finite, sure end. We find a figure abandoned by society.

The Ten of Swords is the ending that is anything but an engaged aesthetic excellence. It is the absence of consciousness. Represented is that worry that we'll somehow lose track of ourselves. It is the looming danger nonwhite people face in losing their identity by close relation to white people and whiteness. White supremacy has infected the water. Even if it is latent, this pathology poses a constant threat that would have us first turn on ourselves and then everyone else around. This cannibal of white supremacy cannot be condoned nor tolerated. There is no redemption when the Ten of Swords shows itself. The only option to survive, to inoculate ourselves and prevent the spread of this virus, is to quarantine. With the Ten of Swords, the only way we can deal with someone who is completely unwilling to be held accountable for the harm they are causing is to cut them out of our lives. And it hurts, but it helps you live. You don't need an audience nor a profit to make sense of your suffering. What you need is healing from compounded trauma. A body in ruins needs therapy and care. The air must fill with peace, rest, and renewal. In a Ten of Swords state, fully understanding the magnitude of the damage done is no simple task. Enduring unrelenting everyday abuse and intimate terrorism is what turns our lives into social horror. What you need is to change the cast of characters in your life, or at least your characterization of them. Rename them to reframe them. Cut the insanity and stop the same people from inflicting the same pain over and over again.

The Ten of Swords takes the reader to the mind's *nigredo.* Agonies dissolve here. This is death to the dopplegänger, a repolarization with your shadow, whereby the only way to make it out of this trip to hell is to return to God. The Swords suit sees its characters grappling with how accurately and reliably their perceptive logical faculties function, often obfuscated by how big or small to make their ego. The ego's shadow and light intertwine like bramble, difficult to contain or define and impossible to kill. You thought for certain *that's* how it was going to end, but it's not, so you're forced to imagine something you never saw coming. You get this card and you endure a death that ends up becoming the cocoon from which you bloom come spring, where only lovers are left alive.

James Baldwin once said, "You've already been bought and paid for, your ancestors already gave it up for you. It's already done. You don't have to do that anymore. Now you can love yourself. It's already possible."[23]

As with all the Tens, this card concerns legacy. It's about the ones that fell on the sword for us. The ones that gave into their addictions and darkness. It's the ones we survive. It's the way our stories are surrendered to the changing cultural mindset across time. When you commit an atrocity you never thought you were capable of, your sense of alienation can seem insurmountable. The only word to describe finding forgiveness is grace. But it only comes after you experience the full fall and fire of unbecoming. Shame, hatred, and humiliation are real consequences for abominable actions. This is no little misdeed; this is horrific. Taking responsibility for these real fatal feelings becomes the door that will get you through redemption.

You can postpone the bitter confrontation, but sooner or later it will be just you in your own company. And would you—if you weren't pushed, if you weren't stripped down and made very lean, and if all your self-definitions weren't made suspicious—would you ever see exactly who you are? Because it is when you see yourself bone bare that you somehow make peace with what and who you find. Though this is difficult, its absolute necessity cannot be denied. For in facing it, your maturity finally arrives.

Ten of Wands

In essence, the migrant body is made to betray itself. Specifically because of perceptions of ethnic difference and body position in labor, the migrant body is seen as belonging in its position in the very agricultural labor hierarchy that then leads to its deterioration. These mechanisms of rendering inequality invisible are potentiated by internalization into Triqui forms of pride. The structural violence inherent to segregated labor on the farm is so effectively erased precisely because its disappearance takes place at the level of the body, and is thus understood to be natural.[24]

The reading attunes to scale, measuring the inner environment in relation to the social landscape one exists within. So we know that in the Ten of Wands it is hard and heavy not because of a personal punishment but because the circumstances are challenging for everyone struggling to transcend dehumanizing labor. The hero hold of the ten wands makes the main figure faceless, nameless, impersonal, common. In the historical psychosocial map that the tarot is, the serfs lie at the bottom of the feudal hierarchy. Off in the distance may be the castle of the aristocratic vampire, waiting for nightfall to feed on the commons. In the royal court there is scale and sight and grandeur, and while the court is in eyeline of the common laborer, their burden obstructs their path and their perception. And just the same we can't see them from either direction. Entire classes of bodies are hidden from social perception, as is their labor we take for granted. The structural nature of labor hierarchy disregards the burden of all the cleaning, cooking, caring, picking, and packing certain bodies are forced to perform as if they possess some magical ability to manage such stress, to get these jobs done. The body is not disconnected from the mind, but certain bodies may be made invisible to reproduce the domination and exploitation of those bodies.

The body does not survive the economic structure of neoliberal capitalism without injury or ache. The dedication demanded of this labor is often debilitating. This is the card of fieldwork, and it is the body that labors in the field, and the field demands physical strength and endurance. Each wand becomes the fault lines of power, tending to fall along categories of race, gender, class, citizenship. The Ten of Wands is a card showing body position(ed) in labor, as class commentary. "Position" holds dual meaning, as both a stance of the body and a post of employment. The jobs that are executed standing or walking are less esteemed, because through their bodily association they are considered less intellectual. "At the same time, these standing bodies are understood as humans of solid standing. This basic respect is seen in the phrases 'upstanding citizen,' 'upright character,' and 'standing up for oneself.' Finally, the jobs at the bottom of the hierarchy that require bodies to kneel in dirt or bend over in the bushes are the least respected. Like animals, these workers are seen 'on all fours.'"[25]

The Ten of Wands depicts the conditions of alienated labor that the oppressed endure. The colonial capitalist society subjugates body to mind, so you see the workers bent over all day in the Ten of Wands as the lowest level of the working class, suffering the most regular physical violence of empire. These are the bodies strained, sweltering, and often sick. They work without break while extremely exposed to pesticides, with the least control over their time, and the most fearful of the government.

The social structures of labor produce very specific bodily dispositions. The ruling class works us to the bone, drains us dry, but also entices us toward an aspirational wealth. The castles of contemporary times are global corporations thriving by grinding up workers' bodies and spirits, still feasting on the fruits harvested from the peasants' bent, bruised body. Certain bodies are forced to bend upon the social categories inscribed upon them. The racialization of bodies, as a tool of domination, reserves for the migrant, undocumented Indigenous body the most physically dangerous, psychologically stressful, and undervalued labor by naturalizing their fitness for such positions. Their biceps are big and their back strong, so shouldn't they be the ones doing this work? The Ten of Wands surveys the scope of such violent, symbolic perception. Perception of bodily difference falls across ethnoracial lines that impress a blue collar on Black and Brown bodies. So as ethnoracial perception shapes labor practices, our labor occupation must be teased apart from unconscious prejudice. The structure of this laboring oppression is reinforced through ethnic pride that internalizes class position in perceiving white bodies as delicate, weak, and more susceptible to pesticides than the Brown, native bodies considered strong, bearing, enduring, and able to hold out.

In the Ten of Wands is a catalyst to consider all occupations within the labor hierarchy as expressive of the structural political violence of ongoing colonial regimes. The habits of the body and its disposition are layered by the social world, and our cuts and cracks demarcate their difference. In our world there is no labor that does not exist within a historic spectrum of enslavement and servitude. The Ten of Wands demarcates the children of Saturn as described by Abu Ma'shar. The many obstacles that block individuals and institutions from fueling the challenger movement of the Ten of Wands exist on structural, cultural, social, and psychological levels. Strategic action for social liberation entails a critique of the symbolic order, or a politics of representation, but its aim should encompass many forms and actions of pragmatic solidarity. The Ten of Wands offers critical and reflexive embodied prophecy toward these aims. To establish effective coalitions working to eradicate empire, the hierarchies of domination must be seen as socially and historically constructed and thus malleable. Tarot can raise consciousness, but it only becomes true literacy when the word of prophecy inspires, directs, and guides the physical movement, the body's action, the social will. Tarot thus works upon the symbolic structure reinforcing the material structures of domination.

After the vision is witnessed in the Eight of Wands, with a faith to follow, and a firm stance of survival in the Nine of Wands, a refusal to give up the vision or the right to dream, the Ten of Wands is the capacity to materially manage this inner fire's realization. Having the energetic resources, the support to get where you want to go, is a Ten of Wands measure, a capacity that is always also a bodily consideration. It is hard enough to pronounce a vision, to claim a set of beliefs, but it is all the more challenging to put our bodies in alignment toward the vision and to work day after day after day to get there, this free, liberated, fulfilled future that our motivations promise is a real possibility. Maintaining this capacity requires a *re*-orientation in this culture of extraction and hyperphysical labor, so that you are sustained over the long haul, caring enough for the common work and the common worker. This might mean taking many water breaks, or asking for help, or getting more regular rest so you don't become despairing or distraught in feeling like you'll never get there, or burnt out on the passion that fueled your pursuit in the first place. Ambition, achievement, and performance can make the fire insatiable, ensuring that nothing will be left in its wake. At a certain point you'll get tired of carrying heavy shit, of always having to be the strong one. Don't you need a deep-tissue massage if you're pulling this card? You'll get tired of being the Ten of Wands muscle man if you don't stop to see the forest for the trees, to clarify your motivations, your position, where your reprieve comes, and where your fruit falls.

When it is a wound of passion you suffer gladly. Fire is honest. You work hard when you love the work, when you own the means of production. When it is an alignment with your soul integrity, you can go to great lengths to see it through. Pleasure can be found in the grit and tenacity of pursuing a vision, of breaking perceived limitations. If I know I am going toward this goal that has value or meaning to me and is part of the larger trajectory of my self-concept, my own sense of soul success and development, I can make sacrifices, I can put in the extra hours, I can carry a heavy load because I am drawing on a different source to fuel me.

Knowing how to restore your spirit is perhaps the most intimate lesson the Ten of Wands represents. Small successes accumulate over time. It takes so much inner validation when your work is not glamorized, when you're doing work that no one sees but that is deeply necessary. Certainly, this is the workaholic card, but some labor requires a certain level of completion before there can be rest, and this is all the more frustrating. The challenge in self-belief, in giving the body rest, lies in affirming the real progress being made.

The world will go on even if we aren't the hero. It's a culture of scarcity that makes us believe we must work hard, perform, or prove ourselves to be valuable, to be worthy of love, validated, or embraced by the world or integrated into community. It's interesting that through overlapping pandemics, the world has begun to call these Ten of Wands workers "essential" and "heroic" as a way to appease classist, consumerist guilt. This guilt must be applied toward political pressure for workers of any industry to be properly paid and protected. These workers live precarious lives not for some noble altruism, but because of economic coercion. Hiding exploitation behind praise and flattery is the most insidious tactic of domination. Closing the gap between workers' social and economic value will not be a one-and-done job. There may not always be the capacity to accomplish long-term liberatory goals, but the disadvantageous position isn't static or eternal. With the Ten of Wands we assess a trajectory where our present actions may make us stronger tomorrow so we can do what we were too feeble to face today. A trajectory where, in the days, months, and years that follow, we are stronger still.

From the wands, we know the fire of devotion is something firm that facilitates flexibility. Power is wielded only after it is built *and* aligned. A caution of the card is to not suffer from the blinders of individualism, the cornerstone of common-sense neoliberal ideology. By removing these blinders we are better able to understand the formation, processes, and agencies of political subjects. The drive of collective political action is a constellation that cannot be mapped using a microscopic lens of an individual rational actor. The figure of this card may endeavor to construct their own visionary, political force, but success and strength come just as much from aligning with parallel, complementary groups and organizations.

"For example, when pre-movement civil rights leaders and their small nascent organizations pulled (i.e., activated) black churches, students, barber shops, etc., from the *passive allies* to the *active allies* category, suddenly all the pre-existing infrastructure, resources, and social capacity of those constitutions and institutions went to work for civil rights, dramatically boosting the burgeoning movement's capacity and reach."[26]

The Ten of Wands understands the imperative to wield political power, but the commoner cannot succeed without more people engaging in aligned political action. The Ten of Wands may be a champion, an icon of the people's power that the reader can meditate on to push past a low plateau. No matter if a person attempts to build the infrastructure, it is still toward a social aim. This wands worker is concerned with expansion and growth. They are at the borderlands, but is this construction site building a border or removing it? Maybe they are clearing a recent reconstruction or putting the framing up for the site, system, and structure soon to be inhabited. Or perhaps they are planting trees, pursuing a *re*-forestation, a repudiation of ecological conquest. Though we face many obstacles, it is possible for there to be differentiation of status without subordination, and for tarot to create an aesthetics of existence where creative power lies in the people's hands. Then the commons can stave off annihilating enclosures.

Your worthiness, deservingness, and lovability do not depend on your capacity to work hard, though life will require you to work hard for the things you love. The Ten of Wands work is in questioning the source of motivation with regard to validation. When the work is about others' acceptance, that inevitably becomes a burden that is unsustainable. But the work that is really meaningful is the work that gets done regardless of how it is perceived. The work your soul came incarnate to accomplish is a bridge toward a time still undetermined. Who knows the larger cultural trajectory of your contributions? Using an immediate marker or reflection of audience response to the vision your work advances can be to the detriment of you walking the path, doing the work, creating as much as you are called to, or believing in yourself. Regardless of the rationale, a different level of strength is inferred when you pull the Ten of Wands. This card sees the challenger with their strength ascending.

When you're overwhelmed, it is hard to do absolutely nothing, to leave the work to someone else, and then make rest, care, and sustenance your primary concern. The beauty of the body's fragile brokenness is that its burden isn't forever. In the absence of your labor's reliability comes a revived political imagination. Insurgency arises from within. And after the scaffolding from our internal renovation comes down, there will be a clear, accessible path for whoever comes after.

Ten of Cups

Osage peoplehood extends beyond Osage inheritance and even Indianness in the embrace of others willing to contribute to communal well-being in this location, displacing racial distinctions in an embrace of humanness as potentially the basis for a shared project of collective groundedness that is given particularity and shaped by "this land." . . . Here, recognizing shared humanness does not suggest a move beyond collective forms of territoriality, and such territoriality does not indicate a drive toward propertied modes of exclusion and violence. Rather, sovereignty as jurisdictional geography and political authority serves as the condition of possibility for having sustained a zone of autonomy that can provide sanctuary to those who have been subject to violence elsewhere, and the resulting relation arises through acknowledgement of the possibility of incorporating new people into extant Osage governance and lifeways. In *Robogenesis,* Wilson indicates that Osage territory has "become a bastion to thousands of people. The spiritual and government leader positions have combined," implying that those non-Osage and non-natives who have come to inhabit this space have successfully integrated themselves into the form of Osage peoplehood that themselves are capacious enough to make room for others.[27]

Like water, belonging is malleable. In the geography of collective life, the social infrastructure offered by the Ten of Cups is one of security, coherence, and harmony. When you pull the Ten of Cups, you're having a homecoming, and if you've never had a home then you will know the Ten of Cups is the dream come true. Geographies of home arise not from bloodedness, nor the markers of race, but from a project of shared survival. And from the desire to secure sacred space is the desire for belonging. As we engage in the collective care of shared lands, thus arises the Ten of Cups.

Indigenous genealogies of placemaking have always existed in a relation of care, responsibility, and reciprocity. Home is made when we treat the lands we inhabit from body to Earth as sacred. This orientation regards home as a determinate space and political entity. In spite of pervasive oppression, displacement, and violent conquest, home exists as an oppositional geography. Home becomes a sanctuary from settler occupation. With open arms, the Ten of Cups calls to us, welcoming us into the place that becomes the heart of the people, those you regard as kin, the ones you keep safe. These heartplaces are models for collective placemaking that ensures native peoplehood endures as imperial empires crumble, for in reconciling with nature a commanding labor of conquest ends.

Place shapes the potentials of being and becoming, and in the intimacy of a connection to place, dwelling becomes a resource for collective well-being and identity within the Ten of Cups. Native nations may have been demolished, disrupted, and/or reordered by colonial infrastructure, but the relation to place remains intact. The domestic space in coloniality is state space, but within a structure of Indigeneity it becomes a sphere of possibility for relationships across many forms of being. The Ten of Cups heartplace becomes an ontological predicate, a wellspring for new modes of life. Home is an altar with animacy. It needs regular sweepings, offerings, cleansings, and blessings.

Sacred space is always honored in the opening of curing ceremonies. Ritual respect to the six directions of a sacred space recognizes the powers of the universe, as our emotional universe becomes centered in order to commune with healing spirits. As a marker of sacred space, the Ten of Cups maintains the links between the seen and subtle worlds. It is the queer oracle that envisions, daydreams, divines a time, a life, a place where heaven on earth is possible. They look into the card and see all these desires for the space-place-time where they will be repressed no more, finally unbound, embraced, and embodied. To onlookers, tarot may appear as a sterile container, but flowering forth from it is a surplus of animacy. Tarot puts the quotidian in alternate frames, exposing the aesthetic dimension of our mundane lives along with the potentiality of our manifest consciousness. Each card is a disco ball, a glittering, revolving, mirrored orb, connecting the threads of culture, consciousness, and revelation.

"On oil dance floors, sites of public sex, various theatrical stages, music festivals, and arenas both subterranean and aboveground, queers live, labor, and enact queer worlds in the present."[28]

The actors upon this queer stage, performing utopia, are not heroes of the Western world. They are delivering a utopian promise. Their open arms embrace alternative, experimental, and outlaw modes of love, sex, sexuality, and relationality. Their image is jubilant and fulfilled. Their gesture is one that offers and receives, which announces and enacts a new social performance. Their shared voice is song, and their shared work is peace. The rainbow primary to the iconography of the Ten of Cups is a reproduction of the natural that renders a queer potentiality imaginable. The ephemerality of the rainbow reminds us that this vision may soon fade, we may need to wait for Sun and Moon to merge once more, but in this card the moment is more than finite. It becomes a blueprint of a better world imaged in the queer aesthetic, imagined by the spiritual practitioner. There is the sense of both distance and closeness, of intimacy and possibility. They bring us hope, potentiality, pleasure, play, and reprieve from coercive work ethics. It might as well be a disco ball, for it functions the same, making the world of this landscape imbued with a tonality of play, dance, and exuberance. It marks the landscapes of ornamentation where the entire emotional range is encompassed, regarded as both natural and divine at once. It is a symbol of salvation under which the masses gather in resplendence, rejoicing hand in hand, arm in arm, in touch and in-tact.

When queers make contact in mass gatherings, the state is always scared. The queer public pronouncement of pleasure makes peace a possibility, even though they glean into this queer future within a repressive heteronormative present that mitigates and suppresses pleasure in service of social control. In a conservative society, the only space to express queer sexuality is within the private sphere. If it must be bridled to be tolerated, true belonging will never be achieved. Likewise, performing sexuality publicly is liberatory so long as it evades being assimilated, manipulated, exploited, or invested in cisheteronormative racist patriarchy. The rainbow, the rejoicing gesture, the held waists and clasped hands perform a care attending in equal parts to flesh and faith, to make future possibilities present realities.

The Ten of Cups utopia is not naive. Rebellion *is* often easily overcome by violent state force, but in the affirmation of shared joy, peace, and soul, divining queer utopias becomes a critique, a refusal of the repressive social order. The critical function of utopia illuminates the art, culture, and ceremony of people yet to be. To be critically utopian is to disidentify with commodity and colonial culture, and to redeploy our mass materia in service of a liberatory project. Lightning strikes, rain falls, and through sunshine we see a politically enabling whole. By sight we access alternate worlds where we all belong. To pull the Ten of Cups is to truly witness the marvelous.

The Ten of Cups presents a landscape where wishes are made manifest. It is an oasis of aesthetic surplus and a reactivation of the erotic imaginary. Meditating upon this image becomes a vehicle for finding a fuller capacity for love and relationality. The children represented in the card, safe and happy and together, are its insistence on surveying the present's dialectical relation to the future. Their shared show of revelry is a modality of meditation. It tells us we can strive toward the future without abandoning the present, because tarot surpasses relegation to any singular temporality.

Without the Ten of Cups, the tarot would not be worth contemplation. Tarot as a system of cartography maps the terrain within and without. We already have plenty of disembodied capitalist models selling futures that never arrive. We need the Ten of Cups to chart and channel the utopic vision, the queer citizenship, the place just beyond the bounds of repressive society. The Ten of Cups tarot reading witnesses new formations within the present that prospect potential, new futures, sprawled across its visual symbolic space. The reading is a type of avant-garde performance conducted between the common people sitting across the cards, making possible queer worlds perceptible. When the reading, a performance, is understood as a mode of labor in service to liberating the erotic future, the reader's body itself becomes a Ten of Cups outpost. The healing facilitated in the ceremony of a reading is typically considered an individual pursuit, but it is really always shared. The personhood of the cards ensures our hands are always held. Medicine circulates in the shuffling cards and becomes a way to participate in the diverse traditions and practices addressing communal healing.

As actors of the erotic imagination, the Ten of Cups caretakers include people of all colors, classes, and genders. The whole gathered are diverse, eclectic, and invigorated by their forming bonds. In their own conscious community, off the grid, over the rainbow, they find in each other a way to thrive. They are within the sphere of some domestic domain, but a vast distance from the spatiality of the Ten of Pentacles, with its densely networked systems and cities. Rather, the Ten of Cups is some rural elsewhere, procuring a new vista onto the world.

Reading tarot becomes a queer aesthetic practice that endeavors to unveil the horizon as always a place with inherent utopian possibility, an everyday existence.[29] All reading is toward the Ten of Cups. Every reading is a ceremony of return, an opening, a utopic performance by which we find pathways to our own best outcomes. With tarot we can tap into the substance of spatiality; relationships to observe the structured symmetry and divergences of all our relations. When we pull tarot, in ordinary places we find a forum to commune with spirits of all sorts, forever marking the location as magical and happening with all sorts of sacredness. The reading accommodates us to blessed landscapes across many dimensions. We learn the parameters of a spiritual existence with every reading conducted. Every time we turn to the deck, we say yes to unforeseen, unusual, and unorthodox possibilities imbued with spiritual powers possessed in the miniature sympathetic universe, contained and yet overflowing from the cards.

The figures we become in the Ten of Cups are medicine people able to read rainbows, able to change the world by presenting it with new paths to follow.

> *It is my hope that Indians will read these stories and know that many powers are available through the ceremonies and rituals of the tribes and that the powers can be applied to our daily lives to enrich our well-being and enhance our understanding of life in the physical world. Unlike other religious traditions, which have an early revelation followed by millennia of critical examination of the premises and substance of the spiritual experience, Indians have access to these spiritual powers here and now. They can be applied in our lives, and, indeed, the validation of these powers must always be in a change in the conditions of the physical world. Indian spiritual powers manifest themselves immediately in healings and prophecies. We would do well to return those roots.*[30]

Tarot is a tool for a generative decolonial stance when it moves away from dehumanizing binary logics. With every reading is movement toward ontoepistemological multiplicity as cards become complex, crowded with meaning, rich in association, full of resonance. Complex solidarities are possible as our capacity for complex meaning-making expands. Each reading threads an interwoven tapestry of foresight, reflection, and critique.

Even without defined communal land bases, native knowing persists as Indigenous peoples maintain ancestral practices to make a way for detribalized, displaced, and de-Indigenized peoples to wholly inhabit the land. Belonging becomes a healing continuity circulating across generations.

The last time I pulled the Ten of Cups I took part in communal *limpia* for the new year. *Limpias* are a ceremonial technology that restores the health of community and repairs the relationships with the powers of life-giving energies. These are the washings that restore relationality. I offered readings and *platicas* alongside acupuncturists, *curanderas,* Reiki practitioners, herbal therapists, *concheros,* and Black queer astrologers. We each came with medicinal practices and joined in prayer, each offering a part of our spiritual genealogies. We helped wash away collective grief and called forth love rain to shower down so it may bless our communal lot, so it may fertilize our fields of hope. Such deep soul wounds of historical and contemporary trauma have enduring effects that require robust energetic strategy. This work comes from complex, distinct, but often overlapping systems of knowledge. There are many ways to call for help from the spirit world. Red medicine is not knowable by mental exercise alone. It is a spiritual heart knowing. We call and are always answered, continuously recognized. These spirits know who we are and so we must know we are never alone. This knowledge is more powerful than the cycles of trauma or the legacies of hurt. Those that are learned in the Ten of Cups know our emotional lives are numinous dimensions, unseen but real with transcendent meaning. These subtle places in our soul are the foundation of our material future and are *marvelous.*

Ten of Pentacles

I learned about the tree of life from other elders who saw the living tree in the placentas of their offspring. Many midwives and women spoke of seeing the tree of life in the placentas as they were "born." Mothers, fathers, and grandmothers spoke of holding up the tree of life in their children's placentas. I'd hear these stories as we were discussing knowledge of birthing and traditional medicine circulating in our Xicana, Indigenous, and Mexican Indian communities. Then I assisted as a birth attendant for a friend of mine who is Choctaw. When the placenta was expelled, I immediately saw the sacred story within the placenta and proclaimed, 'It's the tree of life!' It looked just like a tree, with the veins as its trunk.[31]

The Ten of Pentacles gathers readers round the tree, settling us into the central axis upon which all life revolves. In knowing where your roots are, you see your tree as an agent of orientation, a foundation of knowledge, the pillar of ritual landscape. By knowing the shapers of cultural movements, our creative center becomes fortified. The descendants have a duty as knowledge keepers, inheritors of original relationships, to remind us of our elders' contributions. With the Ten of Cups we honor the spirits, but with the Ten of Pentacles we honor the ancestors, we honor the trees. We reclaim the power of story, we remember, and we retell our stories. The card offers a chance to intervene in our ancestral narratives, to stop the stories that eradicate our ancestral authority. We reinscribe a communal past that has been fragmented to forge collective resistance. This arcanum is a generous reminder of this long and rich practice. With this type of care there will be no unmarked graves, no fading into oblivion or obsolescence. Citation as a type of stewardship exemplifies much of the motivation of this work. It entails reciprocal creative care that ensures the archive of our cultural legacy and impact is respected. Often, this is the work of pentacles.

There is no vacuum we exist, create, or know in. Alienation is a violence because it comes only after acts of erasure, after forced forgetting. So then as Óscar Moisés Diaz says, quoting becomes a quilting tying us back to the world. I hope it's clear that this book is such a quilting, but that the stitching is my design. The naming ceremony that is Ten of Pentacles is personal restoration by a communal reconciliation. It's being named by those you name. When knowledge claims are named, they can be shared rather than possessed. No more are we no-name; now we are known. This politic of recognition breaks the Five of Swords curse of being deadnamed, with all its Five of Pentacles material consequence.

This card knows that all the old concerns are still so contemporary, and there is no new knowledge. But as we engage in a process of self-conscious traditionalism, these concerns can be addressed in the import of our ancestors' language, vision, and values.[32] To align with Indigeneity is to be in relationship with time as a living entity. It is to know that time itself is our elder, our inheritor. We are a people removed from cultural, ceremonial references, but we can reposition ourselves in the cycles of continuous creation as we work with the Ten of Pentacles. It turns to tell us we can heal the past, we can retrieve lost knowledge of the soul and experience life from the coherence of a community that exceeds the human. The Ten of Pentacles, as with all other cards, is an image vehicle, where every symbol of its body is toward the act of remembering, the care of continuing. Tarot offers these image bodies to drive us through the thresholds of knowing, edging epiphany. The imagination is anything but frivolous; it is the faculty that helps us touch the Divine, and to read the tarot is to engage the interplay between the image and the imagination. Words must simply be awoken by activating the human sensorium evoked by the image body. Materially and symbolically imprinted on our bodies are the visual, textual, and oral narratives of colonization. By re-presenting these images of loss, they are made whole. The medicine of this *Red reading* is that it interrupts the rupture of colonization, which is a consciousness overrun with the aesthetics of white supremacy. Then the multibody coherence emerges. Original teachings are stored in the multibody, pronounced in poetic verse, so that no matter where we wander, migrate, or move, song will always call us back home.

The naturally occurring arrowhead etched into the foothills of my homeland marks it as sacred, so I always knew I was native even though I had no official status or formal tribal recognition. Still, I grew up with access and in proximity to tribal territory. Though certain distinctions within knowledge, practice, and categorizations vary from family to family, I was able to repair a dislocated, dislodged relationship to Indigeneity through the generosity of shared ceremonies, traditions, and material investments. At critical junctures where my growth was dependent upon access to institutions gatekept by wealth, the tribe invested in my education, in my material well-being. The Ten of Pentacles represents this compassionate sharing of cosmo-logic technologies between relatives, restoring the ruptured relationship with originality. With such generous power, de-Indigenization is reversible. Made visible in the Ten of Pentacles's dispensation, handing down intergenerational knowledge is this principle of regeneration.

It is the elders who consider inheritance, who meditate on legacy as mortality confronts them. While the primary motive of settler colonialism is territory acquisition, the wealth represented by this card is always *shared.* Nothing will be acquired if it is not given. The decision to share is based upon appropriate relationships, trust, and intimacy. This is domestic medicine; it begins in the home. When the elders confer trust upon us, we become bearers of familiar knowledge. As each pentacle is passed through each generation, communal identity is maintained by the Ten of Pentacles.

Cultures are adapted, tongues change, and ethnic markers shift over time, but those whose beings gather round sacred relationships will never be known as less than. They are known by the land, they are known by those they name. My relationship with the mestizo miscellany has always been fraught. There are aspects of its fluid hybridity that have assisted me strategically as I left home and engaged self-inquiry in shifting, potentially dangerous environments, ever a new context of settler colonialism. It was in higher education institutions that the language of transgression fueled my pursuit of liberatory knowledge. I think I was drawn to the identity marker because I felt disempowered in my mixed heritage making my Indigeneity not real enough. And while it has valorized anticolonial political resistance, I found its critique as a project validating the language of bastardization, de-Indigenization, and anti-Blackness vital.

> *Neither my great-uncle, nor my grandparents, nor my uncles and aunts who identity as Kickapoo, Comanche, or "Aztec" would ever agree that they were post-anything, or an afterthought of Indian, or a shell of Indigeneity, living some postmodern fragmented existence. They were not "subaltern" subjects on the margins of systems created through dominance. They lived at the center of their own existence, grounded by a spiritual sense of order, while simultaneously living among and positioned within these various structures of meaning and power.*[33]

Concern has been expressed about using transgressive subjectivity as a mediator for coalition building within the Indian community, for its potential of presuming a continued exile of tribal people in a homogenizing notion of *mestizaje* that undermines the cultural authenticity and distinctiveness of tribal peoples.

Certain language of critical subjectivity may be part of the fundamental lexicon of Western imperialism so long as it dispenses with the vitality of remaining tied to place, people, original knowledge. The library may be walled, but that doesn't mean its books deserve to be burned. And then I think of Adrienne Rich writing frustrated poems of needing the oppressor's language to talk to you, but it being unable to touch you. Any language will do when they're always trying to cut your tongue out, though the words will always be born of a wound, a naked pain.

The Ten of Pentacles points to the connection between economic oppression, environmental destruction, and the wealth power of bearing titles to territories. For critical theorists to engage a praxis that does not ignore the cultures geographically and historically placed and rooted in tradition, any notion of change that is theorized, called upon, or envisioned should not further market imperatives but rather should enhance our subjectivity in relationship to the larger environment. Our sense of liberation should not be achieved in an emancipation from nature, land, or place. The loss of land as a political and economic disaster is presented in the Five of Pentacles as a spiritual displacement, wherein the real exile is in the destruction of ceremonial life that accompanies the loss of land, the body that is an archive, a library landscape. Restoring the environment is vital to treating the soul loss within the land we are dependent upon. This process pictured in the Ten of Pentacles is found in the act of re-placing ourselves into sacred landscape. Traditional ecological knowledge manifests in symbolic formula, cultural rites, and wellness practices. These practices regard the body as a ceremonial site all its own.

The borders that protect tribal land, resources, treaty rights, and intellectual property must be respected to move toward effective coalition and enact effective methods of border crossing. And so we see in the card a guard with an outward stance that becomes an inward posture of self-reflexivity, an awareness of what knowledge is shared and when. This inward accounting engages the pair looking toward the elder, ready to be received. Then commences a ceremony of memory, and both the future and the present peer into the past, opened and extended. The prophecy is "fulfilled" or rather emerges in the interplay between seeing and being seen. The reading can't complete if you are left all alone. It's a practice of connectivity and a process of relational repair. The Ten of Pentacles shows an enduring interdependence with place that continues to shape and define generational identity as the law of regeneration is activated and upheld in the bodyimagesong of pastpresentfuture. After estrangement, the Ten of Pentacles is the recovery of ancestral land, affirmed in the borders that protect land against further colonial encroachment. This is the harvest of the prophet.

What a secularized, colonialist consciousness regards as alienable private property, natives know as *mother, father, grandmother, grandfather.* The Ten of Pentacles ties these contrasting considerations together. Power, wealth, and status are signaled by the elder, the possessor of property, the sign of capital. But by reorienting to the land and its fruits as a harvest of spirit and family, we reenter sacred society. The communal infrastructure offered by the card is one of stewardship, suggesting that caring for each other ensures there is enough to go around. Success within a stewardship schema is framed as meeting the needs of the most vulnerable, not as hoarding wealth and resources for individual, privatized gain. Our interdependent reality lives on only if each generation upholds their rights and responsibilities, no matter if they are people of the North or people of the South. Survival is in sustaining and reclaiming originary custom, language, and land. It is the land where sovereignty is in dispute, and the dispute is between commodification, privatization, and sedentary settlement on the one hand, or sacred stewardship and commonality on the other.

> *While now asymmetrical, the two enclosures—of the Indigenous world, and of the commons in the West—are metaphorically and metonymically linked. The same class that took over the land in Europe also took over Indigenous land outside of Europe. The privatization of the English commons preceded that of the Irish commons, which preceded that of the Indigenous commons of the Americas. . . . In both countries, nation-states destroyed long-existing systems of communally held land in favor of Dawes Act deeds of private ownership.*[34]

The alter-native fourth of space of Indigeneity is profoundly inter- and cross-disciplinary. So in José Esteban Muñoz's articulation of the "brown commons" as something more than skin; as a sense, a phenomenology of proximity, I see a renewed native way of knowing and finding conspiratorial alignment across all movements and investments. The Brown commons is an attunement of our nearness to others. The image offered by the Ten of Pentacles is a poignant depiction of Muñoz's final offering before his death, something more slowly, steadily developed, distinct from the urgency that steered *Cruising Utopia*.

The organic matter of our Brownness replenishes the earth. Brown is the basis. Brownness is generative as it is generous, there's overflowing enoughness so it's passed around, it's there for seconds and thirds. It's warm and fills you up till you fall asleep. It's made with the intention of being shared, and in sharing, the economy of social bodies becomes common wealth.

> *I am drawn to the idea of a brown commons because it captures the way in which brown people's very being is always a being-in-common. The brown commons is made of feelings, sounds, buildings, neighborhoods, environments, and the nonhuman organic life that might circulate in such an environment alongside humans, and the inorganic presences that life is very often so attached to. But first and foremost, I mean "brown" as in brown people in a very immediate way, in this sense, people who are rendered brown by their personal and familial participations in South-to-North migration patterns. I am also thinking of people who are brown by way of accents and linguistic orientations that convey a certain difference. I mean a brownness that is conferred by the ways in which one's spatial coordinates are contested, and the ways in which one's right to residency is challenged by those who make false claims to nativity.... But we know that some humans are brown in that they feel differently, that things are brown in that they radiate a different kind of affect. Affect, as I am employing it in this project, is meant to address a sense of being-in-common as it is transmitted, across people, place, and spaces. Brown affect traverses the rhythmic spacing between those singularities that compose the plurality of a brown commons.*[35]

The Ten of Pentacles is the allure of the commons, the fortunate invitation to take your place in the vast, vibrant, ever-expanding whole. Weighing the present, past, and future in the commons is to consider more than the century of one's bloodline. The quality of life takes precedence, rather than its length; proximity succeeds mastery. Mysteries may remain between us, but they are no barrier to knowing our commonality. The spiritual and physical safety of home is that no one is trying to harm you, and when you need help, everybody responds, no matter if they like you or not.

The old one in the Ten of Pentacles is the prophet of the political imagination. We see them foresee commonality as they peer back into history. The hope offered is defiant, extravagant. This prophet's offering is a luxury like bread, a poetry that is for everyone.[36] With this card we are reminded of the various altars of place that establish sacred geography, the places where our relationship to the world is renewed. Prayer is the places where cleansing rites are performed. Prayer is fashioned into the bedroom, the home, the kitchen, the garden. We pull cards and come into common consciousness. Wherever we plant ourselves, we make vines of vital connection from the decaying ones of displacement, diaspora, and migrations. We plant ourselves and repair our lineages. From everywhere we now stand, innumerable trees will take our place. Our foresight will be the fruit offered new life.

Conclusion

If tarot is a mirror to understand lived experience, it is far from self-explanatory. The function of a prophet is inspired utterance. The oracle risks a different relationship to uncertainty, possessing a radical spontaneity. They gamble with meaning, meaning that divination is less about fixed outcomes and more about liberation. The augury is always arriving, always shifting, and profoundly unstable. Sometimes the spread subverts your intended, imposed order. The cards keep changing as you keep shuffling. This is fantastic because it means no one masters tarot; this is not the point of the reading. This is not to say the reading has no barometer of success, no meaningful consequence nor any practical application. Rather, this helps the reader work against the fixed fatalism of being appropriated by the Western imagination. Instead, be a devotee, be willing to experiment with the most prescient and pressing work of your healing. Imbibe with divination, dance with it like a lover. It'll keep you on your toes, flexible and with full range. And what a wonderful romance it is to always arrive reverential before the beloved.

The cards are one tool of prophecy, but each card is a key to an archive of archives. The living archive of the prophet's body meets the shattering network of catacombs contained within each card, opening a dynamic emergent space for miraculous modes of knowing to arise.

For it to be a tool of transcendent knowing, it must transgress. The *Red* reader must work against the deep structures of Western thought. They must read the cards to nourish emancipatory knowledge that undergirds all revolutionary praxis. For any meaningful prognostication, the cards must unpack and undo the West's naturalized land claims, the internalized acquiescence to the colonial order. It'll take cutting the deck thousands of times before the psychoaffective attachments to the colonial condition are ruptured.

My aim in offering this work, as a detribalized trans native, is to expand the borders of Indigenous intellectualism by supplying a divinatory text with a language that acknowledges the broader relations of power, historical domination, the ongoing struggle against colonialism, the ruptured spiritual lineages, knowledges, and practices. *Red-dening* the divination tool that is tarot is to work against the West. The Western imagination focuses on a future-centered hope toward an ever-expanding empire that is territorially acquisitive in perpetuity. This fictional future of the West is always made from ongoing practices of Indigenous dispossession. *Red* reading, writing, and thinking can reclaim a precolonial, sacred relationality. So embodied inquiry is necessary to read *Red.*

Any reader, diviner, or writer who wishes to seriously heal and imagine a future that is not predicated upon colonial divisions must actually lift the veil. They must address, in every reading, behind every card, the symbolic violence that "renders the crushing materiality of systemic violence invisible, appear natural, acceptable."[37] This means attuning, with the cards, to the subtle responses to any tableau or small gallery of prophetic images arranged before the reader. In a social world that is constantly overriding our felt sense, tarot reading becomes a practice of learning to trust the intuition, the instincts, the sensorium. Beyond unveiling, the *Red* reader uproots colonial consciousness within all the relations it has so destructively saturated.

This project seeks to model a citation practice that is multifarious and polyvocal. I hope I have woven a tapestry well enough that the intellects engaged in anti-imperialist and anticapitalist commitments to decolonization, emancipation, and revelatory renewal may be further engaged and explored with each syncretized card. Through each card I aim to underscore the need for continual engagement between and across scholars and advocates for Indigenous intellectualism and critical pedagogy. This works upon the foundation of Red pedagogy that emerges "from a collectivity of critique and solidarity between and among indigenous peoples, other marginalized groups, and peoples of conscience."[38]

A *Red* reader is a revolutionary agent. They reinvent themselves, they are in a symbiotic relationship with the more-than-human nature of the cosmos as a sovereign entity. They interrogate the overlapping historical stratum of cultural identifications, the liminality within which people of any diaspora must navigate claims of authenticity in the crossroads of the postmodern social reality and the postcolonial imagination and future we push for. The augury here is related to the materiality of social life and its incumbent power relations. *Red Tarot* is but an admittedly humble step toward that insurgent poetic prophecy of our sovereignty, our emancipatory transformation.

Prophets are also a place, a house of prayer. And more and more it's privatized. Where do we publicly mourn or celebrate? Prophets are the agency, the medium of a divinity. The cards become a compass to navigate the neocolonial landscapes many urban queer and trans natives precariously exist within. For my clients, which include my family, I have helped them evade and handle cop encounters, to deal with divorce and death, to strategically and successfully plan conception, to look into the welfare of a child taken by an abusive adult. I have used the cards to process with these children their traumas, their sadness, their dreams, their dangerous perception. I have foretold fire and rain.

"Mountains and abysses, such is the relief of the grotesque body; or speaking in architectural terms, towers and subterranean passages."[39]

The city is always in a fraught relationship with Indigeneity, as it is an explicitly non-Native space. Entering the city is entering the colonial imagination. Conceiving of cities as *civilized* spaces has meant that cities have been made with very pained efforts to expel Native presence. From violent expulsion came the carefully managed spatial containment of Native excess, joining the other racialized "other" zoned into the inner city, the ghetto, the place where the state puts all and anything deemed disreputable. This means that Native space, Native being, Native imaginaries and cosmologies, languages and knowledge forms, are "waste" lands to the state. We impede the West's progress. This persistent existence meant the theft of the Native land base became a project of state assimilation and subjection. Now gentrification is further dispossessing Native spaces in the city. We are wild birds awkwardly perched in an urban setting. Thankfully, tarot teaches me to read a stranger's book. We are edge dwellers traveling together. When bodies are moving, the risk is always a question of *how far*. Only through the play of our bodies will we become aware of what's outside this dominating social decorum.

I have grown up with access to land-based communities, so I take seriously the ancestral responsibility of land stewardship; but I also have found the need to reconceptualize Indigenous identity with *Red Tarot* so that its system may serve the urban natives who pick up the cards, cut off from the communities and homelands that otherwise ground Indigenous identities. It's affirmative, self-reflective revitalization. With it, I renew the will to live.

Red Tarot offers a divergent method of relating to and with the world with a unique modality of knowing. Each card shapes overlapping aesthetic engagements with materiality and its metaphysical conceptualizations. To redefine our engagement with the tarot requires a reconfigured aesthetic to animate the shadow mirror with renewed agency. Tarot is a centuries-old divination tool that has had significant influence on twentieth-century Western occultism. In an unsurprising classic colonial, orientalist move, the late eighteenth-century European intellectuals would link tarot's iconography to Egyptian mysticism to bolster the cards' credibility. And so it's all the more vital to stress that tarot has no single culture of origin; rather, embedded within its history is a project of cultural hybridity arising from cross-cultural exchange, migration, and importation.[40] And yet as every civilization or precivilization began with art, the image catalyzes literacy. Tarot takes our tongue, our perception, our interpretation and praxis into greater breadth and depth. So often a reading engages generative frustration as we struggle to comprehend the augur, the omen, the silent language of the image or the chart. Divination demands patience. But it also is humorous, incisive, and uncanny. It puts power into the hands of the people themselves. Within its history we also find it as a representative technology of class mobility, thus providing a uniquely useful tool to navigate our contemporary economic precarity with a deck that can be irreverent and satirical in its reflective value estimations. The cards are a critical mirror to contemplate the dark reflection of the Western world power play as well as the different solutions various cultures have engaged to keep alive their tradition and identity in a world of homogenizing globalization. They are a deployment of excess that fuses the high and low. They become a joyful purging.

If you respect prophecy, it will alert you to electrifying opportunities for spiritual and emotional epiphany. It is the regular, daily reading that transforms awareness, that presents daily a chance for meaningful catharsis. Reading is ritualistic, and ritual structures regular reverence. Constructing this space in the home, in the spirit, in the hands between reader and querent, we share an exploratory space of sanctuary. In this space we position ourselves to directly experience the numinous; we open a powerful energetic channel that releases both pain and potential.

By endeavoring toward a dehierachalized relationality we may discover many openings toward a thriving multiplicity. Native peoples in a colonial landscape continued to worship their pre-Columbian deities by way of syncretic realignment. Forced conversion was more apparent than real. Indigenous rituals, rites, and "idolatry" were celebrated clandestinely in the wake of colonial conquest. The tangible dimension of practicing a decolonized, divinatory life is to be seemingly invisible while in plain view of the colonial gaze. Considering invisibility and social exile is to consider that the stranger of the state has an unknowability. Visibility within a dominating white world is dangerous, where the mechanisms of sight are so extremely geared toward surveillance. The cards tell us that the oracle is opaque, and strategically so. When our logical mind reaches toward too tight of a grip, the oracle veils itself.

There is a native relationship between the celestial sphere and objects of brilliance, luster, and luminosity. The enlightened object shines due to its possession of soul. There are many kinds of enlightened materials, and their valuation is unlike European mediums of commercial exchange. Copper, for instance, was preferred over pure gold. The entire universe inhabited by Native consciousness shimmers with spiritual essence. The glow or luster of nature and its phenomena, many objects of minerals, metals, and mirrors, are light solidified, immanent forces of spirit. Underlying all of the vast and varied manifestation of brilliant materials across culture-specific manifestations among the Indigenous was an ascription of sacrality. Light forges a link between objects and soul. The more reflective and chromatic, the more soul these shiny materials possessed and the more value was ascribed to them. These objects of power are a medium of *brilliance.* They are agents of light. Tarot is one such object. Moreso, tarot is the obsidian mirror, the dark divinatory light that allows me to psychically see the soul, the inner process, the hidden connections between all things. Tarot, like or as obsidian, alters our engagement with materiality. Inevitably much meaning is lost in translation, and as light illuminates it also obscures. With each lens overlaying another, the center becomes more opaque. So it's about making the black mirror shine.

Only within an Indigenous syncretic cosmology does brilliance characterize the shamanic experience. For in visions aglow with celestial light, shamans sojourn between physical and spiritual realms. Shamans must be able to not just see and observe more, but to understand more. The light spectrum they can perceive is like possessing night vision.

Many are first-timers. They approach cautiously, fearful to look into another mirror, with another light that so many generations of colonial conditioning taught them was idolatrous, fetishistic. Sit with them and share a parallel luminosity, and perhaps for the first time show them a mirror that reflects their dignity, their brilliance, and their truth.

NOTES

Chapter I: Zero

1 Seth Holmes, *Fresh Fruit, Broken Bodies* (Berkeley: University of California Press, 2013), 157.

2 Patrisia Gonzales, *Red Medicine: Traditional Indigenous Rites of Birthing and Healing* (Tucson: University of Arizona Press, 2012), 3.

3 Gregory Cajete, "Philosophy of Native Science," in *American Indian Thought,* ed. Anne Waters (Hoboken, NJ: Wiley, 2004).

4 Mariana Ortega, "Cámara Queer: Longing, the Photograph, and Queer Latinidad," in *Theories of the Flesh,* ed. Mariana Ortega and Jose Medina (New York: Oxford University Press, 2020).

5 Sandy Grande, *Red Pedagogy* (Lanham, MD: Rowman & Littlefield, 1993), xviii.

6 Cajete, "Philosophy."

7 Mark Rifkin, *Fictions of Land and Flesh: Blackness, Indigeneity, Speculation* (Durham, NC: Duke University Press, 2019), 10.

8 Jose Esteban Muñoz, *Disidentifications: Queers of Color and the Performance of Politics* (Minneapolis: University of Minnesota Press, 1999), 29.

Chapter II: One

1 Toni Morrison, "The Site of Memory," in *The Source of Self-Regard* (New York: Knopf, 2019), 237.

2 Morrison, "The Site of Memory," 236.

3 Patrisia Gonzales, *Red Medicine: Traditional Indigenous Rites of Birthing and Healing* (Tucson: University of Arizona Press, 2012), xx.

4 Gonzales, *Red Medicine,* 126.

5 Gonzales, xii.

6 Tillie Olsen, "Foreword," in *Black Women Writers at Work*, ed. Claudia Tate (Chicago: Haymarket Books, 2023), ix.

7 Morrison, "The Site of Memory," 237.

8 Gonzales, *Red Medicine,* xxiii.
9 Morrison, "The Site of Memory," 239.
10 Robin Wall Kimmerer, "Learning the Grammar of Animacy," in *Braiding Sweetgrass: Indigenous Wisdom, Scientific Knowledge and the Teachings of Plants* (Minneapolis: Milkweed Editions, 2015), 9.
11 Kimmerer, "Learning the Grammar of Animacy," 7.
12 Kimmerer, 6.
13 Chicome Itzcuintli Amatlapantli, *Tarot Yohualli Ehécatl* (Mexico City: Papalota Negra, 2021), 26.
14 Zora Neale Hurston, *Dust Tracks on a Road* (New York: HarperPerennial, 1996), 1.
15 Paula M. L. Moya, "Remaking Human Being: Loving Kaleidoscopic Consciousness in Helena Maria Viramontes' *Their Dogs Came with Them,*" in *Theories of the Flesh,* ed. Andrea J. Pitts, Mariana Ortega, and José Medina (New York: Oxford University Press, 2020), 138.
16 Moya, "Remaking Human Being."
17 Moya, 147.
18 Ytasha Womack, *Afrofuturism: The World of Black Sci-fi and Fantasy Culture* (Chicago: Lawrence Hill Books, 2013), 42.
19 bell hooks, "Eating the Other," in *Black Looks: Race and Representation* (Boston: South End Press, 1992), 3.
20 Leyla Rael and Dane Rudhyar, *Astrological Aspects* (Santa Fe, NM: Aurora Press, 2018), 5.
21 Terry Eagleton, *The Significance of Theory* (Oxford: Blackwell Publishers,≈1990).
22 Kimmerer, "Learning the Grammar of Animacy," 9.
23 Paulo Freire, *Teachers as Cultural Workers* (Boulder, CO: Westview Press, 2005), 52.
24 bell hooks, *Teaching to Transgress* (New York: Routledge, 1994), 172.
25 hooks, *Teaching to Transgress,* 174.
26 Antonia Darder, Rodolfo D. Torres, and Marta P. Baltodano, *The Critical Pedagogy Reader* (New York: Taylor & Francis, 2003), 500.
27 Joseph Campbell, *The Hero with a Thousand Faces* (Novato: New World Library, 2008), 280.
28 Pedro J. Dipietro, "Hallucinating Knowing," in *Theories of the Flesh,* ed. Andrea J. Pitts, Mariana Ortega, and José Medina (New York: Oxford University Press, 2020), 220–34.
29 Dipietro, "Hallucinating Knowing."

30 Stephanie Rivera Berruz, "Stylized Resistance," in *Theories of the Flesh,* ed. Andrea J. Pitts, Mariana Ortega, and José Medina (New York: Oxford University Press, 2020), 239–50.

31 Thelma Sullivan, "A Scattering of Jades: Stories, Poems, and Prayers of the Aztecs," in *Red Medicine: Traditional Indigenous Rites of Birthing and Healing,* ed. Patrisia Gonzales (Tuscon: University of Arizona Press, 2012), 83.

32 Luz Calvo and Catriona Rueda Esquibel, *Decolonize Your Diet* (Vancouver: Arsenal Pulp Press, 2015), 37.

33 Cherríe L. Moraga, *A Xicana Codex of Changing Consciousness* (Durham, NC: Duke University Press, 2011), xvii.

34 Gloria Anzaldúa, "Speaking in Tongues," in *The Gloria Anzaldúa Reader* (Durham, NC: Duke University Press), 169.

35 Paulo Freire, *Pedagogy of the Oppressed* (New York: Continuum Publishing Company, 1993), 68.

36 Barbara C. Sproul, *Primal Myths* (New York: Harper One, 1991), 3.

37 Ed Hirsch, "I've Known Rivers: Speaking of the Unknown Places in Poetry," in *The Lover of a Subversive Is Also a Subversive*, ed. Martin Espada (Ann Arbor: University of Michigan Press, 2010), 57.

38 Paul Christopher Johnson, *Diaspora Conversions: Black Carib Religion and the Recovery of Africa* (Berkeley: University of California Press, 2007), 13.

39 Edgar Garcia, *Signs of the Americas* (Chicago: University of Chicago Press, 2020), xv.

40 Carol Deppe, *The Resilient Gardener: Food Production and Self-Reliance in Uncertain Times* (White River Junction: Chelsea Green Publishing, 2010), 10.

41 S.R. Lyons, "Rhetorical Sovereignty: What Do American Indians Want from Writing?" *College, Composition and Communication* 51, no. 3 (2000): 457.

42 Amatlapantli, *Tarot Yohualli Ehécatl,* 213.

43 Erika Buenaflor, *Curanderismo Soul Retrieval: Ancient Shamanic Wisdom to Restore the Sacred Energy of the Soul* (Rochester, NY: Bear and Company, 2019), 129.

Chapter III: Two

1 Richard Delgado and Jean Stefancic, *Critical Race Theory: An Introduction* (New York: New York University Press, 2017), 82.

2 Delgado and Stefancic, *Critical Race Theory,* 89.

3 Edgar Garcia, *Emergency: Reading the Popol Vuh in a Time of Crisis* (Chicago: University of Chicago Press, 2022), 28.

4 Garcia, *Emergency,* 30.
5 bell hooks, *Wounds of Passion: A Writing Life* (New York: Henry Holt and Company, 1999), 59.
6 Jean-Louis Chrétien and Dominique Janicaud, *Phenomenology and the "Theological Turn": The French Debate* (New York: Fordham University Press, 2000), 167.
7 hooks, *Wounds of Passion,* 105.
8 Toni Morrison, "Nobel Lecture," The Nobel Prize, December 7, 1993, https://www.nobelprize.org/prizes/literature/1993/morrison/lecture/.
9 Earl M, Maltz, "The Fourteenth Amendment and Native American Citizenship," *Constitutional Commentary* 289 (2000), https://scholarship.law.umn.edu/concomm/289.
10 Johnson v. Mclntosh, 21 U.S. (7 Wheat.) 543 (1823). The historical development of the justifications for the treatment of Native Americans in the antebellum era is described in detail in Robert A. Williams Jr., *The American Indian in Western Legal Thought* (New York: Oxford University Press, 1992).
11 June Jordan, *Some of Us Did Not Die* (New York: Basic/Civitas Books, 2002), 163.
12 Nicholas J. Saunders, "A Dark Light: Reflections on Obsidian in Mesoamerica," *Archaeology and Aesthetics* 33, no. 2 (2001): 220–36.
13 Mary Miller and Karl Taube, *An Illustrated Dictionary of the Gods and Symbols of Ancient Mexico and the Maya* (London: Thames & Hudson, 1993), 145.
14 Alessandra Raengo, "Holding Blackness: Aesthetics of Suspension," *Liquid Blackness* 4, no. 7 (2017): 8–33.
15 E. Y. Washington, "I Won't Grow Up, but I Will Grow Sideways" (lecture, Fresh Voices in Astrology conference, Los Angeles, CA, September 6, 2021).
16 Gloria Anzaldúa, *Luz en lo Oscuro: Rewriting Identity, Spirituality, Reality* (Durham, NC: Duke University Press, 2015), 62.
17 Raengo, "Holding Blackness," 18.
18 Raengo, 27.
19 Raengo, 13.
20 Jordan, *Some of Us Did Not Die,* 145
21 W. E. B. Dubois, "The Strivings of the Negro People," *Atlantic Monthly,* August 1897, 194–97.
22 Jordan, *Some of Us Did Not Die,* 58.

23 Iain Matthew, *The Impact of God* (London: Hodder & Stoughton, 1995), 44.
24 bell hooks, *Writing beyond Race* (New York: Routledge, 2012), 92.
25 Martin Espada, *The Lover of a Subversive Is Also a Subversive* (Ann Arbor: University of Michigan Press, 2010), 28.
26 June Jordan, "The Dance of Revolution," in *Life as Activism* (Sacramento, CA: Litwin Books, 2014), 15.
27 bell hooks, *Belonging: A Culture of Place* (New York: Routledge, 2009), 69.
28 Erika Buenaflor, *Cleansing Rites of Curanderismo* (Rochester, NY: Bear & Company, 2018), 70.
29 Jordan, *Some of Us,* 163.
30 Joan Cocks, *The Oppositional Imagination* (London: Routledge, 2012).
31 Maria Lugones, "Hablando cara a cara/Speaking Face to Face: An Exploration of Ethnocentric Racism," in *Making Face, Making Soul/Haciendo caras,* ed. Gloria Anzaldúa (San Francisco: Aunt Lute Books, 1990), 47.
32 Lugones, "Hablando cara a cara," 47.
33 Mark Rifkin, *Fictions of Land and Flesh: Blackness, Indigeneity, Speculation* (Durham, NC: Duke University Press, 2019), 6.
34 John Welwood, "Honesty: Be True to Love," quoted in bell hooks, *All About Love: New Visions* (New York: William Marrow, 2001), 31.
35 Zain El-Roubaei, *Fanon's Love Letter* (Sydney: University of Sydney, 2021), 2.
36 Sara Alicia Ramírez, "Subjects of Trauma" (Ph.D. diss., University of California, Berkeley, 2016), 56.
37 Rumi, "Hand of Fatimah," quoted in Alana Fairchild, *Rumi Oracle* (Glen Waverly: Blue Angel Publishing, 2019), 187.
38 Karen Gregory, "Negotiating Precarity: Tarot as Spiritual Entrepreneurialism," *Women's Studies Quarterly* 40, no. 3/4 (2012): 264–80.
39 bell hooks, *Belonging,* 16.

Chapter IV: Three

1 Sallie Nichols, *Tarot and the Archetypal Journey* (Newburyport: Red Wheel Weiser, 1980).
2 Alice Sparkly Kat, *Postcolonial Astrology* (Berkeley, CA: North Atlantic Books, 2021), 148.
3 Paulo Freire, *Pedagogy of the Oppressed* (New York: Bloomsbury Publishing, 1970).
4 bell hooks, "Eating the Other: Desire and Resistance," in *Black Looks: Race and Representation* (Boston: South End Press, 1992), 24.
5 Kat, *Postcolonial Astrology,* 137.

6 Michael J. Morris, *The Strology Show,* podcast audio, February 9, 2022, https://open.spotify.com/episode/0GER5V9U1slcvo6MEYAsWQ?si=803b4fee82cb43fc.
7 Maria Mies and Vandana Shiva, *Ecofeminism* (London: Fernwood Publications, 1993), 14.
8 Kat, *Postcolonial Astrology,* 131.
9 Mies and Shiva, *Ecofeminism,* 19.
10 William Edward Burghardt Du Bois, *The Souls of Black Folk* (Chicago: A. C. McClurg & Co., 1903).
11 Toni Morrison, *Beloved* (New York: Random House, 1987).
12 Joseph Campbell and Richard Roberts, *Tarot Revelations* (San Anselmo: Vernal Equinox Press, 1979), 116.
13 Morrison, *Beloved.*
14 Karla FC Holloway, *Passed On: African American Mourning Stories* (Durham, NC: Duke University Press, 2002), 7.
15 Veronica Iglesias and Anne Key, *The Jade Oracle: Deities and Symbols of Ancient Mexico* (Albuquerque, NM: Goddess Ink, 2019).
16 Itwari Devi, "The Chipko Women's Concept of Freedom," in *Ecofeminism,* ed. Maria Mies and Vandana Shiva (Melbourne: Fernwood Publications, 1993), 250.
17 Larry Mitchell, *The Faggots & Their Friends between Revolutions* (New York: Calamus Books, 1977), x.
18 Jose Esteban Muñoz, *Disidentifications: Queers of Color and the Performance of Politics* (Minneapolis: University of Minnesota Press, 1999), 23.
19 bell hooks, *Teaching to Transgress* (New York: Routledge, 1994), 59.
20 Audre Lorde, *Uses of the Erotic: The Erotic as Power* (New York: Crossing Press, 1984).
21 Lorde, *Uses of the Erotic.*
22 Taube Miller, *An Illustrated Dictionary of the Gods and Symbols of Ancient Mexico and the Maya* (London: Thames & Hudson, 1993), 60.
23 Réal Grisélidis, *Carnet de bal d'une courtisane* (Paris: Verticales, 2005).
24 Juana Maria Rodriguez, *Puta Life: Seeing Latinas, Working Sex* (Durham, NC: Duke University Press, 2023), 14.
25 Mies and Shiva, *Ecofeminism,* 124.
26 Toni Morrison, interview by Bill Moyers, *A World of Ideas,* PBS, March 11, 1990.
27 bell hooks, *All about Love* (New York: William Morrow, 2001).
28 hooks, *All about Love,* 182, 186.
29 hooks, 178.

30 Maria Lugones, "Playfulness, 'World'-Traveling and Loving Perception," *Hypatia* 2, no. 2 (summer 1987): 3–19.
31 Mark Rifkin, *Fictions of Land and Flesh: Blackness, Indigeneity, Speculation* (Durham, NC: Duke University Press, 2019), 7.
32 Rifkin, *Fictions of Land and Flesh,* 7.
33 Selah Saterstorm, *Ideal Suggestions: Essays in Divinatory Poetics* (Berkeley: Essay Press, 2017), xiii.
34 bell hooks, *Belonging: A Culture of Place* (London: Routledge, 2009).
35 "Toni Morrison and Junot Diaz," interview, 1:22:20, December 13, 2013, https://www.youtube.com/watch?v=J5kytPjYjSQ.
36 Ricky Tucker, *And the Category Is* (Boston: Beacon Press, 2021), 128.
37 Patrisia Gonzales, *Red Medicine: Traditional Indigenous Rites of Birthing and Healing* (Tucson: University of Arizona Press, 2012), 122.
38 Gonzales, *Red Medicine,* 123.

Chapter V: Four

1 Mark Rifkin, *Fictions of Land and Flesh: Blackness, Indigeneity, Speculation* (Durham, NC: Duke University Press, 2019), 6.
2 Paula M. L. Moya, "Remaking Human Being: Loving Kaleidoscopic Consciousness in Helena Maria Viramontes' *Their Dogs Came with Them,*" in *Theories of the Flesh,* ed. Andrea J. Pitts, Mariana Ortega, and José Medina (New York: Oxford University Press, 2020).
3 Rifkin, *Fictions,* 10.
4 B. Binaohan, *Decolonizing Trans/gender 101* (Toronto: Biyuti Publishing, 2014), 40.
5 R. W. Connell, *Masculinities* (Berkeley: University of California Press, 2005), 77.
6 Janet Mock, *Redefining Realness* (New York: Atria Books, 2014).
7 Paul Hoch, *White Hero, Black Beast* (London: Pluto Press, 1979).
8 Binaohan, *Decolonizing,* 40.
9 R. W. Connell, *Masculinities,* 68.
10 Connell, 211.
11 Gary Zukav, *The Heart of the Soul* (New York: Free Press, 2002)
12 Rifkin, *Fictions,* 10.
13 Chicome Itzcuintli Amatlapantli, *Tarot Yohualli Ehécatl* (Mexico City: Papalota Negra, 2021), 341.
14 Rifkin, *Fictions,* 16.
15 Glen Sean Coulthard, *Red Skin White Masks: Rejecting the Colonial Politics of Rejection* (Minneapolis: University of Minnesota Press, 2014), 156.

16 Coulthard, *Red Skin White Masks,* x.
17 Coulthard, 107.
18 Coulthard, 15.
19 Sallie Nichols, *Tarot and the Archetypal Journey* (Newburyport: Weiser Books, 2019), 251.
20 Paulo Freire, *Teachers as Cultural Workers* (Cambridge: Westview Press, 2005), 25.
21 Freire, *Teachers,* 41.
22 bell hooks, *The Will to Change: Men, Masculinity, and Love* (New York: Washington Square Press, 2004), 167.
23 Coulthard, *Red Skin White Masks,* 128.
24 hooks, *The Will to Change,* 118.
25 Amatlapantli, *Tarot Yohualli Ehécatl,* 91.
26 John Mohawk, "The Art of Thriving in Place," in *Original Instructions: Indigenous Teachings for a Sustainable Future,* ed. Melissa K. Nelson (Rochester, NY: Bear & Company, 2008), 129.
27 Ohki Siminé Forest, "Return of the Ancient Council Ways," in *Original Instructions: Indigenous Teachings for a Sustainable Future,* ed. Melissa K. Nelson (Rochester, NY: Bear & Company, 2008), 237.
28 Coulthard, *Red Skin White Masks,* 125.
29 bell hooks, *All about Love* (New York: William Morrow, 2018), 187–88.
30 Chela Sandoval, "Feminism and Racism: A Report on the 1981 National Women's Studies Association Conference," in *Making Face, Making Soul/Haciendo caras,* ed. Gloria Anzaldúa (San Francisco: Aunt Lute Books, 1990), 65.
31 Rifkin, *Fictions,* 2.
32 Sandoval, "Feminism and Racism," 66.
33 Roland Barthes, *A Lover's Discourse* (New York: Hill and Wang, 1977), 39.
34 Jeffrey Wolf Green, *Pluto: The Evolutionary Journey of the Soul* (St. Paul: Llewellyn Publications, 2011), 2.
35 Barthes, *A Lover's Discourse,* 40.
36 bell hooks, *Belonging: A Culture of Place* (New York: Routledge, 2009).
37 hooks, *Belonging.*

Chapter VI: Five

1 Joseph Campbell, *The Hero with a Thousand Faces* (Novato: New World Library, 2008), 81.
2 Jean-Louis Chrétien and Dominique Janicaud, *Phenomenology and the "Theological Turn": The French Debate* (New York: Fordham University Press, 2000).

3 Online Etymology Dictionary, s.v. "Religion," accessed June 15, 2023, https://www.etymonline.com/word/religion.
4 Chrétien and Janicaud, *Phenomenology.*
5 bell hooks, *The Will to Change: Men, Masculinity, and Love* (New York: Washington Square Press, 2004), 135.
6 Chrétien and Janicaud, *Phenomenology.*
7 Vine Deloria Jr., *The World We Used to Live In* (Golden: Fulcrum Publishing, 2006), xix.
8 Paulo Freire, *Pedagogy of the Oppressed* (New York: Continuum Publishing Company, 1993), 48, 55, 58.
9 Toni Morrison, *Playing in the Dark: Whiteness and the Literary Imagination* (New York: Vintage Books, 1993), 59.
10 Morrison, *Playing in the Dark,* 39.
11 Morrison, 37.
12 Henry Giroux and Peter McLaren, "Teacher Education and the Politics of Engagement: The Case for Democratic Schooling," *Harvard Educational Review* 56, no. 3 (1986): 213–38.
13 Morrison, *Playing in the Dark,* xi.
14 Morrison, 17.
15 Freire, *Pedagogy.*
16 Liz Greene, *Saturn: A New Look at an Old Devil* (San Francisco, London: Weiser Books, 2011), 10.
17 Chela Sandoval, "Feminism and Racism: A Report on the 1981 National Women's Studies Association Conference," in *Making Face, Making Soul/Haciendo caras,* ed. Gloria Anzaldúa (San Francisco: Aunt Lute Books, 1990), 67.
18 Toni Morrison, interview by Bill Moyers, *A World of Ideas,* PBS, March 11, 1990.
19 Freire, *Pedagogy,* 72.
20 Jose Esteban Muñoz, *Disidentifications: Queers of Color and the Performance of Politics* (Minneapolis: University of Minnesota Press, 1999), 1.
21 Glen Sean Coulthard, *Red Skin White Masks: Rejecting the Colonial Politics of Rejection* (Minneapolis: University of Minnesota Press, 2014).
22 Tucker, *And the Category Is* (Boston: Beacon Press, 2021), 3.
23 Tucker, *And the Category Is,* 3.
24 Richard Tarnas, *Cosmos and Psyche: Intimations of A New World View* (New York: Viking Penguin, 2006), 14.
25 Robert Firestone, *The Fantasy Bond: Structure of Psychological Defenses* (Santa Barbara: Glendora Association, 1987), 129.
26 Susan Sontag, "Illness as a Metaphor," *New York Review of Books,* January 26, 1978.

27 Sarah Jaquette, "Vulnerable Bodies," in *Theories of the Flesh,* ed. Andrea J. Pitts, Mariana Ortega, and José Medina (New York: Oxford University Press, 2020), 281.
28 Stephanie LeMenager, "Vulnerable Bodies," in *Theories of the Flesh,* ed. Andrea J. Pitts, Mariana Ortega, and José Medina (New York: Oxford University Press, 2020), 290.
29 Coulthard, *Red Skin White Masks,* 114.
30 Muñoz, *Disidentifications,* 31.
31 Larry Mitchell, *The Faggots & Their Friends between Revolutions* (New York: Calamus Books, 1977), ix.
32 Mark Rifkin, *Fictions of Land and Flesh: Blackness, Indigeneity, Speculation* (Durham, NC: Duke University Press, 2019), 13.

Chapter VII: Six

1 Ofelia Schutte, *Crossroads and In-Between Spaces: A Meditation on Anzaldúa and Beyond* (New York: Oxford University Press, 2020), 2.
2 bell hooks, *Wounds of Passion* (New York: Holt Paperbacks, 1997), 68.
3 bell hooks, *All about Love: New Visions* (New York: William Morrow, 2001) vi.
4 Iain Matthew, *The Impact of God* (London: Hachette UK, 2010), 112.
5 Matthew, *Impact of God,* 112.
6 Nick Estes, Melanie Yazzie, Jennifer Nez Denetdale, and David Correia, *Red Nation Rising* (Oakland: PM Press, 2021), 129.
7 Thavolia Glymph, *Out of the House of Bondage: The Transformation of the Plantation Household* (Cambridge: Cambridge University Press, 2008), 106.
8 Frantz Fanon, *The Wretched of the Earth* (New York: Grove/Atlantic, 1961), 1.
9 Estes et al., *Red Nation Rising.*
10 Jose Esteban Muñoz, *Disidentifications: Queers of Color and the Performance of Politics* (Minneapolis: University of Minnesota Press, 1999), 32.
11 Muñoz, *Disidentifications,* 26.
12 Schutte, *Crossroads and In-Between Spaces,* 2.
13 Paulo Freire, *The Pedagogy of the Oppressed* (New York: Continuum Publishing Company, 1993).
14 Louis Althusser, "Ideology and Ideological State Apparatuses (Notes towards an Investigation)," in *Lenin and Philosophy and Other Essays,* trans. Ben Brewster (New York and London: Monthly Review Press, 1971), 142–47, 166–76.
15 Ricky Tucker, *And the Category Is* (Boston: Beacon Press, 2021), 154.

16 Tucker, *And the Category Is,* 158.

17 Hanif Abdurraqib, "Surviving on Small Joys," in *They Can't Kill Us Until They Kill Us: Essays* (Columbus: Two Dollar Radio, 2017), 282–83.

18 Paul Christopher Johnson, *Diaspora Conversions: Black Carib Religion and the Recovery of Africa* (Berkeley: University of California Press, 2007), 2.

19 Freire, *Pedagogy of the Oppressed,* 44–45.

20 Rob Breton, "Ghosts in the Machina: Plotting in Chartist and Working-Class Fiction," *Victorian Studies* 47, no. 4 (2005): 559.

21 Julie Avril Minich, "Vulnerable Bodies: Juana Alicia's Latina Feminism and Transcorporeal Environmentalism," in *Theories of the Flesh,* ed. Andrea J. Pitts, Mariana Ortega, and José Medina (New York: Oxford University Press, 2020), 281–91.

Chapter VIII: Seven

1 Oren Lyons, quoted in "Ely Parker 1844–1865," accessed June 20, 2023, https://www.pbs.org/warrior/content/timeline/opendoor/roleOfChief.html.

2 Wesley Morris, "These Walls Can Talk," in *Black Futures,* ed. Kimberly Drew and Jenna Wortham (New York: One World, 2020), 109.

3 "Quotes," Harriet Tubman Historical Society, accessed July 20, 2023, Harriet-tubman.org.

4 Edgar Garcia, *Emergency: Reading the Popol Vuh in a Time of Crisis* (Chicago: University of Chicago Press, 2022), 75.

5 Jace Clayton, "Invasion of Privacy," in *Black Futures,* ed. Kimberly Drew and Jenna Wortham (New York: One World, 2020), 325.

6 Clayton, "Invasion of Privacy," 323.

7 Ira Shor and Paulo Freire, *A Pedagogy of Liberation* (Westport: Bergin & Garvey, 1987), 57.

8 Jose Esteban Muńoz, *Cruising Utopia: The Then and There of Queer Futurity* (New York: New York University Press, 2009), 32.

9 bell hooks, "Facing Difference: The Black Female Body," *Art Forum,* September 1993, 95.

10 Muńoz, *Cruising Utopia,* 30.

11 Muńoz, 25.

12 Muńoz.

13 Walidah Imarisha and adrienne maree brown, *Octavia's Brood: Science Fiction Stories from Social Justice Movements* (Chico, CA: AK Press, 2015), 4.

14 Imarisha and brown, *Octavia's Brood,* 3.

15 Ricky Tucker, *And the Category Is* (Boston: Beacon Press, 2021), 131.

16 J. E. Cirlot, *A Dictionary of Symbols* (New York: Philosophical Library, 1962), 163.

17 Julio Cammarota, “A Social Justice Approach to Achievement: Guiding Latina/o Students toward Educational Attainment with a Challenging, Socially Relevant Curriculum,” *Equity & Excellence in Education* 40, no. 1 (2007): 87–96.

18 June Jordan, “The Difficult Miracle of Black Poetry in America or Something Like a Sonnet for Phillis Wheatley,” in *Some of Us Did Not Die* (New York: Civitas Books, 2002), 175.

19 bell hooks, *Teaching to Transgress* (London: Routledge, 1994), 169.

20 Brontez Purnell, *100 Boyfriends* (New York: Farrar, Straus and Giroux), 3.

21 Antonia Darder, “Teaching as an Act of Love: Reflections on Paulo Freire and His Contributions to Our Lives and Our Work,” in *The Critical Pedagogy Reader*, ed. A. Darder, M. Baltodano, and R. Torres (New York: Taylor & Francis, 2003), 497–98.

22 Sharon Salzberg, *Real Love* (New York: Flatiron Books, 2017), 3.

23 Anne Crampton, “A Literacy of Armed Love: Confrontation and Desire in Aesthetic and Critical Projects,” *Studies in Social Justice* 13, no. 1 (2019): 97.

24 bell hooks, *Belonging: A Culture of Place* (London: Routledge, 2009), 21.

25 Darder, “Teaching as an Act of Love,” 508.

26 Luis C. Moll, Cathy Amanti, Deborah Neff, and Norma Gonzalez, *Fund of Knowledge for Teaching* (London: Routledge, 2005).

27 Tucker, *And the Category Is*, 163.

28 Thavolia Glymph, *Out of the House of Bondage: The Transformation of the Plantation Household* (Cambridge, MA: Cambridge University Press, 2008), 111.

29 Larry Mitchell, *The Faggots & Their Friends between Revolutions* (New York: Calamus Books, 1977), x.

30 Jose Esteban Muñoz, *Disidentifications: Queers of Color and the Performance of Politics* (Minneapolis: University of Minnesota Press, 1999).

31 Muñoz, *Disidentifications*, 12.

32 Tucker, *And the Category Is*, 28.

33 Marlon Riggs, “Tongues Untied,” in Jose Esteban Muñoz, *Disidentifications: Queers of Color and the Performance of Politics* (Minneapolis: University of Minnesota Press, 1999), 15.

34 Faka, “On the Illusion of Safe Space,” in *Black Futures*, ed. Kimberly Drew and Jenna Wortham (New York: One World, 2020), 474.

35 “bell hooks - Are You Still a Slave? Liberating the Black Female Body | Eugene Lang College,” May 7, 2014, video, 1:55:32, https://www.youtube.com/watch?v=rJkohNROvzs&t=0s.

36 Cherrie Moraga, *A Xicana Codex of Changing Consciousness* (Durham, NC: Duke University Press, 2011), 185.
37 Moraga, *Xicana Codex,* 175.
38 James Hillman, quoted in bell hooks, *The Will to Change: Men, Masculinity, and Love* (New York: Atria Books, 2004), 179.
39 Laura Perez, *Chicana Art: The Politics of Spiritual and Aesthetic Altarities* (Durham, NC: Duke University Press, 2007).
40 Salzberg, *Real Love,* 27.
41 Muñoz, *Disidentifications,* 12.
42 Martin Espada, *Poetry Like Bread* (Stevens Point: Curbstone Press, 2000), 9.
43 "Teaching to Transgress Today: Theory and Practice in and outside the Classroom," October 8, 2014, video, 1:56:58, https://www.youtube.com/watch?v=m_9OgVs19UE.
44 Munoz, *Disidentifications,* 74.
45 bell hooks, *Art on My Mind: Visual Politics* (New York: New Press, 1995), 127.
46 Jess Romeo, "The Taínoes Refused to Grow Food. The Spanish Starved," *JSTOR Daily,* October 12, 2020, https://daily.jstor.org/the-tainos-refused-to-grow-food-the-spanish-starved/.

Chapter IX: Eight

1 J. E. Cirlot, *A Dictionary of Symbols* (New York: Philosophical Library, 1962), 165.
2 Joseph Campbell and Richard Roberts, *Tarot Revelations* (San Anselmo: Vernal Equinox Press, 1979), 18.
3 *Green Leaf,* season 5, episode 8, "Behold," directed by Clement Virgo, aired August 11, 2020, on OWN.
4 Audre Lorde, *Sister Outsider: Essays and Speeches* (New York: Crossing Press, 1984).
5 Barbara Frederickson, *Love 2.0* (New York: Plume, 2013).
6 Sharon Salzberg, *Real Love* (New York: Flatiron Books, 2017), 96.
7 Judith Halberstam, *The Queer Art of Failure* (Durham, NC: Duke University Press, 2011), 183.
8 Halberstam, *The Queer Art of Failure,* 184.
9 Bernadette Brady, *Brady's Book of Fixed Stars* (York Beach: Samuel Weiser, 1998), 5.
10 Jose Esteban Muñoz, *Disidentifications: Queers of Color and the Performance of Politics* (Minneapolis: University of Minnesota Press, 1999), 5.

11 Gloria Anzaldúa, *Light in the Dark/Luz en lo Oscuro: Rewriting Identity, Spirituality, Reality* (Durham, NC: Duke University Press, 2015).
12 Toni Morrison, *Playing in the Dark: Whiteness and the Literary Imagination* (New York: Vintage Books, 1993), 37.
13 Toni Morrison, *Home* (New York: Knopf, 2012).
14 Roland Barthes, *A Lover's Discourse* (New York: Hill and Wang, 1978).
15 Morrison, *Playing in the Dark*, 51.
16 Wendy Travino and Chris Chen, "Mexican Is Not a Race," *The New Inquiry*, April 6, 2017, https://thenewinquiry.com/mexican-is-not-a-race/.
17 Morrison, *Playing in the Dark*.
18 Chandra Talpade Mohanty, *Feminism without Borders: Decolonizing Theory, Practicing Solidarity* (Durham, NC: Duke University Press, 2003), 3.
19 Mohanty, *Feminism without Borders*, 3.
20 bell hooks, *Art on My Mind: Visual Politics* (New York: New Press, 1995), 125.
21 Mohanty, *Feminism without Borders*, 4.
22 Hettienne Grobler, *The Mysteries of the Black Madonna Tarot Deck* (Cape Town: Her Grace Sacred Art, 2021).
23 bell hooks, *Teaching to Transgress* (London: Routledge, 1994), 23.
24 Iain Matthew, *The Impact of God* (London: Holder & Stoughton, 1995), 94.
25 Grobler, *Mysteries of the Black Madonna*, 14.
26 Joseph Campbell, *The Inner Reaches of Outer Space: Metaphor as Myth and as Religion* (Novato: New World Library, 1988).
27 hooks, *Art on My Mind*, 117.
28 LaVerne Wells-Bowie, quoted in hooks, *Art on My Mind*, 149.
29 Morrison, *Playing in the Dark*, 17.
30 hooks, *Art on My Mind*, 147.

Chapter X: Nine

1 *Rodgers & Hammerstein's Cinderella*, produced and directed by Charles S. Dubin, teleplay by Joseph Schrank (2001; Culver City, CA: Columbia TriStar Home Entertainment).
2 Rob Breton, "Ghosts in the Machina: Plotting in Chartist and Working-Class Fiction," *Victorian Studies* 47, no. 4 (2005): 559.
3 Breton, "Ghosts in the Machina," 559.
4 Vine Deloria Jr., *The World We Used to Live In* (Golden: Fulcrum Publishing, 2006) 14–16.
5 Bernadette Brady, *Brady's Book of Fixed Stars* (York Beach: Samuel Weiser, 1998), 4.

6 Patrisia Gonzales, *Red Medicine: Traditional Indigenous Rites of Birthing and Healing* (Tucson: University of Arizona Press, 2012), 142.
7 Deloria Jr., *The World We Used to Live In*, xxiv.
8 Iain Matthew, *The Impact of God* (London: Hachette UK, 2010), 28.
9 Deloria Jr., *The World We Used to Live In.*
10 Edgar Garcia, *Emergency: Reading the Popol Vuh in a Time of Crisis* (Chicago: University of Chicago Press, 2022), 86.
11 Garcia, *Emergency,* 89.
12 Toni Morrison, *The Source of Self Regard* (New York: Alfred A. Knopf, 2019), 117.
13 Alice Sparkly Kat, *Postcolonial Astrology: Reading the Planets through Capital, Power, Labor* (Berkeley, CA: North Atlantic Books, 2021), 43.
14 Amy Allen, *The End of Progress: Decolonizing the Normative Foundations of Critical Theory* (New York: Columbia University Press, 2016), 3.
15 Morrison, *The Source of Self Regard,* 126.
16 Melanie Reinhart, *Chiron and the Healing Journey* (London: Starwalker Press, 2009), 45.
17 Antonia Darder, "Teaching as an Act of Love: Reflections on Paulo Freire and His Contributions to Our Lives and Our Work," in *The Critical Pedagogy Reader,* ed. A. Darder, M. Baltodano, and R. Torres (New York: Taylor & Francis, 2003), 499.
18 Chandra Talpade Mohanty, *Feminism without Borders: Decolonizing Theory, Practicing Solidarity* (Durham, NC: Duke University Press, 2003), 7.
19 Nick Martin, "The Military Views Poor Kids as Fodder for Its Forever Wars," *The New Republic,* January 7, 2020, https://newrepublic.com/article/156131/military-views-poor-kids-fodder-forever-wars.
20 Paulo Freire, *The Pedagogy of the Oppressed* (New York: Continuum Publishing Company, 1993), 161.
21 Mohanty, *Feminism without Borders.*
22 Mohanty, 6.
23 Octavia Butler, *Blood Child and Other Stories* (New York: Seven Stories Press, 2005), 202–4.
24 Gonzales, *Red Medicine,* 172.
25 Gonzales, 172.
26 Mark Allen Peterson, *From Jinn to Genies: Intertextuality, Media, and the Making of Global Folklore* (Logan: University Press of Colorado, Utah State University, 2007), 93.
27 Matthew, *The Impact of God,* 33.

28 bell hooks, *Art on My Mind: Visual Politics* (New York: The New Press, 1995), 125.

29 Larry Mitchell, *The Faggots & Their Friends between Revolutions* (New York: Calamus Books, 1977), x.

Chapter XI: Ten

1 Mark Rifkin, *Fictions of Land and Flesh: Blackness, Indigeneity, Speculation* (Durham, NC: Duke University Press, 2019), 52.

2 Mariah Carey, *The Meaning of Mariah Carey* (New York: St. Martin's Publishing Group, 2021), xiii.

3 Jeanne Schepper, *Moving Performances: Divas, Iconicity and Remembering the Modern Stage* (Rutgers, NJ: Rutgers University Press, 2016).

4 Vlado Kotnik, "The Adaptability of Opera: When Different Social Agents Come to Common Ground," *International Review of the Aesthetics and Sociology of Music* 44, no. 2 (December 2013): 303–42.

5 Schepper, *Moving Performances.*

6 Aria Dean, "Toward a Black Circulationism," in *Black Futures,* ed. Kimberly Drew and Jenna Wortham (One World: New York, 2020), 299.

7 Dean, "Toward a Black Circulationism," 297.

8 Patricia Hill Collins, *Black Sexual Politics: African Americans, Gender and the New Racism* (New York: Routledge, 2005), 27–28.

9 Schepper, *Moving Performances.*

10 Judith Halberstam, *The Queer Art of Failure* (Durham, NC: Duke University Press, 2011), 187.

11 Mary Miller and Karl Tube, *An Illustrated Dictionary of The Gods and Symbols of Ancient Mexico and the Maya* (London: Thames & Hudson, 2015), 63.

12 Jose Esteban Muñoz, *Disidentifications: Queers of Color and the Performance of Politics* (Minneapolis: University of Minnesota Press, 1999), 3.

13 Sean Carleton, "Drawn to Change: Comics and Critical Consciousness," *Labour/Le travail* no. 73 (spring 2014): 153.

14 Paulo Freire, *Pedagogy of the Oppressed* (New York: Seabury Press, 1970), 19.

15 Carleton, "Drawn to Change," 165.

16 Jameel Mohammed, "Nomads at the End of Empire," in *Black Futures,* ed. Kimberly Drew and Jenna Wortham (New York: One World, 2020), 272.

17 Sandy Grande, *Red Pedagogy: Native American Social and Political Thought* (Lanham, MD: Rowan & Littlefield, 2015), 114.

18 Carey, *The Meaning of Mariah Carey,* 23, 258.

19 Patrisia Gonzales, *Red Medicine: Traditional Indigenous Rites of Birthing and Healing* (Tucson: University of Arizona Press, 2012), 213.
20 Seth M. Holmes, *Fresh Fruit, Broken Bodies: Migrant Farmworkers in the United States* (Berkeley: University of California Press, 2013), 43.
21 Toni Morrison, *The Source of Self Regard* (New York: Alfred A. Knopf, 2019), 122.
22 Schepper, *Moving Performances.*
23 Toni Morrison, interview by Bill Moyers, *A World of Ideas,* PBS, March 11, 1990.
24 Holmes, *Fresh Fruit,* 175–76.
25 Holmes, 174.
26 Jonathan Matthew Smucker, *Hegemony How-To: A Roadmap for Radicals* (Chico, CA: AK Press, 2017), 158.
27 Rifkin, *Fictions of Land and Flesh,* 140.
28 Jose Esteban Muńoz, *Cruising Utopia: The Then and There of Queer Futurity* (New York: New York University Press, 2009), 49.
29 Muńoz, *Cruising Utopia.*
30 Vine Deloria Jr., *The World We Used to Live In* (Golden: Fulcrum Publishing, 2006), 214.
31 Gonzales, *Red Medicine,* 122.
32 Grande, *Red Pedagogy.*
33 Gonzales, *Red Medicine,* 224.
34 Grande, *Red Pedagogy,* 269.
35 José Esteban Muñoz, *The Sense of Brown* (Durham, NC: Duke University Press, 2020).
36 Roque Dalton, quoted in Martin Espada, *Poetry Like Bread* (Stevens Point: Curbstone Press, 2000), 14.
37 Glen Sean Coulthard, *Red Skin White Masks: Rejecting the Colonial Politics of Rejection* (Minneapolis: University of Minnesota Press, 2014), 177.
38 Grande, *Red Pedagogy,* 8.
39 Mikhail Bakhtin and Helene Iswolsky, *Rabelais and His World* (Bloomington: Indiana University Press, 1984).
40 "Co Witchcraft Offerings with Michael J. Morris," accessed July 19, 2023, https://www.michaeljmorris.co/.

INDEX

U

V

W

Z

ABOUT THE AUTHOR

CHRISTOPHER MARMOLEJO, MA, is a Brown, queer, and trans writer, diviner, and educator. They use divination to promote a literacy of liberation. They were born and raised in San Bernardino, California, among the pines, in community with the Yuhaaviatam clan of the Maara'yam (Serrano). With nine-plus years of experience as a trained educator focused on cultivating classrooms of emancipatory possibility, they work with students around the world to plant and nurture the seed of a divinatory practice, finely weaving tarot, astrology, and *curanderismo* with critical, decolonial Black queer feminist epistemology. They are available for readings, and they are enrolling students in ongoing divination classes at www.theredread.com. Follow them on Substack (substack.com/@theredread) for more writing.

ABOUT NORTH ATLANTIC BOOKS

North Atlantic Books (NAB) is a 501(c)(3) nonprofit publisher committed to a bold exploration of the relationships between mind, body, spirit, culture, and nature. Founded in 1974, NAB aims to nurture a holistic view of the arts, sciences, humanities, and healing. To make a donation or to learn more about our books, authors, events, and newsletter, please visit www.northatlanticbooks.com.